On Transforming Philosophy

On Transforming Philosophy

A Metaphilosophical Inquiry

Kai Nielsen

Westview Press

A Division of HarperCollinsPublishers

To Hugo Meynell—
who will say,
"No, No."

And to Stanley Stein—
who will say,
"Yes, but..."

Copyright © 1995 by Westview Press, Inc., A Division of HarperCollins Publishers, Inc.

Published in 1995 in the United States of America by Westview Press, Inc., 5500 Central Avenue,
Boulder, Colorado 80301-2877, and in the United Kingdom by Westview Press, 12 Hid's Copse
Road, Cumnor Hill, Oxford OX2 9JJ

A CIP catalog record for this book is available from the Library of Congress.
ISBN 0-8133-0666-3

The paper used in this publication meets the requirements of the American National Standard for
Permanence of Paper for Printed Library Materials Z39.48-1984.

10   9   8   7   6   5   4   3   2   1

Contents

v

Preface

For Students and Their Professors

When I first conceived of this book, I intended to write a short book and one, the great philosophical figures of the past and a few very eminent contemporaries aside, which made no reference to other philosophers and contained no quotations, footnotes and the like. I ended up doing neither. Indeed I went nearly to the exact opposite. I wrote a rather long book with, among other things, extensive discussions of my contemporaries and near contemporaries.

Not doing the first is easier to explain than not doing the second. Metaphilosophy is too tangled, ramified and varied a subject for a persuasive brief treatment. Where obsessions about what one is doing, or should be doing, in doing philosophy, and about the very point of doing it, grip one, one will become entrapped in metaphilosophy. There are people (people who will probably not read this book unless they have to for some reason) who think they know perfectly well what philosophy is and just resolutely set about doing it. Their metaphilosophical account, if they were ever to give one, could (and probably would) be very brief indeed. But not so for the poor souls who are perplexed about philosophy itself and its point (if any). I am one of those poor souls and have been for a long time—from almost the time when I began to study philosophy. Sometimes my metaphilosophical passions have raged stronger than others. But, submerged or not, they have always been there. It is, at least for now, impossible for me to write a short book on metaphilosophy.

The second failure or about-face is less easy to explain. I will approach it indirectly by first speaking of the audience for which this book is designed and of some of the problems that generates. I envisage it principally for two kinds of audience. First, as a text for a variety of students, I see it, very centrally, as a text for undergraduates who have had two or three or preferably more courses in philosophy. The ideal place for them to encounter it is in a middle level or upper level undergraduate or undergraduate/graduate course or seminar devoted in whole or in part to metaphilosophy. I also see it as a text for graduate students who either are in such a seminar or are, philosophically speaking, in a situation similar to that of Stanley Cavell when he was a graduate student, namely, a situation in which they are split in their intellectual and philosophical identities. They are, that is, the sort of student who studies with intense interest both Church and Tarski, on the one hand, and Nietzsche and Foucault, on the other, with a little Kripke or Nagel thrown in for good measure. Their philosophical loyalties and their conceptions of what to try to do in philosophy are pulled in several at least apparently conflicting directions. So primarily I envisage it as a text for students–I would wish that they would all be Stanley Cavell-like convoluted–in such courses or as a book for their solitary and subversive reading. (Subversive, hopefully, for if this book is not thoroughly disliked by some philosophers, I will have failed in the writing of it.)

Secondly, I see it as a book for my peers; that is to say, for other professors of philosophy either in conjunction with their teaching (perhaps for use in a course or seminar such as I described above) or just for reading on their own. And here I envisage it primarily for other poor souls who do not know, or at least are not so sure about, what philosophy is and even wonder sometimes, while being thoroughly entangled with it, if it has much point.

My initial wish not to discuss other philosophers or cite from them (to come at this point the long way around), other than by passing references to the great figures of the past and a very few contemporary giants, e.g., Russell, Dewey and Wittgenstein, was to try to have the book not be off-putting to students. For it can be off-putting to have many names on parade: philosophers or positions (e.g., Strawson or metaphysical realist) of which one may have virtually no knowledge. Such references are too much like name dropping and they can be bewildering and discouraging.

Philosophy, particularly in North America, is very varied. Which philosophers are studied and admired or held in contempt or just ignored will vary considerably from department to department. What flies, or part of what flies, at M.I.T or U.C.L.A. will not fly at Northwestern or Virginia, and vice-versa. What flies, or part of what flies, at Calgary or Edmonton will not fly at Ottawa or Queen's, and vice-versa. There is not, particularly among contemporary philosophers, much in the way of either a common canon to be studied or a common set of problems with which most undergraduates will have to come to grips. What their philosophy professors admire and socialize, or attempt to socialize, their students into admiring will vary extensively from place to place. When undergraduates, and to a certain extent graduates as well, read this book they will come across philosophers they have never studied and in some instances may have never even heard of. Similar things will even be so of at least some of their professors, just as there are philosophers not mentioned in this volume who are not in my repertoire. This is inevitable, given the number of philosophers writing and the diversity of their backgrounds. Then there are also those philosophers we have been taught to be proud of not having read. Moreover, who they are will depend on where we have studied. Tell me the university in which a professor, fresh out of graduate school, has studied and I can tell you, with some considerable, but thankfully not altogether deadly accuracy, the philosophers he admires and those he disdains or of which he is ignorant.

With this background, it should be evident why I wished not to refer to or discuss contemporary philosophers. For you students, who, for good or for ill, are set to studying this book, there will be philosophers mentioned and sometimes discussed that you will know little, or perhaps even nothing, about. That, as I remarked, is inevitable and perfectly natural and there is nothing at all untoward about it. I have been studying philosophy for over forty years and that is true of me as well.

Still, when you know nothing or next to nothing about the figures discussed or used as representatives of certain ways of looking at and doing philosophy, you cannot know whether I have represented these various views with even a reasonable accuracy. Given the range of views, conceptions and philosophers discussed in this book, it would be close to a miracle if sometimes I do not unwittingly distort, perhaps even badly distort, the views I discuss. Where you have a reasonable first-hand knowledge of them yourselves, you can correct at least any gross errors of mine. And, of course, your professors can and will do so as well. But your professors, as they would be the first to acknowledge, are also not omni-competent. It is unlikely that any—or, to play it safer, many—of us are small Goethes. So there is, or at least should be, a natural skepticism, or at least unease, on your part about, for example, my discussion of such foundationalists as Roderick Chisholm or C. I. Lewis or my discussion of John Mackie or of metaphysicians like Alfred North Whitehead or Brand Blanshard.

It is also the case that all this range of reference may be intimidating. Hence my initial desire to avoid such reference, quotations, examination of the arguments of others, and the like. But, as I got into my subject, I found, again and again, for certain positions I wished to discuss, that certain philosophers with certain conceptions of doing philosophy expressed these things very adroitly. They were the very things I wanted to come to grips with in one way or another and they put them very well. To more or less paraphrase them without reference would hardly be honest; to make arguments or state positions that were somewhat in the ball park of these positions would not be philosophically as adequate in trying to give the best reasonably short statement readily available of the position to be discussed.

So, quite against my initial inclination, and with unease, I end up discussing an array of contemporary philosophers.

However, that, as I originally feared, may also make for the alienation from my text. My suggestion for the overcoming of that alienation (if it exists) is this: what is most important in this text are the positions and conceptions articulated and discussed, not the doing of explicative justice to the owners or occupants of those positions. I have tried, of course, to get the accounts right of the philosophers I discuss, but when I discuss Chisholm's, Rawls's, Blanshard's, Mackie's, Rorty's, or Gibbard's position on something or other, it is primarily *the position, articulated as I articulate it* that should be fastened on *here* and not that it is Blanshard's or Rawls's or whomever's. If you have not read the philosopher in question, or have only read her superficially, just take the position as X's or Y's position and note carefully what it says (that is, how I articulate it) and see how it fits in with the flow of the narrative and the structure of the overall argument in the text. Gain that understanding and then reflect critically on it. Ask about the soundness of the arguments and their point. Think about alternatives and the soundness of the arguments for them and their point. Try to make comparisons between the various conceptions of philosophy I set out and ask whether the alternatives are really alternatives that one must choose between or whether they can, and, if they can, whether they should, be combined in some way. And always look for the place of the claims being made in the unfolding narrative of my account. (Remember the arguments could be sound and still have little point.)

Doing these things is the important thing here. There are, moreover, references in the notes to the authors discussed. Where you are taken by or challenged by a philosopher or a position or are both interested in and perplexed by what I say about a given philosopher or position, you may very well find a more adequate, certainly a fuller, account of it than I have been able to give in the text by tracing down the references I provide. It is, moreover, to stress the general position or conception, rather than the exact thought of the philosopher (whom I may not be an expert on), that has led me frequently to use phrases like Cartesian, Lockian, Kantian, Deweyian, Wittgensteinian, Rawlsian, and the like.

For Everyone

I have lots of intellectual debts, far more than I can remember with any accuracy. Debts go long ago to my teacher, Everett Hall. Among his many virtues was a fine metaphilosophical sense. Debts also spring back to friends of long ago: Alice Ambrose, Charles Baylis, William Bean,

Thomas Flynn, Arthur Dow, Joseph Epstein, Gertrude Ezorsky, Ramon Lemos, Morris Lazerowitz, William Kennick, Sidney Morgenbesser, Wade Savage, and, more recently, to Shabbir Akhtar, Barry Allen, Rodger Beehler, Andrew Brook, Steven Burns, Richmond Campbell, Wesley Cooper, Jocelyne Couture, Adel Daher, Dennis Fissette, Andrew Lugg, Bruce Jennings, Arthur Caplan, Russell Cornett, Ruth Macklin, Peter Rossel, Stanley Stein, Y. K. Shih, Béla Szabados, Bertell Ollman, Stanley Malinovitch, Michel Seymour, Terence Penelhum, Tziporah Kasachkoff, David Copp, Hugo Meynell, Henk Hart, Justus Hartnack, John Collier, Brian Walker, Mike Kubara, T. Y. Henderson, Robert Hoffman, Jack Glickman, Rodney Peffer, Sidney Gendin, Steven Patten, and to my colleagues at New York University, the University of Calgary, the University of Ottawa, as well as going way back to Hamilton College, Amherst College, Brooklyn College, and the State University of New York at Binghamton. I am also in debt to discussions of years ago with James Moulder at Rhodes University and to my colleagues at Queen's University when in 1986 I was James Milton Scott Visiting Professor. But by far my greatest debt goes to my students, both graduate and undergraduate, principally at Hamilton College, Amherst College, New York University, the University of Calgary, and the University of Ottawa. Discussions with them and the experience of their probing questioning and counter-arguments and alternative ways of looking at things and articulating them gave vibrancy to my intellectual life.

There are intellectual debts of another sort, some of which should be evident in the text. I refer to the philosophers who have molded my thought. First there were John Dewey, George Santayana and C. S. Peirce; later the logical empiricists, most particularly A. J. Ayer, Charles Stevenson and the Swedish philosopher Axel Hägerström, and, at about that time also, and somewhat conflictingly, C. I. Lewis. Only a little later and, as for me, as a *volte face*, came the post-*Tractatus* Wittgenstein, G. E. Moore *apres Principia Ethica*, and what was called ordinary language philosophy or Oxford philosophy, including such maverick figures as Peter Winch, Frederick Waismann and Stuart Hampshire. (Among the ordinary language philosophers in moral philosophy, Stephen Toulmin and Kurt Baier had a great influence on me.) But here, for a way of viewing philosophy, the most decisive influences were those of Moore and Wittgenstein. Later, considerably later, and from a very different direction, came Marx, later Marxists (principally, but not exclusively, the analytical Marxists or, as I would prefer to call them, analytical Marxians), the Frankfurt School critical theorists, and Jürgen Habermas. And, again from a different direction, the work of John Rawls powerfully influenced me. Lastly, and rather later in the day than for most philosophers, the work of Richard

Rorty, Arthur Murphy, Donald Davidson, and Hilary Putnam has strongly influenced my views, particularly my metaphilosophical views.

Those influences are rather a mixed bag and it leaves me, not unsurprisingly, with a lot of philosophical loose ends and ambivalences and perhaps my metaphilosophy shows it. I have tried here to forge a distinctive thing out of it, but centrally, as the citations at the beginning of each of the three parts (the major divisions of the book) reveal, the influence of Wittgenstein, Rorty and Dewey cut deepest in matters metaphilosophical.

There are two things important to my thought that I have not been able to integrate into my text and so they have been ignored. They are my feminism and my Marxianism. I gradually became aware, perhaps around fifteen years ago, of the importance of feminist thought. Feminism, as a political and social movement, had long before impressed itself on me, but I did not think of it as having much philosophical relevance. However, reading and discussions concerning such issues with Marsha Hanen, culminating in the volume we jointly edited, _Science, Morality and Feminist Theory_, were of lasting value to me. The work in feminist theory of Annette Baier, Seyla Benhabib, Susan Moller Okin, Sandra Harding, Marylin Friedman, Martha Nussbaum, Cora Diamond, Lorraine Code, Nancy Fraser, and Linda Nicholson has been important to my philosophical development. What they have said about ethics and social theory has crucially pushed my own thinking along. The contextualism, historicism, distrust of a stress on principles, distrust of theory (particularly of grand theory), and of appeals to reason that many of them evince seem to me insightful and right. It fits in very well with the conception of philosophy developed in Part III. I am more skeptical, however, of talk about a feminist epistemology, metaphysics or philosophy of science. Since I am skeptical of any of these philosophical enterprises, I will, of course, be skeptical of feminist versions as well. I am generally happier and more confident that we are displaying "the realistic spirit" when we get with these thinkers a deconstruction of philosophy as a distinctive discipline in favor of social critique and articulation. But the books on feminist theory keep piling up on my shelves and, from the reading I have been able to do, I am convinced that there is important work being done and to be done there. When I have been able to more adequately fit such ideas into the web of my thinking and sensibilities, my metaphilosophical outlook may shift. But right now it seems to me that a proper metaphilosophy for feminism, context-sensitive and theory-wary as it is, would be that of broadly Deweyian philosophy as an examination of the problems of life: philosophy as social critique and articulation.

Ditto, I would say, for the metaphilosophy appropriate to Marxism. There is nothing about Marxism in this volume. But my analytical

Marxianism remains as firm as ever in an age where many people are forgetting about Marx and Marxism (if they ever knew anything about such matters in the first place) and where socialism and communism for very many no longer seem either a threat or a hope, but a joke. The reason I have not discussed Marx or Marxism here is that I have never thought of Marxism as a philosophy, any more than I think of Weber's or Durkheim's systematic empirical social theories as philosophies—though their work, as Marx's, is very important for philosophy. (Perhaps, on my part, this is but a carry over from my more puristically analytical days?) But I have never been taken by Marxist accounts of philosophy. I much prefer Marx's and Engels's own scornful remarks about philosophy in their *The German Ideology*. (Remarks that many Western Marxists regard as their positivist remainders, anathema, they have it, to the true Hegelian spirit of Marxism.) I am particularly unimpressed by dialectical materialism, appeals to a "dialectical logic" and Marxist philosophy of science. But I think that Marxian social theory as rationally reconstructed (though often in somewhat different and sometimes conflicting ways) by G. A. Cohen, Joshua Cohen, Jon Elster, John Roemer, Andrew Levine, Debra Satz, Richard Miller, Erik Olin Wright, Phillipe van Parjis, and David Schweickhart is the most promising systematic social theory, yielding, as well, social critique, that is available to us. And like any good theory, it is capable of being revised and developed. Marxianism should be like Darwinianism. There are no Darwinists and there should be no Marxists, but there are Darwinians and likewise there should be Marxians. And I remain unabashedly a Marxian.

It might be said, given my transformation of philosophy into social theory and critique, that I should think of both feminism and Marxianism as philosophy as well in being social theory and critique. In that sense, if we are careful to so construe philosophy, I am perfectly content to regard Marxism and feminism as philosophy and would regard my own attempts to contribute to Marxian social theory as in *that sense* philosophical. Perhaps we should follow Quine's advice about not sharply demarcating philosophy from other activities. (His advice is one thing; his own practice is another.) Still, Marxianism's best *metaphilosophical* articulation seems to me to be a pragmatist one. The same thing, I think, is true for feminism.

However, *inside* social theory, there are important questions of scope. Marxians, including analytical ones, believe in the need and viability of having a systematic social theory. In that they are one with critical theorists. Pragmatists, along with Foucault, are skeptical of systematic social theory and stick more to smaller scale problem oriented theorizing. The particular conception of metaphilosophy I articulate and defend here takes no sides on such issues in empirical social theory and critique and is compatible with both. Here, it seems to me we should proceed by trial and error. Repeated efforts to construct critical social theories at various levels of generality and specificity should again and again be tried on for size. Methodological restrictions or dicta will just get in the way of good work here.

Finally, there are two further debts of another kind that I would like to acknowledge. I would like to thank Merlette Schnell for her expert preparation of the manuscript for this book and for her shipping and receiving various versions and portions of this book as they went back and forth between Montréal and Calgary, and later between Calgary and Aix-en-Provence. And I would like, as well, to thank the Philosophy Department of the University of Calgary and its Head, Brenda Baker, for its generous secretarial support to an Emeritus Professor both at sea with and terrified by what is regarded by some as the benefits of our new technology.

Kai Nielsen

INTRODUCTION

Viewing Philosophy

I

Philosophy is a strange subject in that "What is philosophy?" is a persistent, endlessly contested question of *philosophy* itself. It plainly poses tendentious philosophical problems. Philosophers, both through most periods in the history of their subject and at the present time, have hotly, and without achieving much by way of agreement, disputed what philosophy is. In an introductory physics, biology, geology, or chemistry text, if it is at all representative, as well as such a text in any other firmly established science, a broad characterization of the field can, and typically will, be given in the introductory chapter or preface that generally would be accepted by practitioners in the field in question as at least roughly characterizing what the field is. Some, with a penchant for niceties, might demur at this or that phrasing, but, if the text is at all a standard one, there would be no wholesale repudiation of its characterization of what the field is. Moreover, what is "standard" is not just a matter of some local consensus, but is accepted throughout the scientific community: that is the worldwide community of physicists or the worldwide community of biologists and the like. But this is not so in philosophy. What is philosophy? How should it be characterized? What is its scope and subject matter? What, properly, is it? All these questions are vigorously contested. And, concerning what should be said, we gain nothing more than some local and transient consensus.

It is so local that these matters are often conceived rather differently from philosophy department to philosophy department in universities in Canada and the United States, to say nothing of the very deep differences between France, Germany and Italy, on the one hand, and the Anglo-American and Scandinavian culture-areas on the other. We get even more of a tower of Babel when we extend our gaze to South America, Africa,

Russia, and the Indian subcontinent. By contrast, physics, chemistry, biology, geology, and the rest of the "hard sciences" are pretty much the same across all these culture-areas and indeed throughout the world. A chemist trained in Uganda, for example, may be a little less up to date than a chemist trained in London; if the Ugandan chemist goes to London to work or study, he probably will have some catching up to do. But it is just catching up. It is not that he is faced with a whole new, or almost wholly new, subject matter, a radically different methodology and ways of conceptualizing things. But a student from France or Germany soaked in Kant, Hegel, Marx, Husserl, Heidegger, Sartre, Foucault, and Derrida, but ignorant of logic and analytic philosophy, coming (assuming she could get in) to the philosophy department at UCLA or MIT, or even at Oxford or Harvard, would feel very much at sea. It would be like she was no longer studying the same subject. And the same would apply to the student from MIT who found herself at Heidelberg or Padua or Nanterre. Jacques Derrida and George Boulos go about very different things in very different ways, as did Martin Heidegger and Bertrand Russell.

It is natural to respond that when philosophers look at the great philosophers of the past—Plato, Aristotle, Augustine, Aquinas, Scotus, Descartes, Locke, Hume, Reid, Kant, and Hegel—they share a common heritage. This, of course, is in a way so. But, even here, when Karl Jaspers, Martin Heidegger, Karl Popper and Gregory Vlastos talk about Plato, for example, very different things get said; what is appropriated from the great figures of the past is radically different. They sometimes hardly seem to be talking about the same people. Similar things sometimes should be said for their appreciation of their worth. For Russell, Ayer and Popper, Hegel is a figure of fun, a charlatan, who should not be taken seriously, while for John Dewey, Charles Taylor or Alasdair MacIntyre, Hegel is a very deep and centrally important philosopher in the Western tradition from whom we still have much to learn. In short, philosophy divides into schools, sometimes warring, often contemptuous of each other, sometimes just utterly indifferent to each other. Fashion seems to rule the day; ideological clashes are deep and pervasive, while the theoreticians of the various schools are usually firmly convinced that they are doing things rightly and that the others are mistaken. Not infrequently, they believe that some of them—typically those most distant from them—are completely beside the track. They acknowledge, of course, that there are deep and perplexing philosophical problems, but they also think that they have, in general terms anyway, the right way of going about things and ways very different from theirs are just thoroughly misguided. There are analytic philosophers who think that proper philosophy, or at least proper contemporary philosophy, *just is analytic philosophy*. The Continental stuff, they believe, is bullshit. Continental philosophers of the traditional sort return the compliment by claiming that analytic philosophy is utterly superficial, arid logic-chopping. And so it goes and with it the whirligig of fashion and of stubborn, often uninformed, ethnocentrism.

However, it should also be said that there are many philosophers now on either side of the philosophical iron curtain who are not so rigid and, to borrow from talk about music, there are now many crossovers—philosophers who can and do play it both ways with a foot in both camps. And much *very contemporary* French philosophy, turning against its own traditions, seems very subservient to Anglo-American philosophy, as if French philosophers, Anglo-American preconceptions to the contrary notwithstanding, have lost their own voice. But it is also the case that what philosophers with a foot in both camps take philosophy to be, with the widening of their vision, tends to become amorphous and variable from philosopher to philosopher. So fashion, ideology and radically different conceptualization continue to rule the day. And this is not just a matter of our confused and conflictual times, for it is not new to philosophy, but is something that has repeatedly happened throughout most of its varied history.

Most philosophers simply ignore such considerations, but, if pressed with a kind of sociological account of their subject matter, they, rather grudgingly, will acknowledge this tower of Babel phenomena, while at the same time trying to extinguish any real impact from it on them. Having conveniently swept the phenomena under the rug, they, never taking the matter to heart, go about business as usual—in fact, their quite different businesses as usual—as if nothing were rotten in the Kingdom of Denmark.

Perhaps nothing really is rotten, but surely all this diversity—this thorough lack of consensus, this absence of cross-cultural and transhistorical paradigms—strongly suggests that something is askew. It is difficult to see how philosophers in good faith, in the face of this, can just go on as usual without some measured response to it or at least a wary skepticism about what they are doing. It is certainly hard to regard such diversity as the glory of philosophy and it is hard not to think of it as a scandal in philosophy.

Yet the need, or at least the desire, to philosophize is very pervasive across cultural space and historical time. People have repeatedly been driven to it, even though it is anything but clear whether there is anything that gives these diverse activities a unity or whether they have any tolerably clear conception of what they are being driven to or what they are questing for. It is, that is, not evident what we are doing when we do philosophy. Indeed it very much appears that there are many different things that people are doing when they do philosophy and that there is no essential underlying rationale for, or underlying unity to, all these diverse things. But appearances may be deceiving; perhaps there is something, or some cluster of things, that is the task or the tasks of philosophy when it is *properly* done? (There is here, of course, a *normative* intrusion and is this, to go around the mulberry bush again, proper?)

We shall be looking into that, trying to get some grip on that. "Philosophy" is not the name of a natural kind. In that way it differs from "oak" and "tide" and is more like "gender" or "pessimism". There is nothing there in the social world that we could discover that philosophy must be. Rather, philosophy is what that diverse lot of people who call themselves philosophers do. Moreover, their activities are so diverse that there is nothing that we could sensibly call the task of philosophy. But it is possible, and may even be true, that there is something, or some cluster of related things, that, when we reflect carefully on why we want to philosophize, we will, at least from where we now stand in history, come to regard as the most humanly engaging and intellectually demanding (perhaps they will not come to the same thing?) task or cluster of related tasks of philosophy. When we think carefully and searchingly and take our reflections to heart is there anything we will agree on here? Is there any reasonably distinctive sort of thing that we will really want to do that we will take to be the center of philosophical activity? There hasn't been in the past, but *maybe* things will be better in the future? (The skeptic in me says, "I wouldn't bet my ranch on it.")

Given the very many different things that philosophy has been, and is, and in the skeptical spirit that diversity should generate, there is good reason to ask whether we can, in anything but an implicitly partisan manner, discover or articulate some cluster of things that is philosophy's central task: its deep underlying point or at least its point for us standing where we stand now in cultural history. We shall in this volume, in trying to get a grip on this, first have a look at some diverse traditional conceptions of "the central task of philosophy" and then argue, though not without trepidation, for a transforming of philosophy that will yield a distinctive conception of a central, and humanly important, task of philosophy.

II

In considering these matters, we should keep firmly in mind what we have just stressed, namely, that the very idea of philosophy is problematical (what once was called essentially contested) and that the force of this is particularly strong in our time. Perhaps that is just an effect of a scientistic culture, but the very idea of some distinctive philosophical knowledge or justified philosophical beliefs or philosophical truth is very problematic. Philosophers ask questions like what is knowledge, truth, causation, goodness, justice, ultimate reality, genuine evidence, morality, mind, body, God, freedom, and the like. Philosophical questions tend to be very general and in that way abstract. Biologists tell us about causal connections between events of certain sorts, physicists tell us about causal connections between events of other sorts. The philosopher, by contrast, asks about causal connection *in general*. She asks about what it is for one event to cause another. Similarly, she will ask, with utter generality, what consciousness is, what truth is, what justice is, what ultimate reality is. By contrast, a physicist will tell us that there are neutrinos, a neurologist that there are synapses, a historian (perhaps) that there are classes, a botanist that there are no ferns in Greenland, a mathematician that there are no end of prime numbers. But the philosopher—going for complete generality—will want to know what sorts of things there are altogether.

However, it is not clear, when we get *so general*, what it is that we are asking. In asking, in such a general way, what causation is, what truth is, what reality is, what goodness is, what could we be asking other than asking how "cause", "truth", "reality", "good", and their equivalents in other languages are used? We are asking, that is, a question that is an empirical question about our linguistic regularities, but (at least supposedly) marking uses that go so deep that they would mark linguistic regularities in any language. But philosophers, or at least most of them, particularly the traditional sorts, think that they are asking something other than that, or at least something somehow more than that. They do not want to be caught up in what they regard as linguisticism. But what is this "more" or "other" that they are asking for—what does "more" or "other" come to in this context? What would it be like to answer these questions is by no means crystal clear. We are unclear what it is we are supposed to be doing here. We do not even have a firm understanding of what we are asking. It looks like philosophers have dropped too much context and generalized at least once too often. But, sensible or not, such generality is very characteristic of philosophy. Without it we do not seem to be doing philosophy at all.

III

I will now abruptly shift contexts while continuing to fasten on the question "What is philosophy?" We have, or so at least the logical positivists (logical empiricists) thought, only two secure, well regulated types of knowledge. Deductive knowledge attainable in the formal sciences of logic and mathematics: where starting from axioms and utilizing rules of formation and transformation, we deduce *theorems*. *Given these axioms*, we can establish purely deductively and uncontroversially that certain other propositions must be true. This is one secure and well regulated source of knowledge yielded by logic and mathematics. In these disciplines we can really prove theorems and not just discursively and dialectically argue for so and so in ways that are invariably inconclusive and typically contested. The other source of secure knowledge is experimental and observational knowledge where from hypothesis construction, experiment, observation, and induction, we can really establish that certain things are so or at least probably so. We form hypotheses, make deductions and observations, and gather evidence. Through these procedures we increase our knowledge of what the world is like.

These are the two great sources of secure knowledge. The logical positivists, but not only the logical positivists, concluded that these are the *only* sources of secure knowledge that we have or indeed could even come to have. They may be the only sources of knowledge we have *period*. But philosophy is anomalous with respect to both. Facing this, a few philosophers have proposed to reduce philosophy to logic, but that has been a non-starter as those who proposed it soon realized themselves (e.g., Bertrand Russell). (It is one thing to say, truly or falsely, that logic is sometimes a useful tool for philosophy; it is an altogether different thing to say that philosophy is logic.) Some few others (a very few) have tried to construe philosophy as an experimental science. But just as there are no theorems proved in philosophy, so philosophy has no experimental results such that we can sensibly speak of the experimental results established by philosophy. Indeed, as it is a humbling experience for philosophers to try to list the theorems proved in philosophy, so it is equally humbling for them to list the established results of philosophy, experimental or otherwise. "Every event has a cause" is a plausible enough sounding claim as perhaps is "There are only particulars." But they certainly do not function as or even like empirical hypotheses or empirical observation statements (to be pleonastic). "Every event has a cause" is not like "Every winter it snows in Montréal" or "Every April the swallows return to Regina." We understand perfectly well what it would be like for the latter two propositions to be false. There is nothing *conceptually* anomalous about the swallows not returning in April to Regina or about it not snowing one winter in Montréal. But we are not clear about what it would be like to observe a causeless event or even whether there could be one. "Causeless event" is not, or certainly does not seem to be, self-contradictory like "causeless effect". But still the very notion is *conceptually* anomalous in a way a snowless winter in Montréal is not. Similarly, while we understand what it would be like to establish experimentally and observationally that there are only speckled trout in Meech Lake or that there are only sparrows around Bill's bird feeder, we have not the remotest idea what it would be like to establish or to disestablish *experimentally* or *observationally* that there are only particulars.

In short, philosophical propositions seem neither to be truths of logic or of mathematics or like such truths, nor experimental hypotheses or propositions establishable experimentally or observationally. The two firmly established and regulated sources of knowledge seem not to yield anything philosophical. Philosophical knowledge or warranted assertions, if there are either, certainly do not seem to be theorems of logic or mathematics or like those theorems or experimental hypotheses or simply empirical observations. So we are left at a loss as to what kind of knowledge or warranted assertion, if any kind, they can yield. They seem to be very anomalous and problematic propositions. We are in the dark as to how to establish or disestablish their truth or falsity or even how to ascertain or determine what counts for or against their truth.

It could be replied that this is a too scientistic way of looking at things and indeed even an old fashioned, Pre-Quinean way of being scientistic at that. It in effect takes too uncritically the distinction (alleged distinction) between the analytic and synthetic of *the a priori* and *the aposteriori*. As we shall see in Chapter 2, not all sentences, including plainly meaningful sentences in science and everyday life, are naturally so classifiable and yet they, not infrequently, state things we plainly often know. The division between formal and non-formal science may not be as sharp as it was pictured as being above. There are propositions not clearly, on the one hand, true by definition or in virtue of "their meaning alone" or, on the other hand, experimentally or observationally true, which are none the less unproblematic bits of knowledge, if anything is, e.g., "Orthodox Jews fast on the Day of Atonement." If on a given occasion a Jew does not fast on the Day of Atonement, it does not follow that he is not an Orthodox Jew, but the truth of the statement "Orthodox Jews fast on the Day of Atonement" is not established experimentally or experientially either. Yet the proposition is unproblematically true. So it may be that the logical positivist conception of the sources of secure knowledge, as commonsensical and tough-minded as it at first seems, is too narrow. I may be—and this will become important in Part Three—that there is nothing anomalous at all in saying that we know that pain is bad, torture is vile, that we should normally tell the truth, even though these propositions do not fit into either model of secure knowledge: logical and mathematical knowledge, on the one hand, or experimental and observational knowledge, on the other.

IV

However, distinctively philosophical propositions, e.g., "There are only particulars," "Forms are the ultimate reality," "Pleasure and only pleasure is intrinsically good," "God exists," or "Every event has a cause" are all very problematical. In beginning to see how they are problematical, it may well be valuable to see that they are neither of a type, on the one hand, with the propositions of logic or mathematics, nor, on the other hand, with

experimental hypotheses or observation sentences, such as "The cow is in
the corn." When it is also noted that they are not uncontroversially
establishable as true or false, as are scientific statements which do not fit,
or at least do not fit comfortably, in the analytic/empirical division, such as
"Kinetic energy is equal to one half the product of mass and velocity
squared" or "All physical laws much be Lorentz-invariant," we come to
realize that, even with the abandonment of the analytic/empirical dichotomy, they still remain problematic.

So philosophical principles lack the secure establishability of scientific
and many commonsense propositions of everyday life, e.g., "Frustrated
people are often aggressive" or "Around eight in the morning on a weekday
the subway is normally crowded." So while we might be able to demarcate
philosophical propositions from scientific ones (formal and non-formal) and
commonsense empirical propositions and plain moral propositions, the
problematicity of the philosophical propositions is revealed in that very
demarcation. We seem at loss as to how to establish, or even weakly
confirm, the truth of clearly philosophical propositions. At the very least,
to take only a part of this, philosophy, whatever it is, does not appear to
be a science, either formal or non-formal. A naturalism (a scientistic
naturalism) that ties itself to so construing philosophy seems at least to be
plainly mistaken.

V

So in this volume we will concern ourselves most centrally with the
philosophy of philosophy. We will ask what philosophy is, what it has been,
what, if anything, it can reasonably be, and, finally, what it should be.
Following what has become a rather common practice, I shall call this
inquiry *metaphilosophy.* Some philosophers object to this label denying that
there is, or even can be, any such thing, or at least any such coherent thing,
as metaphilosophy, for the philosophy of philosophy remains firmly
philosophy. When we ask what philosophy was, is, reasonably is, properly
is, what it should become, we are asking *philosophical* questions. To
assert—or, for that matter, to deny—that philosophy is, properly is, or
should be so and so is to make a philosophical claim and to engage *in*
philosophy itself and any such claims, or attempted claims, will themselves
be bits of philosophy and not something *meta-to-philosophy.*

Notoriously, "What is philosophy?" is itself a philosophical question and
a question *in* philosophy. Philosophical positions are taken about what
philosophy is or should be and philosophical arguments are deployed for
or against these positions. This being so there can be no such thing as a
metaphilosophy as something standing before or above or underpinning
philosophy, saying what it is, properly is, or should be. All such claims are

themselves *philosophical* claims and claims *in* philosophy. *There is no philosophically neutral standing back and answering these questions without engaging in philosophy itself.* (In this way metaphilosophy is very different than metaethics. Metaethics—or at least most metaethics—is really meta-to-ethics, though this is not to deny that it is philosophy, but it is to deny that it is ethics or at least that it is typically ethics.)

Thus, while strictly speaking there can be no metaphilosophy, we will, as a convenient short-hand, call the *philosophy of philosophy* "metaphilosophy". That is to say, I shall take as metaphilosophical questions that cluster of philosophical questions or perplexities concerning "What is philosophy", "What is it, properly?", "What should it be?", "What (if anything) is its point, purpose, or task?", "What is its proper subject matter, scope, method or methods?", "What is its nature (if indeed it has one)?", "What kind (if any kind) of discipline is it or should it become? Is it a science? Can it become a science and, if so, in what sense?", "What, if anything, are the data of philosophy or is that even the right way to conceptualize things in speaking of philosophy?". Is there, or can there even be, something *external* to philosophy, such as science, logic, common sense, religion, tradition, that philosophy can or must appeal to in trying to check its claims or that it must presuppose or assume in the very doing of philosophy? These and similar questions are themselves philosophical questions about philosophy—though some of them may be philosophical pseudo-questions. Though still, pseudo or not, they are also questions *in* philosophy. These questions, and questions like them, I shall call metaphilosophical questions. The inquiries in this volume, though sometimes only by indirection, will all be metaphilosophical.

VI

Getting Straight About Philosophy is divided into three parts with two chapters in each part. Part One, entitled "Philosophy as Metaphysics," first looks at philosophy construed in very traditional terms as having its center in Systematic Speculative Metaphysics. This way of conceiving of philosophy, and of centering it and articulating it, is now both in the Anglo-American-Scandinavian ambience and on the Continent much out of favor. This is even true for philosophers who do analytical metaphysics. Still it is a way of conceiving of philosophy that historically has had a very powerful influence. It well might be called the classical tradition, a tradition running from Plato to Hegel and even finding impressive contemporary representatives in the work of Alfred North Whitehead, Brand Blanshard and Bernard Lonergren. Moreover, it is a conception of philosophy that attracts many to philosophy and just seems to some of them what philosophy really is or at least should be. If they cannot have this, they want done with philosophy. It also has its defenders in the Thomistic-Aristotelian tradition of Catholic philosophy and from academics and intellectuals from outside of philosophy such as Leo Strauss and his followers.

I attempt in Chapter 1 to articulate the core conceptions that are common to such speculative metaphysics, show its attraction and rationale, and then to show why such a way of conceiving and doing philosophy cannot be sustained. In the chapter following that—Chapter 2 of Part One, "Metaphysics and *a priori* Knowledge"—I turn to philosophers, many of whom are of a more Kantian orientation than those discussed in the first chapter, who seek clearly to demarcate philosophy as an autonomous discipline distinct from other disciplines and from other activities. They seek to do this by circumscribing a domain of knowledge of the requisite general sort: a knowledge which is both *a priori* and synthetic. Philosophical propositions, and metaphysical propositions in particular, are, they argue, synthetic *a priori* propositions, categorially distinct from both analytic propositions—John Locke's "trifling propositions"—and the empirical propositions of science and of everyday life. I argue that the very notion of a synthetic *a priori* proposition is a non-starter. What has made it seem otherwise to some philosophers is either that they have an overly narrow conception of analyticity (say, a strictly Kantian one) or fail to recognize the force of the arguments deployed by W. O. Quine, Mortin White, and Hilary Putnam designed to show that both in science and everyday life there are many sentences which are not straightforwardly empirical without being *a priori*, or at least unproblematically *a priori*, either. The idea that all sentences or propositions must be one or the other (empirical or *a priori*) is, or so at least I shall argue, an unempirical dogma.

The argument for this leads me to some discussion of the analytic/synthetic distinction itself and to the challenges to it coming from Quine. When this is sorted out, as I think Putnam has done very well, there is no place left for the *synthetic a priori* or any kind of metaphysical necessity. Yet the case for metaphysics, or at least a transcendental metaphysics (if that is not a redundancy), stands or falls with the case for the *synthetic a priori*. My argument shall be that it falls.

I conclude Part One with a brief discussion of *scientistic* metaphysics which eschews the *a priori* and all transcendental argumentation and takes itself to be continuous with science and to be its most abstract, general and theoretical side. I argue that that last claim is a conceit and that such a metaphysics is hardly a metaphysics at all. It is in reality conceptual analysis and conceptual analysis with a dubious point. Genuine metaphysical philosophizing will take a transcendental turn, but, or so I shall argue, there are good reasons for believing that no transcendental arguments can be sound. So the conclusion of Part One shall be that, while philosophy construed as metaphysics has its evident attractions in giving us an argument-rooted comprehensive vision of the world, including our place in such a world, such visions are as impossible as the logical positivists, pragmatists and Wittgensteinians took them to be.

I turn in Part Two to philosophy as epistemology. While the stress on philosophy as metaphysics comes from the classical world, was continued by the Medievals and by Spinoza and Leibnitz down to Hegel and the Absolute Idealists following in his wake, philosophy as epistemology, or, more cautiously, as centered in epistemology, is an invention, or at least a stress, of the modern world, starting with Descartes, finding its full flourishing in the British empiricists, going on to Kant (though there mixed with much else as well), and continuing into the contemporary period with such foundationalist philosophers as Bertrand Russell, Moritz Schlick, C. I. Lewis, and A. J. Ayer. Sometimes it is linked with a dualistic metaphysics (as with Curt Ducasse or C. D. Broad) or with metaphysical realism. But often it takes itself to be free of metaphysics. I examine it on its epistemological side only as the claim to provide us with secure foundations of knowledge which would defeat global epistemological skepticism, after posing in clear terms the challenge of a global epistemological skepticism, and provide us with a foundation of knowledge such that we will have a criterion, or criteria, for determining in any domain (religion, science, morality, our common life) whether we have there genuine knowledge or not.

Classical foundationalism from John Locke to C. I. Lewis would find this foundation in primitive sense certainties, a more modest foundationalism in basic empirical statements that are intersubjectively available. Philosophy, foundationalists of all sorts believe, if it is not to be lost in a holistic fog, must so ground itself. Philosophy most fundamentally should concern itself with the clear articulation and defense of such foundations. If we construct a metaphysics, as *some* of them believe we should, it must be solidly grounded in such a foundationalist epistemology. If, like Moritz Schlick and A. J. Ayer, we eschew metaphysics, we still should articulate a foundationalist epistemology to exhibit the real ground of our genuine knowing.

In Part Two I articulate this foundationalist conception of philosophy, argue that on its own terms it cannot defeat global skepticism, and that, skepticism apart, it fails in both its classical and modern forms to articulate a viable conception of the foundations of knowledge. That foundationalist project is a characteristic project of modernity and of the empiricist temperament. But for all its attractions—or so I shall argue—it is an impossible project replete with errors, some of them deep and ineradicable. But I shall also argue that we do not need foundationalism to defeat global skepticism. The two take in each other's dirty linen. Moreover, in rejecting foundationalism, as Otto Neurath, John Dewey, W. O. Quine, Richard Rorty, and Donald Davidson all well argue, we need not, and indeed should not, abandon the empiricist temper of modernity. But this is an empiricism that does not conflict with a commonsense realism (with the realistic spirit) though it does set aside metaphysical realism.

In Part Three there is a sea change in thinking about what philosophy not only is, but about what it can and should be. I pass from nay-saying against the Tradition, with its conception that at the core of philosophy there is either metaphysics or epistemology or both, to a yea-saying where I argue for a transformation of philosophy away from its metaphysical and epistemological past to a conception of philosophy as social critique and articulation. Philosophy, I argue, should not concern itself with the perennial problems of philosophy, but with the problems of human beings and most particularly, for us, as we philosophize, with the taxing social, political and moral problems that face us in our epoch. This goes in a roughly Deweyian pragmatist, contextualist way, but it also owes much to the later work of John Rawls, such as we find in his *Political Liberalism* and in a series of essays preceding it, where he deliberately travels philosophically light, setting aside, for the purposes of his social theorizing, metaphysical and epistemological issues. Dewey's broad conception of scientific method, what he sometimes calls the method of intelligence, is not at all scientistic, and comes to very much the same thing as Rawls's method of wide reflective equilibrium. If one were to take a slogan for my conception of a transformed philosophy, it would be that of philosophy as grappling with the problems of life within the limits—the methodological limits—of wide reflective equilibrium alone. In Chapter 5, I describe, elucidate, illustrate, and defend that conception of what the office of philosophy should be.

In Chapter 6—the concluding chapter—I face the objection that this is too narrow and partisan a conception of philosophy. And I also, and I believe even more centrally, carefully examine the understandable arguments behind the reaction that philosophy construed as concerning itself with the problems of life inescapably requires either one or two things (more likely both) if its arguments are to be sustained. The first is that it will require deep foundations in a normative ethical theory or at least the acceptance and defense of general normative ethical principles requiring a normative ethical theory for their justification. The second is the claim that such a pragmatic philosophy makes metaethical assumptions which require a metaethical theory for their proper articulation and defense. Without, in short, the claim goes, a metaethical underpinning and a foundation in normative ethical theory, the Deweyian-Rawlsian turn will be baseless and arbitrary. Philosophy cannot escape so easily, if at all, its ancestry.

I argue that it is a mistake to try to find a basis for such a pragmatic approach in systematic normative ethical theory of either a foundational or non-foundational sort. Such theorizing, I shall argue, standardly suffers from the ills of foundationalism as well as other more destructive ills which apply to both its foundationalist forms (which are its most characteristic forms) and its non-foundationalist forms as well. Metaethics, particularly in its most contemporary forms, is less evidently irrelevant to philosophy as an examination of problems of life than normative ethical theory. Indeed in its most modest underlaborer forms it is not irrelevant at all, for conceptual clarification is often, though less often than many philosophers believe, of crucial importance. But—or so I shall argue—metaethical theory, no more than normative ethical theory, can provide the grounding for the pragmatic turn in philosophy that I defend. However, intrinsically interesting some metathetical problems and theories may be, they are better left to benign neglect by a philosophy bent on social critique and articulation. Both metaethical theory and normative ethical theory or some amalgam of them are wheels that, in this respect at least, turn no machinery.

VII

I do not explicitly address questions in the philosophy of language and the philosophy of logic in this volume. Much of the work here, often of an awesomely technical sort, has by now passed over, and rightly so, I believe, into science. What started as philosophy became, with its development and greater precising, science and this is just as it should be. That some people, practicing their science, are still housed in philosophy departments is an accident of history. Such theorists so theorizing will, probably in the next fifty years or so, have departments of their own. There are, however, for the time being, still some philosophical residues and I, in effect, concern myself with them by considering what such theorizing can and cannot do in philosophy.

I do not consider issues in the philosophy of mind or the philosophy of religion. Traditional issues such as dualism, materialism (eliminative or otherwise), or epiphenomalism are tied up in the viscitudes of metaphysics and metaphysics, I argue in Part One, should be set aside. Present day work in cognitive science has its philosophical cheerleading and *perhaps* can sometimes profit from some underlabour elucidations, but it neither requires nor can it come to have philosophical foundations. Foundationalism is as bankrupt here as elsewhere.

Philosophy of religion, to move on to the other subject I do not discuss, traditionally has been utterly entangled in metaphysics. Its core claims are cosmological-metaphysical claims and sometimes of the most obscure sort. Philosophies of religion of the traditional sort and those theologians attempting to do natural theology fall with the fall of metaphysics. They may fall anyway even if some metaphysical view is viable (say, a materialist one), but a necessary condition for their viability—the viability of such traditional philosophy of religion and natural theology—is the viability of metaphysics. Their fate, that is, is tied up with the fate of metaphysics.

However, some contemporary philosophy of religion is anti-foundationalist, and some of it seems at least to travel light metaphysically. Where this anti-foundationalism in the philosophy of religion takes a Wittgensteinian turn, it drops all cosmological claims and becomes in effect, whatever its author's intentions, a kind of moral articulation, a way of facing and attempting perspicuously to display the problems of life. As such it goes into a broadly Deweyian hopper and, in effect, whether its practitioners are aware of it or not, casts religion in an *entirely secular* frame. In its non-Wittgensteinian and non-empiricist forms, by contrast, anti-foundationalism in the philosophy of religion does not travel metaphysically light. It simply appeals to, or presupposes, the old cosmological-metaphysical claims of a theistic outlook as unargued dogmas: as dogmas they deliberately do not argue for. They just proclaim, in a way which fits badly with their supposed anti-foundationalism, that they are *properly basic*. Indeed they invoke them as such dogmas in their crudest forms. Such metaphysical propositions are simply accepted dogmatically without defense. It is, at least in effect, an aggressively assertive metaphysics without argument. But a metaphysics without argument, as John Passmore has observed, is nothing, or at least nothing rationally defendable. Indeed it hardly deserves the label "philosophy", yet metaphysics is intertwined in philosophy of religion as traditionally understood. In shying away from argument, such theistic anti-foundationalism—even proclaiming what they call a "standard theism"—in effect claims the worth of metaphysics, as traditionally conceived, without incurring its risks and its costs. Such philosophers of religion may succeed in showing that these metaphysical claims can have no foundationalist underpinnings and that *foundationalist* atheistic or empiricist critiques, what they call atheology, are ineffective against the claims of religion. But not all secular critique is foundationalist critique. And, most centrally, these theistic metaphysics-encumbered alleged anti-foundationalists in the philosophy of religion just proclaim their fundamental cosmological-metaphysical claims without facing arguments concerning the intelligibility of such metaphysical claims or questions about what reasons we could have for believing them to be true or even for understanding what could count for or against their truth so that we could have some understanding of these claims. They make, to put the matter curtly, no effort to show that these cosmological-metaphysical claims can reasonably be taken to be true or taken as true. They also believe that any secularist critique of the claims of religion presupposes some form of foundationalism when it does not. Secular, including explicitly atheistic critique of religion, does not stand or fall with foundationalism. Such anti-foundationalist Christian or Jewish philosophers cannot so easily dispose of skepticism over religion.

Wittgensteinian anti-foundationalism in religion is, as I remarked, a form of moral articulation embedded in narratives (Christian or Jewish or Islamic stories) touched with emotion. It is in reality an utterly secular view of the world, misleadingly calling itself a perspicuous representation of Christianity, Judaism or Islam *from the inside.* Non-Wittgensteinian theistic anti-foundationalism in the philosophy of religion, by contrast, genuinely sets itself off from secular conceptions. But it mistakenly thinks that a secular view of the world, involving a critique of religion, must be foundationalist and then just dogmatically, without argument, proclaims against it a crude form of transcendentalist metaphysics. We get, like in the good-old-time-religion, proclaiming here rather than argument or elucidation. But strangely enough it comes from philosophers of a sometimes analytical bent. But since secularism need not, and indeed should not, be foundationalist, the situation is not that of setting dogma against dogma and letting faith (religious or otherwise) take its pick: decide which it will take to be properly basic, where anything goes.

VIII

So, to pull the threads of these preliminary matters together, I shall try here to see something of how philosophy and the vocation of a philosopher has been conceived, and is now being conceived; I seek critically, as well, to examine these conceptions and finally to set out a certain somewhat new way in which—or so I shall argue—philosophy should be conceived and practiced. I will, that is, articulate and argue for a certain kind of transformation of philosophy. My conception, as any such conception would be, is tendentious and so the burden of proof rests on me. However, in shouldering this burden, and trying to make such a case for what philosophy should be, it is crucial to take into consideration not only the strength of my own case, but the strengths and weaknesses of the alternatives as well. I seek, I hope accurately and as persuasively as they can be made, to set out the core claims and styles of reasoning of these alternative ways of conceiving of the office of philosophy and to make clear their rationales. All philosophy is contentious and metaphilosophy most particularly so. Any attempt to say what philosophy properly is should be viewed with considerable suspicion: taken, that is, with a grain of salt. I, of course, do not exempt my own claims here. It is, however, time to end the sketchings and proclaimings of an introduction and to turn to the alternatives themselves set in narratives, but narratives rooted in argument.

PART ONE

Philosophy as Metaphysics

Where does our investigation get its importance from, since it seems only to destroy everything interesting, that is, all that is great and important? (As it were all the buildings leaving behind only bits of stone and rubble.) What we are destroying is nothing but houses of cards, and we are clearing up the ground of language on which they stand.

— Ludwig Wittgenstein

All that philosophy can do is destroy idols. And that means not making any new ones—say, out of "the absence of idols."

— Ludwig Wittgenstein

A common sense person, when he reads earlier philosophers, thinks—quite rightly—"Sheer nonsense." When he listens to me he thinks—rightly again—"Nothing but stale truisms." That is how the image of philosophy has changed.

— Ludwig Wittgenstein

1

Speculative Metaphysics

What drives or leads people, particularly young people, to philosophy is, as we shall see, varied. However, one particularly persistent thing is their trying to see life as a whole. They want to see how things hang together and whether they hang together coherently. Things in their personal lives or in their society or both perplex them, indeed in some instances painfully worry them. Things can seem very crazy; nothing seems to make sense; many of "the rules of life"—the expected ways of behaving and thinking—seem to them to be unreasonable. They are told by their elders how they ought to live, or they see just by their elders' behavior—the way they live their lives—how it is that they are expected to live and it can come to seem to them, and sometimes actually does, that there are no good reasons for living in that way or even sometimes worse still that these ways of living and thinking are positively unreasonable. But then what is reasonable, what is a good or a bad way to live or the right way to think and act? And how could we determine these things if, indeed, we can at all? Are all things, or at least the really significant things in life, subjective or relative? Is there no answer, beyond a subjective response, to these and similar questionings? People turn to philosophy in the expectation, or at least in the hope, that philosophy can provide answers to, or at least something in the way of enlightenment concerning, these and similar questions. They look to philosophy to show them how things—the various elements of our lives, our society and our world—hang together, or can be made to hang together, in a coherent way and how we can ground claims about what it is reasonable to do and believe. They want—and indeed we want—to see if we can get a reasonable understanding of the sorry scheme of things entire. They want to see if they can make some sense of it and with that of their own lives.

That I think is the dominant and most persistent thing that leads people, and sometimes drives people, to philosophy in the first place, though it may not, in all instances, be what keeps them there. But it is not the only thing that leads people into philosophy. When in school they study plain geometry they may come to wonder what makes the axioms true or how we could establish the truth of the axioms. With the axioms we can prove theorems. But what, if anything, grounds the axioms? They may come to study mathematics and, in effect generalizing the plain geometry case, come to wonder if mathematics has any underpinning foundations, any grounding, that can show that the various axioms in the domain of mathematics are true. Or are these just postulations or posits that mathematicians make in games that mathematicians play either for pragmatic purposes (as a tool for science) or just for the fun of it? What yields the objectivity of mathematics? Are its axioms just arbitrary postulates and are its procedures just arbitrary procedures? But to say that seems very strange indeed given its intimate link with science. Such a claim, it appears, couldn't be quite serious. But how do we determine the truth of its axioms? What is the link between mathematics and the world? So some, feeling perplexity here, look to philosophy to show, if indeed any such thing can be shown, the real foundations of mathematics and some would as well extend this even to logic. We need, they think, to articulate the philosophical foundations of mathematics and logic.

Similar things obtain for people studying the sciences (the non-formal sciences, if you will). Someone studying economics, if she goes at all theoretical, will study (for good or for ill) decision theory and game theory. This will give her a picture and conception of what rationality is. But it also seems—or can come to seem—remote from the world and from what we would ordinarily, or indeed on reflection, mean by rationality or by reasonableness, if indeed these two things are the same or closely similar. But what then is rationality and what is it to act rationally, to behave reasonably and to have reasonable beliefs and a reasonable outlook on life? Some people look to philosophy for enlightenment here, hoping that by its study they can come to understand what it is reasonable to do or what it is reasonable to believe and what rationality really is. Again, very relativist and subjectivist worries come quickly to the fore.

Psychology can lead to philosophy as well. Consciousness seems to either remain, on the one hand, very unanalyzed or, if thought about, very mysterious or, on the other, in the study of psychology simply to be ignored or to be "reduced" out of the way. We seem at least to have a direct access to the contents of our own minds in a way that we do not have, and cannot have, to the minds of others. For others we infer their mental states from their behavior, including, of course, their verbal behavior. A similar thing is true of our knowledge of the natural world. That, too, is, or so it is often thought, inferential. But we do not, in our own case, observe ourselves thinking, feeling, intending, and the like. We just have sudden thoughts, pains, tickles; we form intentions; we have moods. But the having of these things does not seem to be a matter of observational knowledge in the way my knowledge that you are in pain, that you are depressed, or that you are thinking or worried or unhappy is, or in the way that I observe that the tide is coming in or that it is raining and the like. But what then is this consciousness that we have? What sort of thing is it and is it the basis for our knowledge of the world of nature, of society, and of the minds of others? Again we are led into philosophy. This time from psychology.

The study of physics is another fertile source of philosophy. When we want to know what the world is like, how things work in nature, what the fundamental building blocks (the basic particles) are, physics seems the reasonable place to go. It would seem—or so it seems to most of us educated in modern societies—unreasonable to go any place else for such knowledge. But still the fundamental particles are very strange entities indeed and within the history of physics what they are taken to be keeps changing. How then do we know that what physics at a given time (say, our epoch) claims to be the fundamental particles really are the fundamental particles, and how do we know that its fundamental laws are true or even approximately so? Things have changed in the course of the history of physics. There seems to be nothing like, or even any possibility of, something like, "the final physics," though from time to time something like that gets exhuberantly claimed, or at least expected.[1] Should we, or can we, go to philosophy for answers to such questions about fundamental particles? That seems, to put it mildly, rather unlikely, for isn't it more reasonable to be more confident in what physics tells us about these matters than what philosophy or theology or anything else tells us? Yet what physics tells us is the case about what are the fundamental particles and about what are the laws of nature varies over time. It is certainly reasonable to expect that what physics will tell us in two hundred years, if it is still around, will be rather different than what it tells us now, no matter how much hype we are getting now about the Higgs particle. So how can we know what the world is really and truly like and what ultimate reality is? But we—or at least some of us in certain moods—would like to know these things and we would like to have certainty here. Religion seems to give us, where it attempts this at all, only a mythical or illusory answer rooted in an ungrounded claim to certainty. Can philosophy yield what physics (the sciences more generally) and religion cannot? Or do we even have any coherent idea of what we are talking about when we speak of ultimate reality; could we come to have such an idea if we took careful thought?

Social and cultural anthropology also sometimes provide a push to philosophy, though in a rather different way than psychology or physics. We, in studying anthropology, study some very exotic cultures with very different beliefs and belief-systems: radically different cosmologies, different religions, different moralities, conceptions of marriage and the family, and the like. The ways various cultures organize their lives and conceptualize who they are are not infrequently strikingly different. Moreover, it is also tolerably clear that there is a method in all our various cultural madnesses: all tribes rationalize their behavior, that is, they have a rationale for their various ways of living: their, if you will, various experiments in living. It is easy enough, given its pervasive hegemony and remarkable success, not to have relativistic worries about Western science and the physical cosmology and technology that goes with it. But anthropologists have made clear enough that a superior science does not entail, or in any way assure, superiority in morals, religion, art forms, family relations, or political organization. It is anything but obvious that Balinese art is inferior to Flemish art, Buddhism to Christianity, or the morality of the Hopi inferior to the morality of the British. Here the *de facto* differences between peoples (cultural relativism) inclines us to normative relativism (the belief that no one culture's morality, form of political organization, family structure, art forms, religion, and the like is superior to another's) or to skepticism, namely, to the belief that we have, at least as yet, no objective ground for believing that one society has a superiority in any such forms to another. Attempts to claim this, it is easy to believe, are invariably ethnocentric. They just presuppose, though sometimes in rather unconscious ways, that the norms of one's own society are the correct norms. But, unfortunately, there is no non-ethnocentric ranking of cultures, including, what is perhaps most important to us, a cross-cultural ranking of moralities. Our illusion of superiority, it is not infrequently felt, is just the usual ethnocentrism of all peoples, plus a recognition that the superiority of Western natural science and technology has enabled us to conquer and dominate the world. But that superiority in science in itself yields no legitimation to any claim to superiority in other respects. We must, we are inclined to feel, realize that, if we wish to be non-evasive, we must just acquiesce in this belief in a deep relativity. But we also want to ask whether morality just comes to the mores of our tribe or whether a more universal and a more tolerant morality, sensitive both to cultural differences and to more universalistic aspirations, is possible and somehow reasonably defendable. But perhaps there is a catch in the little word "reasonably." Again it is possible to hope that philosophy might, if pursued carefully, lead to some enlightenment here. So again the study of a science, this time anthropology, can incline us to philosophy.

Literature rather than science leads some people into philosophy. The reading of literature, most typically certain kinds of novels or plays, generates reflection about life and society and, with that, reflection concerning morality and often about religion as well. These various things sometimes lead to philosophical reflection. Sometimes the reading of literature generates thoughts about the self and thoughts about self-deception or thoughts about history, society, politics, religion, and about relations between people. They are thoughts, as Jean-Paul Sartre put it, about what the world is like, meaning by that our social world. Think, for example, of the not unlikely impact of reading Turgenev, Tolstoy, Chekhov, Flaubert, Kleist, Fontaine, or Proust. Novelists construct narratives and paint verbal pictures—sometimes deep and troubling pictures. Moreover, they *sometimes*, as in Thomas Mann's *Magic Mountain*, have characters arguing, and arguing philosophically, with each other. But it is hardly the novelist's or dramatist's business to present arguments, let alone systematic arguments, but to paint a picture, construct narratives, and to reveal a world and human beings and their reflections on and responses to this world and, sometimes, indeed characteristically, to reveal a viewpoint on this world, sometimes even a worldview, if we want to speak in a pretentious way. Sometimes people soaked in literature, or at least extensively dipped in it, can come to wonder if there is a more systematic, more reasoned, more argument-based way of articulating and perhaps even defending (something odd for literature to do) a view of the world, a way of seeing how things hang together, or a way of seeing who we were, are or who we might become than they gain from literature. So from literature some people turn to philosophy.[2]

So, besides the rather pervasive desire to see how things hang together, to make sense of life, society and the world, there are, typically, but not invariably, from people coming from one or another of the sciences or the arts, a concern, not so much for seeing how things hang together, but a desire to get clear about, and to come to see the truth about, what some one or another central category in life is: rationality, mind, ultimate reality (through the fundamental particles), truth, morality, God (if there is one), identity, causality, and the like. But this will frequently lead back, until, in many instances, later specialization and professionalism freezes one, to trying to get a grip on the big picture of how things hang together in the most general sense of that term. Psychology, for example, can lead us to philosophy by leading us to reflect on the relation between mind and body. This can in turn lead us to think about what ultimate reality really is. Is it through and through physical such that mental phenomena (sudden thoughts, pains, moods, and the like) must be brain processes, functional states of the body or—as in the case of moods or cogitations—distinctive forms of behavior, so that the whole category of the mental can be shown to be material? Or are there, as dualists think, two distinct kinds of ultimate reality—the physical and the mental? If the former—if some form of materialism or physicalism, as it is now usually called by philosophers, is true—is the correct account of the world, then how is it, if it is at all, that we can be free or have autonomy? Materialism (physicalism) seems at least to require determinism and determinism seems to undermine human agency (freedom, autonomy) and that in turn seems to undermine morality and the very possibility of any kind of reasonable politics. But it is also the case that to claim such implications seems at least absurd; still it looks like, on the face of it, that there are such connections. But materialism might not require determinism and determinism might be perfectly compatible with freedom, properly understood, and not undermine morality at all. Indeed genuine human agency, and thus morality, *might* require determinism. So we can naturally be *led* from being perplexed by psychology, first to some closely related problems (mind, consciousness, the self) to, in turn, being led to consider a whole nest of at least seemingly interconnected problems and through this to try to get at what ultimate reality really is and at how things in the most general sense of the term hang together in the most general sense of the term and how coherently. Any of the specific problems generated by some particular science or by literature might generate the same search for a big picture and/or ultimate reality. Indeed the two (a big picture and ultimate reality) might go together. Still, some people driven to philosophy by one or another of the sciences might be more obsessed by one philosophical problem or cluster of problems than another. Someone puzzled by problems about fundamental particles or quantum mechanics might be more concerned with problems about ascertaining the ultimate constituents of the world than with the relativity of morals and visa-versa for those coming to philosophy from anthropology. Similarly, to mention a case we have not yet discussed, someone with political passions and an acute sense of the depth of ideological distortions in political life might be indifferent to problems about the objectivity or the foundations of mathematics generated from thinking about mathematics in a certain way, though she characteristically would be interested in questions about the relativity of morals and about what (in certain domains at least) it is possible for us to know. Yet frequently the consideration of one philosophical problem leads to a consideration of another and that to another until it is possible to come to feel—no doubt quite mistakenly—that it is necessary to solve them all before we can solve any of them. So in being driven or just led into philosophy, even from a particular perch, it is natural to want what many with philosophical inclinations want straight off: to see how things hang together and what the nature of ultimate reality is.[3]

II

Systematic metaphysics or speculative philosophy, an enterprise that until rather recently has been thought to be at the very heart of philosophy, and without which philosophy would lose its deepest rationale, is an extension of, and a systematically articulated statement of, the attempt to achieve the most extensive seeing of how things hang together. Indeed, or so the belief goes, it yields a necessary system: a system that *must* be the way the metaphysician characterizes it to be, if his account is the right one. It is such a system that speculative metaphysicians believe to be achievable. Moreover, this is something philosophy must achieve, they claim, if it is to achieve its proper end.

Metaphysics sought to give such a coherent total view of how things hang together and sought as well to say what ultimate reality is and to give us a true comprehensive account and conception of how the scheme of things entire must hang together, including giving an account of the place of value in the world of fact and of our place in nature and society. This is a more articulated conception of what it is that drove people to philosophy in the first place when they wanted, though rather inarticulately, to see how things hang together and what reality really is like beyond all conventions and historically and culturally relative constructions. This is what the metaphysical quest is most fundamentally about and, while it may require a careful logical or conceptual analysis or elucidation of our fundamental categories and concepts, it seems at least to be something more as well. It wants to know what ultimate reality is and what the necessary structure of the world, including the world of values, is. In knowing this it wants to understand the world of human beings with their aspirations and sense of purpose, so that we can see how things hang together in a *rational totality*. The thing we most want to know is what is ultimate reality—something, given neither by common sense nor by science, but, if by anything, or so the claim goes, it is something we gain by metaphysical philosophizing. This quest is a powerful motivating force that drives many people to philosophy, only for them to discover that not many contemporary philosophers believe that anything like this is at all possible, including people, they discover, to be careful and reflective thinkers. Even contemporary analytical metaphysics, they will soon also discover, will not answer, or even attempt to answer, to this need. It can perhaps provide a systematic description and analysis of our fundamental concepts. It perhaps can give us an analysis, or an elucidation, and with that the possibility of a systematic display, of our fundamental concepts or categories: truth, value, cause, identity, mind, God, nature, and time.[4] But this kind of analytical metaphysics, descriptive and elucidatory of our fundamental concepts, will not answer to the philosophical thirst in question. We do not want merely an analysis and perspicuous display of our concept of God or our concept of mind or our concept of value, but we want to know whether God is a reality at all and whether mind and values are fundamental realities or rather somehow derivative or partly or perhaps even wholly illusory conceptions.[5] We want to know the *true necessary* system of the world and with that what ultimate reality is.

In different ways some philosophers have been telling us that such a quest is utterly impossible. That message was conveyed by Montaïgne modestly a long time ago, by Hume, Kant and Kierkegaard more robustly somewhat more recently, then by the logical positivists, by Russell, Wittgenstein, by James and Dewey among the pragmatists, and by neo-pragmatists such as Rorty, Fish, and Putnam more recently. But when students coming to philosophy are told, or given to understand, by their professors that something like this is so, they are often deeply disappointed. The very rationale for studying philosophy has, they feel, been yanked out from under them. If they are convinced by their professors by what they say about the anti-metaphysical thrust of philosophy, they will typically lose interest in philosophy and either turn to religion or some pseudo-religion or lose all interest in such speculative questions. In the latter case they will give up all attempts to see how things hang together or to see the sorry scheme of things entire. Indeed they give up philosophy with the giving up of metaphysical philosophizing.

I think that contemporary Enlightenment thinking, rooted in what by now is conventional wisdom, is right here and that such speculative philosophizing cannot come to anything. I shall not, however, just dismiss it, but will show some of the reasons why *such* philosophizing is so generally, though by no means universally, set aside and will, as well, toward the end of this chapter, show (a) something of what is lost when such metaphysical enterprises are abandoned and (b) show what is sensibly left (deeply demythologized) of such endeavours that we might reasonably ascribe to without crucifying our intellects and good sense. I shall argue that the desire to see how things hang together is not without point and import and can and should be defended as a reasonable and relatively unproblematic endeavor.

III

I shall start by a little more exacting characterization of what systematic metaphysics and speculative philosophy come to. Many now will say that the only function, or the only proper function, of philosophy is the analysis of concepts or the elucidation of our uses of language. The thing is to analyze or elucidate what we mean by truth, God, good, or freedom and not to try to discover what is good and whether there is, or even could be, to take a key example, the reality we refer to, or supposedly refer to, as God. It is not the function of philosophy to discover new truths or new facts or even a more ultimate truth than anything available to common sense or science, let alone something very obscure called *The Truth*, but to analyze and perspicuously display what we already know to be so and to more perspicuously arrange the facts and beliefs that science and common sense yield. It is not, to repeat, the function of philosophy, taken as analysis or elucidation, to discover new truths or more ultimate truths. That, many analytic philosophers take it, is the function, or at least a function, of science. The function of speculative philosophy (systematic metaphysics), by contrast, is to discover truths, including new truths, about the universe as a whole: truths about how the various things that there are *are* and *must* be arranged. There is a strong drive for both necessity and completeness among metaphysicians; what is wanted is to finally have a total account of reality as a necessary system and with that also an account, an account, established reflectively and speculatively, to be true, of what ultimate reality is.

Some have said that speculative philosophy (metaphysics) is distinguished from science by its greater generality. It wants to establish propositions which are true, some metaphysicians claim, not of some limited domain such as physics or biology or politics or mathematics, but propositions which are true of everything in the universe or perhaps even of all possible universes as well as the actual universe. Sometimes these propositions are said to be true *a priori* or somehow to be necessarily true. A genuine metaphysics, they claim, will give us, in a way that science can never do, a true account of the *necessary* structure of the world. It will contain necessary propositions which are necessary without being empty and purely formal as tautologies are. Such, for example, to give some plainly empty ones, as if A is to the right of B and B to C then A is to the right of C or puppies are young dogs. These empty, or nearly empty ones, are John Locke's trifling propositions. The propositions metaphysicians are interested in, by contrast, and are also said to be known *a priori*, are somehow seen to be necessarily true, but, unlike the above propositions, their propositions are substantive propositions supposed to be revelatory of the very necessary structure of the world and are propositions which stand consistently together in a necessary total system of the world. They will tell us what the universe is like and why it is and *must* be like this. They will not just, as G. E. Moore thought philosophy should do, "give a general description of the whole of the universe," but will also attempt to give an argued description of how the whole of the universe not only is but *necessarily must* be.[6]

Sometimes the ultimate reality claimed by metaphysicians is said to be a hidden reality, hidden behind the veil of appearances or beyond all possible experience and whose claims are incapable of being, either directly or indirectly, experientially tested or warranted. Metaphysics, so conceived, makes statements which no conceivable observation could either directly or indirectly confirm or infirm or warrant such that we would have empirically testable grounds for assenting to such claims. But not all metaphysical systems make claims about a hidden reality behind what could be even in theory experienced. The objects or subject matter of metaphysical inquiry, as the subject is construed by some metaphysicians, need not be something hidden beyond the veil of experience. They need not be something noumenal. If the views of Spinoza, Bradley, Bergson, or Whitehead—all paradigmatic metaphysicians—are false, or worse still, incoherent, it is not because they are making claims, or trying to make claims, which are beyond the realm of all possible experience.

It is also not the case that speculative philosophy (metaphysics) need be, G. E. Moore to the contrary notwithstanding, making claims about everything in the universe. As we have already remarked, it sometimes is, but it need not be trying to establish propositions which are true about everything in the universe. Theories about the nature of God or the reality of universals are not about everything in the universe, though they standardly would be taken to be metaphysical. Rather, metaphysics concerns itself with the universe as a whole, with everything in the universe, only in the rather Pickwickian sense that it tries to give reasons why the universe is, and must be, as it is, and to identify the entities which are the ultimate or final actualities of the world. It further affirms that what is true of them must also be true of everything that is ultimately and finally actual. Everything which lacks such final actuality is either in reality merely a phase or aspect of such actual or final entities or is dependent for its existence on these final entities. They are the only ultimate realities.

This is characteristic of Alfred North Whitehead's metaphysical system (one of the very last great systematic metaphysicians), but what is crucial to see here, with Whitehead's philosophy being taken as an example, is that in addition to giving a systematic account of how things do and indeed must hang together, and of how the universe is and must be, a metaphysical view gives with this a conception of *ultimate reality*. But it need not be a doctrine of ultimate reality that claims that ultimate reality is a cluster of noumenal realities or even of a single noumenal reality that is beyond all human experiencing: a hidden reality that stands behind experience. That is one kind of metaphysics, typically linked with supernaturalistic religions, and the target of much empiricist, logical positivist and pragmatist attack. But it is not the only kind of metaphysics and it is not a requisite for having a view of how the universe must hang together. What is definitive of something being a metaphysics is that it is a systematic account of how the universe hangs, and allegedly *must* hang, together, along with an account of what the metaphysician believes the universe must be like, and with, as well, a conception of what the metaphysician takes to be ultimate reality. *It gives us the one true description of how the world is and indeed must be.*

One difficulty concerning such a view is in ascertaining what it could mean to say, and, beyond that bare claim of intelligibility, to give any warrant at all for claiming, that such and such entities are the finally real things of which the world is constituted.[7] How can, or can, such propositions be established and can there be any evidence or reasons in their favor? It seems at least that we have no idea of what it would be like to have evidence or reasons here. Some metaphysicians will say that ultimate reality, final actuality, all truly real being, is changeless or eternal. The empirically discoverable facts of change, they will say, cannot be accepted as characterizing ultimate reality, however obvious and ubiquitous it may be as an empirical phenomena.[8] Other metaphysicians will say, on the contrary, that the real being of anything that is fully and concretely actual is becoming. What appears to us as changeless or eternal must be seen as a phase, not ultimately real, of the temporal and not as real or actual on its own account. Real being is process. Reality is ceaseless change. But no hint at all has been given as to how we can ascertain which of these claims about ultimate reality is true or even probably true. We can paint various word-pictures here, give different narratives, but we have no idea at all of how to establish which of these claims, if any, are true or even probably true.[9] A metaphysician such as Whitehead is not just saying, paradoxically, that whatever does, did, or will exist not only changes but possesses feelings. He is saying that whatever did not possess feelings would lack ultimate reality: would not be ultimately real. It is no longer just a matter of whether we can experientially specify (locate)—itself a very problematical conception in such contexts—whether everything in the world around us has feelings, but whether what is ultimately or finally actual has them and indeed must have them. But it very much looks like that here we have no reason to make one claim or believe one thing rather than another. Different people with different attitudes, different affective dispositions or stances to the world, or perhaps with different aesthetic sensibilities will say one thing rather than another about what *ultimate* reality must be like. The claim that one metaphysical view rather than another is the right one seems to come to nothing more than an incitement to treat some areas of experience as deeper, more humanly reliable, closer to the way things really are, nearer to the heart of reality, than other areas. But that seems to be little more than emotive talk—talk expressive and evocative of our feelings about or attitudes toward the world and our lives.

With such attitudes we organize other of our experiences in accordance with them. But this yields no metaphysical knowledge—no distinctive philosophical knowledge or even any warranted assertions of any sort. It reveals rather different emotional stances toward the world, different ways we feel about things. Attitudes toward experience will not yield substantial information about the world, let alone knowledge about the nature of everything that did, does, or will exist, to say nothing about what must exist. Speculative philosophy or metaphysics purports to give us such knowledge, but there is no good reason to believe that it actually succeeds.[10] If philosophy is identified with metaphysics, at least so construed, or taken essentially to be *a quest for ultimate reality*, then we have good reasons to be very skeptical indeed about philosophy as a cognitive enterprise and to be very doubtful if it has any intellectually sustainable future. And *if* fundamental particle theory in physics makes the same grandiose claims, it succumbs to the same malady. Indeed it, in making such claims, in effect becomes speculative metaphysics. The quest for finality dies a slow death; fallibilism, for some, is hard to accept. There remains a nostalgia for the Absolute.

IV

Speculative philosophy or metaphysics is, as Alfred North Whitehead has put it, "the endeavour to frame a coherent, logical, necessary system of general ideas in terms of which every item of our experience can be interpreted."[11] We have seen that there is good reason to believe that no such metaphysical knowledge or justified belief can be attained. Still, while metaphysicians tell us stories, paint verbal pictures, construct often rather complicated narratives, they also characteristically offer arguments of some sort or another in support of their assertions and their theories.[12] I have argued that these arguments are too loosely framed or articulated to come to anything. But perhaps there is a somewhat different understanding of metaphysics in which it is, after all, a significant endeavor. Metaphysicians will typically say that neither science nor reflective common sense, or some lucid combination of both, are "the final thing." They both need a rational underpinning which will reveal and clearly display the deep rational foundations of the viable parts of common sense and science. As well, a proper metaphysics will give us rational grounds for criticizing certain stretches of science and common sense, perhaps revealing that some stretches of science (e.g., behaviorism in psychology) or common sense do not succeed in making true claims and are incompatible with a true account of the world.[13]

Is it at all plausible to think that we can have such an account of the world? Can metaphysics provide us with factual knowledge of what exists or can exist, a knowledge which science is unable to provide? Do we have any understanding of what it is to talk about "the final thing"? Is metaphysics really a source of knowledge of reality?[14] Perhaps our existing apparatus of concepts is in need of radical reform and a revisionary metaphysics could yield a new framework, a revised cluster of concepts, which would yield the one true characterization of the world and tell us what ultimate reality really is. It will not, to be genuine metaphysics, *just* be an alternative way of reconceptualizing things but will, as well, be a genuine source of knowledge of reality.[15] We will not just reconceptualize what we already know, *perhaps* giving ourselves a more perspicuous representation and/or a more unified characterization of that knowledge.[16] The metaphysics we construct will give us, the claim goes, a new and extended knowledge of the facts telling us what true being actually is.[17]

This is a nice flight of fancy, but how can metaphysics actually go beyond natural science? How can, or can, metaphysics second guess or go beyond physics in determining what ultimate reality is really like, what the true description of the world really is? Even to ask that question is to make metaphysics look absurd.[18] Perhaps talking about characterizing ultimate reality or what the building blocks or the true structure of the world is is absurd, but why, alternatively, cannot metaphysics go beyond the various special sciences, each concerned with certain aspects of reality, by concerning itself *with reality as a whole?* In doing this it will drop talk about ultimate reality or true being. But what could this concerning itself with reality *as a whole* come to other than succinctly and clearly to describe the various parts of reality discovered by common sense and the various sciences? But this would come to no more than a creation of what in effect would be a kind of encyclopedia setting out the various sciences and common sense practices that there are, showing what claims in their various domains the practitioners in question believe are true or at least the most plausible of the claims in their domain, and, as well, showing how they connect with one another. But the philosopher, metaphysician or not, has no special expertise here. Indeed for the various sciences, the scientists, working in the various areas, in the various domains of knowledge, should do this job. Making the connections is more problematical. It would require a team of scientists working together, typically with a broad range of expertise, in various sciences. But writing such compendia and reference books has very little to do with philosophy. It is not even remotely philosophical, but it does require for it to be properly done people with a broad education and clear heads.[19]

It sounds more philosophical, and in particular more metaphysical, to suggest that it is the aim, or at least an aim, of the metaphysician to *integrate* the theories and beliefs of the particular sciences and, as well, of the beliefs and practices of common sense (our ordinary life together), what some Continental philosophers call the lifeworld, into a coherent and unified world-picture.[20]   But, even leaving aside the fact that "world-picture" is a metaphor that could profit by a literalist paraphrase, what form is the desired world-picture to take? It could take the form of a scientistic metaphysics (a metaphysics within the limits of science alone) that would attempt the integration by reducing all intelligible common sense beliefs and practices and all the other sciences to physics. Physics, the master science, integrates them by showing what is really true in them. It is the basic science, and to carry out this reduction would be to procure the integrated world-picture which tells us, in accordance with what physics tells us, what the world is like. What physics cannot tell us we cannot know about the world. What is not displayable in terms of the concepts and structures of physics is not coherently conceivable. But then the physicist, not the philosopher, would be the person in a position to tell us what the true picture of the world is. The philosopher, *qua* logician or analyst, might perhaps show us how the reduction was carried out and in that way help carry out the integration. But the discovering of new facts, the depiction of ultimate reality, the characterizing of the one true picture of the world, namely, what, at a given time, comprehensively physics takes to be so, would be done by the physicist, or at least whoever does it would be doing physics. Moreover, it would certainly seem to be the case that the only person competent to do it, if anyone is, would be a physicist. There is here an activity for the physicist and for the logician (analyst) working together, but no room at all is left for the metaphysician. Again metaphysics drops out.

Alternatively we might say that metaphysical systems, and thus the work of metaphysicians, embody visions of the world which act as *stimuli* to scientists in their setting out of hypotheses or articulating theories, theories which in turn scientists eventually so elaborate, and so precise, so as finally to have empirically testable hypotheses. There is, on such an account, no such thing as a metaphysically or ontologically true view of the world. Rather a particular way of looking at the world, an *anticipatory* vision, stimulating scientific inquiry or perhaps a moral or political conception of life (a *Weltanschauung*), is a disguised set of *rules* for depicting whatever is observable or imaginable or perhaps deemed indispensable.[21] But, as a set of *rules,* they are not the sort of things that can be true or false, but, since they are rules, they are only capable of being adopted or abandoned, as useful or useless, or perhaps somehow in some other way as being helpful or not helpful, in stimulating scientific inquiry or the coming to take a moral, political, or religious stance. No one of these metaphysical systems, embodying visions of the world, could properly be said to be truer or closer to the truth than another. They could no more be true than any other rule or cluster of rules could be true for that is not the sort of thing a rule could be. They could not yield a true or coherent account of how the world is, let alone the one true account of the world. But if we know something, really know it, then what we know is true. But *metaphysics as vision* is the articulation of rules for viewing the world. But then it cannot be making any truth-claims or any other kind of knowledge-claims. As far as providing knowledge is concerned, metaphysics must give way to science and everyday observation, e.g., it rains a lot in Normandy or the food is generally better in France than in England. The only way of increasing our knowledge of the world is through ordinary observation and empirical science and, as well, though more problematically, by the nuanced and reflective descriptions of novelists, poets, and dramatists.

However, someone trying to defend a metaphysical conception of the world might still, even in the face of this, take the following tack. We have in our lives a number of practices other than scientific practices and ordinary observational practices. Besides engaging in scientific inquiry, we engage in moral, political, and artistic practices—we make moral judgments and engage in aesthetic creation or appreciation and some of us even engage in religious practices. It has been said that "through exercise of these activities various views of the world are nourished and develop."[22] As scientific inquiry leads to a scientific view of the world, so religious practices lead to or embody a religious view of the world and moral and aesthetic practices lead to moral and aesthetic views of the world. As is perhaps clearest with the various religious views of the world, they have features integral to their very articulation which are non-empirical. They do not, that is, consist in the articulation of empirical theories or the setting out of empirical hypotheses. They do not have the same structure as scientific views of the world. There remains, of course, our old skeptical query concerning how they could be making factual claims and how, if at all, they could add to the knowledge about the world or indeed yield any kind of knowledge. This is particularly pertinent for religious views of the world.[23] But for almost all of us, for example, moral practices are part of the web of our lives. And this is true for political practices as well. We have things here, whether "cognitive" or not, that we will not readily give up, namely, moral, political, religious (including anti-religious) views of the world. It is not unnatural, if we would reflect a bit, to consider examining what relations obtain between these various views of the world with an aim to arriving at and articulating a coherent and unified view of the world rather more holistic, rather more interconnected and comprehensive, than simply having a scientific or moral or political view of the world. It may well be that we, or at least many human beings, need, or at least reasonably would want, (if we can get one without evasion, mystification, or incoherency) such a view in which our diverse convictions and beliefs about the world and human life reasonably cohere. We would like to see, if we could, how things fit together into a coherent conception.

This—just like that—does not get us to a *total* or *complete* view about the world or a view about the whole of the universe or the universe as a whole: views that metaphysicians seek. Perhaps such notions do not make much sense. But any such less extravagant view of the world—partial, limited, and subject through and through to revision—is not thereby rendered senseless. We can see here that philosophy could have, in so proceeding, a synthesizing function and not only the analytic one of analysing or elucidating concepts or conceptions. And here, some philosophers think we have the beginnings of a speculative metaphysics. But, metaphysical or not, here we have a task which appears at least not to be scientific, for it is the integrating of religious (anti-religious), moral, aesthetic, and political views of the world with scientific ones. A scientific outlook on the world is something which constitutes but "one factor or element in the varied material which gives rise to the felt need for synthesis."[24] But, since this is so, this integrating task—or so some think—can "hardly be satisfied in terms of empirical science alone."[25] Thus, this integrating task looks like a philosophical task, or at least a task of reflective inquiry, though we still have a long way to go before we can establish it to be a metaphysical task.

How tight the coherence should be is an important question. Are we only talking about consistency here or are we talking about something more as well? We also would seem to have a conception of coherence where we could have more and less coherent views here. But we must, if we are to have anything of value, at least have consistency and that cannot be a matter of more or less. The articulated worldview is either consistent or it is not. But this aside, there is also the matter of the cognitive value of such worldviews. Various silly or even incoherent views can be made consistent. A good logician might be able to axiomatize Christian Science. When we consider all the elements in these worldviews and not just the empirical scientific and common sense empirical elements, how are we to distinguish them with respect to their truth-claims? How can we establish their truth or the degree to which they approximate being true? We can set aside those with contradictions that are so central as to be, non-excisable and thus unavoidable and similar incoherences. But where their claims are not incoherent, or at least not plainly incoherent, and do not involve inconsistencies, how do we assess their degree of warrant: the grounds for believing that they are true or probably true? We do not have the tests of empirical warranteability characteristic of scientific views. But how then do we determine which ones are true or the more likely to be true? Is there any kind of test here?[26] And even here, *perhaps* world-views with incoherencies might in other respects express insights that views without incoherencies do not. Moreover, a consistent and coherent worldview might still be false or otherwise mistaken—or so it is natural to argue—for it might not give a true description of the world or faithfully mirror reality.[27] Still, natural as this metaphor is, it is one of which we should be suspicious. It may lead us down the garden path. We shall return to this in our third chapter. For now, we shall take it for what it may well be, namely, a harmless metaphor. The present point is that a view of the world could be consistent and coherent and still say things which are false. But then how do we determine the truth or the viability of metaphysical views? It looks like we have no resources here.

Metaphysics begins to come in if the person who sets out to develop a coherent view of the world makes the assumption, or at least the provisional assumption, that the world (the universe) is a coherent whole. Metaphysicians tend to *assume* just that: assume that that just must somehow be so and that it is their task to show that. But that anything like this is so, or even a coherent conception, is anything but clear. It is quite unclear what it means to say that the world itself is either a coherent whole or is not a coherent whole; it is not clear what, if anything, such talk comes to. Moreover, we should recognize that any pattern you like could be reasonably viewed as having coherency. Drop pieces of multicolored paper on a white surface (say, a floor) and *no matter how they fall* we can trace patterns, see coherency. There is no way for the combination of bits of paper *not* to have a coherent pattern. And this means that there is little sense in talk of coherency or incoherency in such a context. The same obtains for the world. What would it be like for the world as a whole to be incoherent? No clear sense has been attached to this question. At most we can make some arbitrary stipulations here.

Edging more toward metaphysics, we not only look for worldviews which are consistent and coherent, we also look for worldviews which are *comprehensive*. And here we plainly have something which admits of degrees. We do not, however, know what an absolutely comprehensive or total worldview would come to, but we do, at least seemingly not unreasonably, seek a worldview which will cover the aspects of reality we mentioned above. A worldview which only accounted for mathematics and science would, everything else being equal, be inferior to a worldview which accounted for morality, politics, and (in some way) religion as well. Still, we should note, old matters returning like the repressed. We are lacking anything like a clear conception of what it would be like for such widespreading worldviews to be, on the one hand, either true or false or, on the other hand, for, one of them, where they all pass consistency tests, to be more adequate than another.

However—and this, I believe, is of central importance—as will become clear, I hope, in Chapter 5—even a comprehensive worldview need not be a metaphysical worldview. This has been acknowledged and clearly articulated by even such a resolute metaphysician and distinguished historian of philosophy as Frederick Copleston. Copleston writes

> ...some philosophers would probably be prepared to claim that the genuine metaphysician is concerned with displaying the basic structure of reality, which underlies and is presupposed by the various different kinds of phenomena, whereas the author of a worldview is concerned with constructing a coherent and unified picture of changing aspects of the world and human life, a picture which, by the nature of the case, is itself subject to change.[28]

Pragmatists, new and old, for example, articulate worldviews of this non-metaphysical sort while resisting the construction of metaphysical world-views.[29] The attempt to get a coherent conception of our life together – to see how these things hang or fail to hang together – is a crucial aspect of a reflective life and may be reasonably engaged in even by someone who believes, as I do, that metaphysics is moonshine. Moreover, attempting to see how things hang together, and even in succeeding a bit in so seeing things, can be rather less august than even the creating of non-metaphysical worldviews. Still it is not unreasonable to wish it to be a part of the creating of a coherent and unified interpretation of how our world is. But again this can be something less than a construction of a metaphysical system, or even the committing oneself to some metaphysical conceptions, without it being an endeavour without worth.

Notes

1. A distinguished theoretical physicist, Steven Weinberg, enthusiastically articulates what he thinks may turn out to be an ultimate theory of nature: a *final theory*. It would be a theory from whose principles all the laws that govern the workings of the universe could be deduced. For fundamental particle physics, he postulates something called the Higgs particle, which is his candidate for "ultimate reality." Steven Weinberg, *Dreams of a Final Theory* (New York: Pantheon, 1993). Roger Penrose, another distinguished theoretical physicist, gently throws cold water on such claims, concluding "Whatever the status of such grandiose ideas, we are, at best, a very long way from any kind of ultimate understanding of the nature of our universe." Roger Penrose, "Nature's Biggest Secret," *The New York Review of Books* XI, no. 17 (October 21, 1993), 82. Yet hope seems to spring eternal even with Penrose, for he remarks, "Without the kind of soaring global insights of an Einstein, I do not myself see how any real progress to anything approaching a final theory could be achieved." *Ibid.* But that leaves us with a claimed possibility (an Einstein may be just around the corner), while the reality of the matter is that we do not understand what it would be like to have a final theory and we do not know what we are talking about in speaking of ultimate reality. Moreover, and that aside, the history of science should make us very skeptical

indeed about claimed discoveries of *"the fundamental particle."* The Higgs particle may be our best candidate now, better than the positron, omega-minus, neutrino, anti-proton, tau-particle, or the top-quark. But a sense of the history of science or just a fallibilistic consciousness (some critical common sensism) should make us very wary indeed of any such claims. Is it very likely that in fifty years, or perhaps even in ten years, physics will still be so privileging the Higgs particle, to say nothing of what physics will look like (if it is still around) in two hundred years? Just a touch of a sense of history would make that seem astronomically unlikely. Belief in a *final theory* runs against our sense of how science, or more generally, knowledge, progresses or at least changes. The very notion of a final theory is *religiose.*

2. It might go the other way as well or there might be a complex interaction. The relationships between philosophy and literature are much more complex and nuanced than has usually been recognized. See the symposium on morality and literature in *Ethics* 98 (1988), 223-340; Martha Nussbaum, "Literature and Ethics" in Laurence Becker, ed., *Encyclopedia of Ethics* Vol. II, (New York: Garland Publishing, 1992), 728-31; Martha Nussbaum, *Love's Knowledge: Essays on Philosophy and Literature* (Oxford: Oxford University Press, 1990); Cora Diamond, *The Realistic Spirit* (Cambridge, Massachusetts: MIT Press, 1990), 309-18 and 267-81; Anthony J. Cascardi, ed., *Literature and the Question of Philosophy* (Baltimore, Maryland: Johns Hopkins University Press, 1987); and Iris Murdoch, "Philosophy and Literature" in Bryan Magee, ed., *Men of Ideas* (Oxford: Oxford University Press, 1982), 229-50.

3. As we shall see later in this chapter, and more extensively and from a different angle in Chapter 5, it is possible to want the former while believing talk of the latter makes no coherent sense.

4. P. F. Strawson, *Analysis and Metaphysics* (Oxford: Oxford University Press, 1992); P. F. Strawson, "Ma Philosophie: Son Développement, Son Thème Central et Sa Nature Générale," *Revue de theologogie et de philosophie* 120 (1988), 437-52; P. F. Strawson, *Skepticism and Naturalism* (London: Methuen, 1985).

5. Are there certain concepts of ours which, while being concepts which are a fundamental part of our common life (e.g., God, freedom, and immortality), still are concepts that are defective concepts or is the very notion of a concept so centrally placed being defective mistaken? See G. J. Warnock, "Analyses and Imagination" in Gilbert Ryle, ed., *The Revolution in Philosophy* (London: Macmillan, 1963), 111-24 and A. J. Ayer, "Metaphysics and Common Sense" in W. E. Kennick and Morris Lazerowitz, eds., *Metaphysics: Readings and Reappraisals* (Englewood Cliffs, New Jersey: Prentice-Hall, 1966), 317-30.

6. G. E. Moore, *Some Main Problems of Philosophy* (London: Allen and Unwin, 1953), 1.

7. P. F. Strawson gives us something of a demythologized conception of that. See his *Analysis and Metaphysics.* Talk of "finally real things," "ultimate reality," or "final theory," whether by philosophers or physicists, is of very doubtful intelligibility. Hopefully, the genuinely experimentally based part of physics engages in no such extravagance. When physicists do, they become metaphysicians. See note 1.

8. A. E. Murphy, "Can Speculative Philosophy be Defended?" *Philosophical Review* LII (1943), 138.

9. A. E. Murphy, "Can Speculative Philosophy be Defended?" 135-43 and W. E. Kennick, "The Enigma of Metaphysics" in Kennick and Lazerowitz, eds., *Metaphysics*, 1-14. Morris Lazerowitz, *The Structure of Metaphysics* (London: Routledge and Kegan Paul, 1955), 23-79.

10. A. E. Murphy, "Can Speculative Philosophy be Defended?" 139.

11. Alfred North Whitehead, *Process and Reality* (New York: Macmillan, 1929), 4; A. E. Murphy, *Reason and the Common Good* (Englewood Cliffs, New Jersey: Prentice-Hall, 1963), 142-62.

12. John Passmore, "The Place of Argument in Metaphysics" in Kennick and Lazerowitz, eds., *Metaphysics*, 356-65. Bernard Williams, "Metaphysical Arguments" in D. F. Pears, ed., *The Nature of Metaphysics* (London: Macmillan, 1957), 39-60.

13. *Ibid.* and Passmore, "Philosophy" in Paul Edwards, ed., *The Encyclopedia of Philosophy* Vol 6 (New York: Macmillan and Free Press, 1967), 216-26.

14. Frederick Copleston, "Ayer and World Views" in A. Phillips Griffiths, ed., *A. J. Ayer: Memorial Essays* (Cambridge, England: Cambridge University Press, 1991), 65.

15. A. J. Ayer, "Metaphysics and Common Sense," 317-30 and Brand Blanshard, "In Defense of Metaphysics" in Kennick and Lazerowitz, eds., *Metaphysics*, 331-35. Ayer, of course, criticizes such a conception, while Blanshard defends it. See here, as well, the debate between A. J. Ayer and Frederick Copleston reprinted in A. J. Ayer, *The Meaning of Life* (New York: Charles Scribner's Sons, 1990), 18-52.

16. It will not just be the metamorphized metaphysics characterized by John Wisdom, "The Metamorphosis of Metaphysics" in J. N. Findley, ed., *Studies in Philosophy* (London: Oxford University Press, 1966), 213-40.

17. Brian Magee, "The Ideas of Quine: A Dialogue with W. A. Quine" in Brian Magee, ed., *Men of Ideas*, 143-44.

18. It is even questionable whether such an activity has much, if any, value. See Stanley Fish, *Doing What Comes Naturally* (Durham, North Carolina: Duke University Press, 1989), 1-33 and Richard Rorty, "Putnam and the Relativist Menace," *The Journal of Philosophy* XC, no. 9 (September 1993), 443-61.

19. Passmore, "Philosophy," 216-26. See also D. F. Pears, ed., *The Nature of Metaphysics*, 4-8.

20. Brian Magee, "The Ideas of Quine: Dialogue with W. A. Quine," 143-44. See also Frederick Copleston, "Ayer and World Views," 63-75. Philosophers as very different as Quine and Copleston come together here.

21. Frederick Copleston, "Ayer and World Views," 63-75 and Fredrich Waismann, *How I See Philosophy* (New York: St. Martin's Press, 1968), 1-38.

22. Frederick Copleston, "Ayer and World Views," 67.

23. Kai Nielsen, *Scepticism* (New York: St. Martin's Press, 1973); Kai Nielsen, *An Introduction to the Philosophy of Religion* (London: Macmillan Press, 1982); and Kai Nielsen, *Philosophy and Atheism: In Defense of Atheism* (Buffalo, New York: Prometheus Books, 1985).

24. Frederick Copleston, "Ayer and World Views," 68.

25. Frederick Copleston, "Ayer and World Views," 68.

26. This was not only a worry of the positivists, but of rather more traditional philosophers as well. See W. T. Stace, "Can Speculative Philosophy be Defended?" *Philosophical Review* LII (1943), 116-26; Ralph M. Blake, "Can Speculative Philosophy

be Defended?" *Philosophical Review* LII, (1943), 127-34; and A. E. Murphy, "Can Speculative Philosophy be Defended?" 135-43.

27. Frederick Copleston, "Ayer and World Views," 70.

28. Frederick Copleston, "Ayer and World Views," 74.

29. See, for example, Richard Rorty, *Consequences of Pragmatism* (Minneapolis, Minnesota: University of Minnesota Press, 1982).

2

Metaphysics and *A Priori* Knowledge

I

It might be said I made things too easy for myself in the previous chapter. Such an ancient and persistent, even obsessional, enterprise as metaphysics, taken by so many philosophers to be so central to philosophy, cannot so easily, and indeed so high-handedly, be disposed of as I essay to do in what we have just seen. Perhaps grand metaphysical schemes—systems of systematic speculative philosophy, after the fashion of Spinoza, Hegel, Bradley, McTaggart, Whitehead, and Blanshard— can justifiably be set aside on the grounds I put forth in the previous chapter. But not all metaphysics is systematic speculative philosophy. Sometimes metaphysics limits itself to articulating and elucidating what are alleged to be synthetic *a priori* necessities of thought which are presupposed—or so the claim goes—in science and everyday life. It is one thing whether there are these fundamental *a priori* propositions, which are necessarily true for our world and for all possible worlds as well, and thus, as synthetic and necessary propositions, tell us what reality is and *must* be like. It is another thing again whether they form a comprehensive and necessary system. These two matters, that is, are distinct and should be kept apart. It may be that the establishment of the former is necessary for the establishment of the latter. But it is certainly not sufficient. There may be synthetic *a priori* truths without there being a system, let alone a "necessary system," of such *a priori* truths. Whatever I may have shown against comprehensive speculative systems, what I have not shown, in doing so, is that there cannot be true metaphysical propositions: synthetic *a priori* truths—truths whose truth is independent of experience, propositions which are established to be true by pure thought, holding for all possible worlds, but still extending our knowledge of reality and not merely unfolding our understanding of what we already know, e.g., triangles have three sides, where the idea of threesidedness is already contained in the very idea of triangularity: if we understand the meaning of "triangle" we know that triangles must have three sides.

Immanuel Kant was the great articulator and defender of the thesis that there are *synthetic a priori* truths. In contemporary philosophy, with a few notable exceptions, most philosophers, even philosophers in many ways very close to Kant such as C. I. Lewis, have not followed Kant here, but have gone in either of two ways. The first was to argue, as did the logical empiricists and many other linguistic philosophers, that all *a priori* truths are analytic (true in virtue of their meaning alone and independent of fact) and, as such, do not extend to our knowledge of the world, but merely make manifest what is implicit in our concepts (in the meanings of our uses of our words).[1] Thus, in being told—in normal circumstances pointlessly—that puppies are young dogs, we do not learn anything more than what we already knew about puppies in understanding the concept puppy or in understanding the use of "puppy." We do not extend our knowledge of puppies by knowing such truths about our meanings or uses of language as we do when we come to know that they are usually easy to housebreak, that in cold climates their hair grows longer if they are left outside than if left inside most of the time, that they are not seriously trainable until they are six months old, and the like. These statements, if true, extend our knowledge of puppies. But in learning that they are young dogs, that they are animals, that they are canines, and the like, we are merely learning what is already implicit in the very idea of a puppy; we are, as they used to say, merely unpacking the term "puppy"; we are not learning more about puppies and more about the world, except for learning linguistic facts about the use of "puppy." It is in this sense that analytic *a priori* propositions are said to be empty and to tell us nothing about reality: they do not extend our knowledge of reality (linguistic reality aside).

Synthetic *a priori* propositions, if there are or even can be such, share with *analytic a priori* propositions the feature of their truth not being dependent on experience and of their both being necessary truths. But, unlike the analytic ones, they are (1) supposed to extend our knowledge of reality while remaining *a priori* and necessary truths and (2) their denials are not self-contradictory. They yield new truths, or at least distinctive truths, about the necessary nature of reality. By now, to put it sociologically, belief that there are synthetic *a priori* propositions is out of fashion; it is widely believed among philosophers that, if there is any *a priori* knowledge at all, it is analytic. But logical empiricists and most linguistic philosophers do believe that there are *a priori* truths, but they think they are all analytic.

A second approach regards this dichotomy—this dualism of truths of reason and truths of fact—as a dogma. These philosophers are a very strong current of thought at present in North America. Following W. V. Quine's lead, these philosophers believe either that there are no *a priori* truths, period, or at least that there are none that are not trivial and philosophically useless.[2] All such Quineans agree that all truths or at least all significant truths—all non-trifling propositions—are empirical truths of one sort or another, with different degrees of embeddedness in the fabric of our belief, and are held with different degrees of vulnerability to disconfirmation or infirmation. All necessity is some type of empirical necessity. There is, on the strongest formulation of this stance, no knowledge at all to be had *a priori*, for all our knowledge is empirical knowledge. So-called analytical propositions are propositions which we all accept but accept for no reason, yet hold come what may, or at least, if subject to revision or abandonment at all, would be the last propositions we would revise or abandon under pressure from our other propositions.

I am inclined to go in this general Quinean, Putnamian, Davidsonian, and (I believe) Wittgensteinian direction and to believe that there is no hard logical must—no *a priori* necessities in any absolute sense, namely, necessities that are not conceptual scheme dependent.[3] What necessities we have are dependent on there being certain linguistic practices—perhaps pancultural linguistic practices (i.e., practices that in certain core features all languages have)—in virtue of which, in learning these practices, we just learn that certain things are necessary for these practices to be as they are, e.g., that bachelors are unmarried, while other things are not necessary for there being these practices, e.g., that bachelors are stingy or sexually frustrated. But nothing is *necessarily* necessary—indeed such a phrase has no plain sense or perhaps no sense at all—such that some claim just holds quite independently of whatever practices we have or could have and which all practices just must conform to in order to be intelligible practices at all. I will argue that we have no practice transcendent criteria of intelligibility; there are no necessities of thought which hold quite independently of our having any practices at all. We can describe ways in which we do think and act and we can argue that there are certain ways we should think and act, but there are no ways—or at least we could not know that there are—we just must think and act for anything else is unintelligible, not even consistently thinkable. None of our practices are so stringent. Moreover, and more centrally, we have no idea of what it would be like to stand outside of our practices altogether and make such judgments and have such an understanding. Or at least—to moderate my claims so as to offer the fewest hostages to fortune—nobody has been able to show that we have such capacities and that there are such hard necessities: *"necessary* necessities."

I, like many others, do not think that there are any such necessities. But again we should keep in mind something that is hard for philosophers to keep in mind, namely, the possible fact that most philosophers may be wrong. There have been different fashions before in philosophy, different ways of conceptualization, different styles of reasoning, and perhaps the currently fashionable and dominant one is mistaken. Philosophers have been very mistaken in the past. Why not now? In any event, the very possibility of metaphysics—or so, at least, it seems—depends on there being synthetic *a priori* truths. We should not forget that some very able philosophers as different as, in the history of thought, Immanuel Kant and Henry Sidgwick, and, among contemporary philosophers, Arthur Pap, Roderick Chisholm, and Brand Blanshard, have believed that there are synthetic *a priori* truths and have argued carefully for their beliefs.[4]

With such *a priori* truths, if such there be, we could establish that there are self-evident propositions (at least self-evident upon careful reflection) about the world which yield knowledge about the world which is certain and beyond even possible revision in a way no scientific or merely empirical knowledge could be. They would yield, if there are any such truths, the foundational axioms, so to speak, which show us not only what thought *must* be like, but what reality *must* be like as well. They would be the underpinning of science, morality, everyday life, religion, politics, and the like. They would show us what it is that is ultimately real: rational necessities that just must (logically must) be the case.[5]

I shall examine some arguments—key representative arguments—for such metaphysical necessities, arguments which try to establish that certain propositions are synthetic *a priori* truths. I shall argue that we have no good reasons for believing that there are any such truths and that there are not even any sound reasons for believing there even could be any. My argument will not depend on the strong claim that there are no *a priori* truths: that belief in the *a priori* is an illusion. But I shall argue instead that all the alleged *synthetic a priori* truths are really more plausibly construed as analytic or as very general deeply embedded claims *of various sorts* very often not readily or plausibly classifiable as either *a priori* (including analytic) or brutely empirical or in some other way sometimes empirical. But I shall also argue that it doesn't follow that if such propositions are not empirical, or clearly empirical, then they must be *a priori*. At its most concessive, my argument shall be that all claims to self-evident, synthetic *a priori* truths are all themselves less than self-evident. I do not know of any argument that can *prove* that there can be no synthetic *a priori* truths. But what can be shown—or so I shall argue—is that to believe that there are such truths is very implausible indeed. On no occasion—no matter what dialectical gyrations we may make—do we reach a point where we have some absolute self-evident presuppositions which tell us what reality must be like and which are beyond all question so that finally we would have an Archimedean fulcrum rooted in self-evident certainty.

Metaphysicians, that is, defenders of synthetic *a priori* truths of sufficient generality and interest to give us—supposedly give us—insight into the fundamental nature of reality, all rely on *transcendental arguments*. That is to say, they rely on arguments of the form: if so and so (some fact of the matter) must, logically must, be the case, then such and such must, logically must, be the case. But so and so must, logically must, be the case and thus such and such must, logically must, be the case. To use an example: "If every event must have a cause, then the occurrence of a quantum particle must have a cause. But every event must, logically must, have a cause. So the occurrence of a quantum particle must, logically must, have a cause as well. There is no need for experimental investigation; we just know that this must be the case." So here, we have a transcendental argument that the indeterminacy of quantum mechanics is false: indeed an argument which purports to show that the indeterminacy thesis is *a priori* false. We have, if such arguments are sound, proved *a matter of fact* from purely *conceptual* considerations. This, if successful, would yield a sound transcendental argument.

In 1957 a number of distinguished British philosophers carried on, over the BBC, a discussion concerning the nature of metaphysics. At its conclusion, Gilbert Ryle, then "the dean" of Oxford philosophers, confidently summed up the discussion thus:

> We have also agreed pretty well in our appreciation of the things the big meta-physicians of the past did. First, they ontologized; that is, they essayed to prove assertions of existence from conceptual considerations. This was a mistake.[6]

Ryle was quite sure of this and there was no demure from his fellow philosophers. Hardly startlingly or originally, I also think ontologizing is a mistake. And most other contemporary philosophers, at least of a more or less analytical sort, do as well. The Quinean-Davidsonian revolution and the return to "scientistic metaphysics" *à la* David Armstrong and David Lewis has not altered that belief at all. Such ontologizing is out.

However (and this always happens in philosophy), not everyone has gone along. There have remained a few dissenting voices. Norman Malcolm, a linguistic philosopher of distinction, with a way of philosophizing rather similar to Ryle's, came up, to everyone's surprise, only a few years after Ryle made his confident pronouncement, with a transcendental argument which he took to be both sound and important; and he referred to the no ontologizing thesis as a dogma and not something rooted in actually attending to how our thought and speech works, attending to what our linguistic practices actually are.[7] To the shock and disbelief of most philosophers close to Malcolm in general philosophical methodology, not to say of those distant from his Wittgensteinianism, Malcolm argued that a form of St. Anselm's famous ontological argument for the existence of God is sound. If God is a being than which no greater can be conceived, then God necessarily exists. But God is a being than which no greater can be conceived. So God necessarily exists. Here, Malcolm claimed, ontologizing is in and soundly and justifiably so.

Here again we have a transcendental argument purporting to establish, from purely conceptual considerations, not just the existence of something but its necessary existence. This is plainly metaphysics in the service of religion, though Malcolm was rather reluctant to admit that. Predictably, a host of refutations flooded in, for a time almost filling the pages of many of the philosophical journals.[8] Malcolm's argument touched a raw nerve, not only philosophically, but religiously as well. One just doesn't prove, it was widely felt, things like that in the way Malcolm thought he could. That goes against all the lessons of contemporary philosophy, including those of Wittgenstein, Malcolm's mentor. I think—and I have argued—that indeed some of these refutations did decisively refute Malcolm's argument.[9] But that is not centrally to the point in the present context. What we want to know here, along with an examination of whether there are synthetic *a priori* truths, is whether there are, or can be, any sound transcendental arguments. Of course, if Malcolm's arguments stands, there is at least one sound transcendental argument, but the failure of his argument would not show that there can be no sound transcendental arguments or synthetic *a priori* truths. What we need to do is to examine whether such ontologizing is ever justified and whether we are ever justified in believing that there are any synthetic *a priori* truths at all and, if so, whether any of them are of the sort that would establish the truth of any metaphysical belief.[10]

II

Still, this may not be all that is involved in the claims of metaphysics. Perhaps, on the one hand, there can be a *descriptive* metaphysics which describes and perspicuously represents the inter-relations of our governing concepts or our ultimate categories or, on the other hand, a revisionary metaphysics which, finding some, or even *perhaps* all, of our governing concepts or ultimate categories defective, revises them, and with it our conceptual scheme, to, to a greater or lesser extent, provide us with a new, or partially new, set of governing concepts or ultimate categories which can then be used to provide an alternative description of our world, perhaps yielding a more perspicuous representation of our world than our old one.[11] This revisionary account would plainly be parasitical on there being a descriptive metaphysics, but perhaps not illegitimate on that account.

Peter Strawson and Stuart Hampshire are distinguished articulators of a descriptive metaphysics. They both took part with Ryle in the BBC discussion previously mentioned on the nature of metaphysics. Having them in mind, and gesturing in the direction of descriptive metaphysics, Ryle, continuing his summarizing of the discussion of the nature of metaphysics, remarked, "Secondly they [the big metaphysicians of times past] tried, as we try, to trace and relieve logical stresses between the organizing ideas of everyday and technical thinking; and from their work in these fields we have valuable lessons to learn."[12] So at least descriptive metaphysics, and perhaps revisionary metaphysics as well, is, Ryle would have it, in.

Descriptive metaphysicians try to describe the structure of reality or the structure of the world. They try to give us a better understanding of our fundamental governing concepts or ultimate categories. They seek to give us, that is, systematic categorial elucidation.[13] I refer here to the concepts of existence, knowledge, identity, truth, and value. A descriptive metaphysics would elucidate such fundamental concepts and trace their connections. These concepts, and *perhaps* with them, space, time, causality, person, mind, and morality, are central governing concepts or organizing notions of any system of thought and action. We could hardly be or act in the world without them. They are concepts, with the possible exceptions of person, mind, and morality, which, in *their core*, are ahistorical. They are as vital to a stone age person as to a contemporary Parisian or to a peasant in Turkey. Our lives are necessarily organized around such concepts. No matter how historicist we are, and in my view legitimately are, we need to recognize that descriptive metaphysics, or just philosophy, if you prefer, endeavors to give us a more adequate understanding of them and of their interrelations and that these concepts (these categories) in their core are not just concepts (categories) of a particular time or place or cluster of times and places. They are panhuman.

If we give the "necessarily," in "necessarily organized around such concepts," a relaxed, empirical reading, we have in this descriptive metaphysics something which is legitimate enough and reasonably unproblematical. Though it is, as Simon Blackburn has remarked, more *descriptive* than metaphysical.[14] Still, it is an empirical and rather straightforward activity that shows no signs of being incoherent. It may be pointless or of a very small point, as pragmatists and Wittgensteinians would argue.[15] But that is another matter to which we will return in a later chapter. But unlike transcendental metaphysics—the real full-bodied stuff—such descriptive metaphysics ("metaphysics without metaphysics") is plainly enough something philosophy could legitimately be.[16]

However, if the "necessarily" in "necessarily organized around such concepts" is interpreted as having the sense of "logical necessity," or some other very strong sense of "necessity," such that the claim that is being made makes a claim to a structure that could not conceivably be otherwise, a structure that just *must* obtain in any conceivable (consistently thinkable) world, such that it would not make sense (would be completely unintelligible) to deny that in any conceivable (consistently thinkable) world our lives would have to be organized around them, then we have an *a priori* claim and seemingly a synthetic one as well and we have with it all the props of transcendental arguments back on stage and with them the claim to synthetic *a priori* necessities.[17] We thus, for example, have an argument of the following form: "If we are human beings then we must organize our lives around notions like truth and falsity. We are human beings. Thus we must so organize our lives." Where the "must" is an empirical "must," or even in a broad sense a moral "must," the argument seems a good one, but then it is not a transcendental argument yielding ontologizing metaphysical truths. Where, however, the "must" is treated as a logical "must," we have no reason to think "Human beings must organize their lives around notions of truth or falsity" is a logical or conceptual truth. It does not even look like the kind of proposition that would even be a plausible candidate for a logical truth or any kind of *a priori* truth. We should not confuse a very strong empirical necessity with an *a priori* proposition. Or, if this indicates that the category of "*a priori* proposition" is not well defined, then we should say that we have nothing here which yields a transcendental metaphysics, namely, a metaphysics of the recognizable sort which establishes factual or substantive necessities from purely conceptual considerations, and thus uses transcendental arguments, and relies on synthetic *a priori* propositions. Perhaps there are no *a priori* propositions or even any intelligible notion of what we are talking about here and instead we have grades of empirical necessity and contingency.[18]

III

So the vindication of metaphysics (where "transcendental metaphysics" is a redundancy) rests on being able to establish the truth of synthetic *a priori* propositions and indeed synthetic *a priori* propositions of sufficient importance to count as metaphysical propositions yielding metaphysical knowledge. I now turn to some defenses of metaphysics which maintain there are such propositions.

Metaphysicians claiming *synthetic a priori truths* are, by contrast with empiricists, rationalists. By this I mean that unlike empiricists they do not believe all our knowledge is derived from experience or from experiment and observation, but that some of our knowledge—including all of our metaphysical knowledge—is rather established by reason. Our reflective capacities—simply the use of our minds, unaided by experiment or observation or even the attending to our sensations or feelings—can yield knowledge of how things not only are but must be. Reason itself, the claim goes, can yield substantial knowledge of the world.

In saying this metaphysical knowledge is not derived from experience, we mean that it is not based on or *justified* by or grounded in experience. The rationalist, as Kant saw, need not deny that all knowledge *arises* from experience or *comes from* experience. Rationalists, as much as empiricists, could claim that we come to know what we know through experience. Indeed, she could consistently maintain all knowledge—even mathematical knowledge or our knowledge of logical truths—arises from our experience and that we would not have it if we did not have some such experience. The distinctive empiricist claim is not that, but that it is experience which *justifies* or grounds all our substantive knowledge claims. Rationalists, by contrast, will claim that at least some substantive knowledge claims require an appeal to reason and cannot be justified by making certain observations or by relying on experience or by being inferential knowledge derived from knowledge based on such experiential knowledge. There are some things, they have it, that just our reason secures as true. We may learn them through experience, but it is not experience which justifies them.

The world, such rationalists believe, is not just the events, processes or things that just as a brute matter of fact happen to be, as the empiricist assumes, but there are some things that just must be the case. Some things just could not be otherwise; the only really possible world is the actual world. There are, that is, synthetic necessary features of reality corresponding to propositions which are synthetic *a priori* truths which careful reflection will reveal to be self-evident truths. In that way we can come to recognize the intelligibility of the world and its rational necessity. We, by pure reflection, can discover features about the universe that not only are the case but must be the case and indeed must be the case in any consistently thinkable world. That is the force of the claim that the actual world is the only possible world. It is what is involved in Hegel's obscure maxim "the rational is the real and the real is the rational." We not only have synthetic *a priori* propositions, but we have synthetic necessary realities answering to them.

Metaphysicians, in a full-bodied sense of "metaphysics" (i.e., transcendental metaphysics), are rationalists and they minimally want there to be certain propositions about ultimate reality that are absolutely certain. Maximally, they want a *total system* that is completely comprehensive and is known with absolute certainty to be "the total truth." But we will stay here with the (comparatively speaking) minimal rationalist claim to absolute certainty concerning some claims about ultimate reality. They will not in their search here be content to achieve "mere empirical certainty." To discover and systematize some empirical propositions that are always as a matter of brute empirical fact so, even when there is not the slightest actual reason to doubt that they are true, is not enough for them. They want rather absolute certainty: what such metaphysicians would call rational necessity. They want truths of reason that are also truths of fact: but absolutely necessary fact that could not conceivably be otherwise. But still they want facts and not just ways we choose, or even are driven, to represent facts. They want to be able to show that there are rationally necessary synthetic *a priori* truths and thus that there are absolutely indubitable truths revealing rationally necessary features of the world: synthetic necessary existences and relations.

Brand Blanshard is perhaps the last in line of such rationalist metaphysicians.[19] He is also one of the clearest and most self-consciously defensive of such metaphysicians and has forthrightly argued for their being synthetic *a priori* truths and rational necessities in the universe. I will examine how Blanshard constructs his case for there being synthetic *a priori* truths including synthetic *a priori* truths of plain metaphysical import.

Consider first what Blanshard takes to be relatively unproblematical examples of synthetic *a priori* truths, namely, "Two straight lines do not enclose a space"; "Whatever is colored is extended"; "A thing cannot at once have a property and not have it." These are necessary truths alright, but they are not synthetic for their necessity rests on the meanings, the uses, of words in English and equivalent expressions in other languages. It, for example, is things which are colored and things are by definition extended such that "an extended thing" like "four-sided square" is a redundancy. And if, *à la* Quine, it is thought that there is too heavy a reliance here on unanalyzed notions of synonymity and definition, then the *a priori* status of these sentences is impugned. Either way, we do not have the necessity Blanshard is after. Or consider what Blanshard calls the "propositions of vast importance, which the scientist makes use of every day of his life" and which, Blanshard has it, the metaphysician must show to be necessary truths revealing synthetic necessary features of the world:

1. We can learn the facts of the physical order through perception.
2. The laws of our logic are valid of the physical order.
3. There is a public space and a public time in which things happen and to which we all have access.
4. Every event has a cause.
5. That under like conditions the same sort of thing has always happened and always will.

6.   That we ought to adjust the degree of assent to any proposition to the extent of evidence for it.[20]

Like "All colored things are extended," these six propositions are supposed to be synthetic *a priori* necessary truths. They only differ from "All colored things are extended" in being less obviously self-evident necessary truths. We may not immediately recognize them to be self-evident, but careful philosophical reflection will, Blanshard believes, show them to be such. But when we actually inspect these six propositions we see that they are a mixed bag and that none of them has the kind of absolute certainty and self-evidence that Blanshard claims.

Propositions 2, 4, and 6 have been thought to be false by able philosophers or logician-mathematicians.[21] Intuitionists in mathematics and logic have argued that the law of the excluded middle far from being self-evident and applying to our world does not actually hold. We should, they argue, reject it. That such a fundamental law of logic could be so challenged should make us cautious about the status of the others. Beyond that, and I expect more importantly, it is not clear what it means to say that they are valid of our world other than what it means to say that arithmetic and geometry are valid of our world. And that comes to saying that they have useful applications in empirical science. That they can be fruitfully applied to our physical order seems a well-established *empirical* fact, established quite unproblematically by showing how useful and indispensable they are to our reasoning and calculations when we do science. But that is an empirical fact and we do not require metaphysics, or anything *a priori* for its support. Proposition 4, to go to another of Blanshard's propositions, is now thought to be false by many philosophers of science when they consider quantum mechanics. That quantum mechanics can be given deterministic readings only shows that things are problematic here. We do not have anything like a *seen* necessity, if we have any necessity at all. That we sometimes think we do may result from confusing the definitional truism "Every effect has a cause" with proposition 4.

Proposition 6 is also problematic though in a less familiar way. But anyone strongly influenced by Ludwig Wittgenstein's *On Certainty* will have a sense of how problematic, indeed possibly false, it is. Take the propositions "Human beings have heads"; "If they lose their heads new ones will not grow on them"; "I have a head"; "Water boils when heated"; "Water is wet"; "There is an external world": "There are several human beings"; "Human beings do not turn into turtles"; "Ice is colder than fire"; "Bare hands put on red hot coals will burn." All these propositions, with the possible exception of "Water is wet," have at least the look of empirical propositions. They certainly do not seem to be true by definition or by stipulation. Yet we do not adjust our assent to these propositions to the degree of our evidence for them. We are certain of them, even though they are not analytic, yet the idea of giving evidence for them seems at least to be very strange.[22]   Indeed to some of us it seems absurd. Anything that could count as evidence for these propositions would be no more certain than they are and we have no idea of what it would be like to have evidence against them.[23] Anything I could give as evidence for my not having a head would, to understate it, be much less certain than the proposition that I have a head and the same thing is true for the generaliz- ation "Live human beings have heads" as well as the other propositions I listed.   They have the look at least of empirical propositions but it is entirely unclear whether we adjust the degree of assent to these proposi- tions to the extent of our evidence for them. We are certain of them but we do not seem to have any evidence for them at all. What some might call "evidence" is such that were we to try to give it, it should be concluded that we had gone insane rather than to take that as evidence, e.g., talking about my feeling around my shoulders and concluding that after all I really didn't have a head any more.   Some might remain unhappy with this Wittgensteinian turn here. They might, though I believe mistakenly, take it to be an evasion. We know what it would be like to observe live human beings without heads.   Perhaps there is some such tribe that we might discover on some remote island.   Absurd, of course, but perhaps intelli- gible.[24] But this is only a further reason for saying we are far from having a self-evident seen necessity here. Certainly they do not have the look of *a priori* propositions of any sort. But it is also absurd to speak of searching for evidence for or against them. Their status is anomalous, but we can hardly claim of them that they be *a priori* rational necessities. Such being the case, we can hardly be confident of the truth of 6. We clearly cannot claim it is a synthetic *a priori* truth.

Proposition 3 may be true by definition and non-substantive. "Public space" and "public time" are arguably redundancies. They just, being what space is and time is, are public. And by definition space is the place where things happen and "a timeless intrinsically private happening" is a contradic- tion in terms or at least so it is not implausible to argue. And if they are in public space they are by definition things to which we all, in principle at least, have access. So on the most natural reading proposition 3, though less clearly so, should, like "All colored things are extended," be a definitional and non-substantive truth. But it is vague enough to perhaps be taken as some other kind of claim, probably an empirical claim, but certainly not as a seen rational necessity: an *a priori* synthetic truth, carrying the alleged certainty of such a truth.

Proposition 5 is sufficiently vague that under certain readings it is false, under other readings it is like a very vague definitional truth, and under what is probably the most natural reading the first part is a true empirical generalization and the second part, i.e., "and always will," a prediction that is probably true. Take "Jasper always gets drunk after a fight with his wife." The like condition is that "Jasper has a fight with his wife" but it may be false that Jasper always get drunk when he has a fight with his wife. If so, it is not, as a matter of fact, true that under like conditions the same thing always happens. If in turn someone says, "Well, if the same thing doesn't happen, then the conditions are not like," then he is turning it into a definitional, perhaps implicitly stipulative definitional, non-substantive truth. What is more likely is that he will treat it as a proposition that could be false, but that just in fact turns out in all the examined cases to be true and he makes a plausible guess about the future and predicts that it will hold in the future.

Finally, proposition 1 seems to me truistic but all the same ambiguous. It is either a disguised definitional commonplace or an empirical commonplace about how we learn about many things, but no self-evident seen synthetic *a priori* necessity. But even its alleged common-place status is not plainly true. Phenomenalists, subjective idealists, and some kinds of realists think we only perceive sensa or sense-data and infer (mistakenly or otherwise) physical objects from these data of sense, data which are not physical objects or part of the surface of physical objects. In any event, it is not plainly a seen substantive rational necessity. It looks like to learn about the physical order at all we have to allow for perception or else we would not understand what it would mean to learn about the physical order. If we might, as we might, wish to leave that open, then we either have an empirical claim or just some kind of muddle where we do not know what is going on. In any event we do not have a rational self-evident *a priori* necessity. Where we get something that seems like a rational *a priori* necessity here we get something like a definitional truth.

What we have here (*pace* Blanshard) with this mixed bag of propositions is not a cluster of self-evident truths presupposed by science and without which science totters. We have no reason (again *pace* Blanshard) to believe that metaphysics is the continuation of the career of reason "into regions that science leaves unexplored" and which provides the rational "foundations on which science builds arches and vaultings that hold its structures together."[25] Instead, what we have are sometimes propositions so vague that nothing very definite can be said about them, at other times (and under certain readings) empirical truisms that could be false (though they are highly unlikely to be) and which yield no *absolute* certainty, at other times empirical propositions that are very likely false, and at still other times putative disguised definitional truths which taken in a certain way are indeed definitionally true but then are non-substantive. In any event, we do not have here the metaphysical truths or even metaphysical falsehoods of vast importance claimed by rationalistic metaphysicians.

What metaphysicians wish to establish is that there are some propositions that are (a) self-evident, (b) necessary, (c) *a priori*, and (d) substantive (synthetic). But no clear examples have been given concerning which there is anything like a consensus. But to say this may only show such propositions may be very hard to establish, especially against what some metaphysicians may regard as the strong and pervasive empiricist bias of our philosophical and of our intellectual culture more generally. The *Weltgeist* goes against the easy acceptance of such beliefs. Whether or not there is anything to that, it is indeed true that lack of consensus does not prove there can be no such propositions. But where there is no consensus and where there is, as well, no known or even envisaged method for establishing self-evident truths, no even near agreement about what it would be like to gain them, no consensus on whether there even *can* be such self-evident *a priori* synthetic necessities, or, even for people who think that such knowledge may be possible any consensus about instances of such knowledge, the case for such propositions looks dauntingly bleak. (It should also be noted, in passing, that there is something which is at least paradoxical and problematical about speaking of a *method* for establishing self-evident truths. If they are really self-evident—or so it seems—we would not need a method for establishing their self-evidence and, if we have a method for such establishment, self-evidence is perhaps superogatory.)

IV

However, I think that it will become evident that something even stronger of an anti-metaphysical nature can, and should, be said, if we attend to the upshot of the unfolding discussion of the critique of the analytic-synthetic dichotomy initiated by W. V. Quine and Morton White around 1950.[26] The upshot of this discussion is that we do not have any very clear or very satisfactory elucidation of even the clearest cases of so-called *a priori* propositions (sentences, statements, beliefs), namely, the analytic ones. When we turn to synthetic *a priori* propositions, we are even more lost in the foggy, foggy dew. There is no clear distinction between, on the one hand, the analytic or *a priori* or, on the other, the empirical or *a posteriori*. There are, to be sure, clear cases of both. "All bachelors are unmarried" and "There is a book on this table," Hilary Putnam observes, show us, beyond any reasonable philosophical argument, "as gross a distinction" as we could ask for. They are, that is, as plainly distinct as "any two things in the world, or at any rate [as] between any two linguistic expressions in the world...."[27] And Putnam goes on in the spirit of H. P. Grice and Peter Strawson, two early and influential critics of Quine, to remark "and no matter how long I might fail in trying to clarify the distinction, I should not be persuaded that it does not exist. In fact, I do not understand what it would mean to say that the distinction between two things *that* different does not exist."[28] Quine, in denying in "Two Dogmas of Empiricism" that the distinction exists, was, as Putnam avers, just wrong.[29] However, what he was getting at, Putnam goes on to remark, was very important and right, but his literal claim that no such distinction exists was false.[30] Quine, however, no longer denies that there is such a distinction and it probably was the case that he never meant to be taken so literally. In a retrospective essay written thirty years after "Two Dogmas of Empiricism," Quine remarks: "Analyticity undeniably has a place at a common sense level, and this has made readers regard my reservations as unreasonable. My threadbare bachelor example is one of many undebatable cases. It is intelligible and often useful in discussion to point out that some disagreement is purely a matter of words rather than of fact."[31] But it is also important to make a point Quine powerfully argued in "Two Dogmas of Empiricism," as did Morton White at about the same time, and as did Hilary Putnam much more thoroughly later. The point is that we have no non-arbitrary way of going through the corpus of our indicative sentences and putting them all into either an *a priori* bin or an empirical bin. If we try to do this, we will find great masses of often plainly meaningful sentences that cannot be so sorted. It is not the case that we only have a few anomalous leftovers, such as "Orthodox Jews fast on the Day of Atonement." Non-fitting sentences pop up all over the place. What is important to recognize, Quine, White and Putnam argue, is that we have no clear criterion or criteria for demarcating the *a priori* from the non *a priori* or the analytic from the empirical. It is not just that there are borderline cases, but there are masses of sentences living well regulated lives in our discourses that are not, except arbitrarily, so classifiable.[32] There is no reason to think they are really *a priori* (analytic or otherwise) or that they are just plain empirical sentences: synthetic sentences, if you will. Even if we agree, as Quine has now come to, that there are plain paradigms of analytic sentences (e.g., "Bachelors are unmarried men" or "Dogs are animals") and plain examples of empirical sentences (e.g., "Snow is falling now" or "There is a duck in the pond") that accomplished speakers of English immediately recognize as instances of such types of sentences, we still have no good explanation or explication of the difference and no criterion or criteria to use to decide when a sentence is *a priori* or analytic. It is one thing to be able in practice to recognize a distinction; it is another thing again to have an analysis or an account of what that distinction is. We have, in short, no criterion for *a priori* knowledge so that we can clearly say what it is we are having when we have it. Though, even without being able to articulate a criterion, sometimes we can be confident that we can recognize case by case such a distinction, i.e., know when it is we know something *a priori* and when it is we know something empirically. We have a sense of it, that is, even when we are quite unclear what exactly it is that we are having when we have it. However, we have no way of separating out, even with this case by case knowledge, the *a priori* sheep from the *a posteriori* goats. The whole demarcation thing is hopeless and pointless, for there are multitudes of sentences in all sorts of domains that are not untendentiously classifiable as one or the other. And for myriads of cases in many domains, we do not know, looking at them specifically one by one, which, *if either*, bin they belong in.

Consider, in coming to see this, the following more or less randomly selected list, "True Christians believe in the trinity." "Nothing can be both red and green all over." "Moral judgments are impartial," "Beliefs to be justified require evidence," "There is a past," "Kinetic energy is equal to one half the product of mass and velocity squared," "All physical laws must be Lorentz-invariant," "A straight line is the path of a light ray," "The world did not come into existence five minutes ago replete with false memory traces," "There are atoms," "Light rays travel in a curved space," "No well adult needs ten hours sleep a day," "Every substance has some solvent," "No one ever really knows the thoughts of another," "Dreams have no logic," "Without social solidarity social life is fragmented," "Alienation is inescapable," "Language acquisition is an innate capacity," "A society without classes is impossible," "Jealousy is a natural feeling." These sentences do not even sort into the *a priori* and the empirical bins or, to put it more cautiously, most of them do not plausibly so sort and only by a forced and arbitrary sorting can they be so arranged. However, many of the above examples have been thought by someone or another to be problematic candidates for the *a priori*. But the key point here is that none of them go clearly into either bin. We simply do not have a principle of demarcation here. We can, of course, stipulate, but we do so arbitrarily.

"There is a book on the floor" can in a straightforward way be empirically confirmed or disconfirmed by simply looking and seeing. "There is a past" cannot. There is, as Bertrand Russell argued, no just looking and seeing that the world did not come into existence five minutes ago replete with false memory traces. "There is a past" is not confirmable in the straightforward way in which "There was a duck in the pond this morning" is. Yet it is implausible to think "There is a past" is an analytic truth or in any way *a priori*.

"All physical laws must be Lorentz-invariant" is a central claim of contemporary physics. Before Einstein it was not generally held or even conceived of. It is certainly not analytic or *a priori*. It is not like "All bachelors are unmarried" or "All vixens are foxes." But it is not clear what would confirm it or disconfirm it either. Certainly no isolated experiment or observation or cluster of isolated experiments or observations would do so. It is not at all like "All swans are white" brutely empirical and unproblematically disconfirmably by "There is a black swan in this pond," as it was disconfirmed by the European settlers observing black swans in Australia. "All physical laws must be Lorentz-invariant" is not so disconfirmable. It is tied up with all kinds of things contemporary physicists believe. It is a deep element in their thought and could only be abandoned or revised by a very great change in our whole system of physics. But it is still not *a priori*. It is not held completely independently of what is observed or observable and unlike "All bachelors are unmarried" its denial is not self-contradictory and it is not true by definition or in virtue of the meaning of the constituent terms alone. It is more like "Atoms are indivisible" (strictly speaking its Greek equivalent) was for the ancient Greek cosmologists, where, what is now known to be empirically false, had at that time a near *a priori* status. Perhaps, after a bit, for contemporary physicists, "The Higgs particle is the fundamental particle" will come, for a time, to have a similar status. Similarly there may in a hundred years or so, or perhaps even less, be a deep scientific revolution and Einstein's claim may come to be abandoned. It is not a strict *a priori* truth—or literally an *a priori* truth at all—but it is not, at least in any plain and straightforward sense, an empirical truth either. The dichotomy simply doesn't work here. There are many places where we cannot demarcate.

Consider a more homespun example, from my more or less random and certainly heterogeneous list, "Beliefs to be justified require evidence." Suppose I cannot find my watch and suppose to make the case simpler I am imprisoned in a small house and cannot leave or even open the windows or the door and no one else can come in. I look all over the house very diligently several times, but I cannot find it. A friend calls me on the phone and I tell him "My watch disappeared." He responds, not unnaturally, "You mean you cannot find it?" to which I respond decidedly unnaturally, "No, it just disappeared. It vanished into thin air. Moreover, nothing made it disappear. It just disappeared." He, in turn, responds, confidently and correctly, "Watches just do not disappear like that. You must have somehow mislaid or accidentally, and unnoticed by you, flushed it down the toilet or dropped it down the sink or something like that." He does not have evidence for his belief that watches cannot just disappear like that and he doesn't seek any. And the "evidence" that I might give about having looked very carefully and the like does not shake his confident belief. Things like that just do not happen. Indeed they cannot happen. To admit to that possibility would upset his, and our, whole system of belief.[33] It is like, in this respect, "Physical laws must be Lorentz-invariant" in contemporary physics and not at all like "There are no black swans."

His confident and unswerving belief is justified and yet he has no evidence for it. Any so-called evidence would be less certain than the belief itself. Evidence that seemed to count against it would be confidently set aside or reconceptualized so as to not conflict with his belief. It is only if cases like this became very numerous that things would become unsettled and we would, for a time, be at a loss as to what to think. So "Beliefs to be justified require evidence" is probably not even true, but certainly it is not *a priori* true or even very near to being *a priori* true.³⁴ But it is also not clearly empirical either, not even empirically false. It is not a plain empirical statement like "Beliefs about marriage often vary from culture to culture." Moreover, "Watches just do not disappear like that, vanishing into nothing" is also not clearly an empirical statement. It is also anomalous with respect to being either empirical or *a priori*. It superficially looks like an empirical statement, but it does not function like one. It is not like "Watches usually have metal parts." But it certainly is not *a priori* either. It is not self-contradictory to say "My watch just disappeared." "Watches can't disappear like that" is not true in virtue of its meaning alone.

Let me take one final example from my bundle of sentences, namely, "Moral judgments are impartial." It is easy to think that it is *a priori*, perhaps even analytic, the securest, perhaps the only, type of *a priori* sentence we have. Something would not count as a moral judgment, we are tempted to say, if it were not at least thought to be impartial. But parents faced with the prospect of either saving their own child or someone else's child from a burning house might very well form the intention and act on it: "We must save our own child first." This certainly has at least the look of a moral judgment and many would think it a justified one as well. But, justified or not, it seems at least not to be impartial. Someone wishing to hold onto the claim that moral judgments must be impartial will say that it only superficially looks like a failure of impartiality, for that parents should in such situations put the interests of their children first is itself generalizable (universalizable) and impartially defendable. So, after all, moral judgments must be impartial. Others will respond that this is not what it is for a moral judgment to be impartial and that sometimes justified moral judgments are not impartial.

I am not, of course, trying to sort this issue out here, but to use it to show that "Moral judgments must be impartial" has no very clear logical status. We do not know which, if either bin, it should be put into. It is not like our clear analyticity "Bachelors must be unmarried." Someone who is married couldn't possibly even count as a bachelor. It, as they used to say in pre-Quinean days, is true in virtue of its meaning alone. But not so, or at least not clearly so, for "Moral judgments must be impartial." But "moral judgments must be impartial" is plainly not either an empirical or a contingent moral judgment like "Nationalism is always a bad thing." It is not at all like "Moral judgments are often taxing." Indeed, it may not be a moral judgment at all, but an implicit definition or some kind of "grammatical remark." But that claim is also very problematic. So again our dichotomy does not fit the facts—or at least not unproblematically fit the facts—and again we are at loss for a principle of demarcation.

It is not that the statements I have mentioned fall into some third category distinct from the analytic and empirical. Perhaps the category of synthetic *a priori*? We have nothing like that. Rather, as Putnam well puts it, they "fall into many different categories. Over and beyond the clear-cut rules of languages, on the one side, and the clear-cut descriptive statements, on the other, are just an enormous number of statements which are not classified as either analytic or synthetic."[35] When we get a statement (sentence, proposition) that does not seem to be either analytic or empirical, we should not rush to the conclusion that then it must be synthetic *a priori*. It could be any of a number of quite different sentence types. Putnam again, and relatedly to the above, is quite on the mark when he remarks: "Some statements in natural language [e.g., French, English, Urdu, Japanese] really are analytic; others may be *construed* as analytic; still others really are synthetic; others *may be construed* as synthetic; still other statements belong to still other categories or may be construed as belonging to still other categories."[36]

V

The above might come, perhaps with a little more filling out, to the making of a good case for *not* believing that all indicative sentences are either analytic or empirical (where "synthetic empirical" is a redundancy) and that there are not other kinds of indicative sentence (proposition, statement). However, even if this is so, as I think it is, this still does not mean, as we have assumed above, that we have no way of demarcating the analytic ones from all the heterogeneous others. So let us look anew at the problem of demarcation. Quine agrees that if we had an understanding of what in natural language "logical impossibility" comes to, we could use this to explain the analytic. But he thinks the notion of logical impossibility is no clearer than that of the notion of analyticity itself, so that it cannot be appealed to in understanding analyticity or used in demarcating analytic sentences from other kinds. Grice and Strawson argue that Quine is mistaken here. We can distinguish logical impossibility from causal impossibility in perfectly adequate, though informal, ways.[37] Suppose I utter the following two utterances to you about my three year old daughter. (1) "My three year old child understands calculus" and (2) "My three year old child is an adult." At first you, perfectly naturally, take it that in both cases I am engaging in hyperbole, using language in some figurative sense to make exaggerations not intended to deceive or to be taken literally.

To (1) you might respond by saying "You mean she is precocious or unusually bright for a three year old." If I respond "No, I mean literally what I say; she can do, and with good understanding, calculus." Your natural response would be that I am putting you on and for you not to *believe* me. It is impossible for a three year old child to do calculus. But, if I brought my daughter into the room where we were talking, and if you gave her calculus problems of a varied sort and she did them correctly, explained correctly what she was doing, and, as well, explained to you what calculus is, you certainly would in the end be forced to admit that what I said was literally true. Your confident disbelief, faced with such behavior on the part of my child, would turn into perplexed, but still secure, belief and finally into an acceptance that what I said in uttering (1) was in fact true.

Now, by contrast, consider (2) "My three year old child is an adult." Again your initial response would plausibly be that (2) was to be taken as a hyperbole. You would think I meant to say something like my child is remarkably mature for her age or remarkably sensible for her age or in some other way very advanced for her age. But if again I insist that I am speaking quite literally, that I meant exactly what I said, it wouldn't be—assuming you thought I was sincere in my avowal—that you do not *believe* me, but that you just do not *understand* what I am talking about. "My three year old child is an adult" is like "I am a bachelor but married." I contradict myself in saying either. With "adult" I unsay what I say with "child." It isn't that you do not believe me, but that my remark does not make sense. (1) states a *causal* impossibility, (2) a *logical* impossibility. So we have a plain distinction, revealed in our linguistic behavior and reflective acknowledgement of that behavior, between a causal impossibility and a logical impossibility. When I utter (1) and (2) you naturally think I am engaging in hyperbole. But where I insist that I am speaking literally, for (1) the appropriate response is disbelief and for (2) it is incomprehension. In the latter case you just do not understand me. You do not understand me in the specific way that I unsay in that very sentence what I started to say and you see that I have contradicted myself: in no possible world could my sentence correctly be used to make a true statement. You cannot make sense of what I say when I try to speak literally in uttering (2). With (2) we have a clear case of a logical impossibility and with (1) we have a clear case of a causal impossibility and thus we have demarcated analytic sentences from empirical ones or at least some kinds of empirical ones. And we can see how we can identify a class of sentences as analytic and as distinct from the heterogeneous lot of the others whose denials do not express logical impossibilities. Further and varied examples of the same general type can easily be generated and are similarly unproblematically true. They show clearly that we recognize that distinction in our language—it is built into the logic of our language, so to say—and we have informal ways of explaining the distinction, a distinction which enables us in practice to demarcate between the analytic and a heterogeneous lot of other sentences whose denials are clearly not self-contradictory. There is the distinction and it is plainly teachable and recognizable providing us with a principle of demarcation.

However, it is also important to recognize that it is not a sharp demarcation, for there will be troublesome intermediate cases. "My watch vanished into thin air," "Not all events have causes," unlike "All effects have causes" or "My watch is not a watch," do not seem to be, or at least not clearly, expressive of logical impossibilities. But they might, all the same, in some unobvious way, after all, be logical impossibilities. We should not assume that all logical impossibilities are easy to recognize or, if they are really not logical impossibilities, that they cannot be something close to logical impossibilities and difficult to distinguish from them. But that notwithstanding, we can show that in our language there are some clear cases of logical impossibilities and some clear cases of causal impossibilities, and that practiced speakers can correctly sort them out in a large number of instances. As Grice and Strawson put it,

> The distinction in which we ultimately come to rest is that between not believing something and not understanding something.... It would be rash to maintain that *this* distinction does not need clarification, but it would be absurd to maintain it does not exist.[38]

A way of understanding an analytic statement is to understand it as a statement whose denial expresses a logical impossibility. Such a criterion marks off the analytic ones, and at least one clear species of the *a priori* ones, from all the rest. The rest being a variable lot. But however varied they are, they are alike in it being the case that their denials do not express a logical impossibility, though again there are, as we have seen, troublesome cases that are indeterminate in this respect. We do not know, for these cases, whether their denials express a logical impossibility or some other kind of impossibility, not all of which are easily accommodatable as causal impossibilities. When I say "My watch just disappeared" and you try to take it literally is it that you do not understand me or that you do not believe me? It is not clear what we should say here. My hunch is that you do not understand me. But that is just a hunch. Maybe our language gives us no clear guidance here. Indeed it may give us no guidance at all.

Quine or a Quinean might respond by saying (a) that sometimes, given the limpidity of natural languages, we do indeed not know, and perhaps cannot know, whether we have a causal impossibility or a logical impossibility or perhaps some other kind of impossibility and (b) sometimes it does not matter at all what we say or believe here: whether, in the one instance, we say we have a logical impossibility or a causal impossibility or, on the other instance, whether we say, and think, that we do not understand what is being said or say, and think, instead, that we do not believe what is being said. Suppose I say that no one can be in Paris and London at the same time. I am inclined to say that that is just an obvious causal or physical impossibility. Suppose someone, with what I think is a rather bloated conception of the analytic, says "No, it is a logical impossibility." It, after all, is logically impossible to be in two places at the same time. But, still, if I were big enough—a giant Paul Bunyan—I might be in both Paris and London at the same time. One foot might be in Paris and the other in London. *Perhaps* (as a case of (a)) we cannot decide, or at least have no good grounds for saying which it is, if either, but (à la (b)) do we really have any good reason to care? It is impossible, that is clear, so does it matter which kind of impossibility we say it is or whether we by stipulation or by conceptual discovery come to an understanding or at least an acceptance of which it is? We may have no firm understanding of whether our utter non-acceptance rests on incomprehension or utter disbelief. It is clear that an unmarried man is married or that a bachelor is married are logical impossibilities and we, if we understand English, immediately recognize them to be so. But this linguistic competence of ours does not extend to a recognition of whether "Bush sleeps faster than Clinton" or "Procrastination drinks melancholy" express logical impossibilities, though, again relying on our linguistic competence, we are inclined to believe, in some unspecified sense, that they do not make sense. Indeed in a way they make even less sense than clear logical impossibilities. But they in turn are different from each other, just as "He was in Paris and London at the same time" is different from the last two mentioned sentences. It is even less clear, with the last two examples, whether we have a gross physical impossibility or a logical or some other kind of impossibility; but it is also not clear that it makes any, or at least very much, difference which kind of impossibility it is.

Similar problems emerge about two more philosophically interesting examples, namely, problems concerning what kind of impossibilities they express, if they express impossibilities at all. Though, if they do express impossibilities, it is much less clear whether it is important to try to figure out whether the impossibility is logical or in some other way conceptual, as I am inclined to think, or whether the impossibility is of another kind and, if so, exactly what kind. The examples are "All moral beliefs are in error" and "There is an infinite, non-material individual transcendent to the universe."

However, while "Bush eats faster than Clinton" and "Bush walks faster than Clinton" are empirically true or false propositions; it is unclear what kind of propositions "Bush sleeps faster than Clinton" or "Bush dreams faster than Clinton" are. *Perhaps* the latter, after all, is a rather disguised empirical proposition. Still we do not know how even to begin to establish their truth or their falsity, and we do not know whether they are self-contradictory or express logically inconsistent beliefs, as do "Unmarried men are married" and "Bachelors are married males" clearly do. What this at least seems to show is that while we have clear paradigms of analytic and empirical statements, we do not, with the notion of logical impossibility, have much in the way of a criterion, and thus much in the way of a principle of demarcation, for picking out analytic statements from non-analytic ones because it is too often unclear whether what we have is a logical impossibility or some other kind of impossibility. What it looks like we have is what Morton White said we have, namely, we have a continuum between the analytic and the empirical with some statements being more or less analytic. Rather than having sharp differences, we have all along the line indeterminate cases. We have a few clear paradigms, but we lack sharply delineated clear categories. Quine is right in thinking that we lack a clear criterion here. Grice's and Strawson's arguments do not undermine Quine's central claim here.

VI

I think it is important at this point to step back and note what philosophers, contemporary and otherwise, wanted the distinction, or a kindred distinction, between the analytic and empirical (typically simply said to be the synthetic) to do for them. The distinction we have been discussing, or something in the neighborhood of that distinction, has been variously expressed by diverse philosophers from several traditions. It has been called the distinction between the analytic and the synthetic (empirical), the necessary and the contingent, the *a priori* and the empirical, between rules of language and empirical facts, between logical impossibilities and causal and other physical impossibilities, between what is incomprehensible and what is unbelievable, between being a fact about language and being a fact about the world, between truths of reason and truths of fact.

I do not mean to suggest that all these distinctions come to exactly the same thing, are equally general, equally important or equally clear or otherwise perspicuous. But philosophers from Locke, Leibnitz, Hume and Kant to Ayer, Carnap, Reichenbach and Strawson thought it important to draw some such distinction. The sharpest use came with the logical empiricists (Ayer, Carnap and Reichenbach, among others) who used it as a critical weapon to eliminate metaphysics and to give a coherent account of necessity within an empiricist framework. The task was to draw a sharp line between the *a priori* and the empirical and to show that all other sentences are cognitively meaningless. It is the thrust of Quine's and White's critiques to show that this empiricist conception is a dogma, indeed an unempirical dogma, resting on a mistake. Putnam's critique, which is also as naturalistic as Quine's and White's, argues that, even if there is a coherent conception of an analytic sentence, as he argues there is, and with that a genuine distinction to be made, that it remains the case, given the multitude of different types of sentences used for different purposes (sometimes for very different purposes) and their being in a complicated and heterogeneous continuum between the analytic and the brutely empirical, that these things render the positivist (logical empiricist) programme of placing all cognitively meaningful sentences into either the analytic bin or the empirical bin, hopeless and, to add insult to injury, pointless as well. This is even so for someone with a broadly naturalistic orientation. Indeed, perhaps most particularly so for someone with a naturalistic orientation. Something very close to this is, also, I believe, Quine's current position.

However, not everyone who drew the distinction between the *a priori* and the empirical, and thought the distinction of philosophical importance, used it for such a logical empiricist programme. Kantians and extreme rationalists such as Leibnitz and Blanshard, drew the *a priori*/empirical distinction as the distinction between truths of reason and truths of fact. Truths of reason included both analytic statements and synthetic *a priori* statements and matters of fact referred to empirical facts. But extreme rationalists such as Leibnitz and Blanshard went even further. They shared, paradoxically enough, Quine's one time belief that the distinction is illusory or, as they would put it, not ultimately real. It was alright, they thought, to start at the common sense level by making such a distinction, but thorough dialectical examination would reveal that it was not ultimately real. There are, they thought, no genuinely empirical truths for all true propositions, when properly understood, would be seen to be the necessary truths or truths of reason. This indeed, as we have seen, would yield a systematic speculative metaphysical system. But many other metaphysicians, of a more modest broadly Kantian orientation, wished, less exuberantly, first to show that the possibility of metaphysics turned on their being synthetic *a priori* propositions and, that established, they then went on to argue, that there were indeed synthetic *a priori* propositions—synthetic *a priori* truths—and that some of them were of vast metaphysical importance. But they did not try to show, as the extreme rationalists did, that all truths are really necessary truths.

It, as I remarked earlier, is this broadly Kantian metaphysical position that I am concerned with here. It is a position that marks a distinction between truths of reason and truths of fact and argues that metaphysical philosophy is concerned with those truths of reason (those *a priori* truths) that are synthetic. Naturalistic philosophers, such as Quine, White and Putnam, are as unreceptive to the synthetic *a priori* as the logical empiricists. Indeed they just seem to assume that if a proposition is synthetic it can't be *a priori* and that, if there is any coherent conception of the *a priori*, it will be that of the *a priori* and the analytic coming to much the same thing.

However, it might be thought, that in spite of that pre-conception, with Quine's and Putnam's treatment of some logical laws and some mathematical truths (including geometrical ones) as being non-analytic, room has been made again for the synthetic *a priori*. I shall argue that this is an illusion. Paradigms of analytic propositions are the familiar ones "Unmarried persons are unmarried," "Bachelors are unmarried adult males," "All dogs are animals," "Every vixen is a fox," "Every brother is a male sibling," "Every brother is a male." They are Locke's trifling propositions; propositions whose denial expresses a logical impossibility. However, Quine and Putnam take a more nuanced view for logic, arithmetic, geometry and for some scientific principles than did the logical empiricists. The basic laws of logic are regarded as analytic in the same straightforward conception of analytic. "Anyone," Quine remarks, "who goes counter to *modus ponens*, or who affirms a conjunction and denies one of its components, is simply flouting what he learned in learning to use 'if' and 'and'."[39] And *perhaps*, he adds, the logic of truth functions, quantification and identity are also analytic. But for other areas of logic, Quine avers, it is not quite so clear. Even something as basic as the law of the excluded middle has not always been thought to hold come what may. Intuitionist logicians have rejected it. So we see here how deeply revision can cut even in logic. Perhaps, Putnam and others have worried, the revision can go even deeper in logic. There may be no unrevisable propositions even in logic and mathematics. At least, or so it seems, the very notion of their being revisable does not seem to rest on a mistake. Here we have propositions of systematic interest, but we do not seem to have the at least apparent utter unrevisability of the trifling propositions: our paradigms of analyticity. Yet it would be absurd to regard logical and mathematical laws as empirical propositions. So what we seem to be left with is the fact that some of them do not seem to go either into the analytic or empirical bin. Yet they are certainly more like analytical propositions than empirical ones.

The principles of Euclidian geometry, or for that matter any geometry, are interesting cases. They for us now are empirical statements though of a very formal sort. But for Newton and for Hume, they were virtually analytic. As Putnam puts it, "Before the work of nineteenth-century mathematicians, the principles of Euclidian geometry were as *close* to analytic as any nonanalytic statement ever gets."[40] For Newton and for Hume, it was analytic, or virtually so, that if two straight lines are perpendicular to a third, the two straight lines do not meet. No experiments with light rays concerning how light tracks, no experiments with tape measures, no careful looking and seeing or anything of the sort could "have overthrown the laws of Euclidean geometry before someone had worked out non-Euclidean geometry.... Principles as central to the conceptual system of science as laws of geometry are simply not abandoned in the face of experiment *alone*. They are abandoned because a rival theory is available."[41] People, in Newton's and Hume's position, in their place in history, could not conceive of their falsity. Hume and Newton would not take a straight line to just be the path of a light ray. For them it would have been impossible to form a conception of a straight line that did not conform to the principles of Euclidean geometry. The denial of these principles would have seemed to them to result in propositions which express logical impossibilities. Any conception of a straight line not conforming to the axioms of Euclidean geometry would not coherently or properly be called a conception of a straight line. Euclidean geometry defined what a straight line was. Experimental results, *assuming* that "straight line" means "path of a light ray," and establishing experimentally that two light rays both perpendicular to a third light ray meet would not, even if the experimental results were established, be taken by Hume or Newton as falsifying or even infirming Euclidean geometry. Rather, the experimental results would be explained by supposing that light rays travelled in a curved path in Euclidean space. After the development of Riemanian and Lobachevakian geometry, it was plausible to treat, as Albert Einstein in effect and Hans Reichenbach explicitly did, the axioms of Euclidean geometry as synthetic and empirical. "Straight line," Reichenbach claimed, if correctly analyzed, means "path of a light ray" and, with this analysis accepted, the principles of geometry are now construable as principles which are experimentally testable. We have in the non-Euclidean geometries alternative systems of representation. So we have alternative systems and conceptions of the representation of space. Which represent space the more accurately is to be decided, or partially decided, experimentally. What for Hume and Newton were the analytic, or nearly analytic, principles of geometry, are for Einstein and Reichenbach empirical statements subject to confirmation and disconfirmation, though still not simply by isolated experiment or observation as "All swans are white" can be disconfirmed. Experimental results by themselves, without a new theory to integrate them, will not disconfirm the geometrical principles, but experiment, together with a coherent new integrating theory of superior or equal perspicuousness, can overthrow them.

Similar things should be said for "Atoms are indivisible." For the Greek cosmologists it was virtually analytic, for modern physicists it is a plainly false empirical statement. And again a similar thing obtains for the principle of physics that force equals mass times acceleration. Prior to relativity theory, it was virtually analytic; after relativity theory, its status changed and it is now an empirically false statement, though certainly not falsifiable by an isolated experiment no matter how many times it is repeated.

So, unlike—or so at least it appears—clear paradigms of analyticities ("Bachelors are unmarried," "Vixens are foxes," "Brothers are male siblings"), which are true in any consistently thinkable world, the principles of geometry, the fundamental principles of physics and perhaps even some of the principles of logic are not so firmly analytic: so true of all possible worlds, that timelessly their denials are not consistently thinkable; they do not, independently of some adopted system, express logical impossibilities. They are mistakenly thought to be analytic or perhaps synthetic *a priori*—because, unlike low level generalizations such as "All the books in my library are in French or English" or "All swans are white" or "All libraries in Montréal close at six o'clock," they cannot be overthrown by an isolated observation or experiment. Still they do not hold, come what may. They are overthrowable for there can be good reasons for overthrowing them; and there are good reasons for overthrowing them, as Putnam puts it, where we have presented a rival theory, to the theory in which these principles are embedded, which contains "the denials of these principles, plus evidence of the success of a rival theory."[42] Quine, White and Putnam all stress, as good fallibilists, that, as Putnam puts it, any "principle in our knowledge can be revised for theoretical reasons"; although some principles probably will never in fact be revised and "many principles resist refutation by isolated experimentation."[43] They can seem for a time self-evident and their denials impossible and this gives rise, where we have an overly narrow empiricism, to the belief that they are *a priori*.

Putnam argues, and Quine now agrees, that the claim about any principle being revisable, at least in principle, applies only to most of the principles of science, including the formal sciences, such as mathematics and logic. But not to what "is really an analytical principle in the trivial sense in which 'All bachelors are unmarried' is an analytic principle."[44] There are some of these in science and some in logic such as *modus ponens*. But, and this is the centrally important point, principles with deep theoretical import are all at least in principle revisable. But some, which have been extensively confused with properly analytic propositions, are those principles which will never be abandoned by scientists merely because of experiments. These are the ones which are prone to be taken, but still are mistakenly taken, to be *a priori* propositions, either unwittingly in an extended sense of "analytic" or as synthetic *a priori* propositions. But again, as Putnam puts it, there "is all the difference in the world between a principle that can never be given up by a rational scientist and a principle which cannot be given up by rational scientists merely because of experiments, no matter how numerous or how consistent."[45]

VII

What it is important to keep in mind here is that the foregoing discussion of the analytic/synthetic was not carried out for its own sake, but as something instrumental to a critique of metaphysics and in particular to a critique of the metaphysician's appeal to synthetic *a priori* knowledge. What I shall argue is that all the alleged synthetic *a priori* principles, those which are plainly incoherent aside, e.g., "Being noughts nothingness," are in reality either, on the one hand, genuinely analytic or, on the other, are *non-a priori* principles of the sort we have been discussing, namely, the principles of Euclidean geometry or some very deeply embedded, during certain periods, principles of physics such as, for the Ancient Greeks, "Atoms are indivisible," or for modern pre-relativity physics, "Mass equals force times acceleration." They are not true in virtue of the meanings or uses of their constitutive terms alone; they are not true in all possible worlds so that their denials do not express logical impossibilities. But they are principles that no experimental results, *taken by themselves*, could falsify and, given this relative unrevisability, they have been mistaken for *a priori* principles albeit of a somewhat mysterious sort. Hence the appellation "synthetic *a priori*."

I have already argued that Blanshard's attempt to articulate synthetic *a priori* principles of metaphysics underlying and grounding science fails. But one swallow doesn't make a spring or one fine day. Perhaps there are other and better examples. Synthetic *a priori* propositions (statements, sentences) are propositions, if such there be, whose negations are consistent and entail nothing inconsistent, yet they are also propositions whose truth is somehow known *a priori*, i.e., grasped intuitively or established by pure reflection (pure reason) independently of experience, observation, inference from such experience or observation or experiment.

Is there "anything that is known *a priori* to be true expressible only in statements that are synthetic, i.e., in statements that are neither analytic nor logically true?"[46] Most frequently the question "Is there any synthetic *a priori* knowledge?" is taken to be the question "Is there any knowledge which is not empirical and which is expressible only in synthetic statements?"[47] If the intermediaries talked about by Putnam, Quine and White on the continuum between the strictly and plainly analytic ("Bachelors are unmarried") and the brutely empirical ("There is a watch on this table" or "All swans are white"), such as the principles of geometry, some logical principles and some basic scientific laws, are said to be non-empirical and, *if* non-empirical, *therefore a priori*, then there is some accepted knowledge that is also synthetic *a priori* knowledge. But, as Quine in particular brings out, who regards himself as an empiricist, it is only by using "empirical" in an arbitrarily restricted way that we get *a priori* knowledge here, for such knowledge is dependent, though not only dependent, on how the world as a matter of fact turns out to be, i.e., what it turns out to be like. And, he adds, we do not gain any knowledge of how the world turns out to be only by rational insight or "intuiting essences" or just by reflection or just by thinking hard and carefully or anything of the kind. *Pure reason does not establish anything to be the case.* If, instead of utilizing Quine's broad use of "empirical" (a use common to all the pragmatists), "empirical" is taken more narrowly, as the British empiricists took it, to be only that which is knowable directly by experience or inferable from what we know directly by experience alone or anything inductively supportably by the foregoing, then it is not clear, again from what we have brought out regarding the Quinean-Whitean-Putnamian continuum, whether the only other kind of knowledge, contrasted with empirical knowledge so narrowly construed, should be classified as *a priori* and it is further not plain that we can have any such purely *a priori* but synthetic knowledge.

However, and be that as it may, let us turn again to some alleged examples of synthetic *a priori* propositions. This time Roderick Chisholm's examples will be examined together with his arguments for so construing them. They have the added attraction of having been culled by Chisholm from the writings of American philosophers concerned to defend such notions and writing from the Second World War until around 1960, a period in which such discussions received extensive play. Chisholm gives seven fairly standard examples, examples we can justifiably take as paradigms.

1. Anything that is red is colored.
2. Nothing is both red and green.
3. If anything is orange, then it has a color that is intermediate between red and yellow.
4. Anything that is colored is extended.
5. Anything that is a cube has twelve edges.
6. Seven and five are twelve.

Of the list Chisholm remarks: "If we wish to show that there is no synthetic *a priori* knowledge, then we must show, with respect to each of these statements, either that it is analytic, or that it expresses what is known but not known *a priori* or that it does not express what is known at all."[48] I shall argue that for all six of his statements one or another of these things obtain.

(1) is rather plainly analytic. It is only a problem for Chisholm because in its examination he employs a rather narrow conception of analytic, but, if one uses the non-extravagant and non-eccentric one used by Grice and Strawson, namely, that an analytic statement is one whose denial expresses a logical impossibility, then "It is red but uncolored" goes the same way as "My three year old child is an adult." If we try to employ either we realize that someone hearing us will not understand what we are saying. His state will not be one of disbelief but of incomprehension, for what is said to be the case is a logical impossibility. Someone who understands our linguistic practices knows that he cannot say that "It's red but uncolored," for saying that is unintelligible because self-contradictory. In saying it he is unsaying what he says.

(2) is different than (1). On one construal it could be empirical. There could be a thing with a sheen or a gloss such that on the surface it was red but when one looked at it with a little care it was seen to be green deep down. It is like clear still water in a lake that looks colorless near its surface but looked at deep down it looks bronze. If, in turn, it is replied that that was not what was meant by "Nothing is both red and green," then, in turn, it can be replied that the sense of the sentence is not sufficiently fixed such that we know what kind of proposition is being asserted. Perhaps its denial expresses a logical impossibility and perhaps it does not. But where it does not, or does not clearly do so, there is no reason to think that we just directly intuitively know it—know it by "the eye of reason"—to be true independently of any experience, including our understanding of the linguistic regularities that we gain in mastering a language. Moreover, that our concept of color *might* be sufficiently indeterminate that we cannot ascertain that nothing can be both red or green all over surely does not even suggest that it might be a synthetic *a priori* truth. The only plausible construal of it as *a priori* is to construe it as analytic.

(3) seems similar to (2). The sentence might be plausibly construed as analytic or empirical or, in some settings, like the principles of geometry, it might be unclear how to construe it. It might, like "Orthodox Jews fast on the Day of Atonement," be neither *a priori* nor empirical. (Do not say that it *must* be one or the other. As we have seen that does not fit the facts.) If someone had repeatedly seen orange things but never red or yellow things, he might not understand that orange is intermediate between red and yellow. Indeed, whether it does may be a matter of looking and seeing. That suggests a gloss where (3) is construed as empirical. But some speakers, thinking of some different contexts, might very well assert,

and their linguistic behavior would confirm their assertion, that they just use "orange" as a term for a color intermediate between red and yellow. That, of course, counts toward (3)'s analyticity. It all depends on who is using (3) how and where. In that way it is like the principles of Euclidean geometry, force equals mass times acceleration or atoms are indivisible. We have no good reason to believe that (3) is a synthetic *a priori* proposition.

(4) "Anything that is colored is extended" is a poor candidate for being synthetic *a priori* for different reasons. If in "anything" we, in thinking of *a thing*, are just thinking of the sort of thing that could be colored, as a bit of paper, a pencil, a wall, a string, then (4) is plainly analytic, for "a bit of paper is extended," "a pencil is extended," "a wall is extended" are all analytic and plainly so. It is just these sorts of things that we have the word "extended" to apply to. But "thing," particularly in "anything," is not always so physically understood. Thing understood geometrically as being exemplified by a geometrical point is not extended. If it had extension it would not be a purely geometrical point. But it is also true that a geometrical point—it seems analytically—could not be colored or it wouldn't be a geometrical point, though, of course, a point of light would be extended. Indeed any physical point (something a point of light is)—just to be a physical point—must be extended. And to be colored, the thing must be physical, so it must—logically must—also be extended. "Physical things are extended" is analytic.

Now consider (5) "Anything that is a cube has twelve edges." The logician C. H. Langford argued, Chisholm reports, that while (5) was plainly *a priori*, it was not analytic and so he concluded it must be synthetic *a priori*.[49] His argument seems to me both curious and mistaken. He argued that many people who know what a cube is, who recognize dice and the like, who even recognize that cubes have six equal square sides, do not recognize that being a cube requires its having twelve edges. From this Langford deduced (thought he deduced) that "the notion of having twelve edges can be no part of the notion of being a cube" and hence that the proposition "Anything that is a cube has twelve edges" cannot be analytic. But such things about the *psychology* of our notions cannot be the fundamental tests for analyticity, for an examination of our use of language shows that "Its a cube but it does not have twelve edges" is a contradiction. It expresses a logical impossibility and hence its denial is analytic. Whether everyone recognizes this or not is irrelevant. (Some people do not recognize the validity of *modus ponens*.) That no more undermines its analyticity than the analyticity of a long arithmetical calculation is undermined because many people are not sure of what the answer is or make mistakes in calculation. If a statement expresses a logical impossibility that is enough to show that it is analytic. If we (where "we" refers to the community of native or practiced speakers) do not know whether it does or not, then we do not know whether it is *a priori* or not. "A cube has twelve edges" is analytic and is known in such communities to be analytic. That is the way it is now implicitly defined in our linguistic practices. Whether a given person knows that or not is a different matter entirely.

(6) "Seven and five are twelve" is an example of Immanuel Kant's of a synthetic *a priori* proposition. Sometimes it is thought that the analyticity of (6) turns on the truth of logicism, namely, the claim that all mathematical statements can be defined in terms of purely logical principles. But there is no reason to think that some mathematical statements could not be analytic in their own right—quite independently of the truth or falsity of logicism—just as some geometrical statements, e.g., "Triangles are three-sided" are analytic. The logical impossibility of "Seven and five do not equal twelve" ensures that "Seven and five are twelve" is analytic. Failure to recognize the truth of this obvious triviality—another trifling proposition—is probably due either to the mistaken belief that the analyticity of mathematics is tied up with the truth of logicism or to a narrowly Kantian conception of analyticity in terms of subject and predicate sentences. But both those conceptions are rather evidently mistaken. If, in turn, it is denied, absurdly it seems to me, that the denial of "Seven and five are twelve" is a logical impossibility or if it is asserted that we have no good grounds for believing that it is, then it is also the case that "Seven and five are twelve" is not an *a priori* truth or that we have no good grounds for believing that it is. If such is the case, then it may be, as with many of the principles of geometry, some kind of empirical truth or a principle on the Quine-White-Putnam continuum that is neither plausibly classified as *a priori* nor as empirical, but *certainly*, in that case, it is not, like good synthetic *a priori* principles, if there are any such principles, just known by reason to be true and beyond even possible revision.

Reflecting on our arguments concerning these very characteristic examples of putative synthetic *a priori* principles and reflecting back on Blanshard's cases, previously considered, we should conclude that we should be very skeptical indeed over the very possibility of there being any synthetic *a priori* propositions at all. Synthetic *a priori* knowledge seems to be a Holmesless Watson. That there is any such knowledge—knowledge of what must be the case about the world just given through or by pure reason—or that there is the kind of necessity being claimed by transcendental metaphysicians seems highly unlikely. Yet there being such synthetic *a priori* knowledge is a *necessary* condition for the very possibility of a transcendental metaphysics; that is to say for the full-bodied metaphysics that is a part of the tradition. But it is still only a necessary condition and not a necessary and sufficient condition for having true metaphysical propositions, if indeed there are any at all. All metaphysical propositions must be synthetic *a priori* propositions but not only metaphysical propositions are synthetic *a priori* propositions. The (6) putative cases given by Chisholm—the very claimed paradigms of such propositions—are plainly *not* metaphysical propositions. The six propositions claimed by Blanshard to be synthetic *a priori* propositions had the advantage over Chisholm's of being plainly metaphysical propositions or at least evident and rather direct philosophical aids to metaphysics. But their disadvantage in comparison with Chisholm's propositions is that it is even more evident that they are not synthetic *a priori* propositions. The advantage of Chisholm's over Blanshard's is that they are slightly more plausible as candidates for being synthetic *a priori* propositions. The value of his discussion is that, if his arguments had been well-taken, he would have shown us that we can have propositions of a logical type that make way for the possibility of metaphysics. But even if my criticisms of his account are not well-taken, he still would not have shown that there are any metaphysical propositions with such a status.

Suppose now that my arguments against Chisholm's six examples of synthetic *a priori* are way off the mark and we clearly have synthetic *a priori* knowledge. Now let us ask if we have any metaphysical propositions of the requisite sort that it would be reasonable to accept. Let us assume as well that my criticisms of Blanshard cases have been on the mark, so we do not have to step again in that river, and let us now consider other examples of real live metaphysical propositions–propositions which are plainly metaphysical, but are, as well, claimed to be synthetic *a priori*.

1. Ultimate reality is being as such.
2. Ultimate reality is eternal.
3. Ultimate reality is process.
4. Ultimate reality is of the nature of feeling.
5. Universals alone are real.
6. Only particulars exist.
7. All facts are physical facts.
8. To be is to be perceived.
9. Mind alone is real.
10. Matter and energy alone are real.
11. There is both mind and matter and they are distinct substances.
12. The universe forms a purposive order.
13. Reality forms a necessary system of total truth.

The above propositions are real metaphysical propositions alright. They are the very stuff that metaphysics is made of. And real metaphysicians (i.e., transcendental metaphysicians) would try to make out that at

least some of them are synthetic *a priori* propositions. Let us set aside for
a moment propositions 6, 7, and 8, which some might try to make out as
analytic or "analytically false," i.e., expressing logical impossibilities or being
self-contradictory. Consider first only the other propositions on the list.
Though they must, to be metaphysical propositions, be synthetic *a priori*
propositions, they certainly do not seem to be such, though they do not
seem to be analytic or analytically false either, and they certainly do not
seem to be empirical propositions. Perhaps they are just among the many
different propositions not fitting into any of these cubby-holes of which
Putnam speaks. But, unlike his examples, they are also sentences without
a secure use in our language. What is the case, as we saw in the previous
chapter in examining metaphysical systems utilizing such propositions, is
that we do not understand what they mean. They appear at least not to
make sense. We do not understand what we are trying to assert or deny
in asserting and denying them; we do not understand what counts for or
against their truth. It is not that I am turning positivist (logical empiricist)
here and asserting (trying to assert) that a proposition to be cognitively
meaningful must either be analytic or empirical and, then, going to say, in
fine positivist fiddle, that these propositions are cognitively meaningless
because they are neither analytic nor empirical. Rather, without invoking
a general criterion of meaning (or any criterion or theory of meaning at
all), just by examining them, proposition by proposition, we recognize,
without the aid of theory, that they are so problematical (even with the
background of their utterance filled in) that we do not know what we are
talking about in using them. (That was one of the key morals of the
previous chapter.) We note, in so reflecting on them, that they contain
phrases such as "ultimate reality" which are undefined, unelucidated, have
no secure use in our language and concerning which we are quite at sea,
for we have not the faintest idea of how to go about ascertaining what is
ultimately real so that we could say, and be tolerably confident that it was
true, that x (for whatever value "x" takes) is ultimately real. Such phrases,
to repeat, have no even reasonably settled use in our common language.
Moreover, metaphysical sentences in the above list are not, like "All swans
are white" or "Frustrated people tend to respond with aggression,"
straightforwardly empirical or even more generously empirical like "Atoms
are indivisible" or "Force equals mass times acceleration." The latter two
statements are not, as we have seen, confirmable by a single isolated
experiment no matter how many times repeated, but they are, given the rest
of science, similarly treated, confirmable or confutable. They are a part of
a large system of integrated propositions which, taken together, have
empirically testable consequences. Physicists know what establishes or
disestablishes them or at least what counts toward doing so. But this does
not obtain for the above metaphysical propositions. There is no consensus

at all about what would establish them or disestablish them. We do not know what counts for their truth or what counts for their falsity besides saying that their at least apparent incoherence counts for their falsity. One metaphysician says "Ultimate reality is being as such" another says "Ultimate reality is process." We have no idea which metaphysician, if either, is telling it like it is. We do not even have any idea about how to go about trying to find out.

Similar things should be said about 13 "Reality forms a necessary system of total truth." We understand what it is for various statements to be true. And we know some of the plain truths of the world, e.g., "It is colder in Quebec in December than in August" or "Newborn babies cannot speak." We do not, however, have a solid grip on what of talk of *the* truth comes to, but perhaps we can make something of such talk in some determinate contexts. But talk of "total truth" is just as baffling as talk of "Ultimate reality" or "Being as such." It is not unreasonable to think that such talk is unintelligible. At least no determinate sense has been given to it so that we can have any confidence at all that people who so speak know what they are talking about.

We should also not forget that these propositions, to be metaphysical propositions, are supposed to be synthetic *a priori* truths. They are, that is, supposed to be self-evident truths that we just somehow "see" (directly apprehend) to be true or are directly aware of their necessary truth as we are directly aware that if A is to the right of B and B to C then A is to the right of C. We are supposed, after careful reflection, to be similarly directly and certainly aware of the truth of these metaphysical propositions. This might—just might—be true of the so-called synthetic *a priori* truths such as "All red things are colored," "Cubes have twelve edges," or "Anything that is colored is extended." We either just "see" they are true or we do not. Their being true is somehow a matter of direct awareness and not of experimental investigation or any kind of looking or seeing. Their truth, it is claimed, is a matter of intuitive, direct *a priori* insight. It is doubtful whether such talk—such intensional idioms—make much sense, though philosophers as able, and down to earth, as Roderick Chisholm and C. I. Lewis, have employed such idioms. But whether or not, with Quine and a host of others, we should be suspicious of such talk, it is natural enough, so to speak, and, at least with some demythologization, it is not obviously senseless. But what is to the point here, even if we accept such intensional idioms, is that whatever we might say about the self-evidence of "All red things are colored," and its synthetic *a priori* status, none of the metaphysical propositions mentioned above have anything like that status. Far from being self-evident, apprehended to be true in the light of reflective reason alone, we do not even understand what they mean, or at least we have nothing even remotely like a clear understanding of what is being said, and it is not unreasonable to suspect that nothing intelligible is being said. We do not have anything with them that is even remotely in the area of being self-evident or of being directly known, quite beyond question, to be true, as "All red things are extended" perhaps might be. Metaphysical propositions are supposed to be synthetic *a priori* truths. None of the paradigm metaphysical propositions are that. Their obscurity is such that we could never reasonably claim they are directly knowable by pure reason, even reflective pure reason.

It might be responded, to return to what I set aside a few pages back, that 6, 7 and 8 are not so plainly senseless as the others and are not unreasonable candidates for *a priori* truths. Berkeley, the response might continue, did a pretty clever job of producing a transcendental argument to prove the *a priori* status of 8 ("To be is to be perceived").[50] These three propositions are plainly not as opaque as the others. Yet none of them are analytic; their denials are not self-contradictory—or at least they have not been shown to be self-contradictory—and none of them are empirically establishable either, not even in the indirect way that "Force equals mass times acceleration" was once established and has now been disestablished. Philosophers produce transcendental arguments for 6, 7 and 8, but there is no consensus that any of them yield true metaphysical claims, though there is something approaching a consensus about their falsity, incoherence or utter problematicity. There is, to put it minimally, nothing like the consensus we have about "If anything is orange, then it has a color which is intermediate between red and yellow." What we have perhaps is something approaching a consensus that these sentences are at best false.[51]

Transcendental metaphysics—real full-bodied metaphysics—lays claim to establishing synthetic *a priori* truths which are seen to be self-evident by the use of our unaided—experimentally and observationally unaided—reflective reason. I have argued that we have good reason to believe that there are no such metaphysical truths and to be skeptical of the very possibility of discovering or constructing any. I have also argued that there are good grounds for believing that there are no synthetic *a priori* truths of the mundane sort I discussed and that, moreover, we do not even have, in the very idea of a synthetic *a priori* truth, a well formed conception. Synthetic *a priori* propositions are necessary for metaphysics, but the whole idea is built on sand.

VIII

A descriptive metaphysics or even a revisionary metaphysics can be thoroughly naturalistic and, in the broad sense, empirical. We could, as does Quine and as does J. J. C. Smart following him here, see philosophy, including metaphysics, as continuous with, indeed, as Quine puts it, even as "a part of science," differing from "the rest of science" in being "at the abstract and theoretical end of science."[52] "Science," Quine continues, "is a continuum that stretches from history and engineering at one extreme to philosophy and pure mathematics at the other."[53] Philosophy, he tells us, and this presumably includes very centrally metaphysics, "is abstract through being very general. A physicist will tell us about causal connections between events of certain sorts; a biologist will tell us about causal connections between events of other sorts, but the philosopher asks about causal connections in general—what is it for one event or cause another? Or again a physicist or zoologist will tell us that there are electrons, that there are wombats; a mathematician will tell us that there are no end of prime numbers, but the philosopher wants to know, in general terms, what sorts of things there are altogether. Philosophy seeks the broad outlines of the whole system of the world."[54] Or, as Smart puts it, "Metaphysics is continuous with science. As science gets more general and abstract it gets more metaphysical."[55] Metaphysics "is a search for the most plausible theory of the whole universe, as it is considered in the light of science."[56] Where metaphysics is the most abstract and general side of science it, as Smart asserts, "just is science," though it is the more conceptual side of science, as in elementary particle theory and in conceptualizing action at a distance. But, as a part of science, metaphysics is most emphatically not, for Quine and Smart, First Philosophy founding (attempting to found) or grounding (attempting to ground) science. Such conceptions are as unintelligible to them as they were to the logical empiricists. Their naturalistic metaphysics is not like the traditional metaphysics discussed in previous sections and in the first chapter. There is, as Smart puts it, where "metaphysics is properly done" no "attempt to deduce facts about the world purely *a priori*."[57] There are, with Quine and Smart, no transcendental hypotheses or transcendental arguments. Nor is there any appeal to any necessities beyond empirical necessities. As Quine puts it "Metaphysical necessity has no place in my naturalistic view."[58] We, in short, have, as we had in John Dewey, an "empirical metaphysics" inquiring into very general questions, questions, as Quine puts it, "as to what sorts of things there are, as well as what it means to exist, for there to be something."[59] This is all, supposedly, the most general part of science. So we have what Putnam has called, tongue in cheek, metaphysics within the limits of science alone.

I find this whole idea of a metaphysics within the limits of science alone puzzling. Where we get "metaphysics," as a part of Physical Cosmology, we ask was there a Big Bang—a universe wide intensely hot explosion in which space started expanding—or wasn't there? Are there markedly different cosmic regions and how much life is there in the cosmos? Is the universe made up of infinitely prolonged contractions or an infinity of cosmic oscillations: explosions followed by gravitationally produced recollapses followed by new explosions?[60] What we have here are plainly rather speculative scientific questions. It is unclear what, if anything, the philosopher *qua* philosopher can contribute here. A philosopher who knew a lot of physics and astronomy might make some small preliminary conceptual clarifications here, but the arguing for or the elucidating of these claims falls to the astronomer and physicist. You can call this metaphysics, if you like, but the work here is done by physical cosmologists, is plainly a part of established science, and these questions are distant from the questions of traditional metaphysics and the questions we found Quine asking. Philosophy has very little business here or relevance.[61] Realism and anti-realism debates, even granting that they make much sense, have no bite or even relevance here at all. Though philosophers who learn physical cosmology very well, in effect changing disciplines, could, of course, like any scientist so accomplished, make a contribution here, though it is unclear whether any philosophical expertise is doing any work for him in such a context.

When we consider Quine's questions, questions about what it means to exist, or to be a cause, or to be a causal connection, or for one event to cause another or questions about what *sort* of things there are, we seem at least to be asking the kinds of questions that the linguistic philosophers (those resolutely *second-order* chaps) were asking: that is, conceptual questions about the use of terms. Questions requiring analysis and elucidation rather than empirical investigation or theory construction linked with experiment and observation. Their very generality—something Quine insists on—seems at least to rule out genuine experimental examination. What in reality we have instead is the *second-order* activity of conceptual analysis and not an investigation into what our universe is like, e.g., whether there was a Big Bang or whether the universe oscillates. "Every event has a cause" is not like "Frustrated people respond with aggression" or even "Force equals mass times acceleration" or "Atoms are indivisible." Quine's   questions—plainly   standard   traditional   philosophical questions—seem at least to be *second-order* questions (questions about the uses of our talk about the world). They are questions of conceptual analysis: questions about how language works, questions about how "event," "cause" and the like work in our language and how equivalent terms in other natural languages work, the only places where it is even intelligible to speak of their working. If *that* is metaphysics, then metaphysics collapses into *second-order* conceptual analysis. But that is in effect to persuasively define or redefine "metaphysics" and in doing so to so radically reconcept-ualize it that the very subject matter has been changed.

Here it might be responded that I am forgetting the very Quineian-Putnamian lessons I have drawn about the analytic/synthetic in the previous discussion. We should, reflecting on that, take Quine's point that there is no way in general of separating out what in language is made true by our linguistic conventions and what is made true by the facts of the world. I take that point, though, as I shall argue in the penultimate chapter, we can sometimes usefully go *second-order*, as Quine stresses himself, and ask questions about our uses of language, knowing full well that that is what we are asking. But often we cannot. We cannot separate out conceptual questions (questions about language) from factual questions (questions about the world). We should perhaps treat "Every event has a cause" as being about the world *and* about language in a way similar to the way we regard "Force equals mass times acceleration"; but, with the latter, we have a body of developed science, theoretically elaborated and experimentally based. We have nothing like that for "Every event has a cause." What we have is a lot of conflicting philosophical doctrines with no consensus on what is to be said or how we would go about establishing what is true or well warranted here.

Let us, however, not continue to ask about the logical status of these metaphysical claims, but take them (try to take them) as Quine and Smart wish them to be taken, as very general scientific claims open, in the way "Force equals mass times acceleration" is open, to theoretical and experimental test. In this way our "scientific metaphysics," if you will, would seek to describe, including describing the connections, and explain (causally explain?) our fundamental categories, namely, existence, knowledge, identity, truth, value, space, time, causality, and perhaps some others as well. We would get a description of them, an explanation, and an account of how they fit together. This supposedly is to be done in a scientific, that is, in a theoretical-cum-experimental-cum- empirical way.

I can understand this descriptive metaphysics when it is construed as a description and elucidation of these terms, together with a description of how they stand to each other. We get here something empirical enough and testable, in the indirect ways of which Quine speaks; but we do not get the *necessity* sought by metaphysicians. We have eschewed anything like *a priori* or "metaphysical necessity." Existence, knowledge, identity, etc. are our categories. In being socialized—introduced into any culture whatsoever—we gain a working mastery of them; and in our lives they work in empirically describable ways. But we get none, in such descriptions and elucidations, of the necessity that metaphysicians have sought. There is no establishment with such a descriptive metaphysics that we *must*, categorically must, think in these terms or even that we *should* so think or that there can be no intelligible or coherent alternatives to thinking in this way. We get a description of our practices, including, of course, our linguistic practices. When we get very general, we may sometimes get things that are true enough, but where true, and so general, they are platitudinous. We learn things such as "If it is true then it must be so," "Existence is not an attribute of things," "Truth and confirmation are distinct," "If we know something then what we know is true," "Facts and events are distinct," and the like. To break, or at least relieve, philosophical confusions, it, in a good Wittgensteinian manner, is sometimes valuable to be reminded of these platitudes or truisms. (That they are truisms does not at all mean that they are not true.) Moreover, there is nothing unempirical and uncheckable here, but a *system* of such description, or a systematic carrying out of such descriptions, has very little point. It has no metaphysical point beyond the therapeutic one of relieving or breaking philosophical perplexities. Positively, we learn in doing "descriptive metaphysics," to describe what some practices are and how they function in all societies. But we get no metaphysical necessities here. Such description satisfies no metaphysical craving for necessity and certainty. We do not, as Smart wished, get a theory, let alone the most plausible theory, "of the whole universe, as it is considered in the light of total science."[62] We do not, as Quine wished, get a metaphysics which rounds out the system of the world. "Philosophy," as Quine has it, seeks "the broad outlines of the whole system of the world."[63] But in fact we get nothing like that from our "descriptive metaphysics"; we, where we get truth, get a collection of platitudes (truisms) whose value consists in their use to break philosophical confusions such as "We can never know the mind of another?" "We can never know what is true?" "God could not not exist." and the like. But we have nothing like a systematic metaphysical theory here worthy of the name. Where we get strong allegedly *necessarily* necessary metaphysical claims we get incoherence. Where we get accurate description of categories we get description with no clear point or philosophical rationale.

Notes

1. A classic positivist statement of it, and its rationale, is in Hans Reichenbach, "Rationalism and Empiricism: An Inquiry into the Roots of Philosophical Error," *Philosophical Review* (1948). For a non-positivist articulation see C. I. Lewis, *An Analysis of Knowledge and Valuation* (La Salle, Illinois: Open Court, 1946), 35-170.

2. Willard Van Orman Quine, *From a Logical Point of View* (Cambridge, Massachusetts: Harvard University Press, 1953), 20-45; Morton G. White, "The Analytic and the Synthetic: An Untenable Dualism" in Leonard Linsky, ed., *Semantics and the Philosophy of Language* (Urbana, Illinois: University of Illinois Press, 1952), 272-86; and Hilary Putnam, "The Analytic and the Synthetic" in his *Mind, Language and Reality: Philosophical Papers* Vol. 2 (Cambridge: Cambridge University Press, 1975), 33-69.

3. For a powerfully articulated, broadly Wittgensteinian, undermining of this dichotomy, see Fredrich Waismann, *How I See Philosophy* (New York: St. Martin's Press, 1968), 122-207.

4.   Immanuel Kant, *Critique of Pure Reason*, Norman Kemp Smith, trans. (London: Macmillan, 1953), 41-64 and 189-91; Henry Sidgwick, *The Methods of Ethics* (Chicago, Illinois: University of Chicago Press, 1962); Arthur Pap, *Semantics and Necessary Truth* (New Haven, Connecticut: Yale University Press, 1958); Roderick Chisholm *Theory of Knowledge* in Chisholm, et al., eds., *Philosophy* (Englewood Cliffs, New Jersey: Prentice-Hall, 1964), 287-311; Brand Blanshard, *The Nature of Thought*, two volumes (London: George Allen, 1939); Brand Blanshard, *Reason and Analysis* (La Salle, Illinois: Open Court, 1962); Brand Blanshard, "The Philosophic Enterprise" in Charles J. Bontempo and S. Jack Odell, eds., *The Owl of Minerva* (New York: McGraw-Hill, 1975), 163-77.

5.   For a subtle and probing questioning of the very idea of there being such truths see Cora Diamond, *The Realistic Spirit: Wittgenstein, Philosophy and the Mind* (Cambridge, Massachusetts: MIT Press, 1991), 13-72.

6.   These are Gilbert Ryle's remarks in a final summing up of their discussion. See D. F. Pears, ed., *The Nature of Metaphysics* (London: Macmillan, 1957), 164.

7.   Norman Malcolm, *Knowledge and Certainty* (Englewood Cliffs, New Jersey: Prentice-Hall, 1963), 141-62. This is a reprinting of his article, "Anselm's Ontological Arguments," which first appeared in *The Philosophical Review* LXIX, no. 1 (January 1960).

8.   For example, a later issue of *The Philosophical Review* LXX, no. 1 (January 1961) was entirely devoted to criticisms of Malcolm's account. Malcolm characteristically remarks of these and some other criticisms, "I do not know that it is possible to meet all of the objections; on the other hand, I do not know that it is impossible." Malcolm, *Knowledge and Certainty*, 162.

9.   I have assessed Malcolm's arguments in my *Reason and Practice* (New York: Harper and Row, 1971), 156-67.

10.   Some key discussions of transcendental arguments are Barry Stroud, "Transcendental Arguments," *The Journal of Philosophy* LXV, no. 9 (May 1968), 241-56; Charles Taylor, "The Validity of Transcendental Arguments," *Proceedings of the Aristotelian Society* 74 (1978-79), 151-65; Richard Rorty, "Strawson's Objectivity Argument," *Review of Metaphysics* 23 (1970), 27-44; Richard Rorty, "Verificationism and Transcendental Arguments," *Nous* (1971), 3-14; Richard Rorty, "Transcendental Arguments, Self-Reference, and Pragmatism" in P. Bieri, et al., eds., *Transcendental Arguments and Science* (Dordrecht, Holland: D. Reidel, 1979), 77-103; and Richard Rorty, "Epistemological Behaviorism and the De-transcendentalization of Analytic Philosophy" in Robert J. Hollinger, ed., *Hermeneutics and Praxis* (Notre Dame, Indiana: Notre Dame University Press, 1985), 89-121.

11.   For literature on descriptive metaphysics and its contrast with revisionary metaphysics see P. F. Strawson, *Individuals: An Essay in Descriptive Metaphysics* (London: Methuen, 1959), 9-12; P. F. Strawson, *Analysis and Metaphysics* (Oxford: Oxford University Press, 1992), 8-28, 97-108; essays by Strawson and G. J. Warnock in Gilbert Ryle, ed., *The Revolution in Philosophy* (London: Macmillan, 1963), 97-126; Stuart Hampshire, "Metaphysical Systems" in D. F. Pears, ed., *The Nature of Metaphysics*, 23-38; Stuart Hampshire, "Identification and Existence" in H. D. Lewis, ed., *Contemporary British Philosophy* (London: Allen & Unwin, 1956), 191-208; and

Stuart Hampshire, "A Statement About Philosophy" in Bontempo and Odell, eds., *The Owl of Minerva*, 89-101.

12. Ryle in D. F. Pears, ed., *The Nature of Metaphysics*, 164.

13. See references to Strawson and Hampshire in note 11. See also my "On there being Philosophical Knowledge," *Theoria* LVI, Part 3(1990), 193-225.

14. Simon Blackburn, "Can Philosophy Exist?" in Jocelyne Couture and Kai Nielsen, eds., *Méta-Philosophie: Reconstructing Philosophy? New Essays on Metaphilosophy* (Calgary, Alberta: University of Calgary Press, 1993).

15. Richard Rorty, *Consequences of Pragmatism* (Minneapolis, Minnesota: University of Minnesota Press, 1982).

16. This is argued for and illustrated in a rather convincing way by P. F. Strawson in his *Analysis and Metaphysics*.

17. Cora Diamond, working with a very keen understanding of Wittgenstein, gives us very good reasons for believing that there can be no such necessities. Cora Diamond, *The Realistic Spirit*, 13-72.

18. Morton White, "The Analytic and Synthetic: An Untenable Dualism," 272-86.

19. See references to Blanshard in note 4 and see, as well, his "In Defense of Metaphysics" in W. E. Kennick and Morris Lazerowitz, eds., *Metaphysics: Readings and Reappraisals* (Englewood Cliffs, New Jersey: Prentice-Hall, 1966), 331-55 and his "Current Strictures on Reason," *The Philosophical Review* LIV (July 1945), 359-70. For two quite different reactions to such rationalism see Ernest Nagel, *Sovereign Reason* (Glencoe, Illinois: Free Press, 1954), 266-95 and Richard Rorty, "Review of *Reason and Analysis*," *Journal of Philosophy* LX (1963), 551-57.

20. Brand Blanshard, "The Philosophic Enterprise," 170-74. For a critique of such a conception of philosophy see my "Jolting the Career of Reason: Absolute Idealism and Other Rationalisms Reconsidered," *Journal of Speculative Philosophy* (1994).

21. See the discussion of this by J. J. C. Smart, "Why Philosophers Disagree" in Couture and Nielsen, eds., *Méta-Philosophie*. See Michael Dummett, *Truth and Other Enigmas* (Cambridge, Massachusetts: Harvard University Press, 1978), 215-47; G. Priest, R. Routley and J. Norman, eds., *Paraconsistent Logic: Essays on the Inconsistent* (Munich: Philosophia, 1989); and Neil Tennant, *Anti-Realism and Logic* (Oxford: Clarendon Press, 1987).

22. Norman Malcolm, *Thought and Knowledge* (Ithaca, New York: Cornell University Press, 1977), 200-212. See my *God, Scepticism and Modernity* (Ottawa, Ontario: University of Ottawa Press, 1989), 121-33.

23. Kai Nielsen, *After the Demise of the Tradition: Rorty, Critical Theory and the Fate of Philosophy* (Boulder, Colorado: Westview Press, 1991), 91-122.

24. However, see my second thoughts about such groundless believing in my *Philosophy and Atheism* (Buffalo, New York: Prometheus Books, 1985), 223-31 and my "Peirce, Pragmatism and the Challenge of Postmodernism," *Transactions of the Charles S. Peirce Society* XXIX, no. 4 (Fall 1993), 513-60.

25. Blanshard, "The Philosophic Enterprise," 176-77.

26. See references in note 2.

27. Putnam, "The Analytic and the Synthetic," 36.

28. Ibid. H. P. Grice and Peter Strawson, "In Defense of Dogma" in L. W. Sumner and John Woods, eds., *Necessary Truth* (New York: Random House, 1969), 141-59.

29. Putnam, "The Analytic and the Synthetic," 36.

30. Ibid.

31. Quine, "Two Dogmas in Retrospect," *Canadian Journal of Philosophy* 21, no. 3 (September 1991), 270.

32. As well as Putnam, who makes the definitive argument here, see Waismann, *How I See Philosophy*, 122-207.

33. See the references in notes 22, 23, and 24.

34. Ludwig Wittgenstein, *On Certainty* (Oxford: Basil Blackwell, 1969).

35. Putnam, "The Analytic and the Synthetic," 38.

36. Ibid., 65.

37. Grice and Strawson, "In Defence of Dogma," 149-52.

38. Ibid., 65.

39. Quine, "Two Dogmas in Retrospect," 270.

40. Putnam, "The Analytic and the Synthetic," 48.

41. Ibid., 46.

42. Ibid., 48.

43. Ibid.

44. Ibid., 49.

45. Ibid.

46. Roderick Chisholm, *Theory of Knowledge* in Chisholm et al., eds., *Philosophy* (Englewood Cliffs, New Jersey: Prentice-Hall, 1964), 287-311.

47. Ibid., 305.

48. Ibid., 304.

49. Ibid., 305-306. C. H. Langford, "A Proof that Synthetic *A Priori* Propositions Exist," *Journal of Philosophy* XLVI (1949), 20-24.

50. Charles Baylis very briefly and cogently expresses the arguments that might lead us to think Berkeley achieves that and then equally adroitly shows how they do not wash. Charles A. Baylis, "Introduction" in Baylis, ed., *Metaphysics* (New York: Macmillan, 1965), 6-12.

51. Nielsen, "Can there be Justified Philosophical Beliefs?" *Iyyun* 40 (July 1991), 235-70.

52. Quine, "Dialogue with W. A. Quine" in Brian Magee, ed., *Men of Ideas* (Oxford: Oxford University Press, 1982), 143.

53. Ibid.

54. Ibid., 143-44.

55. J. J. C. Smart, *Ethics, Persuasion and Truth* (London: Routledge and Kegan Paul, 1984), 138.

56. Ibid.

57. Ibid., 154.

58. Quine, "Two Dogmas in Retrospect," 270.

59. Quine, "Dialogue with W. A. Quine," 144.

60. John Leslie, ed., *Physical Cosmology and Philosophy* (New York: Macmillan, 1990), 2.

61. What I say here may seem to conflict with what I said in the first note in Chapter 1 about Steven Weinberg and his search for ultimate reality and a final theory which would tell us with *finality* what nature really is like so that we will have at long last found in the Higgs particle the ultimate stuff, so that we will now at least know what ultimate reality is really like. My objection to this is that it is not physics, but metaphysics of a rather wild sort parading as physics and is vulnerable to therapeutic conceptual analysis. But the physical cosmology I described above does not seem to be that. It makes no claim to a final theory or to have discovered ultimate reality. It is just rather speculative physics, but still physics operating under empirical constraints. Finally, as a distinct point: there is a de-mythologized conception of a final theory that would leave it as a coherent possibility. Namely, if talk about ultimate reality, or an unrevisable theory telling us finally what nature is really like is dropped, and the claim to final theory just is the claim to a theory from whose principles all the laws that govern the workings of the universe could be deduced, then we have something that is, perhaps, non-metaphysical and *conceivably* could be true.

62. Smart, *Ethics, Persuasion and Truth*, 138.

63. Quine, "Dialogue with W. A. Quine," 144.

PART TWO

Philosophy as Epistemology

Philosophy solves, or rather gets rid of, only philosophical problems; it does not set our thinking on a more solid basis. What I am attacking is above all the idea that the question "What is knowledge?—e.g.—is a crucial one. That is what it seems to be: it seems as if we didn't yet know anything at all until we can answer <u>that</u> question. In our philosophical investigation it is as if we were in a terrible hurry to complete a backlog of unfinished business which has to be finished or else everything else seems to hang in the air.

— *Ludwig Wittgenstein*

There is no chance that someone can take up a vantage point for comparing conceptual schemes by temporarily shedding his own.

— *Donald Davidson*

...there is no such thing as the way the thing is in itself under no description, apart from any use to which human beings might want to put it.

— *Richard Rorty*

...the appearance/reality distinction [is] useful when confined to relatively narrow contexts (apparent magnitude rather than real magnitude, non-dairy creamer rather than real cream) but is useless when blown up to the traditional philosophical scale. For then it is useless to ask whether one vocabulary rather than another is closer to reality. For different vocabularies serve different purposes, and there is no such thing as a purpose that is closer to reality than another purpose the latter being a purpose which is simply a "finding out how things are" as opposed to finding out how to predict their motion, explain their behavior and so on.

— *Richard Rorty*

3

Epistemology and Skepticism

Traditionally, philosophy has not only been centrally concerned with metaphysics but with epistemology as well. This has particularly been true and insistent during the modern period from Descartes to Kant and coming down, particularly in Anglo-America, into the contemporary period. With a variety of mainstream philosophers, epistemology (theory of knowledge) has remained a central preoccupation. Indeed not a few philosophers believe that if metaphysics is at all possible, it will have to be grounded in a sound epistemology.[1] Others of a more empiricist bent eschew metaphysics, or at least try to do so, but take epistemology very seriously indeed.[2] To avoid relativism and nihilism, or at least the relying on the idols of our tribe, we need, they think, a sound theory of knowledge to ground our beliefs and diverse practices. This, many philosophers believe, can and should be done without an appeal to metaphysical conceptions.

The questions epistemologists ask are "What is knowledge?" "How do we test knowledge claims?" "What criteria do we have for knowledge?" "What is evidence?" "What is the relation between knowledge, belief, evidence, and truth?" "Do we ever have knowledge of the truth?" (This may be just a way of asking do we ever have knowledge?) "Do we ever know anything with certainty?" "Are there any self-evident or self-justifying beliefs that could not be rationally denied?" "When are beliefs justified?" "Indeed are any beliefs ever really justified or do they all rest on animal faith?" "Is there any substantive knowledge that is non-empirical?"[3] These and similar questions are the questions of epistemology, or at least traditional epistemology.

Three often connected but still distinct issues have been focal for epistemologists: (1) What are the criteria of knowledge or justified belief such that, with an answer to this, we could have a kind of litmus paper test to ascertain when we know something or when, if ever, our various practices and beliefs–everyday, scientific, moral, political, legal, and religious–are justified or rationally warranted? (2) Epistemologists have also sought to see if they can refute the skeptic, or otherwise rationally meet the challenge of the skeptic, who says we have not been able to show that we know anything or that any of our beliefs or practices are justified or rationally warranted. Perhaps they are, the skeptic grants. He does not–making a strong positive claim–deny that we have any knowledge or sound beliefs or reliable assessments of what it is rational or reasonable to do and believe and what is not; he only claims that neither philosophers nor anyone else has shown or established that we have better reasons for thinking so than for not so thinking. Our beliefs, even those that appear to be the best warranted, he opines, seem at least to rest on a kind of animal faith. (3) Non-skeptical philosophers, and indeed in a kind of negative way, even skeptical philosophers, have wanted to provide a critique of culture. The non-skeptical ones have wanted to provide a rational foundation for our various moral, political, religious, scientific, and aesthetic practices. Through the use of elaborate arguments, they make knowledge claims, claim certain beliefs and practices are justified, and deny that others are justified. The epistemologist wishes to provide rational grounds for deciding which ones, if any, are really rationally warranted. He wants to provide a *theory* of knowledge which provides genuinely substantive criteria for when we really know something, anything at all. His approach, as befits a traditional philosopher, is perfectly *general*. In some instances–say, perhaps, in religion or politics or even morality–we may never obtain knowledge; indeed, perhaps none of these beliefs or practices are rationally warranted. Perhaps there are no genuine religious knowledge claims, perhaps politics is all ideology (confused, distorted beliefs expressing class or cultural biases), perhaps morality is no more than our projected emotions so that there is, and can be, no genuine moral knowledge or justified moral beliefs. Perhaps it is all a matter of what attitudes we just happen to have. Perhaps, by contrast, science, and science alone, yields genuine knowledge? (Such a belief has come to be called scientism.) The kind of epistemologist I have been talking about sets it, as part of her task, to determine whether any of the above things are really so. The idea is to articulate a *general theory of knowledge or justified belief* which would establish what claims in our various forms of life, including even mathematics and the natural sciences, are really justified, really rationally warranted, so that we could claim truth for them. The epistemological task is to establish, by showing a rational foundation for them, which, if any, of these beliefs are true or have sufficient rational warrant to make them beliefs that any rational, properly informed person must accept.

Philosophy, as this classical foundationalist epistemology, will be an overseer of culture by establishing where, in the various domains of ordinary belief and science, we have genuine knowledge rooted in evident truth: in certain knowledge rooted in self-justifying propositions which cannot be rationally denied. These are not propositions, they also claim, which can be established by the use of experimental hypotheses or empirical research, but only by careful philosophical reflection and analysis. On such a conception, epistemology, something here taken to be at the very heart of good philosophy, is, while remaining purely reflective, still a super-discipline which will ascertain and assess the truth or rational warrant of all other disciplines and human activities. Philosophy is to be the overseer, assessor, and judge of religion, science, politics, morality, and of what is sound in common sense. It is, moreover, on this foundationalist conception, philosophy which, if anything will, will tell us what a just society and a truly humane society is and what a set of rational scientific principles and practices are.

There will be some—indeed in our culture many—who will be unhappy with this conception of philosophy as providing the grounding for cultural critique. They will think this is pure hubris on the part of the epistemologist. Still, while cutting—trying to cut—the epistemologist more nearly down to size, they will continue to see the task of the epistemologist to be that of in some way meeting the challenge of the skeptic by establishing that some of our beliefs are justified and that we really do sometimes have knowledge. To do this, it is frequently believed, the epistemologist must provide criteria for knowledge—knowledge in any domain—or at least justified belief—justified belief in any domain. But, if this can be done, then surely philosophy could be such a super-discipline, such an overseer of culture. To regard this as *hubris*, the traditional epistemologist will say, is just a failure of philosophical nerve, revealing what in effect is skepticism about philosophers having such general criteria for knowledge or justified belief.[4]

II

Why is it that skepticism has been thought, again and again in the tradition of philosophy, to be a problem which a proper epistemologist should closely examine? Philosophical skepticism is, after all, very peculiar and is, at least on the face of it, rather different from the ordinary garden variety skepticisms about morality, politics, personal relations, religion, aesthetic canons, and the like. The philosophical skeptic purports to be skeptical about our knowledge of the external world or of other minds.[5] We might be skeptical about whether there really are neutrinos, the Higgs particle, an id, or whether there are any gods, but, it would seem, on the face of it at any rate, quite impossible to be skeptical about the external world or other minds. But this is precisely what philosophers of the modern period have taken to be the core of the skeptical challenge and have erected an epistemology to meet.

How could any sane person think these are real problems? Yet these problems, in spite of their at least apparent absurdity, have remained persistent in the philosophical tradition. A cluster of them have been put this way:

> Do we really know that there is a world external to us? Are there objects outside us, existing whether perceived by us or not, objects such as chairs, tables, other people, and not only other human beings but minds as well? Can we know more than that these things appear to exist?[6]

If a person were to exist, how could she know that anyone else exists? Let us suppose that I cannot doubt that I think and that therefore I cannot doubt that I am, that I cannot just think that subjectless thinking occurs. (Not "I think therefore I exist" but "Thinking occurs now therefore thinking occurs now.") But even *if* I cannot doubt that I exist, how can I know that anyone else exists or that what I take to be the actually familiar objects of the world actually exist?

Plato asks—or has Socrates ask—in the *Theaetetus*, "How can you determine whether at this moment we are sleeping and all our thoughts are a dream, or whether we are awake and talking to one another in a waking state?" What we take to be the bodies of others may be so many images in a dream. Because of this possibility we cannot deduce or infer from our sense experience the bodies of others. At the beginning of the modern period Descartes similarly asked: how do I know that an omnipotent and omniscient evil genius "has not brought it to pass that there is no earth, no heaven, no extended body...and that nevertheless they seem to me to exist just exactly as I now see them?" Suppose, Descartes went on to ask, an evil genius so extensively deceives me that I come to suppose "that the heavens, the earth, colors, figures, sounds, and all other extended things are nought but the illusions and dreams of which this evil genius has availed himself in order to lay traps for my credulity...." Descartes continues, "I shall consider myself as having no hands, no eyes, no flesh, no blood...yet falsely believing myself to possess these things." In a later *Meditation*, Descartes put the matter somewhat more prosaically. He remarked, "I have never believed myself to feel anything in waking moments which I cannot also sometimes believe myself to feel when I sleep and as I do not think that those things which I seem to find in sleep proceed from objects outside me, I do not see any reason why I should have this belief regarding objects which I seem to perceive while awake... [Moreover] I saw nothing to prevent me from having been so constituted by nature that I might be deceived even in matters which seemed to me most certain...." Berkeley, solidly in the tradition of British empiricism, remarked a few years later, "I say it is granted on all hands (and what happens in dreams, frenzies, and the like, puts it beyond all dispute) that it is possible we might be affected with all the ideas we have now, though no bodies existed without resembling them. Hence it is evident that the supposition of external bodies is not necessary for the producing of our ideas; since it is granted they are produced sometimes, and might possibly be produced always...without their concurrence."

Some contemporary philosophers, taking skepticism very seriously, have made supplementary related arguments which serve further to strengthen the skeptical challenge. Even someone as non-exuberant and hard-headed as A. J. Ayer argued as follows. Suppose I walk into my classroom and I note that there is a lectern before me. But even for such a plain proposition as that there is a lectern before me, I cannot carry out all the tests "which would bear upon the truth of even so simple a proposition...."[7] Though I accept the proposition, he in effect continued, yet, since I cannot carry out all the tests that would bear upon its truth, it still might turn out to be false. No sense-tests by which we try to establish the existence of any physical object will ever constitute conclusive evidence for the physical object. No finite number of observations will be sufficient to establish the existence of any physical object for a subsequent observation might show that the claim was mistaken. However strong my evidence for there being a lectern before me, "there would never be a point at which it was impossible for further experience to go against it."[8] "Only," as Alice Ambrose put it in discussing Ayer, "an infinite number of observations would secure this, and it is impossible that such a number of observations be made—impossible because self-contradictory. For to complete an infinite series of sense-tests is to terminate the non-terminating."[9] She goes on to add, "If now we connect this argument with the Platonic-Cartesian argument, we are driven to the further consequence: even allowing the possibility of making an infinite number of observations, we still would not arrive at knowledge. For, if any finite number of sense-tests could be illusory, so also could the infinite totality be."[10] It looks like we are driven to the extremely paradoxical conclusion—indeed the absurd conclusion—that we never really know, or even can come to know, that any physical object exists.

As a final skeptical argument, supplementing the stock arguments from the 17th and 18th centuries, there is what Ralph Barton Perry has characterized as the argument from the *ego-centric* predicament.[11] I want to know whether my own perception is veridical, but I could only know that if I could compare it with the thing from which it derives. But I cannot do that, for I am always, and unavoidably, enclosed within my own experience. When I try to compare my perception with the thing itself—with what it supposedly is a perception of—I find myself in the *ego-centric* predicament of comparing one of my perceptions with another of my perceptions. A comparison with the external object can never be made. I always find myself within the circle of my own perceptions, memories, and the like.

So we have—to label the classical skeptical arguments—"the argument from the impossibility of distinguishing waking experience from a vivid coherent dream, the argument from the impossibility of an infinity of verifications, the argument from the ego-centric predicament."[12] Together, it has been thought by not a few philosophers, they make a strong case for skepticism. Skepticism, they believe, cannot reasonably just be ignored.[13] We can see from the above argument that every experience we in the normal course of things take to be a veridical experience or, even any experience we regard as veridical period—that is, every experience which we believe is an experience in which what we *in fact* perceive is what we seem to perceive—can be duplicated by an exactly similar illusory experience, an experience in which we do not perceive what we seem to perceive. This being so, there cannot be anything in perceptual experience itself to tell us whether it is veridical or illusory. We cannot use an experiential or experimental method—a scientific method of fixing belief—to refute skepticism and establish that we do perceive the external world (things external to us such as rocks and trees and the like) or other minds. We cannot—or so it would at least seem—(*contra* the pragmatists) use science or the scientific method to refute skepticism and prove or otherwise establish that there is an external world and other minds.

III

There is something paradoxical, and perhaps even worse, in this. In real life (when we are *not* doing philosophy) anyone who had such doubts—wondered, really wondered, whether there really is an external world (whether there are rocks and trees) and whether other people had minds—would rightly be judged to be insane. And the skeptic herself behaves exactly like the person of common sense. She doesn't have different expectations than others. When others think there is a storm brewing she usually does as well. Her skepticism seems unnatural and unreal, and in certain moods she thinks so as well. David Hume, who arguably was the most important philosopher of the skeptical tradition, remarked of himself, "I dine, I play a game of backgammon, I converse, and am merry with my friends; and when after three or four hours' amusement I would return to these speculations, they appear so cold and strained and ridiculous that I cannot find it in my heart to enter into them any further." Similarly, John Locke, writing a few years earlier, remarked, "I think nobody can in earnest be so skeptical as to be uncertain of the existence of those things he sees and feels...The notice we have by our senses of things without us...is an assurance that deserves the name of knowledge." These skeptical challenges–the claim that we do not know there is an external world or other minds–surely seem to most people to be unsubstantiated, entirely unreal, something that, if we have any good sense at all, we will set aside. Still, such natural reactions aside, how do we refute the skeptic? How do we, or can we, answer, or justifiably set aside, his arguments? Are our own firmly fixed beliefs–beliefs we are not about to abandon–simply matters of animal faith? When we think we know do we only very firmly and groundlessly believe? In telling the skeptic to get lost we are not answering him. Yet it indeed seems ridiculous to enter into these questions. To even start such an argument seems to be to commence to play a silly and pointless game. Still, can we refute, or non-question beggingly answer, the skeptic?

One important contemporary philosopher–G. E. Moore–thought he could.[14] With Moore we get a philosopher deploying analytic argumentation rather than just emphatic assertion (foot stamping) in defence of common sense against the skeptic. There is a superficial appearance of naivete and dogmatism, even foot stamping, in Moore's defence of common sense, but that is misleading for in reality a remarkable sophistication in conceptual analysis is being deployed. Moore's technique consisted in taking the words of the skeptical philosopher in their accepted sense (the plain meaning these words have in ordinary life) and then to set out what his statements logically imply and in this way elucidating them: giving them a perspicuous representation. This he often did by a technique that has been called translation into the concrete. (He thought, wisely I think, but against the philosophical grain, that we could generally be more confident about particular matters than about general matters.)

The skeptic says that he does not know, and doubts whether anyone knows, that there is an external world. This must mean that he thinks he does not know that physical objects (rocks, trees, and the like) exist and that he doubts that anyone knows that they exist. And when he is conversing with another he does not know–or so he thinks–that that person has thoughts and feelings. But this in turn must mean that no one knows or is even unassailably justified in believing the following truisms, truisms Moore confidently asserts he knows, namely,

> There is a body which is my body, born at such-and-such a time in the past. It has been for a number of years on or near the surface of the earth. There are a great number of material objects to which it stands in spatial and temporal relations. The earth has existed for many years past.

There are other human beings than myself, each of whom, like myself, has had various experiences. Each of us knows the above statements about himself and his body to be true.[15]

Moore maintained that any philosophical view which implies either the falsity or self-contradictoriness of these truisms and that we do not know these truisms to be true was itself either false or self-contradictory. But how does—or does—Moore know that? Is he not, after all his intentions to the contrary notwithstanding, just engaging in foot stamping—flat assertion—here rather than in argument?

The answer is no, for at this point Moore engages in a *burden of proof* argument. He remarks, "I think we may safely challenge any philosopher to bring forward any argument in favor either of the propositions [the skeptical propositions] being true, which does not, at some point, rest upon some premise which is beyond comparison, less certain than is the proposition it is designed to attack."[16] Moore goes on to say, "It would always be at least as easy to deny the argument as to deny [for example] that we do know external facts," e.g. empirical truisms such as those we have listed above.[17] Moore here is not simply denying the skeptic's conclusion. He is arguing that his arguments are defective for they all employ premises which are less certain than are such common sense truisms. If the skeptic's claims do not involve a self-contradiction, e.g., "We do not know that others exist," they logically imply unacceptable consequences, namely, propositions which are themselves less certain than the common sense propositions they were designed to confute.

Many, perhaps most, philosophers have thought this argument of Moore's to be mistaken. Indeed many think it is plainly mistaken. Some would say it is clearly an argument, if we can even rightly so dignify it, that is question-begging. Moore, the claim goes, did not prove that we know that there are physical objects (rocks, bark, bats, and the like) and thus that we know there is an external world. His argument, utilizing the technique of translation into the concrete, in drawing out what he takes to be unacceptable consequences from the skeptic's position, takes rather the form of a *reductio ad absurdum* argument. The skeptic says that we never know whether there are realities external to ourselves; this has the consequence—it logically implies—that even under the best of circumstances neither I nor anyone else can know that there is a lectern before us. But this is plainly an unacceptable consequence, Moore maintains, because we sometimes do know that there is a lectern before us. To deny that we sometimes know this is absurdly false. So, it is Moore's claim that he has shown that the skeptic has, as a consequence of his argument, a belief which is plainly false, so the skeptic is refuted.

Moore, it has been replied, has given an argument, but in giving his argument he has not argued against the *reasoning* of the skeptic.[18] The skeptical arguments I previously described remain untouched. Moore cites some facts, plain facts, which are, he avers, expressed by some equal plain true propositions. But he cites facts which the skeptic denies to be facts and his *reductio* arguments, resulting from his translations into the concrete, will not be accepted by the skeptic because he sees nothing absurd in the consequences. (This is something that can always be the fate of attempted *reductio* arguments.) It also should be said that Moore cannot *prove* (deductively demonstrate) from premises known with certainty to be true that a given external object exists, and thus he cannot establish his claim to know with certainty that a given external object exists. Moreover, Moore himself concedes as much. In order to *prove* that a given object exists—say, the pencil that is in his hand—he would "need to prove, for one thing, as Descartes pointed out, that he is not dreaming." But how, he asks, "can I prove that I am not?...I have conclusive evidence that I am awake; but that is very different from being able to prove it."[19]

Moore, many think, is not after all so different from the person of common sense who simply rejects the skeptic's conclusions, namely, that we never know—or at least cannot establish that we know—that there is a lectern, a pencil, a rabbit, a turtle, another person there before us. But his "unacceptable consequences" are acceptable to the skeptic. This being so, the argument goes, Moore and the skeptic are at a stalemate. The skeptic could readily grant Moore that in many circumstances, even most circumstances, the evidence is normally taken to be conclusive that, for example, a given person at a given time has a pencil in her hand. But that it is normally taken to be conclusive evidence does not establish that it actually is conclusive. For such matter of fact beliefs, the evidence for their truth, as we saw Ayer and Ambrose arguing, can never be conclusive: that there is a pencil on my desk could always be disconfirmed by some future experience. At any given time my senses may deceive me. Moore is just, the claim goes, asserting something to be a fact—that he knows, and knows with certainty, such and such—that the skeptic denies. Moore has not been able to refute the skeptic or show him to be mistaken. What Moore claims to establish that he knows, and indeed knows with certainty, may simply be a matter of animal faith or trust on his part and, no doubt, ours as well.

This is the standard response to Moore. In broad terms most philosophers think this standard response is right. I am, however, among the few who think Moore comes through this critique unscathed and that his argument, suitably interpreted, is sound and important. As we have seen, and as Moore makes explicit, he is not trying to *prove* (deductively demonstrate from self-evident premises) that the skeptic is mistaken and that we can *prove* that we know that there is an external world and that there are other minds in the strict way that a mathematician or logician, starting with a certain axiom, or set of axioms, can prove a theorem. Moore's argument, as I remarked, should instead be seen as a burden of proof argument. His argument is that the skeptic, in relying on his chain of arguments, relies at some points on propositions which are less certain than the proposition he means to confute. "That I can never be certain that I am not dreaming" or "That I can never be certain that my senses or my memory do not deceive me" are, as we have seen Moore putting it, "beyond comparison, less certain than is the propositions it is designed to attack." "There are other people," "There is soil," "Sometimes the grass is green," and that we know these things is more certain than any argument which would appear to confute such claims. It is more reasonable to believe that some mistake has been made in the skeptic's reasoning or that some tendentious assumption has (perhaps unwittingly) been made than it is to believe that we do not know there are other people or things (e.g., rocks, trees, clouds). No matter how air-tight the skeptic's argument may seem, it is always more reasonable to believe that somewhere along the line there has been a mistake in the reasoning or an assumption has been made more challengeable than the belief the skeptic would confute. It is, that is, more reasonable to believe that than to believe that it has been established that it is either false or meaningless to claim that we know that there are other people or that we know that there are things external to us. The situation is analogous to the puzzle claim that swift-footed Achilles cannot catch up with the tortoise. We see the power of the argument, but we know the conclusion is false. The fun thing is to show what is wrong with the argument. We know that it must be mistaken, but we can't see how. Similarly, with the skeptic's argument which apparently irrefutably shows that I cannot know that other people have minds—indeed that there are other people—or that there is a lectern before me and thus an external world. Like the Achilles case, I know that the skeptic's conclusion is false and thus his argument cannot be sound. But I may not be able to detect an error in his reasoning. But it is more reasonable for me—and for you—to believe there is somewhere an error than to believe that his conclusion is true and that at least some of us do not know there are a few rocks in Iceland. Moreover, if the denial that we do not know that there is an external world is not a denial of that, then it is unclear what it is a denial of. This is one more virtue of Moore's technique of translation into the concrete and his insistence on literalness. (Something very rare but very healthy in philosophy.) When we do not make such translations into the concrete and remain on an abstract, very general level, it is too easy just to mistakenly assume that we understand what we are talking about. A little translation into the concrete has a fine shock effect here in the direction of realism. Moore, unlike many philosophers, pulls us refreshingly down to earth. So here we do not have even an attempt at a formal proof, but we have a powerful burden of proof argument.

I have argued that it is always more reasonable to think that there is either something more dubious about some (at least one) of the skeptic's premises than the common sense beliefs he questions or that it is more reasonable to believe that at some point there must be an error in his reasoning—the deduction doesn't go through—than that he has shown that we do not know that there is an external world or other minds. And it is truistic to say that, everything being equal, we should always believe what is the more reasonable thing to believe. The burden of proof is on the skeptic to show that everything is not equal here or that the reasonability claim is not justified. The more reasonable position is to remain totally unruffled by the skeptic's challenge and to rest content *here* with common sense. What was evident from the very beginning to the plain person should now be evident even to the philosopher.

IV

The tendency may persist among philosophers (mistakenly I believe) to continue to think this reliance on common sense is dogmatic and perhaps unscientific and illogical to boot. Not a few philosophers will think that to have such essentially Moorean convictions—to believe that we know for certain that there is an external world and that we know that there are other people—is dogmatism comparable to believing that the earth is flat or that the earth is the center of the universe and that the sun goes around the earth. People massively and confidently believed those things at one time and indeed reasonably so, but all the same we know now that such beliefs are false or at least we have very good reasons indeed to believe that they are false. What is reasonable to believe in one context, in one age, against a certain cultural background, is not reasonable in another. How do we know that "There is an external world" will not go the same way as "The earth is flat"? Appealing to reasonability here, the argument concludes, is not very conclusive or even telling. The Moorean philosopher, the would-be critical commonsensist, still seems to be stuck in a common sense dogmatism and to not really be meeting the skeptic's challenge. It may be reasonable to believe that there is an external world now, but perhaps a hundred years from now it will not be. (Is it entirely irrelevant that this remark sounds absurd and not even remotely in the philosophical spirit in which questions about the reality of the external world are raised?)

Again, this argument should be resisted. It is true that in part what it is reasonable to believe is culturally, historically and sometimes even individually dependent. What it is reasonable for a child or a mentally retarded person to believe is not identical with what it is reasonable for a normal adult to believe. It was reasonable for the Greeks to believe in animism but not for a contemporary Englishman or Swede. In the seventeenth century most people in the West, including most educated people, believed that they had immortal souls. And it was then not unreasonable to believe that. Now some people believe that, but many others, particularly among the educated, do not. What is reasonable to believe here has become problematic. Not a few believe, including *some* religious people, that for a philosophically and scientifically educated person such a belief is unreasonable. What people two hundred years from now will believe is an open question. Perhaps by then nobody will believe in immortality any more and that that will be a reasonable, perhaps the only reasonable, stance for them. So what is reasonable to believe and to do does, to a certain extent, vary over cultural space and historical time. But not completely so. It was as reasonable for Aristotle or Thales or an Australian aboriginal to believe that water is wet, that people grow old and die, that fire burns, that the nights are often colder than the days, that people converse with each other, and the like as it is for us to believe these things. At any time or in any culture only insane people do not believe these things. What people believe over such matters does not vary, or at least does not vary very much, culturally and historically and what they judge reasonable to believe over such matters also does not vary. There are, as I remarked, cultures and times in which people believed, and reasonably so, that the earth was flat and the sun goes around the earth. But there are no cultures or times where people believed that there was no external world or that there was only one person who had a mind. In some cultures, namely, in our Western cultures, a few *philosophers* thought we could not know such things and some (namely, idealists) believed not only that we could not know that there was an external world but that there wasn't one, and fewer still believed that only one person exists (namely, the person having the experiences). These solipsists, as they were called, supposedly knew that there could only be one of them. But these, including the philosophical skeptical beliefs, were generally thought, and typically by even the philosophers holding them, to be so paradoxical, to be so strained as to be, as Hume put it, ridiculous. Yet they thought, for all their at least seeming unreasonability, that they were somehow driven to them by logic or by careful thought. But, be that as it may, these strange beliefs were the private intellectual property of only a few philosophers; they were never anything like the cultural norm. It is not anything like the once pervasive belief that the earth was flat. We have never had a society of solipsists or (in the proper philosophical sense) of idealists or philosophical skeptics. Only a "brave" little band of philosophers—and then only some philosophers—thought things like this and even then their own behavior belied them and they typically took the matter very ambivalently being fully aware that such beliefs have at least the appearance of being unreasonable and sometimes even incoherent, e.g., there can hardly be a *society* of solipsists.

So while the beliefs that "the earth is flat" and that "the sun goes around the earth" are culturally relative beliefs, indeed way down to the issue of their reasonability, that is not true of the belief that there is an external world or that there are other people. Those beliefs, like the belief that water is wet and that rocks are hard, are culturally invariant both with respect to the culturally ubiquitous extent of these beliefs and the cross-culturalness of their being required as beliefs that reasonable people will have. The comparison with believing the earth is flat and the charge of dogmatism are both quite out of court. What is in court, however, and before the dock and to the point, is whether people can reasonably be philosophical skeptics, idealists, or solipsists. The grand tradition in philosophy has generally assumed such positions are not unreasonable. But this is anything but evident. Such matters, when they are taken, as they are meant to be taken, as factual claims—claims that could be empirically true and not just the adoption of a peculiar way of speaking or viewing things—do seem at least to be very unreasonable.

The skeptic or his defender might still respond: "reasonable" and even "rational" are very vague and problematic terms. There is no consensus on their proper analysis so we do not know, or at least not with the needed exactness, what we are saying and thinking when we use them. This very response makes another mistake that Moore was careful to guard against. We can, and typically do, know how correctly to use terms without knowing their correct analysis (knowing how to define them or elucidate them). I, and most of us English speakers, know how to use "rock," "chair," "pencil," "human being," without having any idea, or at least any clear idea, of how to define these terms or what their proper elucidation is. Yet in most circumstances (not all) I can correctly identify rocks, chairs, pencils, and human beings and make true or false statements using these terms. I can do this, and you can as well, without having a clue as how to analyze them. Indeed only if we, or at least some of us, knew how to use them, and could identify what they refer to, and make true or false statements about those things, could we ever get very far with their analysis. Analysis rides on the back of, is parasitical on, the proper employment of the term or terms to be analyzed. The short of the matter is that we can know perfectly well that there are chairs or human beings and something of what they are like prior to and independently of any analysis of these terms (or their equivalents in other languages). And one of the last things we are going to get is a proper definition or a perspicuous elucidation. But we can very well operate *with* our native languages without being able to operate *upon* them. We are not all linguists and only a very few of us have an acute language-sense even approximating that of Moore, Ludwig Wittgenstein, J. L. Austin, Stanley Cavell, or Zeno Vendler.

The same holds for "reasonable" and "rational" as holds for "chair" and "human being," though less obviously so. What their proper *analysis* is is quite up in the air. There is no non-very-local and rather temporary consensus about what it is or about how these terms are to be characterized let alone defined. (Though, as we shall see in Chapter 5, there are some rather general things we can say at least for people in our culture.) And it is probably true—most evidently for "reasonable"—that no correct non-contextual definition is possible. But still we know how correctly to use these terms and, as the discussion in the paragraphs immediately following this one will show, we can make quite unproblematically true or false statements using these terms. We are not always using "rational" or "reasonable" as ideological weapons.

A reasonable adult normally wired will not, under normal circumstances, run into a fire and he will know that fire burns and that is causes pain. A reasonable person, unless he is indifferent to getting wet, will not, in normal circumstances, walk across town when rain threatens without bringing an umbrella or a raincoat. When a matter is in dispute and there is time to regard the considerations for and against, a reasonable person will give some regard to the evidence or considerations for and against. A reasonable person will not think that he is invincible or that (in an ordinary way) nothing can harm him. Such examples can easily be multiplied and can be taken from a variety of contexts. Without an analysis of "reasonable," we can and do make plainly true statements (as in the above), as well as sometimes false statements, using such terms. To be sure they typically, perhaps even always, at least implicitly, carry with them qualifiers such as "in normal circumstances" and "everything else being equal." And *sometimes* everything else isn't equal and *sometimes* the circumstances are not normal; but very often both conditions obtain and plainly so: the circumstances are normal and everything else is equal and we make perfectly unproblematically true statements about something being reasonable and the like. Maybe we will never get good analyses of "reasonable" and "rational," but this will not impede our making true or false statements using such terms and from coming to have some understanding of what it is reasonable to believe and do.

The skeptic or his defender might, and I think should, concede the above arguments about it being more reasonable to be a critical commonsensist than to be a skeptic. The common sense option is a more reasonable option than the skeptical one: those common sense beliefs are very much more likely to be true and to be known to be true than the skeptical ones. Moreover, the skeptic might even grant that the critical commonsensist case is beyond reasonable doubt and still say, "Though beyond reasonable doubt" it is not *proven*, for we do not *know with certainty* that there is an external world or that there are minds other than our own.

He could point to the relationships (the conceptual connections) between reasonable belief and truth, evidence and truth, well-warranted belief and truth, well-confirmed belief and truth, justified, even best justified, even ideally rational, belief and truth. A belief may be ever so reasonable and still turn out to be false. We might have the best evidence available for a belief and it still might be false. Well-warranted beliefs may turn out to be false and beliefs without warrant, even unreasonable beliefs, may turn out to be true. Even our best justified (best confirmed, most coherently placed) beliefs may turn out to be false. If something is red then it is colored, if something is a square then it is a rectangle, if something is known then it is true, but if something is the best justified belief it does not follow that it is true, let alone that it is known with *certainty* to be true. The connection between truth and justification or rationality is always *contingent* as is not the case with being red and being colored or being known and being true. (If we know something to be the case then we know it to be true.) Even those beliefs which have the best possible justification might, as far as *logical* possibilities are concerned, turn out to be false. However we analyze "truth," it is plain that it does not mean "what has the best justification" or "what is ideally rational." Ideally rational beliefs could be false, though they, of course, could not be *known* to be false, for when we know them to be false they *ipso facto* cease to be rational beliefs for us.

Because of these considerations Moore has not *proven* (indeed, as we have seen, he never tried to) that the claim of the skeptic is false, for, though now we are granting (at least for the sake of this argument) that the skeptic's claim is unreasonable, unreasonable or not, it still might be true. So skepticism has not been refuted—proven to be false or incoherent—when it is shown to be less reasonable than critical commonsensism or even unreasonable period. What—so the claim goes—would refute skepticism, if something like this could be pulled off, is the derivation of a knowledge of the external world and the existence of other minds from *a priori* propositions such as "Puppies are young dogs" or self-justifying (if such there by) propositions such as "I have a headache" or some combination of them. Some foundationalist epistemologists think that something like this could be carried out and thus skepticism refuted and skeptics, of course, as well as many others, think that such a derivation cannot be made. But this, if we could do it, the objection goes, is what it would take to refute skepticism. *Only* this would show that we know with certainty that there are other minds and an external world. Showing that it is more reasonable to reject skepticism than such common sense beliefs or even that skepticism is unreasonable will not do the job. It does not, the claim goes, cut deeply enough.   It does not show that we can have certain knowledge that skepticism is false and that there must be an external world and other minds. Skepticism remains, the argument has it, very much on the agenda.

There are, however, some other twists to the dialectic. It is not so evident the skeptic really has another inning. "Certain knowledge" is not a redundancy. We can, and typically do, have knowledge without certainty. I know the swallows will return next spring to Montréal and I know that in the next ten to forty years I will die, but neither of these things are certain. Most of our knowledge is like that. Certainty is one thing and knowledge is another. We can know that there is an external world and that there are other minds and not be certain of it, just as I know that it will snow next winter in Chicago without that proposition being certain. The skeptic has at most shown that we cannot be certain that there is an external world or that there are other minds; not that we cannot know these things.

However, it is natural, though I think mistaken, to retort that to show that we do not have *certain* knowledge of these things is, for the skeptic, enough. That shows we do not have the *highest* grade knowledge of these plain matters of common sense: these common sense truisms. We can only rely on probabilities here which means we cannot quite exclude the doubt that there really is an external world or other minds.

This line of defense of the skeptic is *at best* superficially persuasive. In asking for certain knowledge here and in asking for the skeptic to be *so* defeated, we are not just seeking to exclude all *reasonable* doubt but all *conceivable* doubt as well. The claim actually comes to the request that to have certainty, or exclude all conceivable doubt, it must be shown that there is an external world and that there are other minds are *necessary* truths: truths whose denials are self-contradictory. They must be like "Red things are colored" or "Ferns are plants" and not like "There are a few trees in the Sahara" or "There are storks in Austria." To claim that we cannot know for certain that there is an external world or that there are other minds comes only to the claim that "There is an external world" or "There are other minds" can be denied without self-contradiction. That is to the claim that they are not like red things are colored. But to be such claims, claims whose denials are self-contradictory, they would have to be analytic and not factual. However, for the thesis that there is an external world or that there are other minds to be substantial and significant, it must be at least in some broad sense an empirical claim, but that means that it can be denied without self-contradiction. It cannot be a logically necessary truth. In order, the claim goes, to have really good knowledge, i.e., certain knowledge, of the external world or other minds, the skeptic is in effect requiring that for this to be so that this knowledge both be a knowledge of a substantial factual (empirical) claim *and* still be the kind of knowledge that could only be *a priori*. But that, as our discussion of the synthetic *a priori* in the previous chapter has made evident, is not like asking for the moon but like asking for the color of heat. For such knowledge to be possible, it would have to be the kind of knowledge we have of logical truths or analytic truths, but then the propositions in question cannot be of the type—empirical factual propositions—the skeptic requires to make his thesis a substantial one. The skeptic wants to say that while the common sense claim is that it is a fact that we know that there is an external world, that, on the contrary, we do not know that that is a fact. But if what is at issue is what are the empirical facts here, then the propositions which either assert or deny the skeptical thesis cannot be propositions whose denial is self-contradictory. The skeptic, if he, as he seems to wish to, pushes matters this far, is then in reality (though, of course unwittingly) asking for something which is self-contradictory, namely, that for an empirical proposition to be certainly true that it then must be a *logical* necessity. But this is in reality asking for an empirical proposition not to be an empirical proposition. If the skeptic tries to stop before this, then he ends up with something the non-skeptic can refute. But if, as seems natural, he persists and instead pushes this far, then he ends up with something which is self-contradictory. Either way the skeptic is undone.

Independently of this, and even if the above argument is somehow mistaken, the skeptic faces the following quite different objection. There is no reason why there cannot be empirical certainty as well as *a priori* certainty, though it is important not to confuse the one with the other or to take "*a priori* certainty" to be redundant and to be the only kind of certainty that is worth the candle. But that is something the skeptic seems at least to be doing. But to so divide things up and so choose one's friends is arbitrary. Empirical certainty trivially cannot be *a priori* certainty, but to call it merely a "practical certainty," as Hans Reichenbach and C. I. Lewis did, is at best misleading. Suppose a professor is teaching a class in epistemology and he asks the class whether there is a lectern before him. If the light is normal, the class normal and reasonably numerous, and some careful checking for a trick has been made, then the professor and the class can be quite certain that there is a lectern in the class room.[20] They can know that with certainty. To pretend to any doubt or lack of certainty about that is pure sham: evidence, as Ludwig Wittgenstein liked to put it, that we are *just doing philosophy*. Empirical certainty is not *a priori* certainty and cannot—logically cannot—be, but so what?

There is still another response to the skeptic. This response has to do with the ethics of belief. If the skeptic admits, as he not infrequently does (recall the quotations given earlier in this chapter from Locke and Hume), that his doubts are ridiculous and unreasonable and if, as we have argued, they actually are unreasonable: that there plainly are other people and an external world and that we know those things—we know, that is, that such matters are beyond reasonable doubt – then we should not doubt them or doubt that we know such things. Reasonable people ought not to have unreasonable doubts and there is no reason or point or sense in normal circumstances in asking "Why be reasonable?" Such global epistemological skepticism (the typical skepticism of the tradition) can justifiably be set aside. We can, with sound reasons and without dogmatism, tell such a skeptic to get lost.

Notes

1. See, for example, C. I. Lewis, *An Analysis of Knowledge and Valuation* (La Salle, Illinois: Open Court, 1946).

2. Moritz Schlick, *General Theory of Knowledge*, Albert E. Blumberg, trans. (La Salle, Illinois: Open Court, 1985) and A. J. Ayer, *The Problem of Knowledge* (Harmondsworth, Middlesex, England: Penguin Books, 1956).

3. It is evident that some of these questions overlap with the questions discussed around *a priori* knowledge in the previous chapter.

4. Roderick Chisholm, *Theory of Knowledge*, 3rd edition (Englewood Cliffs, New Jersey: Prentice-Hall, 1989); Alvin Goldman, *Epistemology and Cognition* (Cambridge, Massachusetts: Harvard University Press, 1986); and Susan Haack, *Evidence and Inquiry* (Oxford: Blackwell, 1993).

5. Barry Stroud, *The Significance of Philosophical Skepticism* (Oxford: Oxford University Press, 1984) and Michael Williams, *Unnatural Doubts* (Oxford: Blackwell, 1991).

6. Alice Ambrose, "Philosophical Doubts," *Massachusetts Review* (1960), 271.

7. A. J. Ayer, "Verification and Experience," *Proceedings of the Aristotelian Society* XXXVII (April 1937), 147.

8. A. J. Ayer, *Language, Truth and Logic*, 2nd edition (London: Gollanez, 1948), 9.

9. Ambrose, "Philosophical Doubts," 274.

10. Ibid.

11. The notion of the ego-centric predicament we owe to Ralph Barton Perry, *Realms of Value* (Cambridge, Massachusetts: Harvard University Press, 1954), 447.

12. Ambrose, "Philosophical Doubts," 275.

13. On advice not to ignore skepticism see Barry Stroud, *The Significance of Philosophical Skepticism* and Christopher Hookway, *Scepticism* (London: Routledge and Kegan Paul, 1990).

14. G. E. Moore, *Philosophical Papers* (London: Allen and Unwin, 1959), chapters II, VII, and IX; Thomas Baldwin, *G. E. Moore* (London: Routledge and Kegan Paul, 1990), chapters VII and IX; and Arthur E. Murphy, *Reason and the Common Good* (Englewood Cliffs, New Jersey: Prentice-Hall, 1963), 108-20. Baldwin's treatment of Moore is both scholarly and masterful, bringing out the central importance of his thought. Murphy's discussion is the best we have on Moore on the topics I discuss here.

15. Moore, *Philosophical Papers*, 33.

16. Moore, *Philosophical Studies* (New York: Humanities Press, 1951), 228.

17. Ibid., 163.

18. Ambrose, "Philosophical Doubts," 281-86.

19. Moore, "Proof of an External World," *Proceedings of the British Academy* XXV (London 1939), 30.

20. Norman Malcolm, *Knowledge and Certainty* (Englewood Cliffs, New Jersey: Prentice-Hall, 1964), 1-72.

4

The Foundationalist Quest

Perhaps I have said enough justifiably to tell the skeptic, or at least the kind of skeptic we have been discussing, who has so long haunted philosophy, to get lost. If so we would also have one good reason for setting aside epistemology, at least as it has traditionally been conceived. However, reverting to the beginning of the previous chapter, we saw that refuting the skeptic, or otherwise rationally disposing of the skeptic, was not the only task of the epistemologist. The epistemologist also wants to set out, if she can, criteria for knowledge or justified (rationally warranted) belief and to resolve, as I pointed out in delineating her subject matter, certain related problems and, with this in hand, as I also pointed out initially, she wants clearly to display secure foundations for our knowledge, to (to steal the title from one of Bertrand Russell's books), make clear, and clearly to establish, the scope and limits of human knowledge. If the epistemologist really shows us that we have such knowledge, that it is certain knowledge, and that we can be certain that we have such knowledge, she will, *on her own terms*, have refuted the skeptic; but, if her achievement has not this degree of certainty, still, if she can carry it out more approximately, she still will have set out the foundations of knowledge and justified belief in such a way that we will have criteria for knowledge and justified belief. With that we will know which of our beliefs give us certain knowledge and how, starting from those beliefs, as they are expressed in propositions, to build a theory of knowledge — an accurate account of what our knowledge is — such that we can show that our other knowledge claims are derived from these basic beliefs rooted in our most primitive, but still our most unchallengeable, sense certainties. We perhaps will not have dissolved the skeptic's skepticism, but we will, the skeptic aside, have gained the basis for a reasonable consensus concerning the foundations of knowledge.

This kind of foundationalist account of epistemology, as it has been called, would, if successful, provide us not only with a true account of our knowledge, but with a rational basis, as so many foundationalists believe or at least hope, for a critique of culture and would, in its strongest forms, successfully end the ancient and persistent philosophical quest for certainty.

Foundationalism is a view which finds expression in Descartes, the British Empiricists, and in Kant and the subsequent Kantian tradition. Among contemporary philosophers it has been articulated, in various forms, by such major empiricist philosophers as Bertrand Russell, Moritz Schlick, C. J. Ducasse, A. J. Ayer, Axel Hägerström, C. I. Lewis, and Roderick Chisholm. And something like this on the Continent was defended, though without strong empiricist commitments, by Franz Brentano and Edmund Husserl. It has had its opponents, as well, namely, Hegel and the Hegelian tradition, Marxists and Marxians, the pragmatists, *some* logical empiricists such as Otto Neurath and Carl Hempel, as well as having very deep going opposition from some other analytical philosophers, most strikingly from Wilfrid Sellars, W. O. Quine, Donald Davidson, Richard Rorty, Michael Williams, and Charles Taylor. Presently, philosophical fashion runs against foundationalism, but fashion, as it frequently is, may be mistaken here or just arbitrary. Moreover, in thinking about what philosophy is, can be and should be, such a persistent tradition in philosophy with such plain attractions cannot reasonably be ignored. I shall try in this chapter to give foundationalism a full inning, or as full an inning as I can in such a book, and in doing so try not only critically to examine it, but to make plain its attractions and its underlying rationale.

I shall in the end argue, however, that, for all of foundationalism's attractions, in this instance current philosophical fashion is not mistaken and that a foundationalism which will be substantiated and answer the quest for certainty cannot be cogently articulated and that furthermore, even if it could be so articulated, the certainty that it would yield will not provide a basis for a critique of culture or an adequate response to the skeptic. If the arguments in the previous chapter have been on the mark, we have already disposed of the skeptic and have done it without presupposing functionalism, so that concern can be set aside. But what remains of interest is whether such a secure foundation of knowledge—foundations of the foundationalist kind—can be successfully articulated and whether, with it, we have a rational ground for the critique of culture such that we can assess our knowledge claims in morals, politics, science, and religion. I shall argue that foundationalism cannot bear any of these burdens and that, surface appearances to the contrary, we are not the worse off for this impossibility: that we have no need for such an epistemology at all and that it in reality just confuses what it is to gain knowledge and what might be useful methodological directions for the conduct of inquiry and the fixation of belief. Foundationalist epistemology, I shall argue, is something we can do without. But this *sounds* like sour grapes, for it is, at least for those with normal philosophical inclinations, natural to think that such a foundationalism, if defendable, would be very desirable. I shall argue that it is neither defendable nor, even if defendable, particularly useful or desirable. But first I need to state rather more clearly what the core claims of such a foundationalism are.

II

Traditional epistemological accounts, including, of course, foundationalism, seek to articulate grounds for an assessment of all our knowledge of the world, including of ourselves. Such accounts seek general criteria for knowing anything at all. Traditional epistemology *seeks* to make a judgment on the world from a position of detachment essentially untangled in cultural and historical biases or preconceptions. Moreover, (*contra* the skeptic) the world, our putative knowledge of which we hope to assess, is taken to be an objective world in which the facts are what they are independently of their being known or believed or said or thought to be that way by anyone.

In seeking to articulate a structure of what this knowledge is, the foundationalist maintains we must start with *experiential* knowledge.[1] Only that kind of knowledge stands any chance of giving us something that is matter of factly substantial (i.e., empirical) and certain. She need not claim that this is the only kind of knowledge we have, but such knowledge, the claim goes, has a priority, when it comes to knowing what is the case, over any other knowledge we may have. The foundationalist wants to sort out, from the jumble of beliefs we humans have, those beliefs which are certain beliefs which yield immediate knowledge rooted in direct basic apprehensions such that when they have linguistic expression they yield incorrigible empirical statements on which all the other corrigible ones—including the whole edifice of science—are based.[2] Those propositions of science and everyday life which cannot be derived from, or otherwise firmly based on, such incorrigible (self-justifying) empirical propositions—the vehicles of our basic apprehension of the world—are thereby shown to be false or incoherent propositions rather than vehicles of knowledge and truth. These basic apprehensions—this basic experiential knowledge—is supposedly knowledge we would have even if we had no knowledge whatsoever about external reality (facts beyond ourselves). In going back to these basic apprehensions we are going back, and tracing all our other knowledge back, to knowledge we should have even if we knew nothing about the world.

An explanation (*contra* the pragmatist or Wittgenstein) of how we might come to have knowledge of the world that depended on our already having some such knowledge would lack the required *generality* to serve as the basis for a theory of knowledge.[3] Philosophers such as John Dewey, the claim goes, who try to set aside epistemology, miss that very point of having a theory of knowledge. And this also makes it clear why we must give, in our foundationalism, or indeed in any legitimate general account of knowledge, priority to experiential knowledge, for it is the only plausible candidate for what would remain as substantial knowledge once knowledge of the world is set aside or bracketed.

However, the aim, of course, is to regain, in a theoretically appropriate way, a knowledge of the world from these direct apprehensions, this immediate incontestable, self-justifying, experiential knowledge: the surest thing we can get in the domain of the empirical. Indeed the surest substantial knowledge we can get anywhere.

The foundationalist also claims that starting with this basic experiential knowledge of what is immediately evident, of what we directly apprehend, we then can go on to order our beliefs or the propositions or sentences expressive of those beliefs or propositions. We show them to be resting on conceptions that we can clearly articulate and survey and that these conceptions and beliefs are under formal ordering principles such as "Whatever is evident is beyond reasonable doubt," "If anything is probable, then something is certain," and "If a person believes himself to be talking with someone, then it is certain for that person he believes himself to be talking with someone," and the like.[4] We start with certain beliefs—instances of knowledge if anything is—we elucidate their basis and then go on to probable knowledge and to surveying and ordering the whole of our knowledge. Only if we can do this can we achieve the generality requisite for an adequate theory of knowledge. To give our beliefs this theoretical epistemological integrity we must show that all genuine knowledge is traceable back to sense experiences which yield us certainty. That must be our common evidential ground. This is our grounding in immediate experiential knowledge. We assume, in so reasoning, that we have a firmer grasp of what is "in" the mind than of what is outside it. For only what is in the mind can be incorrigibly true. But the foundationalist will argue, as we shall see, that this assumption is safe enough. (We shall challenge that assumption later.)

III

This gives us our candidates for basic non-inferential foundational propositions. But we should also recognize, independently of any acceptance of such claimed candidates, that we can and should recognize that foundationalism is also a *formal* conception about the structure of inference. *Formal* foundationalism is the "view that justification depends on the availability of *terminating* beliefs or judgments, which amount to knowledge or are at least reasonably held to without support from further empirical beliefs."[5] But while the kind of foundationalism we have been discussing and the kind of foundationalism that runs from Descartes and Locke to C. I. Lewis and Roderick Chisholm is a formal foundationalism in the above sense, it is also something more. It is, as well, a *substantive* foundationalism. To meet skepticism, to give us an overseer conception of knowledge, to yield us certain knowledge of the external world, it must be a substantive foundationalism. Indeed that is just simply what is usually, and I believe properly, meant by "foundationalism." Formal foundationalism involves the doctrine that inference depends on letting certain beliefs function as fixed points. Substantive foundationalism, as we have in effect seen, gives in addition to that formal point "a distinctive account of the kind of beliefs capable of performing that function."[6] To appeal across the board to our considered judgments, or, as Moore did, to certain common sense beliefs or to, as Wittgenstein did, as a stopping point for justification, to a background of judgments affirmed without special testing—judgments that stand fast for us—is to articulate views which are *formally* foundationalist. But, as Michael Williams well puts it,

> ...there is no suggestion that the functional role of standing fast corresponds to some kind of broad topical or quasi-topical division of our beliefs. This secure standing fast is *just* a functional role, there being no *a priori* restrictions on the propositions that, given appropriate stage setting, can slot into it. Taking foundationalism as a purely formal or structural doctrine, we have no reason to think that a given belief has any particular or permanent epistemological status. Perhaps the same belief can be a fixed point at one time, or in one particular context of inquiry or justification, but a candidate for justification at another time or in another context. Nothing in formal foundationalism excludes this.[7]

For the substantive foundationalist (foundationalism proper), by contrast, things are different. There is for her a class of propositions, supposedly theoretically specified, which give us self-justifying beliefs which have an *intrinsic* epistemological status. It is this status which accounts for their ability to play the formal role of terminating beliefs, beliefs which for all contexts account for, and ground or justify, all our other knowledge or at least all our other empirical knowledge. They, with their basic apprehensions, are just taken to be the beliefs that are epistemologically prior, *period*, and not just with respect to a particular context. This supposedly is not a matter of practice, convention or contextually determined interest or anything of the sort—in that way they are not at all like John Rawls's considered judgments or Wittgenstein's judgments that he says stand fast for us. Rather, they play the role of basic beliefs because *they just are basic*: other beliefs, by contrast, receive inferential justification, and this obtains in any context because they require it and because of their being the kind of beliefs they are. The non-inferential beliefs are certain, evident, self-justifying and terminating; the others, the inferential ones, are merely probable.

The substantive foundationalists—the philosophers of the epistemological tradition from Descartes to C. I. Lewis—believe, all pragmatic considerations aside, our "basic beliefs arrange themselves into broad classes according to certain *natural* relations of epistemological priority. Beliefs to which no beliefs are epistemologically prior are epistemologically basic. Their credibility is naturally intrinsic, as that of all other beliefs are naturally inferential."[8]

When the epistemological priority of a substantive foundationalism is said to be natural, what is intended to be conveyed is that as experiential beliefs they do not depend on the changing and contingent circumstances in which beliefs which are not natural become embedded. This is also why the belief is said to have an intrinsic epistemological status. *The claim is that these experiential beliefs get expressed in what are called basic propositions or statements which simply record the data of experience.* As natural in this way—as simply recording the data of experience—these propositions are not thought by foundationalists to in any way depend on convention or any culturally contingent considerations. Their justifiability is thought to be purely natural as is the justification of the non-basic beliefs that are derived from them. They are also thought to be naturally inferential and in all contexts as having that status. So they too—though it is a different one than that of basic beliefs—have an intrinsic epistemological status. In this way, in not being dependent on contextual, cultural or disciplinary constraints, this foundationalist account can—if it can be sustained—assess our various cultural beliefs, from scientific to religious to political and moral ones. It can show how philosophy can play its traditionally desired overseer function. In giving us the rational foundation for all our knowledge, it affords, as well, it is claimed, the basis for cultural critique.

The sustaining of such claims to naturalness or to intrinsic status (the two go together like hand and glove) is essential to get foundationalism up and running and, as well, to the very taking of philosophical skepticism as a coherent option. For, on the one hand, skepticism about the external world to be a coherent possibility or, on the other hand, to prove, in the way traditional philosophers wanted to prove, if only they could, that there is an external world, it would be necessary to establish that experiential knowledge really is, as a matter of fact, or at least as a matter of "epistemological fact," more basic than knowledge of the external world or any other kind of knowledge of what is the case. That seems to us, brought up in a broadly Cartesian or empiricist tradition, a natural thing to say and to believe to be true. But it is not clear how we would justify such an assumption and without it neither the skeptic's position nor the position of traditional epistemology can get off the ground. For someone not so philosophically enculturated, but who started instead with Vico, Herder, Hegel, and Marx, such conceptions would not seem so natural.

IV

However, for the sake of the argument of this chapter at least, let us make this familiar assumption of the Cartesian-empiricist-Kantian tradition. Certainly it is an assumption which is natural enough for most of us to rather uncritically make who philosophize or learn to philosophize in our cultural environment. But it is an *assumption* that we should recognize we are making. However, that it is an assumption that we are making neither suggests that it is justified nor that it is not justified. But we do see here how hard it would be, if possible at all, to get a presuppositionless philosophy.

Let us now, making that assumption, and pursuing the foundationalist's quest, ask what kind of experiential beliefs, expressed in basic propositions, are taken to be our basic foundational beliefs. Beliefs that are certain, yielding incorrigible, indubitable knowledge, resulting from such natural basic apprehensions. We, on such a picture, justify one proposition by appeal to another and another by appeal to still another and that one in turn by an appeal to another until we come to a *terminating* proposition. If justification is to come to an end, as it appears it must, what then are the terminating points in this chain of justifications? Where do we get the certainty which, classical foundationalists believe, is necessary to have a coherent conception of probability, for if nothing is certain—or so they believe—then nothing is probable either? (They think this is some kind of formal truth like "If nothing is colored then nothing is blue.")

The search here—the foundationalist search—is to look for the place where an empirical proposition or an empirical sentence is just accepted on the basis of direct evidence and *evidence that is its own warrant*. This is the proper experiential basis. But, if and when this obtains, to describe the evidence in question would be simply to repeat the empirical evidence itself. When this obtains—if it ever obtains—we have reached a proper stopping place in the process of justification. Here justification properly comes to an end.[9] We justify such empirical propositions (propositions expressed by sentences) simply be reiterating them. *The proposition's justification is what the proposition says.*

Put in the language of belief, the claim is that there are beliefs whose very occurrence is their own justification. It is indeed natural to be very suspicious of such a notion. It surely sounds suspect and perhaps is. Normally we certainly cannot justify a proposition by reiterating it. That is the very last thing we can reasonably do. If I assert "There were at least three robins in Montréal's botanical gardens all last winter," I better have pretty good evidence for it. Just saying so loudly and emphatically will not help at all. Even for "I see a fly in my soup," my just emphatically reasserting it will not show that it is true, but for "My head aches" or "I think I see a fly in my soup," my honestly avowing it seems at least to settle it. More generally, to the question "What is your justification for *thinking* you know that you *believe* so and so?" there is, some foundationalists claim, "nothing to say other than I do believe so and so."[10] Here we have, the claim goes, a self-justifying proposition and the parallel belief is a self-justifying belief.

The candidates for self-justifying propositions, at least for traditional empiricist foundationalists, are all statements about our own beliefs or other psychological states or attitudes, such as expressed in the following type sentences: "I believe the wine is too cold," "I feel a pain in my left side," "I feel sad," "I hope to come tomorrow." First person present tense avowals that I (where "I" is, of course, any of us) am thinking, desiring, wondering, loving, fearing, hating, and the like are self-authenticating, self-justifying utterances whose honest avowal by the person having the experience, foundationalists at least plausibly have it, establishes their truth. "I seem to remember the restaurant was on Duluth Street" as distinct from "I remember the restaurant was on Duluth Street," or "I think I see a blue jay" as distinct from "I see a blue jay" are such propositions. I cannot, the claim is, be mistaken about "I am hungry" or "I think I see a blue jay" but I can be mistaken about "I see a blue jay." *There are some places where thinking or feeling so makes it so.* If I have a mastery of English, I cannot, the claim is, be mistaken about my avowal "I think I see a blue jay" or "I am hungry" or "I am sad." Perhaps I have nothing to be sad about, but if I feel sad it settles it that I am sad.

Sometimes, of course, we use "appears" as a qualifier to guard a prediction, e.g., "It appears that it will rain this afternoon" and those propositions are not self-justifying. But it is also true that *things just do appear to us in various ways* and we "can alter the appearance of anything we like merely by doing something which will affect our sense organs or the conditions of observation."[11] We want to use "appears" not only to make guarded statements—hedging our bets when we predict—but simply to record how things just appear to us and this is linked with the key epistemological question as to whether there are any self-justifying propositions about the ways things simply and naturally appear to us.

It appears (now "appears" being used in the qualifying sense) to be so from the above. Moreover, it is not just philosophers of the empiricist and Cartesian traditions who have thought so, but even such a traditionalist Christian philosopher as St. Augustine. In trying to refute the skeptics of the late Platonic Academy, St. Augustine wrote, "I do not see how the academician can refute him who says 'I know this appears white to me', 'I know my hearing is delighted with this', I know this has an agreeable odor', I know this tastes sweet to me'...When a person tastes something he can honestly swear that he knows it is sweet to his palate or the contrary, and that no trickery of the Greeks can dispossess him of that knowledge."[12] Commenting on this passage a prominent contemporary foundationalist epistemologist (Roderick Chisholm) remarked: "Suppose, now, one were to ask 'What justification do you have for believing or thinking you know that this appears white to you or that tastes bitter to you?' Here, too, we can only reiterate the statement: 'What justifies me in believing, or in thinking I know, that this appears white to me and that tastes bitter to me is the fact that this does appear white to me and does taste bitter to me'."[13] It is with such matters, such self-justifying beliefs, that justification over matters epistemological properly comes to an end. This is the needed terminating point. This is the empirically given, the primitive experiential certainties that we have, which, when expressed in self-justifying propositions, justify all our other factual beliefs.

The foundationalist claim is that (1) every justified proposition about what we think we know is justified by some proposition which *justifies itself* and (2) there are propositions about appearances, such as the ones I have illustrated, which justify themselves. The knowledge which a person at any given time has is something which is complex and structured, with many parts and stages, which help support each other but the structure as a whole is supported by its own natural foundation. That foundation is the certain knowledge that comes with the self-justifying propositions of the kinds that I have just described. This is the given in experience and it is this which justifies all our other matter of fact knowledge claims. These self-justifying propositions about our own thoughts, feelings, intentions, sensings are the natural foundation, the basis, of all the rest of our knowledge. The whole complex, many layered edifice is erected on such a foundation. This is the culturally invariant given in experience and it is the source and ground of the rest of our knowledge or at least the source and ground of our knowledge of the world, our knowledge of ourselves and of others.

V

Is this foundationalist account of our knowledge—this foundationalist picture—the right account, the true account, or correct or best picture of our knowledge? The long tradition of empiricism, from Locke and Berkeley to Moritz Schlick and C. I. Lewis, has thought that some version of it must be right. But fashions in philosophy have shifted and it is now widely thought to be through and through mistaken, not just in detail but in underlying conception. It is, it is frequently said, a very atomistic unempirical empiricism caught in the myth of the given. There is, it is now widely believed, no such basis for knowledge. Such an epistemology is an impossible task. It will neither succeed in refuting the skeptic or the solipsist nor will it give us a viable alternative account of our knowledge. It will not yield the certainty it promises. Its quest for certainty is fundamentally flawed. Moreover, it is not only an impossibly flawed epistemological project, it is an unnecessary one as well. We can make sense of our knowledge, show how we get a reasonable measure of objectivity here, as a form of intersubjectivity, and how sound cultural critique can, and indeed should, be engaged in, without the assistance of such foundationalism or indeed of any foundationalism. In reality, it is just an impediment to the carrying out of critique.

This is the fashion now. But is something like this fashionable assessment justified or at least the most plausible thing to think? In this case, as I have already remarked, I think the current fashion is justified. But perhaps I am simply caught up in it myself? This foundationalism has had a long and distinguished history and has had in our recent history some careful and extended articulations. Surely Locke, Berkeley, Russell, Ayer, Schlick, C. I. Lewis, and Chisholm are no trifling philosophers. So I will not simply assume that this epistemological way is mistaken but argue against it.

I shall limit myself to four arguments. There are, I should add, a host of other arguments and other pertinent considerations that I shall ignore. I have tried in my characterization of foundationalism to give a rather general characterization of foundationalism, waffling at times between the niceties of particular theories. In doing so, I have tried to avoid the controversial details of certain theories. I have, as perhaps my most crucial avoidance, tried to avoid saying anything which would commit such a foundationalism to *phenomenalism*: a doctrine that very frequently goes with it, but is widely believed to be at best false. By "phenomenalism" I mean the belief that the self-justifying experiential propositions which are at the foundations of our knowledge consists in propositions which record the apprehension by an individual of what has been variously called sense-data, sensations, sense impressions, sense qualia, or phenomena. The account of foundationalism I have given is compatible with phenomenalism, but does not, I hope, require it.

I shall, as I have just remarked, make four distinct criticisms of foundationalism. The first two accept, for the purposes of the discussion, the truth of the thesis that there are incorrigible, self-justifying propositions of our mental states such as I have described, but argue that even so they cannot serve as the foundation for the rest of our knowledge or as the rational foundation for cultural criticism or social critique. The third criticism challenges the very idea that there are self-justifying or incorrigible propositions or beliefs even of our mental states. We can have, I argue, no such knowledge. The fourth criticism considers a modification of foundationalism designed to avoid certain criticisms of classical foundationalism and then criticizes that modified version. The modified version is that of some contemporary foundationalists who abandon the quest for certainty and take their foundational propositions to be corrigible, less than certain and intersubjective.[14] By the latter I mean that they are not taken to be private to the individual having them, in the way that my mental states are private to me and yours to you. (In the appropriate sense I cannot have your mental states and you cannot have mine.) They are, rather, for such a modest foundationalism, public experiential propositions such as "That barn is red with a white trim" or "The moon looks pink tonight." I shall argue that while this more modest, if you will, fallibilistic foundationalism escapes many (though not all) of the difficulties of classical foundationalism, it no more yields a more secure foundation for our scientific, social, and common sense propositions than that which can be had by going directly to them in their regular employments in their various, though sometimes shifting, contexts. They are practice embedded propositions with no claim to a natural, intrinsic epistemological status and priority.

VI

I shall turn now to my first criticism of foundationalism. Something, say a bird, appears blue to me or the wine I drink tastes sweet to me. I know, as St. Augustine put it, that it appears blue to me and I know that it tastes sweet to me and no other person—or so I believe—can gainsay that. I also know that the bird could appear blue to me and not be blue or the wine taste sweet to me and not be sweet. But I also know that if it appears blue to me it appears blue to me or if it tastes sweet to me it tastes sweet to me and that is the end of it. (We can hardly sensibly reject such tautologies.) What justifies me in believing or in thinking I know that it appears blue to me or tastes sweet is just the fact that it does appear blue to me and that it does taste sweet to me.

As I remarked, I am accepting, for the moment, this once widely accepted traditional doctrine. But note first that it does nothing—even if the above remarks are true—to refute the skeptic about the external world or other minds. The having of these private experiences does not justify a belief in the external world or other minds. I could be having them, as in a dream, and there could be no external world and solipsism could be true and there could be no other persons, no other minds, and all my experiences could be intact, could be just the same. When St. Augustine thought he had refuted the skeptic by noting such self-justifying propositions it was not the skeptic that has haunted modern philosophy, starting with Descartes, Locke, and Hume, that he refuted or thought he had refuted. It was not the person skeptical about how we could know there is an external world or other minds. St. Augustine's view here licenses nothing beyond solipsism. It at best would refute the skeptic who said that I could doubt that I knew such things about myself: doubt that I know I have a headache or that there is something which appears blue to me.

So foundationalism cannot refute epistemological skepticism, but there are some classical foundationalists (Chisholm, for example) who do not think that skepticism can be refuted, but still defend foundationalism as yielding a *non-refuting alternative* to skepticism which can give us a coherent account of how our knowledge of ourselves, of others, and of the world could have a secure foundation. It does not refute skepticism: show it to be false, incoherent or self-contradictory or even unmotivated, but it provides an alternative account of knowledge to that of the skeptic. It is claimed that we can in a clear manner, following foundationalist procedures, both exhibit the complicated edifice of our knowledge and show how it is plausible to believe that it rests on a foundation of certain knowledge. In this way we can articulate the rational foundations for all our knowledge or at least all our factual knowledge.

However, for the same reason that the skeptic cannot, from foundationalist premises at least, be refuted, we cannot—or so I shall argue—so foundationally rationally reconstruct our knowledge. Do I know the sky is blue or do I merely know that now it appears blue to me? Foundationalism shows, let us continue to assume, how an individual can know, and indeed know for certain, that the sky *appears* blue to him and thousands of propositions like that. But from such propositions alone we cannot deduce or even inductively infer that we know or justifiably believe that the sky actually is blue or that a table is solid or that there are tables or people who sometimes sit at them. For every private experience expressible in such self-justifying propositions in which, let us assume, we actually perceive what we think we perceive there could be an identical private experience similarly expressible in which we do not. Therefore there cannot be anything in these private experiences themselves, taken individually or taken together, which will tell us whether we actually perceive what we think we perceive.

Suppose I assert that there is a pencil on my desk. I cannot carry out all the tests which would bear upon the truth of even so simple a proposition. In practice, that is, in everyday life, I accept, even when I am being most scrupulous, such propositions after making only a limited number of tests—indeed usually, and not unreasonably, rather cursory tests. But this still leaves open the possibility that the proposition is false. Such experiential tests, as in the previous chapter we noted Ayer and Ambrose arguing, by which we try to establish the existence of any physical object always fall short of constituting conclusive evidence for that or any physical object. And if we rely on less than conclusive evidence, we will not have gained the certainty that classical foundationalists seek and require. Without it their foundationalist program flounders. No finite number of observations would, or could, be sufficient to establish that there is a pencil on my desk because subsequent observations—subsequent sense-experience—may show that the prior observations were mistaken or at least conflict with them so we are at a loss what to say. The truth of my statement that there is a pencil on my desk can never be conclusively established, for, no matter how strong the evidence for it is, there can never be a point at which it is impossible for future experience to go against it. As long as the totality of possible experiential tests (sense-tests) is not exhausted, the existence of my pencil has not been conclusively established. Alice Ambrose puts the matter well when she remarks:

> Only an infinite number of observations would secure this, and it is impossible that such a number of observations be made—impossible because self-contradictory. For to complete an infinite series of sense-tests is to terminate the non-terminating.[15]

With such a foundationalism each of us is imprisoned within our own personal experience. We are in an *egocentric* predicament and relying just on such self-justifying propositions—such primitive sense-certainties—we cannot reconstruct or show the foundations of our empirical knowledge or even show that it has foundations.

Chisholm (a paradigm foundationalist) admits as much when he remarks:

> (1) …there are beliefs or statements about some of our own psychological states and about some of the ways we are "appeared to" which can be said to be "self-justifying" in a sense in which no other belief or statement can be said to be "self-justifying"; thus the statements expressing what we attribute to perception cannot, in this sense be "self-justifying." (2) "Our

senses do at times deceive us"; that is to say, there are occasions when we *think* we perceive that some state of affairs obtains and when, as a matter of fact, that state of affairs does not obtain. And (3) if we make use *only* of premises which are "self-justifying," in the present sense of the term, then we could not construct a good argument, deductive or inductive, for the thesis that any of the beliefs we normally attribute to perception are true."[16]

Where we start from and remain with, for our foundational basis, such primitive sense-certainties, even when spiced by the use of logic or other purely formal principles similarly certain, we cannot erect a foundation for our knowledge. We cannot even establish the truth of "There is a pencil on the desk." There is no good reason for believing that our knowledge is an edifice, or anything like that, supported by appearances alone.

VII

I shall now turn to my second criticism of foundationalism. Let us assume, for the sake of the argument I shall now pursue, that my first criticism is not well taken and that from these self-justifying propositions we can justify our knowledge claims about what we really remember and not just think we do, our claims about actually perceiving dogs, trees, trains, people, and the like and not just thinking we do. Suppose we have justified such beliefs and justified as well other more complicated and general common sense beliefs such as the belief that the tides in the Baltic are not as strong as those in the Atlantic, that people need air to survive, that people get born and die, and the like. These latter more general common sense beliefs, let us further assume, are justified on the basis of simpler ones such as I saw Jim die and I saw the birth of Fred and that these claims in turn are based on self-justifying appearance claims. That is to say, let us assume that we have shown that knowledge claims of the above common sense types are erected on the foundation of our primitive sense-certainties. This is how the chain of justification goes back to terminating judgments. But foundationalism also wanted to provide an Architectonic for knowledge, an Archimedean fulcrum to assess the genuineness and indeed the warrant for our knowledge claims in science, religion, morality, politics, art, and more broadly in everyday life: in what Continental philosophers like to call our life-world.[17] This is, in part, what is meant by saying that philosophy should engage in cultural criticism, including the critique of society, e.g., the unmasking of ideology. This is something that most of the classical foundationalists tried to practice, or at least gestured at practicing, and Kant and Kantians made it clearly a theoretical part of their program. Foundationalism was supposed to yield the rational ground for such a critique. It went with their attempt to give a philosophical articulation of the Enlightenment showing it not to be an ideology (or just an ideology) but a conception of the world and of our place in it that rested on rational foundations. The second criticism—the one I shall now pursue—is simply that even if foundationalism is otherwise successful this does not establish anything about even the possibility of its providing such a ground for the critique of culture let alone show how it succeeds.

Suppose, for the sake of this discussion, we can from purely self-justifying propositions justify that some memory beliefs and some perceptual judgments are true, that some common sense matter of fact beliefs are justified, that (miracle of miracles) there is an external world and other minds. How does—or does—this aid in the critique of culture? How does it help us assess sociobiology, for example? Those who think it is confused baloney, at least when applied to human beings and human societies, will tend to, or very well could where now they actually do not, come to agree with sociobiologists about what perceptual beliefs are justified and about common sense matters of fact. What divides them is not such things, but something much more theoretical, logical, and conceptual. The same thing would be true for disputes about the structure and import of quantum mechanics or disputes about the tenability of historical materialism. Those who accept the dominant atheoriticism in history will not believe we can construct viable theories of epochal social change, Marxian or otherwise; but those who think a genuinely scientific account of epochal social change is possible do not, characteristically, differ from the atheoreticists about which memory beliefs or perceptual judgments are justified and which common sense factual beliefs, so establishable, are true or justified. Historical materialists and their opponents do not differ, or do not essentially differ, on these grounds. The same thing is true concerning disagreement between and with feminists concerning whether human beings are just so biologically wired such that gender differences are important or whether their being important is a result of a certain kind of socialization which is humanly alterable without damage to human beings. Again the rational reconstruction of the foundations of knowledge that foundationalism proffers, even if true, would not give us any grounds for going one way or the other over these and similar issues. Foundationalism is socially inert. In fine, it affords us no basis for arguing for the cogency of scientific theories, for sorting out genuine science from pseudo-science, or for challenging the hegemony of science or the claim that science either does or does not yield a true description of reality.

Similar things can be said about the critical examination of religion or morality. Theists, agnostics, and atheists, at least if they are reasonably sophisticated, do not differ over matters that foundationalism might establish and, we are assuming now, does establish. Establishing that we know that some memory beliefs are justified, that some perceptual beliefs are true, that there are other people and an external world, and that our knowledge here is all rooted in sense-certainties does nothing toward showing that theism is true or that belief in God is incoherent or that (alternatively) belief that God exists is false or probably false or that God is a projection of our emotions and thus thoroughly illusory or anything of the sort.   Christians, Jews, atheists, agnostics can be foundationalists or anti-foundationalists. Acceptance of either does nothing to establish or disestablish their beliefs concerning religion.   The establishment of foundationalism does nothing for the critical examination of religion.

Similar things should be said for morality, art, and politics. Foundationalism, even if true, affords nothing like a rational basis for critique or critical examination of such matters.   The knowledge claims of these activities are not so establishable or disestablishable. So foundationalism, even if true, offers us no basis for a critique of culture, no Archimedean point to determine in any domain, in any discipline or social practice, what is genuine knowledge and what is not.

This being so it is not obvious what, if any, point foundationalism has. It yields no Archimedean fulcrum for determining the legitimacy of knowledge claims in any of the disciplines (philosophy, if indeed it is actually a discipline, aside) such that we could assert or deny, working from foundationalist premises, that psychoanalysis, Marxism, Social Darwinism, or quantum mechanics is incoherent or otherwise mistaken or ill-grounded or well-grounded. Similarly, it provides no basis for a critique of culture such that we could say what the, or even a, just society is, assess popular morality, current democracies, capitalism, socialism, feminism, and the like. It also provides no help in sorting out, reforming, and newly articulating a literary or artistic canon.

It used to be thought that a crucial philosophical task was to provide a critique of culture. That rather disappeared with the thorough professionalization of philosophy and with the hegemony of analytical philosophy. With such an analytic entrenchment most philosophy graduates at the good graduate schools in Anglo-Saxon and Scandinavian universities just took analytic philosophy to be philosophy or at least contemporary philosophy. Moreover, what was good in the history of philosophy needed, it was similarly believed, to be recast or reconstructed on this analytical model. But prior to the cultural entrenchment of analytical philosophy in philosophy departments and academia more broadly, it seemed natural, as it did to John Dewey or Sidney Hook, or in a different ambience, to Simone de Beauvoir and Jean-Paul Sartre, to engage in a critique of culture, to regard philosophy as such a cultural overseer and assessor, to take philosophy to be in some way linked to the search for wisdom. This belief or attitude remained even when there was a lot of skepticism about whether there was anything like this to be even staggered toward.[18] But however desirable such a critical examination of life and society is, however important the search for self-knowledge is, foundationalism does not provide any help in such matters. Perhaps no philosophy can, but foundationalism certainly does not.

There will be some *contemporary* foundationalists who will agree with that and some will even add "And a good thing, too."[19] Foundationalism, they will believe, should rid itself of such Kantian accretions and stick to what it was invented for, namely, to, against the skeptic, establish that we have certain knowledge of a whole range of things and that, beyond these particular things, we also know that there is an external world and that we have perspicuously displayed an edifice of knowledge such that we can see how knowledge claims are founded and related to their basis, how truth is objective, and how metaphysical realism is vindicated. That is enough for one account; we do not need critique of culture as well.

If our first criticism is justified, foundationalism achieves none of these non-critical things and it seems entirely unlikely that it ever could. But—the part about metaphysical realism aside—we are, for the space of our articulation and examination of this second criticism, assuming that foundationalism is true: that it has established these things and in doing so it will show that we can refute the skeptic, the solipsist, and the metaphysical idealist (the philosopher claiming that all reality is really or ultimately only mental). Doing these things would be something of achievement and to have an objective account of truth would as well. These achievements would be particularly impressive where we would have shown how all of this is grounded in primitive experiential certainties of the individual inquirer. We would have pulled off, in a way Locke would have admired, an empiricist defense of common sense and this would be no mean achievement. But it still would not yield a critical philosophy or a critical theory, for what we have here is a rational reconstruction on an empiricist foundation of common sense beliefs against the excesses of skepticism, solipsism, and idealism.

However, it would not even yield *metaphysical* realism or any other metaphysical view. By "metaphysical realism" I mean the claim that (1) there is one uniquely true description of the world which characterizes the objective structure of the world, (2) that all declarative sentences with factual content are either true or false, and (3) that for some of these sentences their truth-conditions are verification *transcendent*: that is to say, the statements expressed by these sentences are true or false, and can be known to be true or false, even though they are not verifiable or testable even in principle: there is no way of empirically confirming or infirming— and thus no way of confirming or infirming—whether they are true or false. Metaphysical realism, if establishable, would be of a not inconsiderable importance. Even if foundationalism does not provide a critique of culture or the basis for a critique of culture, it would be a considerable feather in its cap if it could establish metaphysical realism.

Foundationalism, however, does not establish that there is one set of self-justifying propositions that all individuals have, or can come to have, independently of how they are wired, their interests, purposes, the languages they have learned, the cultures they live in, and the like, which will yield the one true description of the world.[20] The propositions expressing memory beliefs and perceptual judgments about what is the case can also track, foundationalists believe, the one uniquely true description of the world. But such a conception is mythical. Starting from such individual bases in experience there could be many different descriptions with no way of telling which one, if any, is, or even could be, the one true description of the world. Indeed it is not clear that a conception of the one true description of the world has a coherent sense. It certainly seems that the world is, and indeed must be, in some determinate way and thus, it would also seem, there can be no logical ban telling us that it is impossible to give the one true description of the world. It would, if we had such a description, be the one in which the description managed to describe completely accurately this determinate world, for we agree that the world must be in some determinate way. No doubt we would not know it when our description did so luck out. We seem to have no way of discovering the one true description of the world, but why is it impossible that, just by chance, some description should be that, should so luck out? But language does not mirror the world. We have no understanding of what it would be like for it to do so. It is just being caught up by representationalist metaphors that makes us think that it does. Rather, language is more like a tool which we use, for our various purposes, to cope with the world, to get on in the world, to achieve one or another of our ends or goals.

While the above may be, I think is, well taken, it is not the case that the foundationalist must be committed to metaphysical realism. It is not the case that foundationalists need believe that there are truth-conditions that are verification transcendent. Moritz Schlick, A. J. Ayer, and C. I. Lewis were as verificationist as you like and they were all consistent foundationalists. But they were not metaphysical realists or for that matter anti-realists either.

Finally, the foundationalist might have an objective conception of truth consistently linked with a minimalist or deflationary account of truth.[21] It is a conception that is in no sense subjective or relativistic, but it is not tangled in the obscure claims to a correspondence between thought and fact of the metaphysical realist. The sentence "The snow is white" is true if and only if the snow is white; moreover, we can know that the snow is white in perfectly ordinary empirically testable ways, without invoking, or even understanding, the claim that we know what it means for a thought, expressible in a sentence, to correspond to a fact. We have no understanding of how, by comparing them, we could see how thought and fact correspond by having an independent access to them both. Without such an independent access, there is no possibility of comparing them. But with such an independent access, it supposedly is the case that we can just see or note the sentence, the thought or the proposition and, taking another look, see, as well, the fact—the fact-like entity supposedly just there in the world—and then, looking back and forth, compare them so as to see whether the one corresponds to the other. But such talk is absurd; it makes no sense. We have no understanding of what it would be like to do these things. (If it is responded that in the above I have parodied the correspondence relation, I would in turn respond with the challenge to provide a characterization of the correspondence relation that does make sense.)

The most crucial point I have tried to make here is that the foundationalist's Kantian expectations to the contrary notwithstanding, the foundationalist has provided us with no basis for a critique of culture and thus she has not set forth a *critical* philosophy or shown how one, on her foundationalist basis, could be set out. We might, for example, wonder whether religious claims are ever true, or more radically, wonder whether they could ever even be either true or false and thus make genuine knowledge claims. Foundationalism will not help us one iota here. Moreover, it does not establish or disestablish metaphysical realism. It would, if justified, perhaps provide a refutation of solipsism and epistemological skepticism or at least be, in the way I have explained, an alternative to them such that the reasonable thing will be not to be such a skeptic, though one might quite consistently be a religious skeptic or a moral skeptic, for all that we can garner from foundationalism. However, if my Moorean defense of common sense discussed in the previous chapter is on the mark, there is no need to take such a chancy route to the defense of common sense. But, in any event, if my first criticism of foundationalism is on the mark, no such foundationalist account is justified.

VIII

The first two criticisms of foundationalism started by accepting the foundationalist's central thesis that there are self-justifying beliefs and propositions about some of our mental states and then went on to argue that this could not yield knowledge of the external world or knowledge of other minds or give us a critical philosophy that could assess the beliefs of our life-world. I now want, in my third criticism, to turn to an argument which would give us grounds for rejecting the belief that there are any self-justifying propositions at all or any incorrigible knowledge of any sort yielding certainty.

In examining whether there are any self-justifying propositions, I am asking do we have any absolutely certain knowledge of any experiential (empirical) matter? Put otherwise, I am asking, "Are there any incorrigible empirical statements?" And this is, for any interesting epistemological purposes, much the same as asking *"Are there are indubitable items of empirical knowledge?"* I want to argue that, appearances to the contrary notwithstanding, there are none.

First I want to set aside some irrelevancies. The most likely candidates for indubitable items are propositions or statements about our own present sensations such as "I have an itch," "I feel cold," "I am in pain," "This note seems higher than that." The last example, however, might cause raised eyebrows. I am taking it, and to make a plausible claim to incorrigibility it must be so taken, simply as a description of my present auditory sensations and not as even a very tentative judgment about existing sounds. The claim is that when I honestly avow with a firm grasp of the language in question and without mis-speaking myself, that I feel cold that I know, without any risk of error at all, or even the very possibility of error, that I feel cold. The same is true for I feel pain or I have an itch. I cannot be in error about such matters, the claim goes, I just infallibly know when I am in pain, feel cold, or have an itch.

It is important to put in the qualifiers I did above, because lying is always possible and there are always possibilities of verbal error. Someone—a child or a foreigner—who has a very poor command of English might say "I feel cold" when he means to say "I feel hot" or "I feel pain." And a competent native speaker on occasion may mis-speak himself and sometimes we hesitate how to report an experience because we are unsure how to *classify* it. We can, for example, hesitate, and indeed end up in a quandary in deciding what is the right name for the exact shade of color that we seem to see. Still we know what it is we seem to see—that (or so the claim goes) is just given to us—what we do not know, in this instance, is how to classify or accurately describe what we seem to see. But what we have in these cases are further sources of *verbal* error. Once the verbal error is cleared up, the foundationalist is claiming, we know for certain what we feel or seem to see. The claim is that empirical statements of the kind I described, when made in certain optimal circumstances, "are free from all risk of non-verbal mistake."[22] They must, however, be limited to pure reports of present experience to have any chance at all of being absolutely incorrigible and still empirical.

It is this claim of incorrigibility that I wish to contest. "I felt cold" or "I will continue to feel cold until the thermostat is turned up" are not, of course, incorrigible. We can make non-verbal mistakes here and honestly say something which is false while believing it to be true. The claim for incorrigibility is for "I feel pain now" and utterances of that type.

John Mackie makes the important point (a point also put in different terminology by Roderick Chisholm):

> Once we have so restricted the meanings of these statements so that they do more than report or describe a present experience, we shall have to decide either that all of them are incorrigible or that none of them is: their claim to incorrigibility rests simply on features that are common to them all; of these the most obvious is that in these cases there is no distinction between evidence and conclusion, no question of going beyond one's evidence, and therefore no room left for error.[23]

There is certainly something in this claim to incorrigibility: in the belief that sincere reports of one's present sensations are incorrigible. However, it runs the risk of our getting entangled in metaphysical issues, which, if the argument of the first two chapters is right, are better set aside. It looks like such incorrigibility leads us into solipsism or to a mind/body dualism. If the introspective reports of any individual cannot be wrong, it is agreed on all sides that the reports about him by anyone else can be mistaken. We have a plain asymmetry here. But then it is natural to suppose that these introspective reports are about something which is not just contingently but *necessarily* private. But such necessarily private psychological entities cannot be identical with physical entities or objects or processes since the latter are—indeed must be—public and not private. There is no logical requirement that only one person could be aware of them. Still it is to be hoped that somehow the incorrigibilitist, as I shall call the foundationalist relying in individual sense-certainties, could untangle herself from such metaphysical issues for her claim has at least a *prima facie* plausibility in a way the metaphysical claims do not. Again Mackie puts the point well.

> There is undoubtedly at least a *prima facie* case for the incorrigibility of sense-statements. If I say "I feel cold," meaning it, not speaking in metaphor, not being misled by any ignorance of the English language, not intending the deceive myself or anyone else, speaking descriptively and not with any prescriptive or hortative purpose—not, for example, saying that I feel cold in order to keep up my morale at mid-day in a tropical desert—then how could this statement be corrected? How could it be in need of correction? If someone else has checked that I know English and mean what I am saying, that I am speaking descriptively and not either metaphorically or dishonestly, it would seem absurd for him to entertain any further doubt that I am feeling cold. Nothing except a rebuttal of one

or other of these provisos would justify him in saying "No, you aren't feeling cold." My statement it seems is not corrigible by anyone else.[24]

Yet Mackie is one of those who believes that, though plausible seeming as the incorrigibility thesis is, it is mistaken. There are no such statements, he argues; there are no indubitable items of empirical knowledge.[25]

I think the incorrigibilist does not keep firmly enough in mind the difference between what it is to *have* an experience, on the one hand, and what it is to take *notice* of and to *reflect* on the experience one is having, on the other. Having an experience is one thing; contemplating it is another. What is the result of reflection or contemplation, what is the result of taking notice of one's experience, is open to the possibility of error and propositions registering or articulating that taking notice of, that reflection on, that contemplating of, of one's experience are at least in principle corrigible. The reason why there is a reluctance to admit even in principle corrigibility—to concede any possibility of error about the judgment that I am now feeling cold—is our tendency to identify the *having* of the experience with *contemplating* its quality. We tend to think that to feel cold is just the same as to be aware of this experience as of the cold-feeling sort. A. J. Ayer has put the matter well: "In allowing the descriptions which people give of their experiences may be factually mistaken, we are dissociating having an experience from knowing that one has it. To know that one is having whatever experience it may be, one must not only have it but also to be able to identify it correctly and there is no necessary transition from one to the other."[26]

This distinction is not perfectly reflected in our language. "I feel cold," like "I'm cold," may be just an expression of feeling cold and function like uttering "Brrr" when one *has* the experience of feeling cold. If I feel cold I may shiver, hug myself, utter "Brrr," or say "I feel cold." Each of these performs, as Ludwig Wittgenstein has stressed, the same, or at least a very similar, function.[27] That is, each may be a mere expression of the feeling: a mere reaction to the feeling of being cold. But a shiver is not a matter of knowing or of knowledge nor is its linguistic equivalent "Brrr." It is an expression and a reaction, nothing more. It is not a matter of knowledge, not a matter of reflection, contemplation, or even of taking notice or note of anything. Nothing cognitive is going on here. The same thing is true for "I feel cold" where it, as it often does, has the same function as "Brrr" or a shiver. It is indeed something, unlike a shiver or *perhaps* even "Brrr," that has to be learned and goes with having a language, while a baby or infant not yet having acquired a language may shiver though hardly say "Brrr." As Mackie puts it, "Saying 'I feel cold' is no doubt a sophisticated, a learned reaction, whereas shivering is an unsophisticated and unlearned reaction, but it can be a reaction and nothing more."[28] But then Mackie goes on to make an important observation of something that Wittgenstein and Wittgensteinians tend not to take note of. Mackie says: "On the other hand, the remark, 'I feel cold' can perform the very different task of stating an explicit judgment that my experience is of a certain sort, and it is only when it performs this function that it is an empirical statement that is capable of being true or false, or of conveying an item of knowledge."[29] But in that use, where knowledge is involved, we are into the realm of the intersubjective, the communicable; to *know* that one has an experience, one must be able to *identify* the experience correctly. But to even be able to utilize a conception of "being correct" requires memory and memory-statements and criteria; but they are not taken, and cannot plausibly be taken, to be incorrigible. (It is one thing to say "I think I remember the drug store being around the corner" and another thing again to say "I remember that the drug store is around the corner.") In order to compare my present statement "I feel cold" with others I remember so that I can say, as I must to identify it, that it is like such and such others, I must be able to remember such and such others and here I can make mistakes and we have public criteria for what they are. But in order to know that I feel cold I must be able to identify my experience. There is no *knowing that* I have it, as distinct from just *having* it, without such identification. But identification—identifying correctly or incorrectly—involves comparison and thus memory-statements and we are thus immersed in the realm of the fallible, corrigible, and public.

It has been responded that while we *learn* to make such identifications by making such comparisons that, after coming to acquire the capacity to make identifications in that way, *what* we learn "is the link between the word and a quality which is present independently in each subject, and once we have learned to use the word we use it to describe each subject on its own, not to compare it with others."[30] Even if this is so (something which is problematical), we are still, when we are making such knowledge claims, enmeshed in a context which somewhere along the way requires an appeal to memory-statements and so we have fallibility and at least arguably intersubjectivity.

Still this might be too easy a way to dispose of the incorrigibilist. His case would be strengthened if a purely private language—a language that only one person could, *logically* could, understand—were possible. With such a private-language there would be purely private meanings, purely private criteria of correctness, for purely private statements (propositions) that would go along with incorrigibility. There would be some places where an individual would just know something—quite apart from having a public, socially acquired language—and would be certain that she knows it. But the very idea of such a private language is very problematical.[31] We can, and some of us do, think up secret codes, but they all depend on our already having available a public language that we use—the tool with which we do our thinking—when we construct the secret code. So that is no evidence for a private language in the relevant sense. And even more vitally, the secret code must be a code—to be a *logically* private language—that not only in fact no one cracks, but a code, with its essentially private language, that it is logically impossible to crack. But that is an incoherency or a logical impossibility. So it seems at least that there can be no, in the relevant sense, private languages (intrinsically private languages) and that language must be essentially public. But with publicity we get intersubjectivity and space for error for any knowledge-claim.

It might in turn be replied that the above considerations establish another merely *linguistic* corrigibility. What has been shown is that all empirical *statements* are corrigible; but that would not have established the more vital conclusion that all *items of empirical knowledge* are such that they are not certain. Even if it turns out that we can only *talk* about our present experiences by comparing them with others, it, it has been claimed, would not follow that we could be aware of their character only by literally knowing, being aware of, what they are like.[32] But this sounds very much like, and I think is, a contradiction. To be aware of their character is just to know, or at least to know, what they are like. "Character" is a kind term. When I say "I am feeling cold," if I am not just reacting to the cold, but taking note of my being cold, then I am doing something which would enable me to say, if I wish to, that I *know* that I am feeling cold. But to do this I must be able to identify cold. To do this, in turn, I must know the use of "cold" or its equivalent in another language and to know what the character of cold is, in turn, and this is to know what cold is like. Again I am in the intersubjective.

Suppose it were in turn said, as Mackie actually does, that showing that there are no incorrigible empirical statements would only establish that there is no indubitable empirical knowledge, if we could also show that there are no necessarily private objects with their attached private meanings such that an individual could be aware of them and take note of them without using or knowing any language at all. To show that there are no indubitable items of empirical knowledge it is not sufficient, the claims goes, to show that there are no indubitable empirical statements or propositions. It is also necessary, as well, to establish that there is no indubitable empirical knowledge, to show that there are no necessarily (logically necessary) private and indubitable objects that, even without the mastery of a language, we could just be aware of and take note of. But that this cannot be, it is claimed, has not been shown by the above linguistic considerations. We again have, the claim is, the sin of linguistic-ism.

Concerning this, I want to say two things. First, talk of logically or conceptually necessary private objects is exceedingly problematic. It is anything but clear that it has any meaning at all. At the very least it has no stable use or clear meaning such that we can be tolerably confident that we understand what we are talking about here. Being so problematic makes it a very weak base on which to construct a claim for indubitable empirical knowledge of any kind. Secondly, we should not forget what has been previously distinguished, namely, that we should keep firmly in mind the distinction between the expressive-reactive use of "I feel cold," a use which makes no knowledge-claim at all, and its cognitive use. The former use, recall, is merely a linguistic substitute for a shiver. Being neither true nor false, it is not something we can either be in doubt about or believe, for we are not at that cognitive level. There we do indeed have something which doesn't necessarily require language or thought. After all, babies shiver and no doubt when they do they feel cold. Moreover, the same thing, or a very similar thing, could be done with a shiver as is done with the expressive-reactive use of "I feel cold" or a "Brrr." But these things do not involve knowledge-claims. But this must be distinguished from the descriptive use of "I feel cold." It does make a cognitive claim. It claims to be an item of empirical knowledge. Now, I might, of course, know that I feel cold without my saying so. But the very knowing of it involves having a belief that is either true or false, as a belief could not but be, and thus we have something that could be expressed in an empirical statement. Indeed to be a belief it must be so *expressible*. And thus we are in the intersubjective and away from the incorrigible. There is no having an item of empirical knowledge without having something which is expressible in an empirical statement. And there is no claiming it, no claiming we have such knowledge, without making of an empirical statement expressive of that knowledge. As such, it says something which is either true or false. But in being something which is either true or false, it is an item of propositional knowledge. There is, moreover, no non-linguistically grounded knowing of a proposition. But once we get such a knowledge-claim, we do not have something which is indubitable or incorrigible. Moreover, to speak of knowledge is to speak of something that can be communicated and this brings in others and intersubjectivity and with it fallibility.

To fall back on saying that the knowledge that is being spoken of here, as an indubitable item of empirical knowledge, is a knowledge which not only is not, but cannot, be expressed in language or used in communication, is to fall back on a desperate expedient. It is in effect a claim that there is "ineffable knowledge."[33] But to make two familiar steals from the philosophical literature: what we cannot speak of we must be silent about and we cannot whistle it either. If something is inexpressible, incommunicable, ineffable, then it is not and cannot be an item of *knowledge*. Again we must not run together having the experience with taking note of it. Knowledge goes with communication, or at least the possibility of communication, with intersubjectivity, truth and publicity. And with this goes, as well, many sources of error as well as the possibility of truth. But truth is another public notion. "Subjective truth" or "intrinsically private truth" or "ineffable truth" are all contradictions in terms.[34] It is again the confusing of the *having* of an experience with the reflection on, the contemplation of, the noticing of, the taking note of, the experience. It is here, and not simply in the having of the experience, where we can have knowledge of the experience. *Taking the having of the experience to be the same as taking notice of the experience has led to the myth that there is a form of certain—just given to an individual—empirical knowledge: an experiential knowledge that could not be in error and concerning whose claims there could be no intelligible doubt.* But there is no such reality; rather, we merely have a confusion here to be exposed.

However, this still might be thought to be a too short way with a long and distinguished foundationalist tradition. Moreover, it might also be thought, the above cluster of arguments has been too concerned with language, too much of what Mackie once called linguisticism.[35] So consider now, and distinctly, the following argument against incorrigible empirical knowledge given by Mackie himself:

> It is questionable...whether we should call feeling cold a *cognitive* experience. It is not a knowing (or believing) *that* anything. (Obviously, too, it is not a knowing how.) Nor is it a recognition: to feel cold is not to meet anything again and recognize it, for the thing recognized could be nothing other than cold, but when you feel cold the first time you cannot be recognizing it, and yet feeling cold the first time is as genuine a case of feeling cold as feeling cold for the thousandth time. Moreover, within feeling cold itself (as opposed to judging that one feels cold) there is no room for error, there is no question of being wrong and equally no question of being right: the experience simply occurs. As an expression of this experience the utterance "I feel cold" is incorrigible in the same way in which a shiver is incorrigible, but it is then not a statement, it does not express any item of empirical knowledge.[36]

This can, and, I believe, as I have already argued, should be accepted, along with my previous more linguistically based arguments. (This argument seems to me to be linguistically based too. But let that go. However we classify it, it appears to be a sound argument.) Together they show that there are no self-justifying propositions, no empirical statements which are in principle incorrigible, i.e., in which the possibility of error is *logically* precluded, and that there are no indubitable items of empirical knowledge either. This is sufficient to refute classical foundationalism:

that is, the foundationalist on *the quest for certainty*, the foundationalist seeking to isolate the basic empirical statements or propositions to be used to test all other empirical statements or propositions while they remain themselves utterly secure items of indubitable *knowledge*.   They test everything else but they themselves never need to be tested.   Indeed the idea of testing them makes no sense.   But there are no such basic propositions.

However, it should also be said, to take any paradox out of this, that there may be certain sense-statements, experiential statements about our present sensations, which it is very difficult to correct and which it is not very clear what a real doubt concerning them would come to.   When I honestly assert that I am in pain or feel cold, do I know, or understand, what it would be like to feel cold, reflect on that experience, and, in so reflecting, judge wrongly that I was feeling warmth or pain when I was in reality feeling cold?   Even in the best circumstances we cannot get a conclusive demonstration that a particular sense-statement is mistaken. Often we are quite at sea even as to what counts for and against here.   It looks as if we can never make an observation or series of observations that will *compel* the admission that a particular sense-statement was mistaken. It is not that they are incorrigible, but merely that we can never be compelled to correct them.   This is not a guarantee against error but against the *conclusive* detection of error. But to expect conclusive detection of error is just the flip side of the foundationalist search for certainty. If there are no indubitable items of knowledge, no detecting that something is certainly true, there is going to be no such detecting that something is certainly false either.   We cannot find a secure epistemological standpoint—an Archimedean point—in establishing either the certainly true or the certainly false. There are no such facts of the matter or at least we have no understanding of what it would be like to have such facts of the matter. It was a foundationalist error to think that there is or could be or that we could have any coherent understanding of such things. We gain knowledge, but not such certain knowledge beyond peradventure of doubt.

IX

I shall now, turning to my fourth and final criticism, relax what it is to be a foundationalist. I shall still be concerned with an empiricist foundationalism, but it shall no longer be a foundationalism—the classical foundationalism—which takes its basic propositions—the building blocks of its epistemological edifice—to be sense-*certainties* or experiential-*certainties*, to be *indubitable* empirical propositions.[37] There is no longer the quest for certainty. What we are now taking to be our basic propositions can, like other empirical propositions, be mistaken and are open to public, intersubjective confirmation and disconfirmation. They are expressed by simple sentences without "if" or "that" or "or" or "likely" or "characteristically" and the like. Examples would be "that red flower," "the tree over there," "the swan on the lake," "the high note we hear," "the pungent odor we detect," or "that frog there." They are simply empirical propositions recording simple states of affairs of which we all supposedly can be directly aware, can clearly understand, and can readily know the truth-conditions of (know when they are true and when they are false). They are also intersubjectively establishable experiential statements about what we see, or can see, hear, taste, smell, and feel.

It is statements of this type, the modest foundationalist claims, on which we base all our other empirical knowledge. We, that is, test non-basic empirical propositions by them. Our lines or chains of inferential knowledge come to rest on these non-inferential bits of simple experiential knowledge. These propositions record what we directly know, but there is no claim that we know, even with this direct knowledge, *with certainty*. But it is what *we* directly know or can directly know. Still, though there is direct knowledge, there is no claim to certainty. I may claim to know that there is a swan on the lake when there isn't. "There is a swan on the lake" or "I see a swan on the lake" could express basic propositions but they both might very well be false. It could instead be a white goose or a gull or nothing at all. Modest foundationalism does not, as does classical foundationalism, start with primitive sense-certainties or what are thought to be primitive sense-certainties just given to the individual. But like traditional foundationalism, it seeks to give an account that would provide the philosophical foundation for the one true description of the world and it does this by an appeal to experiential knowledge only this time inter-subjectively experiential knowledge. Still the account is fallibilistic. It, to repeat, does not seek certainty. Its basic building blocks—its atoms of knowledge (to switch the metaphor)—one by one or all together—might be false. It bypasses skepticism or solipsism rather than attempting to refute it.

Modest foundationalism also has a number of vulnerabilities along with the distinctively modern virtue of fallibilism. First, how do we decide which type of proposition to take as basic? Do we have a non-arbitrary criterion or method or indeed any criterion or method at all? Similar problems have classically arisen for traditional-quest-for-certainty-foundationalism, though we did not pursue them. One thing, however, is plain: the sentences have, for the modest foundationalist, to be simple empirical sentences used to make intersubjectively verifiable statements about that part of the human and non-human world of which we are or can be directly aware, e.g., "The cat is in the tree," "A bird is on the lawn," "It is raining," "He is in pain," and "She is unhappy," rather than complex sentences such as "The cat in the tree is after a bird" or "If he is in pain then he will be irascible until he gets his medication" or "She is a manic-depressive" or "He is an anal erotic paranoid" or even "He is suffering from intense anxiety." The basic sentences must be grammatically simple, directly descriptive sentences recording the human and non-human world in theoretically unramified ways, e.g., "He is sad" not "He is a manic-depressive." But we plainly get gradations here and isn't there something problematical in ruling out all grades of theoreticity? Isn't "That is H_2O" more accurately descriptive of the physical world than "That is water"? Yet only the latter proposition would be available to a person in the Middle Ages or the Ancient World. It is not obvious which type proposition, if either, should be taken to be basic, though typically, but not invariably, modest foundationalists have taken as basic common sense propositions, propositions, though about the external world, which were also clearly rather brutely experiential: they are propositions about things people do or could see, hear, taste, smell, or feel and they could be characterized in terms that required no scientific or philosophical understanding at all. But it is not clear that such propositions, more than the scientific ones, give an accurate description of what the world is like. In one sense they are more directly observationally (experientially) testable, though this may be offset by the fact that sometimes the scientific propositions, since they are more sharply defined, are the more rigorously testable. The relevant variables are better controlled. It is unclear which type proposition, if either type, should be taken as basic, though foundationalists have typically taken the common sense option. Perhaps in one context one type of proposition is basic and in another, another. But while this would be a *formal* foundationalism, it would not be the context invariant *substantive* foundationalism sought by foundationalists both classical and modest.

Even if we take the route of the common sense experiential propositions or their non-scientific refinements, it is not clear whether we should take that bird has a yellow breast or a more nuanced, more fine-grained description, giving the exact hue, as a basic proposition. That the bird's breast is yellow is a less accurate description than the finely grained one. The fine-grained one, someone with metaphysical inclinations might be inclined to say, is "closer to reality" (whatever that means) than the common sense one. Bird watchers would probably in most situations prefer it. But it is also, because it is more fine-grained, more liable to error than the claim that the bird's breast is yellow. ("That is a bird" is safer than "That is a robin" and that utterance is safer than "That is a young robin." If we say something general enough it is hard to say something false. "There are rocks in the world" is hardly likely to be false.) Moreover, with "The bird's breast is yellow," we are not only less likely to say something false, we are also more likely to get intersubjective agreement than with the fine-grained proposition and with that, to better facilitate communication for people—non-bird watchers in this example—who do not care very much about nuance and accuracy. (But accuracy for what? We have no simple, non-context dependent notion of accuracy here.) Again it is not clear which propositions we should take as our basic building blocks for our theory of knowledge.

There is also a problem that plagues modest foundationalism that—or at least not so obviously—does not plague classical foundationalism. We want a foundationalism to yield *terminating* propositions or *terminating* judgments: propositions or judgments which are our evidence for other propositions but do not require evidence for themselves (or, if you will, they are their own evidence). That I seem to see or think I see a yellow breasted bird or that I am in pain seem to be that kind of proposition. We have found reason to query that, but that is surely how they seem. But "That bird's breast is yellow" doesn't even have that appearance. In most contexts at least it is in place to ask the person making the assertion what is her evidence for it and she will say things like "I see it. The bird is on a telephone wire in bright sunlight." Or, where the circumstances are more dubious (the light is not so good or the like), she will say something like "Well, I think it is yellow. It looks like that to me." So, being able to ask for evidence, and its being in place to ask for evidence, it is not clear how the proposition is basic and the judgment *terminating*. Indeed it certainly looks like that is just what it isn't and that we are again back to the place of the classical foundationalist in search of sense-certainties. With classical foundationalism we see that we cannot get the requisite sense-certainties, but with modest foundationalism we do not get anything which is terminating and thus we do not get anything properly foundational.

The basic facts, the basic propositions, represent (supposedly represent) something we are supposed directly to know. There is supposed to be a direct knowing or, if you will, an immediate knowledge here. When I see a rabbit and assert "The rabbit is white" the idea is that there is a quality-word "white" and that there is a link between that word and a quality which, independently of others, is sensorily present to me, though the assumption is that it is similarly present to any person with normal eyes, situated as I am situated, and who understands English. (Recall the importance for foundationalists of their claim that their epistemic relations are natural.) "White" stands for the quality (property) white and it is being predicated of a rabbit which I am also directly aware of and the word "rabbit" stands for that subject, namely, the rabbit, of which I predicate that it is white. I am, as others can be as well, directly aware of both the rabbit and that the rabbit is white. This is what direct knowledge comes to here and this is a paradigm case of such direct knowledge or knowing.

That *seems* at least to be an obvious bit of common sense. Could there be anything substantially wrong with that? Why should it be thought that such direct knowledge is the least bit problematic? The following will bring out the reasons. The above picture of world-word relations is too simple. "Rabbit" stands for rabbit and "white" for white alright. But this is something we come to learn in learning a particular language. The infant without a language but with developed eyes, when in my arms and looking in the same direction as I am, when I see the white rabbit, surely sees something. But he does not see something he conceptualizes as a rabbit and white. That is something which is learned with the mastery of language. Moreover, different languages conceptualize things somewhat differently. There are languages in cultures different than ours that do not discriminate between black and green. The same word does duty for what we would say are two different colors. There are, as well, all sorts of shades of white. We use a single word for them. But we might not. That is an accidental feature of our language. We could be speakers of a language, users of a system of thought, which had two or more words for different shades of white and no single word for what we call "white"—just as Eskimos have no single word for snow—to cover a range of shades of white. Similar things obtain for the subject term "rabbit." There are different kinds of rabbits; there are also, of the same kind of rabbits, baby rabbits, adult rabbits, rabbits in winter with one color and in summer with another, rabbits sitting, rabbits hopping, and the like. *We* call them all rabbits, but others might not. We do not call a caterpillar a butterfly. But others might have the same name for the insect with different stages at both stages We might simply have called tadpoles frogs, remarking, where some explanation is called for, that they are young frogs. Word-world relations are not a simple given but are many and varied and, as they are varied, people see and conceptualize the world differently.[38] (Note I did not say *completely* differently.)

It is true that people can learn other languages and learn to make the discriminations that others make. But still there is no agreement about which of these languages, with their different word-world relations, correctly, truly, catch the world just as it is, apart from any language or any convention.[39] We have no place to stand which just tells us how to see or apprehend rightly, apart from the adopting of some language or conceptual system.

Moreover, and the above argument aside, when I see a rabbit and see that it is white, I see, at a given time, only a rabbit side or a part of a rabbit and I only see that it is white on one side or on those parts I see. In saying "The rabbit is white" I am making some primitive inferences about its other side or the unseen parts of its surface, its continuity, and the like, so my knowledge is not direct and utterly non-inferential. Again the foundationalist's picture goes wrong. It was to try to escape (though vainly) such problems that led the classical foundationalists to concoct sense-data. So for these reasons, and other reasons as well, the notion of direct, utterly non-inferential knowledge is a non-starter.

Modest foundationalists are almost always, perhaps always, metaphysical realists. They believe that there is one uniquely true description of the world and that that description of the world tells us just what that world is, quite independently of how we happen to conceptualize it. There must, they will assert, be a way the world is. The philosophical trick is to articulate the one true description of the way the world is. Whether a given sentence, thought, belief, statement, or proposition is true depends on something extra-human, namely, the actual world itself. There are these fact-like entities there in the world, that are our truth-makers, and they are to be accurately described by a philosophically appropriate language which, at the level of basic propositions, will, in recording these fact-like entities, reveal simple truth. What makes a proposition or statement true is the way the world is. There are these fact-like entities—these truth-makers—there in the world for true propositions or, if you will, sentences to correspond to.

However, and unfortunately for the modest-foundationalist, the world is not prestructured into fact-like entities. The world doesn't consist in some totality of fact-like entities there to be discovered and counted and to which, one by one, or in any other way, our sentences correspond. Nor is our world prefabricated in terms of kinds of categories. Objects and kinds do not exist independently of conceptual schemes. There is no coherent answer to the question "How many objects are there on my desk?" It makes no sense to say that there must be a determinate number of objects in the universe and thus there is no *logical* possibility, some convention aside, of saying how many objects there are on my desk, in my hand, or in the universe. There are, moreover, no self-identifying objects. The world does not come precategorized, presorted, or presliced. It is the noetic activity of the mind or the establishment of linguistic convention or linguistic practices that produce the categories and categorial systems that we have. To think of truth as correspondence is to assume, perhaps naturally but still utterly mistakenly, that thought or language mirrors the world. But that notion makes no sense, for it assumes, incoherently, that the world comes precategorized in fact-like, self-identifying entities. It is also the case that we can never compare a thought or a statement or a network of thoughts or statements with an unconceptualized reality so as to tell whether the world answers to that thought or statement or network of thoughts or statements.

The metaphysical realist and his epistemological companion, the modest foundationalist, work with the following pretheoretical intuition which they cannot abandon while still keeping their positions intact. The metaphysical realist wants the world *quite* unequivocally to determine what is true and what is false and the modest foundationalist wants to tell us what it would be like to know that this is so and to correctly characterize its basic structure in a theory of knowledge. For this to be so, it must be the case that objects and properties, as things which are just there in the world, determine whether propositions are true quite independently of what organizers or investigators think or what conceptual schemes are extant and accepted. But the metaphysical realist's intuition – natural as it is – is at best false and more likely incoherent. The world does not come in such a precategorized manner. To translate into the concrete: if the proposition that a yellow breasted finch is in the bush, as modest foundationalists and metaphysical realists believe, fits with a certain segment of the world, as it could, then it is true and we need not, in acknowledging that, be concerned over how some cognizers interpret it or what conceptual schemes are accepted. This conception of the simple truth and of (in our bird description) a match of the true description of the world rests on a myth. Language, or, for that matter, thought, does not work in this simple fashion. The phrase "yellow breasted finch," though certainly translatable into French, Italian, German, and the like with ease, does not just pick out an object in the world. There very well could be languages and schemes of thought where it was not so translatable (at least not on the spot and without considerable innovation in that language), where the people with their particular language had no concept of a finch or of the breast of birds (the joints of nature do not come prefabricated and already precategorized). (Remember the factual truth – the true factual statement – that Eskimos have no single word for snow. What we call snow is too important to them to be so coarsely conceptualized.) And a people might have no concept of bush so, lacking these concepts, they do not "read the truth off nature" in the same way we do, or, more accurately, none of us succeeds in "reading the truth off nature" for that very notion is without sense. It is a metaphor we cannot cash and thus it false as a coherent metaphor. (A putative metaphor that even with ingenuity cannot be paraphrased non-metaphorically is not a metaphor at all, for then we cannot say what it is a metaphor of. Very frequently for a subtle metaphor, we cannot, right off, or even sometimes with careful reflection, say at a given time what it is a metaphor of. But, if we abandon the very logical possibility of saying what it is a metaphor of, we at the same time abandon the claim that the phrase is a metaphor or metaphorical.) There is no language which just tells it like it is – just records or depicts or pictures what nature is like.[40] We rather are always, and inescapably, dependent on the societal norms or determinate uses of terms in certain linguistic and social practices (they go together) of a given society or family of societies during a given historical period. It very much appears to be the case that, at least that in that way, society determines what we can say, think and believe and what has the most fundamental epistemic authority.

Metaphysical realist and foundationalist expectations to the contrary notwithstanding, we cannot say *sans phrase*, and make it stick, that there is a yellow breasted finch in the bush. What we can correctly say is that, given a certain interpretation of the sentence expressing that proposition, a certain specification of truth-conditions *and* a certain condition of a part of the world (so specified), that (if *all* these conditions obtain), it is true that there is a yellow breasted finch in the bush. But under other interpretations it is false and under still other interpretations it is indeterminate. There is no, it just being the case, independently of holding some conceptual framework, that there is a yellow breasted finch in the bush. Since this is perfectly generalizable, including to such simpler propositions as "The bird is yellow," "There is a bush there," the commonsensical sounding claims of modest foundationalism have been undermined. There is no just discovering the truth or what it is reasonable to believe is the truth or at least a string of truths—the simple truth or simple truths—there naked to our gaze. There is no just looking and seeing what is the case. There is, of course, indeed there must be, a way the world is—we do not create the world—but we are never in a position to say, independently of human devising, the way that it is. It will be a burden of Part 3 to show, and unparadoxically show, appearances to the contrary notwithstanding, that this does not lead to relativism, conceptual or otherwise, let alone to subjectivism or nihilism, playful or otherwise.

Notes

1. C. I. Lewis adroitly defends such a view. C. I. Lewis, *Collected Papers of Clarence Irving Lewis* (Stanford, California: Stanford University Press, 1970), 258-93.

2. Roderick Chisholm, *Theory of Knowledge*, 3rd edition (Englewood Cliffs, New Jersey: Prentice-Hall, 1989).

3. Ibid.

4. Ibid., 61-62.

5. Michael Williams, "The Unreality of Knowledge" in Jocelyne Couture and Kai Nielsen eds., *Méta-Philosophie: Reconstructing Philosophy? New Essays on Metaphilosophy* (Calgary, Alberta: University of Calgary Press, 1993).

6. Ibid.

7. Ibid.

8. Ibid.

9. Chisholm, "A Theory of Knowledge" in Chisholm et al., *Philosophy* (Englewood Cliffs, New Jersey: Prentice-Hall, 1964), 270.

10. Ibid., 273.

11. Ibid., 276.

12. Ibid. Chisholm cites the passage from St. Augustine's *Against the Academicians*.

13. Chisholm, *A Theory of Knowledge*, 276-77.

14. The most extended sophisticated statement we have of modest foundationalism is Alvin Goldman, *Epistemology and Cognition* (Cambridge, Massachusetts: Harvard University Press, 1986). For a briefer but carefully reasoned statement of modest foundationalism, see Robert Audi, "The Architecture of Reason," *Proceedings and Addresses of the American Philosophical Association*, supplement to Vol 62, no. 1 (September 1988), 227-56. I critically examine Goldman's account in my *After the Demise of the Tradition*, Chapter 5.

15. Alice Ambrose, "Philosophical Doubts," *Massachusetts Review* (1960), 274.

16. Chisholm, *A Theory of Knowledge*, 334.

17. Richard Rorty brings out how this was an underlying concern of foundationalism and in turn trenchantly criticizes it. Richard Rorty, *Philosophy and the Mirror of Nature* (Princeton, New Jersey: Princeton University Press, 1979) and Richard Rorty, *Consequences of Pragmatism* (Minneapolis, Minnesota: University of Minnesota Press, 1982).

18. Kai Nielsen, "Philosophy and the Search for Wisdom," *Teaching Philosophy* 16, no. 1 (March 1993), 5-20.

19. Jaegwon Kim, "Rorty on the Possibility of Philosophy," *Journal of Philosophy* LXXCII, no. 10 (October 1980), 588-97. I criticize Kim's account in chapter 4 of my *After the Demise of the Tradition*.

20. Both Hilary Putnam and Richard Rorty developed nuanced critiques of the coherence of the conception of the one true description or conception of the world. Hilary Putnam, *Realism with a Human Face* (Cambridge, Massachusetts: Cambridge University Press, 1991); Richard Rorty, "Pragmatism as Anti-Representationalism" in John F. Murphy, *Pragmatism from Peirce to Davidson* (Boulder, Colorado: Westview Press, 1990), 1-6; Richard Rorty, "Putnam on Truth," *Philosophy and Phenomenological Research* LII, no. 2 (June 1992), 431-47; and Richard Rorty, "Putnam and the Relativist Menace," *Journal of Philosophy* XC, no. 4 (September 1993), 443-61.

21. Richard Rorty, *Objectivity, Relativism, and Truth*, 126-61 and Paul Horwich, *Truth* (Oxford: Basil Blackwell, 1990).

22. John Mackie, *Logic and Knowledge* (Oxford: Clarendon Press, 1985), 24.

23. Ibid., 24-25.

24. Ibid., 26.

25. Ibid., 40.

26. A. J. Ayer, *The Problem of Knowledge* (Harmondsworth, Middlesex, England: Penguin Books, 1956), 7-8.

27. Ludwig Wittgenstein, *Philosophical Investigations* (Oxford: Basil Blackwell, 1953) and Ludwig Wittgenstein, *The Blue and Brown Books* (Oxford: Basil Blackwell, 1958).

28. Mackie, *Logic and Knowledge*, 35.

29. Ibid.

30. Ibid., 29-30.

31. There is an extensive literature on Wittgenstein's critique of the very idea of a private language. Ludwig Wittgenstein, *Philosophical Investigations*, Sections 202-300; the essays by Ayer, Rhees, and Cook in George Pitcher, ed., *Wittgenstein: Philosophical Investigations* (Garden City, New Jersey: Anchor Books, 1962), 251-323; Saul Kripke, *Wittgenstein on Rules of Private Language* (Cambridge, Massachusetts: Harvard University Press, 1982); Norman Malcolm, *Nothing is Hidden: Wittgenstein's Criticism of His Early Thought* (Oxford: Basil Blackwell, 1986), 157-70.

32. Mackie, *Logic and Knowledge*, 30.

33. Alice Ambrose has powerfully criticized such conceptions. Alice Ambrose, "The Problem of Linguistic Inadequacy" in Max Black, ed., *Philosophical Analysis: A Collection of Essays* (Ithaca, New York: Cornell University Press, 1950), 15-37.

34. Arthur E. Murphy deconstructs the very idea of truth as subjectivity in his *Reason and the Common Good* (Englewood Cliffs, New Jersey: Prentice-Hall, 1963), 173-79.

35. John Mackie, *Contemporary Linguistic Philosophy—Its Strength and Its Weakness* (Dunedin, New Zealand: University of Otago Press, 1956) and John Mackie, "The Logical Status of Grammar Rules," *Australasian Journal of Philosophy* XXVII (1949), 197-216.

36. Mackie, *Logic and Knowledge*, 36-37.

37. See references in note 14.

38. Hilary Putnam, *Mind, Language and Reality* (Cambridge: Cambridge University Press, 1975), 1-32.

39. Nielsen, *After the Demise of the Tradition*, 57-90.

40. See references to Rorty and Putnam in note 20. Barry Allen, *Truth in Philosophy* (Cambridge, Massachusetts: Harvard University Press, 1993).

PART THREE

Philosophy as Critique

...philosophy must in time become a method of locating and interpreting the more serious of the conflicts that occur in life, and, a method of projecting ways for dealing with them: a method of moral and political diagnosis and prognosis.

— John Dewey

The problem of restoring integration and cooperation between man's beliefs about the world in which he lives and his beliefs about values and purposes that should direct his conduct is the deepest problem of modern life. It is the problem of any philosophy that is not isolated from life.

— John Dewey

5

Philosophy and the Problems of Life

I

Since the seventeenth century, the overwhelmingly dominant tradition in philosophy has taken metaphysics and epistemology, and frequently an epistemologically based metaphysics, to be the core of philosophy. It is metaphysics and epistemology that will provide, if we can only get the really true metaphysical and epistemological view, the foundation for life. The really deep underlying foundations for morality, politics, the aesthetic education of human begins, community, and the like must be found in such a metaphysical and epistemological view. Without such philosophical foundations we can make no adequate sense of our lives. I have been concerned in Parts One and Two to resist such a conception of philosophy and such philosophical views. The brunt of my attention has been directed to, and, after elucidation, against metaphysical accounts of the world and against foundationalist epistemology, a conception which is distinctively a part of modern philosophy. (Sometimes they combine, as we have just seen, in metaphysical realism and modest foundationalism.) I shall now argue in Part Three that philosophy should turn away from such foundationalist quests, whether epistemological, metaphysical, or ethical, and center its endeavors on the problems, perhaps always the historically and culturally determinate problems, of human beings. For us, what should be at the center of our attention are the problems of our epoch both in social and political arenas and in our lives as individuals—in our conceptions of ourselves and in our conceptions of how we should relate to others. I will argue that these things stand in need of sustained and careful philosophical reflection, discussion, conceptualization, and sometimes reconceptualization.

This stress puts, against the tide, social, political, and moral philosophy (the latter construed broadly) as the very core of what philosophy should be after the demise of the tradition.[1] What was for some time viewed as rather marginally and optimally philosophical, now, I propose, should become center stage. But moral philosophy here will not be the epistemology of morals, metaethics or an attempt to articulate the "foundations of practical reason." If there is no, as I have argued in Part Two, "epistemology-epistemology" (theory of knowledge), at least of a foundational sort, then there is certainly no epistemology of morals or of valuation or of norms more generally. If the Cartesian-Lockean-Kantian or modern empiricist or rationalist quest for the foundations of knowledge rests on a mistake, a mistake so thorough as to be an utterly misbegotten project, then certainly the effort to articulate, after the fashion of Immanuel Kant, Henry Sidgwick or G. E. Moore, the foundations of morals is equally, or *perhaps* even doubly, mistaken.

In saying that moral, political, and social philosophy should become center stage, I do not have in mind either such foundationalist inquiries or the metaethical inquiries that sprang up after Moore (and was implicit in parts of his work) and still are at the heart of much of the more theoretical work in analytical ethical theory.[2] I mean moral-social-political philosophy done much more after the fashion of John Dewey, Isaiah Berlin, John Rawls, Ronald Dworkin, Michael Walzer, Stephen Toulmin, and Michel Foucault. Their work, of course, is importantly different, but there is enough in comment about how they conceive what moral-social-political philosophy is about to treat them together in this respect, though among them only John Dewey has articulated a general conception of what philosophy should be, after metaphysics and epistemology, and along with it metaethics, have been set aside.

I shall argue that there is no need for a metaphysical-epistemological preface or prologemna to ethics and politics so that with it we can finally be oriented to the real deep truth about such matters. There is in such a non-foundationalist account a seriousness and a care about pressing issues of morals, politics, and of culture more generally, and a commitment to considering such issues intelligently, reflectively, and imaginatively and not to be trapped by ideological illusions. But there is no search for the accurate representation of reality as it is in itself or a quest for the one right answer—some kind of general answer—to moral questions yielding the one true morality. Indeed it is believed that such conceptions dear to the tradition are incoherent.[3] It is not even thought, as some contemporary metaethicists do, that to proceed reasonably here with such substantive moral and political considerations, we first must get reasonably clear about what is meant by "normative matters" and about what the nature of moral or normative inquiry is or about the structure of practical reasoning. We will see how far we can go in reflective moral inquiry and critique by leaving such matters to benign neglect. In taking a normative turn, I am empathically not urging that in effect we turn that normative turn into a meta-normative turn.

II

So let us see where we can go with philosophy conceived as concerned with the problems of human beings and indeed, centrally, with the problems of human beings of a given time and place. Philosophers on such a conception should not be concerned with the perennial problems of philosophers but with the social and moral problems of our time.[4] Only a deeply cynical deconstructionist would say there is nothing to be concerned about there, but not a few, including many, who are not cynical at all, would be skeptical about whether *philosophy* has any useful role to play here.[5] To this it will in turn be said that philosophers have developed critical standards and methods of critical inquiry; they have, as well, conceptions, sometimes even a vision, of human excellence, while remaining concerned with the problems of life—the problems of our time and place, though sometimes perhaps not only of our time and place. In doing so it is part of their vocation to be reflective. If they are doing philosophy properly, they will in a reflective and carefully reasoned manner seek to take a stance and to set out ideas for our consideration—it is not for the philosophers to command or order—that are, if they do philosophy properly, both detached and informed. They want us to take sober and searching second and even third thoughts. Philosophy, whatever else it is, has to be a reflective and critical activity.[6] After all, for Socrates philosophy was the love and pursuit of wisdom. However skeptical or cynical we may have become about the very idea of wisdom, this Socratic conception resonates in us if we have any philosophical inclinations at all.[7] We would like our morality, our conception of society and its social institutions, our sense of life, to be informed, reflective, and critical, as well as sensitive. This will remain so even if the very idea of "a critical morality," "a sense of the meaning of life," "social critique," "a conception of a humane and truly human society" seem very problematic to us. We want not only to be actors and in some way consumers in our world, but to gain a reflective and critical understanding of, and to take a stance toward, our world, meaning by that, most centrally, the human problems that we face in our world. We want a keen sense of the alternatives that are or can be available and a good understanding of how to evaluate them. We want to have a clear understanding of the import they severally have and of their various rationales.

People coming to philosophy, as I remarked at the very beginning of this book, perhaps naively, would like philosophy to provide wise guidance and an integrated outlook on life. If we go at things at all philosophically, we do not just seek to solve or respond to the problems of life one by one, taking them up in isolation, but we will attempt, in solving them or responding to them, to get something of an integrated and perhaps even a comprehensive sense of them.[8] Practically speaking, we cannot, of course, reasonably discuss everything at once. We must at a given time focus on a particular problem or a closely connected cluster of problems, but we should also keep in mind the connections with other not so directly connected problems, keep a sense of the importance of attempting to see how things hang together and to come to have a sense of the good life for human beings, or, if nothing both coherent and non-platitudinous can be said here, at least some sense of the good life for human beings situated at a certain time and place.[9]

Philosophers should concern themselves with the problems of our time — the deepest and most intractable problems that human beings face — but we would also like, were we are doing philosophy, if we can, to view them somehow comprehensively: to give ourselves an integrated and critical conception of who we are, were, and of whom we might become with what social institutions, social practices, and with a reflective sense of our lives together. These, rather than the problems and conceptions of perennial philosophy or foundationalist, even modest foundationalist, epistemology and metaphysics or metaethics, should be the objects of our philosophical investigations.

III

What are the central problems of life for us, standing where we stand now, which should be the object of our critical reflection? Without striving for anything like a comprehensive and exhaustive list, the following are plainly prominent. As we go into the twenty-first century we do not have much of any kind of idea what our lives will be like in the next fifty years. The Cold War is over. Communism everywhere is either dead or dying.[10] The hopes and the fears that it generated are gone. Or at least so it seems. But poverty, exploitation, degradation, just plain massive starvation go on. Destructive, brutal, and indeed rather senseless wars flare up all over the place. And the economies of the capitalist democracies are working very badly. More people lose their jobs and cannot find others; the poor get poorer and more numerous, and the rich get richer, though fewer. The end of communism and the victory of capitalism has not even begun to issue in the rosy dawn of the good or even the just society that many expected. Even in the advanced capitalist societies homelessness is not infrequent and the standard of living and quality of life for most has in varying degrees deteriorated. Stress at work has increased and job security decreased. And vast numbers of people have no prospect of work at all, let alone meaningful work. Along with this, particularly in the United States, but not only there, there is private wealth for a few amidst public squalor, a squalor that affects not only the poor but the wealthy as well. Think, for example, of the sometimes elegant and often expensive houses in the suburbs together with the horrible transportation between metropolis and suburbs and the eyesores that rich and poor must look at when they go from suburbs to metropolis. We have plainly a very inegalitarian and unjust society as well as a society with such arrangements that it surely looks like an irrational society. What can and should be done, and how to do it, is a key cluster of problems of life for us.

Also in societies, where there is anything like democracy at all, democracy increasingly becomes a farce, a kind of television road show, with little in the way of citizenship participation, no clear articulation, let alone citizen debate, of the issues (indeed even the candidates do not debate them in any unrehearsed, unprogrammed way). There is also a narrowing of the alternatives with powerful interest groups setting the agenda and in considerable measure in fact determining the results. Without at all wishing to throw out the little democracy we have, it is hard to be optimistic about the prospects for democracy. A deep cynicism is not at all irrational. Indeed it is very difficult to be anything else but cynical.

Similarly, again most extensively in the United States, our contemporary mass education is in a sorry state. In a few elite universities, a quality education is available; in other universities, though here some places are worse than others, we have, with huge classes and harried professors, a mass education that hardly sustains, let alone develops, the creative and intellectual capacities of students, exercises their imaginations, gives them a reasonable sense of the world they live in and its possibilities, or gives them a sense of the cultural history of the West, to say nothing of the rest of the world, or equips them reflectively and critically to respond to their world. This, all the same, is on the university level. Even counting the lumpen-colleges and universities, we have here a group (actually several stratified groups) in a situation that is relatively "privileged." That is, they are privileged in comparison to those who do not even get near a community college or in some instances even through high school. In the elementary schools and the intermediate level schools, things are much worse than in the colleges and universities. People there lack all kinds of elementary skills. And going through these institutions does little to help them gain them. Many are, and remain, functionally illiterate. Few are equipped with anything like an understanding of the society in which they live, let alone the critical capacity to enable them to respond as effective democratic citizens. Ideological indoctrination, typically of a rather indirect sort, is pervasive. Education is typically to secure, if possible, stupidity and to keep toodle straight on the tracks no matter what. Streetwise kids may circumvent this in certain ways, but street wisdom is not enough. *Perhaps* this characterization of education is too bleak and too partisan, but it is at least arguably accurate, and, in any event, our educational situation is so inadequate that it clearly poses for us one of the problems of life.

There is also the pollution of our environment and the threat of exhaustion of our resources (our fish stocks, for example). We are making human life and other animal life on our planet, if not increasingly untenable, at least increasingly inhospitable. Yet the pollution goes—or at least seemingly goes—with industrial development and industrial development seems at least necessary to sustain population levels at anything like where they are now. Slowly to reduce them, and surely not to increase them, is a very desirable thing, but not by the drastic measures of starvation. It is just desirable in most circumstances that people come to have fewer children, as they probably will anyway with increasing security and affluence. (That in the Third World they do not have that is evident. It is hard to expect population levels to go down in such circumstances.) There is no feasible turning our backs on industrial civilization. Yet it is also plainly true that that civilization, among other things, poses, and poses severely, problems of pollution that are not easily solved. In sections of the Canadian North, to take an example, people are very poor and there is little work. Uranium mining would provide work and strengthen the economy, but it is polluting and contributes to the use of nuclear energy and working conditions in such mines, far beyond the average mine, are hazardous (principally because of radiation). So the choice looks like either no job or a hazardous job which, among other things, contributes, and dangerously so, to pollution.

There are, to shift to another cluster of problems, the difficult relations between the rich capitalist societies, unevenly as their own wealth is spread around, and the less industrially developed parts of the world. There is something which at the very least looks very much like the subordination, domination, and exploitation of the latter by the former. As bad as things generally are in the rich capitalist societies, they are far worse in these other societies. In some of them extreme poverty, mass starvation, and malnutrition are pervasive. There is considerable lack of anything like gainful employment, little in the way of education, deep ethnic and racial hatreds, and the like. In Africa, Latin America, the Caribbean, and parts of Asia people are rotting away while they and the environment in which they live in are being exploited by the West. (Indeed they not only rot away, they starve to death to the tune of fifty thousand per day.)

The problems of life so far described are, broadly speaking, all political problems. Public problems, if you will. There are, as well, somewhat more private problems, though the division is not sharp or uncontested and the individuals whose "private problems" they are are through and through social individuals, as we all are, standing in complex relations of interdependency and subject to the particular deformation of the societies in which we live. From birth to death we human beings are interdependent. The Lone Ranger doesn't exist. Still, the problems I am about to describe have a more personal ring than those described above. People, if they are not to have a very alienated, unflourishing life, need a sense of identity and to experience recognition (the two go together like hand and glove). Without these things they will not have the good of self-respect, which is one of their most fundamental goods without which their lives will be very impoverished indeed. But in our world, our identities are increasingly insecure. We do not know who we are; we—or at least very many of us—have lost our sense of history and cultural identity, and, without a secure "we," without a face-to-face living community, we will usually have a very impoverished conception of ourselves and no secure sources of recognition. For the latter, in such circumstances, we increasingly fall back on the family and that central institution cannot bear the strain. Moreover, with a resolute feminist challenge to male domination, the family is changing and also under severe stress. Both women and men no longer have a clear sense of their station and its duties or a clear sense of their roles. Much of this is in many ways a blessing—we certainly do not want to go back to the patriarchal, male-dominated family—but this change also has its downside, for without reasonably clearly defined roles, without a clear sense of what to expect of others and what to have others expect of us, there is not likely to be much in the way of a living community and without that we will have little in the way of recognition, a sense of identity, and the sense of self-respect that depends on recognition and identity.

In our society, to take another example belonging to the same family of problems, life, particularly for the very old, can be very isolated, devoid of meaningful occupations, with, for the very old, even less recognition than is the norm across the society (where it is anything but extensive), and with a debilitating loneliness and a sense that one is of no use and of no value any more. The old often feel like worn out objects discarded by their society.[11] They have a sense of themselves as being utterly useless and utterly uncared for. And, while things have always been very difficult for the old (though more so in some societies, in some strata, and in some occupations that others), in societies under the conditions of modernity the psychological ills that beset them run deeper than in many more traditional societies. There are, of course, inescapable physical ills, or at least disabilities, that go with aging. But they are exacerbated by the society in which they live and are arguably within limits alterable.

Relations across generations and between males and females are also under increasing strain. Women rightly challenge male domination and men, feeling threatened, react with a backlash.[12] New ways of living together or apart are tried out and homosexual relations, previously thought to be unnatural, enter as live and as increasingly acceptable options, though again there is a violent backlash against them with the murder of gays and the like. And, as gays and lesbians demand both the protection of their rights and recognition, we have a whole domain of personal relations feeling its way through to what can be forms of flourishing life. But doing so is also very conflictual.

Modernity—the increasingly disenchanted world of secular and, as well, rather varied ways of living with its inescapable pluralism—is often blamed for a lot of the world's ills, but it is also a source of its escape from parochialism, ethnocentrism, and confining ways of living. There are lots of ways of life, including many newly emerging subcultures, in some of which we will find, if we enter into them with the effort that success here requires, new ways to live and relate to each other. Still, disenchantment has its costs. Religion provided social bonds, a sense of who we are, were, and how we could find meaning in life. But religion—or so it seems—is increasingly not a live option for people with a modern education. To gain a critical sense, to overcome ethnocentrism, is indeed desirable, but it brings with it, to use a phrase of James Joyce's, the threat of the wolves of disbelief. Is the social cement of religion necessary to secure our identity and the possibility of sustaining a life that has significance, or are there genuinely secure sources of such identity and significance that are purely secular? And, if not, should we return, or try to return (we might not succeed), to a religious orientation even if it requires a crucifixion of the intellect? (Perhaps it does not; perhaps to think so is a modern secular prejudice?)

The cluster of problems of life just described here are more personal than political, though to dichotomize here is problematic. However, linked closely with problems of identity and recognition in modern multi-cultured societies is the problem of nationalism. Individuals find their identities, if they find them, as members of groups, but it is not clear that large multicultural states such as the United States, Canada, the old Soviet Union, India, or a united Europe (if Maastericht becomes a reality) can be the source of such identity. There are, or so it may be, too many distinct cultures (nations) under the umbrella of these multinational states to make these states reliable sources of such identity. But can a culture (an ethnic group, a nation without a state supporting its distinct culture) be secure under modern conditions in a neutral liberal state (behaving even-handedly to all groups) or in an authoritarian multinational empire which did the same? Cultures, under modern conditions, need, or at least seem to need, states reflecting their interests, but often that is impossible and, where possible, it is *sometimes* (where, for example, there is a considerable mix of cultures living together in a given territory), all things considered, undesirable. However, there may be circumstances and conditions (given the protection of the rights of minorities and the like) where it at least seems to be clearly desirable.

In any case, nationalism is growing and has a powerful appeal to many people.[13] Is it always a bad thing? Must it be in conflict with internationalism? Is it unavoidably something that becomes jingoistic and ethnocentric? Sometimes, of course, it becomes far worse. Can it sometimes be a desirable thing and, if so, under what conditions? It appears at least in some situations to be a desirable thing. I have in mind situations where minorities either do not exist or where their rights and possibilities for flourishing are securely protected. Where such things are maintained, a nationalism, not in conflict with an internationalism, is at least arguably a good thing,
for it is necessary—or so it seems—for a secure sense of identity which in turn is essential to secure the good of self-respect. Be that as it may, there are a cluster of problems of life centering around nationalism/internationalism, sustaining a sense of identity, and achieving and sustaining recognition in an increasingly disenchanted world.

IV

I hope I have described a reasonable and somewhat representative sampling of the problems of our time. They are problems which deeply tax human beings, and not just intellectuals. They are often unsettling and perplexing problems which are very difficult even to describe without in one way or another being unwittingly partisan or contentious. Our very choice of vocabulary often puts us on contested ground. The hope, if we are striving to be philosophical about the matter, is that we can, with effort and a steady gaze, using what John Dewey called intelligence in human affairs, state these problems clearly, then face them and either resolve them or dissolve them. *Some* problems, at least when looked at in the terms in which they are usually put, turn out, after examination, to be specious. However, it is clear enough that this is often not so and that we both must use our brains and be sensitively reflective in coming to grips with them. In that sense, Dewey was plainly right about the use of intelligence. But that accepted, it is still not clear, to return to a question posed at the beginning of this section, what *role philosophy* can play here. Public relations acts on the part of applied philosophy standardly obscure this. We need specifically to ask whether there is really any philosophical expertise here and, if so, how it works. Though in asking this, we should also ask ourselves if that is the wrong question to ask. Perhaps putting it in those terms misconceives what a philosopher is or should be about.

I shall now turn to the task of sketching how I think a *proper philosophical* treatment of one of these problems of life should go, trying to show what a proper response to the above considerations would look like as I go along. I shall take, making the selection rather arbitrarily, the last problem described, namely, nationalism. My account here is for illustrative purposes only and will necessarily be sketchy and superficial or else I will not be doing metaphilosophy (examining what philosophical deliberation should be like) but be engaged in trying to solve, by at least a relatively full-scale account, a distinctive non-metaphilosophical philosophical problem.[14] Here I do not attempt any such thing, though I do not suggest that my account is not on the right track. I think it is, but what I want to do here is to show how we should proceed in considering the problem of nationalism philosophically. I seek to illustrate, by my procedures, and my commentary on my procedures, how this way of doing things could apply to the other problems of life as well. What is important here is that I have got the account of how to proceed roughly right. That, not my conclusion about nationalism, is what I want to draw attention to.

Neither the liberal nor the Marxist theoreticians of the 19th and early 20th centuries saw the import of nationalism.[15] It was generally rather optimistically thought that as economic wealth developed, as it became more evenly distributed, as regimes became more democratic, society more tolerant, and as the level of education rose, nationalism would gradually wither away. Perhaps it still is reasonable to believe that, since these conditions are still so far from being met. Since this is so, this confidence may, after all, not be misplaced, but, in any event, nationalistic aspirations have intensified rather than diminished and tolerance has hardly increased in the world. So we live with nationalism in a full-blown manner and, so situated, there is an almost kneejerk reaction among many intellectuals when they think about nationalism. They just take it for granted that nationalism is a bad thing. It is ethnocentric, jingoistically patriotic, intolerant, and sometimes even far worse; and it runs against a proper internationalism and universalism that should be high on our order of commitments.

When I first thought about the matter, I rather unreflectively reacted in this way. Nationalism was just no good. Now I think we must be much more nuanced about such matters.

Certainly, and unreservedly, I want to keep my internationalist commitments; I hope for the day when we will all see ourselves as members of a world community: a community of communities. I want to see a time when we have commitments to local communities harmoniously meshed with such a commitment to a community of communities. I want, that is, our sense of community to be global as well as local. But I have also come to see that we—or at least most of us—gain and sustain our identities and find recognition through local communities. We are not only women and men, we are particular kinds of women and men, belonging to a particular culture with a more or less distinctive scheduling of values and outlooks. We may–and I hope we will (as I have just remarked)–also see ourselves as internationalists. But our internationalism cannot be the whole thing; without local attachments we are adrift. It is not just journalistic rhetoric to say we have a need for roots.

The trick is not to let these local attachments become chauvinistic or ethnocentric. We need to avoid going from a firm acceptance and a taking to heart of the fact that these particular ways of doing things and viewing things mean a lot to us and that we want to maintain them and to pass them on to our children, on the one hand, to the assertion, on the other, that these are the only right ways of doing things and that all other ways of doing things are bad and must be stopped, or at least discouraged, if doing so is not too costly. A lot of people go from the first to the second and it makes nationalism something which is often imperialistic and nasty. Even where such attitudes only obtain in a rather attenuated form, the resultant nationalism, if not actually nasty, is rather oppressive, or at least stultifying. Moreover, recent events, particularly in parts of Eastern Europe and Africa, but in India as well, show clearly enough how horrible and destructive nationalism can be.[16] But we should beware of drawing hasty conclusions from these horrifying cases. Czechoslovakia is not Yugoslavia. It divided along nationalistic lines, perhaps not wisely, but without grave ills or much nationalistic exhibitionism. Similar things, though by no means perfectly, obtained for the Baltic Republics when they split from what was once the Soviet Union. And going back in time a bit to when Iceland and Norway separated from Denmark, this was done without violence, without much injustice, or without the claiming of cultural or any kind of superiority, and by now Iceland, Denmark, and Norway are the best of neighbors. And if Quebec separates from Canada, it will be entirely peaceful and there is no reason to expect that anyone's rights will be trampled on. So nationalist movements, and the forging of new nation states, can, under fortunate circumstances, be entirely nonviolent and without fanaticism, ethnocentrism, or lack of respect for the ways of minorities in the new nation states or the setting aside of internationalist commitments. We must not let the horrifying example of the Balkans, both now (1993-94) and in the war of 1912 and 1913, narrow our conception of what is possible.

Still, why be nationalistic? Quebec can peacefully, and without rights violations, separate from Canada. But should it? Why want your own nation state close to your own sense of nation-hood and cultural identity? Why care about being an American, a Swede, an Italian, a Basque, an Icelander, a Quebecois? The reply should be: because one's very identity and sources of recognition are tied up with it and without these things one's self-respect will be undermined. And to why care about self-respect, the answer is that self-respect is a very central human good; without it life will lack meaning. If self-respect is extensively absent in society, morality in that society will wither. It is essential for the very possibility of a good life for human beings. Why not just cultural identity without a nation state supporting that identity? Why not just a sense of being a people, a nation, if you will, without having your own nation state? Why not go for multicultural states with neutral, tolerant, liberal regimes? Why cannot one be Quebecois, Catalonian, Basque, Scots, Welsh, a Jew, or a Palestinian without having a nation state which gives authority to and specially protects and even nourishes those cultural convictions and ways of doing things? The important thing is to be a part of a state which has the virtues of liberal tolerance and which allows diverse cultures to flourish, if they have the internal steam, without being the representative or nourisher of any particular people or giving any culture an authoritative articulation or *privileged* protective cover. Let many flowers bloom, if they can, but do not have the state in the business of being the gardener. If a garden gets made the state should function to keep others from destroying it or stealing from it. But the state itself should not be in the gardening business.

In some places this may be the best solution. The best thing to go for, in such situations, may be a genuinely neutral liberal state. Where there are many distinct cultural groupings mixed in one territory with no group being in a clear majority long located in the territory, a nation state, representing, protecting, and nourishing the well-being of a given culture, a given national identity, is not the right kind of state to have no matter how rights-respecting it is of others. A U.S.A. for the Wasps or for the Jews or for the Italians would be a terrible thing. But *suppose,* to look at different situations, since the situation in the United States is rather atypical, France, Sweden, Holland, Germany or England were, through immigration into these nations, to come to be threatened with the loss of, or a severe attrition to, their cultural institutions, including most centrally their national languages. Then, in such a circumstance, they would, at least arguably, be justified in taking measures, though without violating the rights of their minorities, to protect their cultural institutions. They could pass, or reinforce if they already exist, laws to protect their national languages: laws concerning, for example, the language of instruction in the schools or the language of workplaces (say, beyond family units). People who come to a country as immigrants can reasonably be expected to adapt to that country: a country of their choice or at least a country they chose to come to. It is not at all like the situation of French Canadians in Quebec prior to the Quiet Revolution being forced to use an alien language (English) in their own homeland. They rightly resented and revolted against that. But with immigrants it is perfectly fair to require them to send their children to schools where the language of instruction is the national language of the country and to expect them to accept that that language will be the language of non-family workplaces. Such cultural protection and furthering is standardly, but not always, essential to protect the cultural identity of a nation. England without English and English cultural institutions would be a very different place than it is now and has been for a very long time. If majorities and cultural commitments shift over time, even where such protection and nourishment is in place, then that is a different matter. A people plainly shouldn't be forced to remain a people. Indeed a little realism will tell one that that is impossible to accomplish anyway. But where the majorities are in place and *value* their language and, where minority rights are protected, such cultural protection is justified. The state in such a circumstance can, and indeed should, be in the culture preservation business. It should be a good gardener, but surely not engage ethnic cleansing. It is perfectly legitimate to want to protect your culture and to have in such circumstances a nation state with such cultural commitments. It is a secure way—arguably the only secure way under contemporary conditions—of attaining and sustaining one's culture. If it can, as it at least arguably can, be done without violating minority rights, then such a state is both legitimate and desirable. A people can want that, to repeat, without thinking themselves a superior people, a favored people, holier than thou, or anything of the sort.

Nationalism is plainly very frequently a bad thing. It often takes one group to be superior, to be a favored folk. And it very frequently will be a favored folk which dislikes, disdains, perhaps even despises, or more typically, simply, with a condescending paternalistic sense of superiority, looks down on other folk, discriminating against them in subtle and often not so subtle ways. This is plainly unacceptable, but things need not be like that; nationalism need not stand against internationalism and tolerance. It does not even have to be paternalistically tolerant with a smiling sense of superiority. There are living examples—the Dutch, the various Scandinavian nations—where people typically have both a firm local identity along with more universalistic commitments. A sense of being a people, and taking steps to be able to securely live as such a people, steadfastly in possession of one's cultural institutions, seems to be essential for having a stable identity and that in turn is necessary for human flourishing. But all these things are perfectly compatible with internationalism and a respect for individual rights. This being so, it seems that *a certain kind* of nationalism is a good thing and that, under certain circumstances, it is desirable that that sense of nationhood—the having of a homeland whose governance is in the hands of the people whose home it is—be realized in a nation state. It is important for a people to have a homeland so governed.

V

It is crucial to remember that I am not trying for an argument that would be even remotely decisive in bringing the argument about nationalism to closure, but to show, I hope not unreasonably, something of how such an argument would go. Stepping back from what I said about nationalism and looking at the character of what I just said, it should be noted that what I said involved a mixture of rather straightforward factual judgments, more interpretive factual judgments, elucidatory and clarificatory remarks and normative judgments of various kinds, i.e., judgments about what is good and bad, right and wrong, desirable and undesirable, and reasonable and unreasonable. There is also no sharp division between heavily interpretive factual judgments and the normative, including moral, ones. It is also the case, as usually happens when philosophy is being done, that there were a number of modestly elucidatory or clarificatory remarks about what nationalism is, its varieties, what a nation or a culture is, what a nation state is, and the like. There is also a describing of options in a clear way and the drawing of relevant distinctions to make those options as clear as it is reasonable to expect they can be. And these clarificatory remarks, as well, blend into the interpretations including the interpretive ones with a rather sociological character.

It is also the case that sociological rather plainly factual claims were made or operated as background assumptions. They were such things as (1) the remark that nationalist aspirations are now very strong in many parts of the world and (2) that typically among intellectuals nationalism is thought to be a bad thing. The second of the sociological factual judgments just recorded *mentions* a moral normative judgment made by many intellectuals, but is not itself a moral judgment but a plainly factual judgment true or false in the rather straightforward way that factual judgments, by appeal to empirical evidence, can be established to be true or false. There is the further factual claim, more deeply interpretive, that nationalism frequently takes an ethnocentric and even a fanatical and destructive turn. Parts of Eastern Europe and India were cited as examples.

Let us follow up on this last remark. Consider what it takes to justify the plainly moral observation that nationalism is frequently dangerous, nasty, destructive, oppressive, and harmful to minorities within its sway. To be justified it is essential that the empirical side to this claim (for it has both a moral and empirical side) be established to be true. Events in Bosnia, religious clashes in India, and killings and oppression in Northern Ireland and Israel seem at least to confirm the claim or at least constitute confirming evidence. It should also be noted that these factual judgments are interpretive. It is hardly like the claim that in the territory that was once called Yugoslavia there are different nationalistic sentiments and aspirations. That is rather brutely factual (though things here are a matter of degree) while the claim that the different nationalistic aspirations in Bosnia have taken a brutal and destructive turn, while equally plainly true, and also plainly factual, is a strongly interpretive claim and, while being factual, it is itself also normative, involving, with the use of "brutal" and "destructive," plainly a moral judgment. That, in what was once Yugoslavia, there are different nationalistic sentiments and aspirations is a blandly neutral remark, though I do not mean to suggest by that that in being neutral it is thereby more accurate than the moral observational rooted in thick descriptions. Indeed it seems the moral observation—a thick description which is also a moral judgment—is clearly equally accurate, if not more accurate. If we want to know what the conditions are like in Bosnia, that last remark points more accurately to what the conditions are like. Our use of the thick descriptive-cum-normative (evaluative) words "brutal" and "destructive" can be in turn justified by giving the journalistic detail that we were given in 1993 about conditions in Bosnia. If those detailed journalistic accounts are not for the most part true, then the thick description-cum-evaluation is not justified. But the thing that is most relevant in the present context is that with them we have sociological factual claims—interpretive factual claims—that are at the same time normative, and that it is essential that these factual claims be true for the moral normative claims I made about nationalism in what was once Yugoslavia to be justified. Moreover, it is also the case that their truth is empirically ascertainable. There is no mystery here.

It is important in this connection to keep in mind that in setting out my illustrative case for nationalism as an illustration of how philosophy should concern itself with the problems of life I sprinkled my text with thick descriptive words (words which are both descriptive and normative). "Fanaticism," "contempt," "stultifying," "nasty," "exhibitionistic," "despise," "disdain," "horrible," "destructive," and "wisely" all occurred. This is par for the course for such discussions. No utilizing of a more neutral vocabulary would, as Isaiah Berlin has well argued, describe the situation more accurately.[17] It is a myth of rather old fashioned analytical philosophers to think otherwise. But this does not mean that these claims, with their thick descriptions, are not themselves empirical claims establishable as true or false in the standard ways empirical claims are so establishable.

I argued that a certain kind of nationalism is a good thing. I argued that it was legitimate to want to protect your own culture (the very conditions for being the people that you are and that you want to continue to be). I also claimed that self-respect is a central human good and that for human beings having a firm sense of identity and achieving recognition and respect for who you are (the particular kind of people that you are) and what you are doing are also vital goods. These things, I claimed, are necessary to sustain self-respect. Moreover, the good of self-respect, a sense of identity and the achievement of recognition, require people with a sense of who they are as a people (a sense of their culture, their history, their nationhood) and that this in modern conditions is not secure without a nation state committed to the cultural protection and enhancement of the people they represent. A liberal neutral state cannot protect the culture of a people as well as a state committed to the ideals and traditions of that culture. (This does not mean the non-neutral state is out to destroy or undermine or is even indifferent to the cultures of the minorities in its domain. Sweden, to take a very progressive example, takes care that their foreign workers and their families learn Swedish. But the children of these workers also get instruction in their mother tongue and learn of the culture they came from and that still plays an important part in their lives.) But to return to the main line of my argument, there is no identity without a local identity, the identity of being a particular sort of person who is a member of a determinate culture. (This is not to deny that a few people in certain culturally complex modern societies will have several cultural identities or that their identity will be in an unstable mix. But that itself is still a kind of local identity.) Furthermore, having such a local identity with the recognition and acceptance that goes with it is vital for the social bonding that is necessary to sustain a morality. There can, under modern conditions, be no secure culture or national identity without a nation state which nourishes it. Moreover, standardly, the protection of cultural identity requires the protection of the language or languages of that culture.

These last claims, though also interpretive, are definitely factual claims and for a case to be made for a certain kind of nationalism being a good thing, it is necessary that these factual claims be true. There is no just establishing moral or normative claims independently of what are the facts of the matter, though it is also true that it is almost invariably the case that there is also no even specifying of the facts of the matter independently of the use of thick descriptions which are both factual and normative. But the key thing to see here is that there is no such thing as *a purely normative inquiry* that could establish that nationalism sometimes is or isn't a good thing. Both moral deliberation and close empirical investigation are necessary and it is vital that they work in an integrated tandem.

VI

There were also in my sample discussion of nationalism claims of connections either causal or conceptual or not clearly one or the other. I claimed that while nationalism was frequently antiinternationalist and ethnocentric it was not necessarily so: that there was nothing in the very idea of nationalism that made it anti-internationalist or even indifferent to internationalist commitments and sentiments. Danes and Swedes, for example, are typically proudly, though not noisily, nationalistic, but they are also generally internationalist as well. You do not have to be a person with no country, no sense of nation, and no local attachments to be a good internationalist.

I also claimed that there can be no self-identity without the cultural identity that goes with local attachments, with the feeling that you belong to a community, and that there was no securing of self-identity without recognition and that they both require, for all people, that they stand in close relations of interdependence to some people of their own particular culture. Without recognition and a sense of self-identity, I further claimed, we will be alienated. We will not be able to sustain a sense that life has much meaning and without such a sense we will not flourish. All of these claims make claims about causal connections and they all require evidence (empirical evidence) if their truth is to be established. They also may require, as I gestured at in my sketch, some elucidation of the key terms involved if the claims are challenged in a certain way. Suppose, to illustrate, that against my claim that we can consistently and coherently have both nationalism with internationalism, it is responded that real or genuine nationalism is always fanatical, oppressing or denying, or at least discouraging or not fully accepting, the legitimacy of aspirations of those different from those who are the people who are hegemonic in the state in question. In its very nature, the claim goes, nationalism is ethnocentric.

I will then have to argue to maintain my causal claim—as I would indeed argue—that this really is to in effect make an arbitrary stipulation about the use of "nationalism," ruling out, by stipulative redefinition, the very possibility that someone could be a proud Icelander, proud of her nation, determined to preserve her cultural heritage and distinctive way of doing things, while still being internationalist in outlook. This flies in the face of the facts, for there are certainly plenty of such Icelanders; that is, Icelanders proud of being Icelandic and still thoroughly internationalist in outlook. To say, then, that they are not really nationalist is just to play with words, arbitrarily restricting the use of "nationalism." To so proceed is to in effect engage in what some philosophers have called arbitrary *persuasive* definition. One persuasively defines "nationalistic" in such a way so that such an Icelander cannot be nationalistic and so that nationalism cannot be a good thing. But that is just word-magic. We cannot regiment reality by so regimenting language.

A more serious challenge to the argument of my sketch is to challenge my claim that nationalism, with a nation state sustaining and enriching the culture of a majority, need not violate individual rights of the minorities in the society with a different cultural outlook from the majority. In making Christmas an official holiday, but not some part of Ramadan or the First of May, the State, some will argue, is protecting the rights of the majority and neglecting the rights of some minorities. Where the cultures are identified, partly along linguistic lines, and further where one culture with one language is much in the majority, and the State, to protect that culture, passes laws about the language of instruction in the schools and the language of the workplace and the language of store signs, then the rights of people, the claim continues, who wish in these situations to use another language, have been violated. The non-neutral state may wish to avoid doing so, but it cannot in fact do so. Such violations of rights just go with the structure of the situation. Indeed—or so it is sometimes said—the free speech rights of these people have been violated. The state, the charge is, cannot both engage in cultural preservation and not violate rights.

I shall now argue that these things need not be so. Let us imagine a certain modern tolerably wealthy industrial state with two distinct peoples (cultures): The Flores, who constitute over three quarters of the population, and the Verlangs. They are economically, educationally, and culturally on a par, but their cultures are in certain respects importantly different and, while crossovers and mixes and assimilations are not forbidden or even culturally discouraged, they do not, as a matter of fact, happen very often. The reality of the situation is that we more or less have two solitudes with each culture keeping pretty much to itself. Suppose further that, while the Verlangs are decidedly a minority in that state, that that state, let us call it Floresland, is surrounded on all sides by a much larger cluster of Verlang states: states with a Verlang culture and with a population that speaks Verlangish. Flores, on the other hand, is pretty much limited to Floresland. The Verlangers outside of Floresland are not aggressively disposed toward Floresland, but by the very fact of the size of the Verlang constellation and, with its greater size, greater wealth, the Verlangish media (television, radio, magazines, books, etc.) flood Floresland. Also, with their greater wealth, Verlang industries penetrate extensively into Floresland. A good portion of the industries in Floresland come to be owned and controlled by Verlangers. However, the pervasiveness of the Verlang cultural influence, including Verlangish, notwithstanding, the Flores still want very much to preserve their culture, including their own language.

Suppose there is in Floresland a long established practice of having state schools in which the language of instruction is Flores and of there being, as well, other state schools in Floresland in which the language of instruction is Verlangish. Suppose further that the two different school systems are equally well kept up and the like. Suppose immigrants coming into Floresland, sometimes Verlangish speakers and sometimes not, tend massively to go to Verlang schools for the quite understandable reason that

that is either already their mother tongue or that, for nonVerlangish speaking and non-Flores speaking immigrants, having their children learn Verlangish and then perhaps, but only as a second language, Flores, will, given the great mass of Verlangish speakers in the greater area surround Floresland, give their children far greater *de facto* mobility than if they were Flores speakers and were assimilated into Flores culture. But suppose the State of Floresland and the government of that state is committed to sustaining Flores-culture *and* the Flores people—who are three quarters of the population in Floresland—very much want their way of life, including their language, protected. Suppose further that demographers point out to the government, and more generally in the society as well, that without corrective legislation, given the normal pattern of immigration, in two hundred years Floresland will no longer be a country with the culture of the Flores, but, in everything except name, it will be another Verlangland. The Flores culture, that is, will be swallowed up in the Verlang Ocean. Coming to see that that is the case, the government, with the support of the majority (it takes a referendum), passes legislation that says that immigrants coming into Floresland (whether Verlangish-speaking or not) must send their children to Flores speaking schools, that the language of workplaces with more than forty people must be Flores, and that store signs and the like, while they may contain more than one language, must have Flores in a prominent place. For the native Verlangish speakers in Floresland, their Verlangish speaking schools are protected and extra funds are provided for second-language instruction in Flores, should the Verlangish school boards wish to use it, though Flores instruction is not required in these schools. Similarly free night schools teaching Flores are provided for immigrant adults, or indeed anyone else, to utilize if they choose.

I claim that in such a circumstance no one's rights, free speech or otherwise, have been violated. When immigrants come to another country—something they choose to do and are not forced to do—they are expected to adapt to that country. If I emigrate from England to the United States, I do not have my rights violated if I have to drive on the right hand side of the road rather than on the left. If I emigrate from Albania to Australia, my rights are not violated if I cannot get bilingual Albanian/English street signs established. If I emigrate from Iran to Ireland, my rights are not violated if I cannot get some days during Ramadan declared a public holiday along with Christmas. If I immigrate from Denmark to New Zealand my rights are not violated if I am forced to educate my children in either English or Maori, though, if I am a native Maori-speaking New Zealander, my rights would be violated if I were forced to educate my children in English. These are just the things that immigrants rightly expect, or rightly should expect, when they choose a new country with a new culture as their homeland. They can keep certain of their old cultural ways if they wish, but they must adjust to the ways of their adopted country as well. So the government of Floresland violates no rights in passing the school, workplace, and sign language legislation I have described to protect their culture. They would violate rights if they passed laws either forbidding or taking away proportionally equal support for Verlangish speaking schools or laws prohibiting nonimmigrant citizens who are Flores speakers from sending their children to Verlangish speaking schools or vice-versa.

If the Flores speakers do not care enough about their culture to keep it from collapsing into the Verlangish culture or actually want to assimilate into the Verlangish culture, so be it. In that case (a rather unlikely one) they should be allowed to do so. The government should not paternalistically act to preserve a culture its members do not want to preserve. That is elementary democracy. What is the far more likely scenario is that the people will wish to preserve their own language and culture. In that circumstance the government can and should act as I have described vis-a-vis immigrants where the Flores-speakers want to preserve their own culture and its is reasonably believed to be threatened without that protection. (Note again how important it is to get the facts right. Moreover, there can be a getting of the facts right even if there is no such thing as the one true description of the world.)

VII

I have argued that self-respect is a very central human good and that both self-identity and recognition are necessary for self-respect being securely in place. But we will not have much in the way of recognition or a firm sense of self-identity if our lives are not in part anchored in local attachments. We may very well also have—and indeed should have—an internationalist outlook and care about the attaining of global justice, but we also need local attachments. We may care—and I think we should care—about what goes on in Africa as well as what is happening in Canada and the United States. But we need local attachments to have a sense of ourselves and for our lives to flourish.

There are empirical claims here, as we have seen, that could be challenged, though I think these challenges could be readily met. But suppose the empirical challenges are successfully met and in that way things are, as I have described them, thick descriptions and all. But even so, this primacy-of-human-problems-philosophy approach—this broadly Deweyian conception—still faces two traditional philosophical challenges: one, as some philosophers like to call it, metaethical and the other normative ethical. If my sketch of an examination of nationalism, plus my remarks about the sketch are kept clearly in view, it will be seen that I carried on the discussion without recourse to anything like traditional ethical theory. Neither metaphysics nor epistemology raised their ugly heads, nor did traditional ethical theory either metaethical or normative ethical. I appealed neither to Utilitarian, Kantian, Hobbesian, or Aristotelian principles or methods nor did I make analyses of moral or other normative terms or sentences or try to display the logic of moral reasoning or normative inquiry. I used a bit of philosophical terminology, namely, "descriptive judgments," "normative judgments," "thick descriptions," and the like. But that was principally a matter of shorthand. I, of course, tried to reason carefully and to make a case for what I was saying. That is to say, I worried about my arguments being sound arguments and I tried to place them in an illuminating narrative. But surely these things are not enough to take us to grand philosophical theory or indeed any kind of philosophical theory at all. I, or so at least I believe, appealed to no metaethical or normative ethical theories, let alone metaphysical or epistemological theories or conceptions. I was resolutely, all along the way, commonsensical and I travelled philosophically light.

The challenge I now turn to is the claim, against what I have been arguing, that the various resolutions available to particular problems of life all actually, at least implicitly, rely on some metaethical and/or normative ethical theory. They are, that is, more tied up in traditional philosophical thinking than I recognize. For arguments for some reasonable resolution to problems of life facing us to be sound, the contention goes, the arguments for some presupposed metaethical and normative ethical theory also must themselves be sound. If they are not, the whole thing collapses. There is, the contention goes, no escaping metaethical and normative ethical theory. I, in turn, think that that is false. I can, and should, for my problems-of-life approach, my broadly Deweyian approach, leave these matters to benign neglect.

The metaethical challenge challenging my claim will go: you appeal to the good of selfrespect, to its being a central good, to self-identity, to cultural identity, to recognition, and to nationalism, nation, homeland, and culture. But until we have a reasonable elucidation or analysis of these terms we really do not know what we are talking about. What do we mean by "self-respect" anyway and how does it differ from "self-esteem" and what do we mean by saying it is a good, let alone a central good? What is it for something to be a central good and what is the difference between a good (a value) and a norm?

Self-identity, the challenge could continue, may even be more illusive than self-respect. Problems in the philosophy of mind make it evident how difficult it is to understand what personal identity comes to let alone something like self-identity which is taken to be a form of cultural identity.

It is entirely unclear what we are talking about here. To know whether self-respect and self-identity play the important moral and normative role you ascribe to them, we first must do our metaethical homework and find out what we are talking about. To be clear about what we mean has always been a central virtue in philosophy. One cannot, to do that, stay on surface, as I am proposing to do; it is necessary to engage in metaethical analysis.

Such strong claims for metaethical theory or metaethical analysis seem to me to rest on a mistake. We very well know what chairs, Germans, and states are and we are able to use these conceptions to make some true claims, and some false claims as well, without knowing, or even having much of a clue about, what the correct analysis of the terms "chair," "German," and "state" are. Normally, to give a *second-order* account of a term (an account of the use or meaning of the term, an account which talks about our talk) we first must have a firm grasp of the use of that term. This need not be true for all terms, but it must be true for most terms for a meta-analysis—a *secondorder* analysis—to even get off the ground. "Self-respect" and "Self-identity" in this respect are like "chair," "German" or "state." We can be in considerable doubt about the proper *analysis* of both these terms, while in many familiar contexts being able to effortlessly use the terms and, as well, being confident, or reasonably confident, about the truth of some claims concerning people's selfrespect or self-identity. Without knowing the proper analysis of "self-respect," we can be pretty confident that the following statements are true, as well as confident about what we would need to confirm their truth: "Being told repeatedly by the other children at school that his mother is a whore and his father a pimp undermined his self-respect"; "The repeated beatings and sexual assaults from her father destroyed her self-respect"; and "Her inability to get a job and her having to live on welfare hurt her self-respect." We know the sort of behavior and attitudes that would count in favor of such claims using such terms and we can be confident about this while being not at all confident—perhaps even at a loss—about their proper *analysis* or *elucidation.* The same thing can and should be said for self-identity and the other remarks I put in the metaethicist's mouth. To do the Deweyian thing, to come to grips (at least for my sample problem, but I think it can be generalized) in a reflective and disciplined way with the problems of human life, we do not, generally speaking, have to engage in metaethical analysis. (Here something parallel is going on to what we said about G. E. Moore's defense of common sense in Chapter 3.)

Only if there was some *real doubt,* and not some merely contrived doubt or some possible doubt (what C. S. Peirce called a "paper doubt"), about what we were talking about, so that because of the doubt we could not get on with our deliberation—our first-order deliberation—or our actual moral inquiry, would we need to engage in an examination of the meaning of the terms in question. (This was one of the great insights of the pragmatists, particularly of C. S. Peirce.) We need a context where we have a real live doubt about what it is we are talking about for such an inquiry to have philosophical relevance. Otherwise, so exercising ourselves is not a display of proper philosophical rationality, but just an arbitrary blocking of inquiry. Standardly, in coming to grips with the problems of life, no such metaethical detour is desirable, let alone required. (I have said very little in my above remarks about metaethical *theory.* Perhaps, after all, it has some kind of foundational or otherwise grounding relevance to such a Deweyian problems-of-life-approach? I return to that in the next chapter.)

VIII

Similar things, I believe, should be said about the normative ethical theory challenge. It might be claimed that by appealing to the good of self-respect, as I did, I was implicitly presupposing a Kantian theory and for that presupposition to be justified I would have to establish the soundness of a Kantian theory and its superiority to any alternative ethical theory or at least to the competitors that are around. I, in turn, deny that I am presupposing or in anyway need a Kantian or any other kind of normative ethical theory. They, I shall argue, actually get in the way of such a Deweyian treatment of the problems of life as much as do metaethical theories. We can and should get along without normative ethical theories. They are impediments, not aids, to a fruitful reflective examination of the problems of life. They lead us on to a variety of false paths of investigation by giving us an illusory sense of what abstract systematization and articulation of principles can achieve. So stressing normative ethical theory leads us, if we take a non-skeptical route, to believe that what is required to solve such problems of life—to get a reasonable resolution about what is to be done—is to find the right method yielding the right principles which will give us the truth about the moral life and the good life for human beings. Careful reflective and rigorously pursued philosophical investigation will yield us a true morality. We need finally to get these matters clear to the light of reason. But this will require, the claim goes, doing systematic normative ethical theory. Alternatively—though still in the same ball game—a normative ethicist might believe that no normative ethical theory can be shown to be true. Philosophers have failed in their attempts to discover the one true morality. Abandoning any attempt to articulate an objective normative ethical theory, she will take a skeptical turn and contend that we have discovered no such moral truth, moral knowledge, or a foundation for the moral life and that indeed—as far as we can see—none is to be found.[18] But, skeptical though she is, she will agree with the non-skeptic that we need such a foundation to rationally resolve the problems of life. The trouble—and that is what makes her a skeptic—is that we do not have it and cannot reasonably be expected—or so she believes—to get it. Still, she also believes that a Deweyian approach, such as I have illustrated, doesn't push matters far enough and rests unwittingly on arbitrary, conventional, and even ethnocentric starting points and conclusions. Surely we want philosophy, the ethical skeptic could claim, to come to grips with the problems of life, but, if it is genuinely to do so, it must push things further than what such a pragmatism dreams of. About this the skeptic and non-skeptic in normative ethical theory agree.

Such a traditionalist claim, in many ways similar to the skeptical and foundationalist epistemological claims we discussed in Chapters 2 and 4, whether skeptical or non-skeptical, seems to me thoroughly mistaken. My appeal to the good of self-respect, even to self-respect being a central good, and to the value of self-identity in sustaining the bonds of morality, does not commit me to a Kantian morality or in anyway presuppose one. A Kantian morality is an extreme form of rationalism seeking to ground morality in pure practical reason. A thoroughly rational agent will come, Kantians believe, to acknowledge that she must accept what Kant calls the categorical imperative if she is to act and live rationally. She must, that is, always, where rules or maxims come into play, act on rules or maxims which are universal: rules which everyone, or at least every rational everyone, in the circumstance where the rule or maxim applies, must accept, and act in accordance with, if we should act rationally. But it is doubtful whether there are any such rules or maxims or at least any with any substance. (And without substance they could not serve as action-guides.) There is certainly no consensus about whether there are, or even could be, such rules or maxims. And, even if there could be such rules, there is no consensus about *what* they are. But what is clear is that a belief in the goodness of self-respect is not derivable from the categorical imperative, and what is even clearer is that someone who takes self-respect to be a very fundamental good need have no notion at all of the categorical imperative or come to believe, when the categorical imperative and its rationale is explained to her, that her moral convictions require such a rationale or that her belief in the good of self-respect is grounded in reason such that any well-informed person who reasons correctly, and is not otherwise irrational, must accept that conviction of hers. Rather she could more plausibly believe that that conviction of hers is one of the convictions—indeed a very central one—that is deeply embedded in the morality of her society and some other moralities as well and that it is something she is firmly committed to and concerning which there is no reason at all to be doubtful. It is true enough that it is not a self-evident principle, so it is *logically* possible to doubt it. But that is true for any other substantive principle as well as for any law of nature or statement of fact. *Possible* doubts are not real doubts and the fact is that there is no actual reason whatsoever to doubt it. Nothing thrown up in inquiry, deliberation, or in living the moral life gives us any reason to doubt it. It fits together with our firm convictions and our beliefs about the world. No conflict actually generated in genuine moral deliberation or in the moral life gives rise to a doubt about it. We do not need the categorical imperative for its support and we have no reason to believe that it presupposes the categorical imperative.

Kant also says that the only thing good without qualification or good without exception is a good will. Similar things should be said here to what I said above. It is not entirely clear what this claim of Kant's means, but it seems to mean, at least in part, that it is intentions which most deeply count in morality. But suppose a person with good intentions—with a good will—is so irrational, so self-destructive, and so dangerous to others that he, like some of the characters in the late plays of Eugene O'Neill, brings great suffering, insecurity, and unhappiness to those he is close to and indeed even cares very much about. It is clear enough that he means well, but he is just too irrational to have a proper control of himself. Perhaps we should not blame him, but we should not say that all that morally matters or what matters most fundamentally is his having a good will. It would be far better that he be just a man of good morals, acting rather conventionally and habitually, but still prudently and reasonably, in accordance with the moral practices of his society (unless his society was something like a Nazi society) and sometimes not from the best of motives, tailoring, as he does, his morals to his own advantage, than to act so irrationally and so self–and others destructively–though, as a man of principle, from good will. Neither type person is very attractive morally speaking. But even if we find the O'Neillian irrationalist the less unattractive (even his mis-shaped integrity counting for something), we would, and should, still prefer the other sort to be around in the world than the O'Neillian. They cause much less suffering and unhappiness in the world than such O'Neillian moralistic irrationalists. The old adage that the way to hell is paved with good intentions is to the point. Happiness and avoidance of suffering isn't everything in ethics and integrity is a very important virtue. But an integrity that generates so much misery is something we could do without. If the choice is between a man of good morals and a man of moral principle who behaves as does the O'Neillian irrationalist, then the reasonable thing to do is to go for the man of good morals.

If, in turn, the Kantian responds that if a person so acts (acts as the O'Neillian irrationalist acts) then he really doesn't have a good will, it then becomes unclear what it is to have a good will. So either good will, on the one hand, is taken rather straightforwardly and it is not always unqualifiedly (exceptionlessly) good or *perhaps* sometimes even good at all, or, on the other hand, it is taken in some rather special way in which it is unclear what is being claimed and why we should take it, so understood, to be unqualifiedly good. The modern common sense view is that there are many things which are good, and indeed some of them are very fundamental goods, but none of them are unqualifiedly or exceptionlessly good. There are contexts in which something which is normally good—a good thing to do or a good attitude to have—is not good or at least not unqualifiedly good. We have a cluster of very important goods which we should consider together and to balance one off against the other.

So we have good reason not to accept Kant's, or some modified Kantian, doctrine. But not accepting it does not at all jeopardize the common sense belief that the good of self-respect is a very great good. And even if, against what I have just argued, we do accept the Kantian doctrine, it does not suffice to establish the good of self-respect. An O'Neillian self-destructive irrationalist might have good will—good intentions—but have only loathing for himself and even further believe, that other people, if they can see beyond their illusions about themselves, will also loath themselves. Self-respect, he believes, is only possible with self-deception—a failure to acknowledge the truth about oneself and of others: to realize what contemptible little animals we really are. Self-respect, given the way we human beings are constituted, can only be attained, the O'Neillian claims, by selfdeception and, like it or not, it is very hard to so deceive ourselves all the time. Our big brains get in the way. Light sometimes will come in, for a fleeting moment, and then we will see, for a moment at least, what despicable creatures we really are. But still, he could maintain, in spite of that, a good will, whether anyone can have it or not, is an unqualified and exceptionless good. It is just that we human beings are so rotten that that is something we seldom achieve. An Augustinian or Jansenist Christian, full of the sense of the utter depravity and sinfulness of human beings, *might* reason in a similar way, though he is less likely to give such weight to good will. So we cannot go from good will to the good of self-respect. Self-respect in this respect stands on its own; it does not presuppose or require a Kantian or any similar doctrine of good will.

There are other Kantian doctrines such as we should see ourselves as members—all with equal membership, all having equal moral standing—of a kingdom of ends where each person is an end in himself and all equally should have that status or standing. This is an attractive ideal, *perhaps* even tied up conceptually with what it is to take the moral point of view, at least in modern societies. But, even more so than the two doctrines discussed above, it is vague and indeterminate. Perhaps really to respect ourselves requires that we respect others as well, regarding them as having the same status or the same moral standing as ourselves. That is part of what it means to believe that we are all members of a kingdom of ends. However, we need to face the fact that in slave societies and in Aristocratic societies, some people–standardly the elite–not infrequently maintained, or at least certainly seemed to maintain, a secure sense of self-respect without any such Kantian belief. They did not think that everyone should have such an equal status or equal standing. Some of them even thought that some people are so animal-like (slaves and the like) that they are not capable of self-respect. There were some beings, they thought, who hardly counted as moral persons. These beings, on their view, had no moral standing. They could, they believed, without moral mistake, do with them what they liked or utterly ignore their needs and interests. (Much later down the historical path, Nazis felt that way about Jews. Most Nazis grovelled at the Nuremburg trials. But some hung in there, revealing a sense of self-respect, showing that selfrespect can take very distorted forms.) Yet these aristocratic slave owners sometimes firmly maintained their own sense of self-respect. Some of us think they should not have and we may very well be right. But now we are on different grounds. I certainly think that it would have been far better if they could have gone to such a Kantian and universalist belief. I do not see the justification for their making a special case of themselves and their peers. But that should not gainsay the fact that they could, and sometimes did, have a belief in the goodness of self-respect and, in spite of, or perhaps even because of, their Nietzschean disdain for the common people–the herd–they maintained their self-respect.

Kantian ethical theory is not, of course, the sole competitor in the field of normative ethical theory or even by any means the clear, or even unclear, winner, if there is, or even could be, any such winner at all. Besides Kantian theories there are various varieties of utilitarianism, Aristotelian ethical theories with their perfectionist and virtue ethics offshoots, and forms of rightsbased or duty-based ethical theory that are pluralistic in the way that Kant's ethics is not. They are, like Kant's theory, what philosophers call "deontological ethical theories," giving the right priority–that is why they are called "deontological"–over the good. They further take it, being pluralistic theories, that we have a cluster of defeasible rights or duties that are foundational, or at least fundamental, in ethics. If the pluralistic deontological theory in question is rights-based, they will, of course, be rights; if it is duty-based they will be duties. Moreover, the pluralist deontology could, of course, though this would be a bit more messy, be a mixed deontological theory appealing to both rights and duties without in general giving either priority. For such deontologists, these rights and duties are taken to be defeasible or *prima facie* rights and duties. *Taken as such,* they are said to be self-evident moral truths that we must just intuitively grasp. That notwithstanding, sometimes they conflict or one applies in a particular situation and another does not. Which *prima facie* duty is our *actual* duty that must be acted on in the situation in question or which *prima facie* right yields an *actual* right that we can categorically rightly and not just conditionally insist on being something that we can act on, if we choose, will be something that requires another rational intuition where we just have to recognize ("see") what, everything considered, is suitable to the situation in question: the thing to do, all things considered, in the case of a duty, or the thing we can act on, all things considered, given a right.

The problems-of-life-account I have been characterizing and am now defending may *seem* on the face of it closer to a pluralistic deontology than to the other normative ethical theories. But that is an illusion. It has no view on the priority of the right over the good or, for that matter, on the priority of the good over the right. It is through and through contextualist and has no such general view. It also makes no appeal to moral intuitions (or any kind of intuitions), has no doctrine of moral truth, and has no systematic account of *prima facie* duties or rights and their relation to our actual duties or rights or to what we should do everything considered.

What they do have in common is a pluralism—the belief that there are many sometimes competing or conflicting views about what is right or good—and a taking very seriously indeed of our common sense moral convictions, convictions that both conceptions also share with Kantians. But the Deweyian view does not share the deontological theorists' (whether pluralistic or Kantian) foundationalism or their epistemology with its appeal to rational intuitions (so-called "rational intuitions") yielding *a priori* necessary moral truths. Deweyians, and Rawlsians as well, benignly neglect such things and there is no good reason to think that their accounts require them.

Similar things hold for the other normative ethical theories vis-a-vis a problems-of-life-account. Ideal utilitarian or perfectionist theories, for example, with their foundationalism, appeal to rational intuitions and a plurality of intrinsic goods (rather than *prima facie* rights or duties). But they have many of the same difficulties as deontological accounts, plus the additional difficulty of accounting for the notion of intrinsic goodness and of the justifying of a strictly maximizing account of morality. Utilitarians want to bring the greatest sum total possible of intrinsic goodness into the world and see that it stays there. But, as distinct from classical utilitarianism, ideal utilitarianism is pluralistic about intrinsic goodness and it recognizes that intrinsic goods sometimes conflict and that, when this obtains, we somehow must just see (intuit) which good, in a particular situation in question, takes pride of place as being productive of the most good. This leaves ascertainment of what is the sum total good (the greatest amount of goodness in the world) very indeterminate and even very problematical. We do not know what it would be like for such a state of affairs to be achieved. It does not look like we have anything very plausible or perhaps even coherent here. Moreover, and centrally here, in appealing to the good of self-respect and to the value of self-identity and recognition, there is no reason to think that I am presupposing such an ideal utilitarianism or perfectionism or any doctrine of, or utilization of, a conception of intrinsic goodness, let alone of maximizing intrinsic goodness. In saying selfrespect, self-identity, and recognition are good, I do not give to understand that I am saying or implying that they are intrinsically good or, for that matter, instrumentally good. I do not buy into that typology, that classification system, and it should not be read into my account.

Similar things even more obviously obtain for classical utilitarianism. My modest Deweyianism is not committed, as are the classical utilitarians, to the belief that pleasure or happiness and pleasure or happiness alone is *intrinsically* good and that the thing to do, morally speaking, is to maximize, or try to maximize, the amount of pleasure or happiness in the world. It is very questionable that pleasure or happiness is the *sole* intrinsic good, though, if anything is intrinsically good, they certainly seem to be. It is also very questionable indeed if maximizing the amount of pleasure or happiness in the world is the sole or even the most important moral imperative. It may not even be a moral imperative at all. To so regard it would require more sacrifices from people than it is reasonable to expect them to make and it neglects, except as an instrumental consideration to get the greatest totals of pleasure, questions of distribution and thus of justice (fairness in who gets what) which is arguably at the core of morality. But the Deweyian with her thoroughly contextualist views need take no position on these controversial matters. In arguing that a kind of nationalism under certain circumstances is justified, I took no view on these matters and my account presupposes no such view.

Some contemporary utilitarians drop talk of happiness or pleasure and speak of maximizing preference-satisfaction no matter what those preferences are. This, as far as I can see, has the same difficulties about justice as the classical view and while there are gains over taking happiness as the sole intrinsic good there are losses as well. Simply to talk of preferences makes the end to be attained very indefinite. We seem with that not to have much of a picture of a good life for human beings. Still, sneaking in an implicit egalitarian principle of distribution, indeed a principle which is not maximizing, the utilitarian claim is that what society should aim at is to bring into existence and to sustain a world in which as many people as possible could have as much as possible of whatever it is that they want that is compatible with all others being so treated.[19] Put otherwise, the

sort of society that we should seek and, if ever we have it, try to sustain is one where there is equal satisfaction of compossible desires for everyone or, alternatively and differently, an equal chance for the equal satisfaction of compossible desires. This, on any of its formulations, links a requirement
of fairness (an egalitarian form of justice) with a maximizing doctrine. This view has all kinds of difficulties, including how we could ever make even a shrewd guess about when as many people as possible have as much as possible of whatever it is that they want.[20] We need also to recognize how problematical the utilitarian belief is that all preferences or desires, or even just all compossible ones, should be treated as being on a par. Some seem just to be degrading or utterly frivolous preferences that do not even seem to count morally. *Perhaps,* where he is taking as morally relevant only compossible desires, the utilitarian should just bite that bullet. No desire *just in itself,* he should reassert, where it can exist harmoniously with the desires of others, should be regarded just in itself as evil or as degrading or something to be shunned. But that he, or we following him here, should bite that bullet is not obvious and again there is no reason why a Deweyian, taking a problems-of-life-approach, should take any position here at all. *Perhaps* something more can be said for something closer to a hedonistic utilitarianism than is usually thought. But a Deweyian contextualism can safely ignore such arcane issues.

Modern non-Thomist Aristotelians are perhaps more in harmony with this Deweyian approach than any other normative ethical theorists, pluralistic deontologists *perhaps* aside. What, Aristotelians claim, we need to think about most centrally in our moral deliberations is about the good life for human beings. To ascertain that, we need to determine the distinctive capacities and needs of human beings and their proper scheduling. What we need to ascertain, these Aristotelians claim, is what is essential to the proper flourishing of human beings, what is essential to their nature as men and as women. Lacking those things, human beings would not be able to function properly, for they would lack something essential to their very nature. So we must ascertain the distinctive human capacities and the distinctive human needs and, as well, their priorities when not all needs can be satisfied.

Classically, such a view has been closely linked with, indeed perhaps even tied to, difficulties (perhaps even incoherencies) about talk of the function of human beings and about their essential nature. Perhaps, not being artifacts or just bodily parts or identifiable with the social roles we have (such as being doctors or mechanics), we, *just as human beings,* have no function: have no built-in purpose. This would seem to be particularly likely if we are not, as we may well not be, created by God for a purpose or indeed created by God at all. But perhaps we could put all talk of the function of human beings aside along with metaphysical talk of essences and the like and just treat human beings as a natural kind and go, in doing so, for a kind of minimal Aristotelianism. Doing that, we then look for distinctive capacities of human beings as well as the distinctive needs that they have—capacities and needs that they all have, or at least all have if they are not seriously incapacitated. We try to ascertain that and then we look for the role these capacities and needs play in human life. It is not implausible to hypothesize that the satisfaction of these needs and the realization of these capacities are necessary for the flourishing of any human life.

To this it can be responded that there is disagreement about the comparative importance of these different needs when they conflict, as they sometimes do, without it being evident that the criteria for making a pecking order of needs can be read off human nature or has a cross-cultural consensus. Moreover, do we have a good theory which enables us to identify needs and, furthermore, why give such weight to needs rather than to wants and why not heed Nietzsche's injunction that man is something to be surpassed?[21] We also have the problem of whether we have a non-ethnocentric account of human needs and of the essential nature of human beings. And what, if anything, would constitute self-realization is not clear. Whether we can expect any consensus about what human excellence consists in is likewise unclear. Perhaps such notions are essentially contested?

I do not mean to give to understand that these problems are so intractable as not to have reasonable resolutions or, in some instances, dissolutions; and I am not saying that contemporary secular Aristotelians such as Martha Nussbaum, Amartya Sen, and Bernard Williams are not well on their way to their resolution.[22] I do not know whether that is so, but it is not unreasonable to think that it might be. But what I do want to say is that again the Deweyian, to come to grips with the problems of life, need take no position concerning these contentious matters. He need not assume that there are good answers to these questions and that we have a good general theory, let alone that he has answers, to say nothing of having a general theory, concerning what human excellence comes to or what would constitute the good life for human beings. Both the Deweyian and, I would further argue, the Rawlsian can legitimately set these issues aside. Indeed they not only can, they should do so, and, free from them, get on with coming to grips with the problems of life. This is the really crucial thing. The belief that we need some general backup theory to ground—really ground—our carefully thought out views about the problems of life is an illusion, indeed a traditional metaphysically inspired illusion. The metaphysical tradition dies slowly.

IX

I want now to point to a way, free of traditionalist conceptions, I would view philosophy as centrally concerned with the problems of human life and thus centrally concerned with moral, political, and social philosophy. In philosophizing we should do this, I have argued perhaps *ad nauseam*, not only free from metaphysical and epistemological concerns, but, as well, we should—and this has been the burden of my arguments in this chapter—just as resolutely set aside the problems of metaethics and normative ethical theory, or at least systematic normative ethical theory. My Deweyian account does not presuppose a position in metaethics, the epistemology of morals or epistemology more generally, in metaphysics, or the acceptance of a distinctive normative ethical theory such as Aristotelianism, utilitarianism, perfectionism, Kantianiasm, or pluralistic deontology. It need not say that all these things are moonshine, but it does say that resolving or taking a stance on such issues is not needed for such a broadly Deweyian account. Involving oneself with them stands more in the way of resolving such human issues than it contributes towards solving them or giving us a rational purchase on them. But such an account does not eschew piecemeal elucidation and clarification where there is a live puzzle about a concept, a claim, or an argument. It also seeks perspicuous representation and clear sound arguments embedded in narratives which are to the point and clearly articulated. Those things, the point about narratives aside, are good residues from analytic philosophy.

This problems-of-life approach is resolutely contextual. Starting with the common sense and scientific beliefs of our time and place—the time and place of the persons whose problems they are—it seeks to resolve our problems, or at least give us a better purchase on our problems, and fix our beliefs concerning such matters. For us (that is, for we moderns in modernizing societies and, as well, for the educated few others in societies on the edge of modernity who, in key respects, have been similarly acculturated), we look in the domain of morals not only to our scientific beliefs and our non-moral common sense beliefs, but also to the most deeply embedded, most firmly held, considered convictions of the actual morality of our society, those considered convictions concerning which there is an overlapping consensus in our society among the diverse reasonable subgroups (subcultures).[23] (It is plain here that we have a very pluralistic society.)

The use of "reasonable" understandably will raise a red flag. I do not intend to define it or to mean anything very precise by it. I do not believe it can be usefully given an utterly context-free and culture-free articulation. Indeed I do not think we can even get very close to that. And within a given culture, it is a very contextual concept. But it is meant to be used to provide a rationale for not trying to get within or into the overlapping consensus cult groups, the KKK, the Aryan League, the Jewish Defense League, and the like. The cutoff point is not sharp. We have here nothing like an algorithm. And it may be wise to have a policy of keeping on talking as long as such groups as mentioned above do not act. But there are limits. The Nazis have made that historically clear. Still there is no sharp cutoff point. Are Christian Scientists, extremely orthodox Jews, and flat earthers beyond the pale? I doubt it, for, while there is obviously much they do not agree with with the more mainstream groups of our culture, they are still a part of our culture and there is also a lot they do agree on with the more mainstream members. That this is so is not very frequently remarked on, for a lot of the things on which there is agreement are in background beliefs of our culture and are so obvious as to not readily occasion even taking note of let alone commenting on. But given those points of agreement in deliberating with them, we can find a toehold for discussion. Starting from where we do agree, we can then proceed, albeit hesitantly and slowly, from there. The going will be shaky; caution and skepticism are in order. But it is not impossible, given good will on all sides, that some consensus about some important issues could be achieved over time. Think how slow the coming of religious tolerance in the stable capitalist democracies was from the exhausted intolerance and the religious hatred that existed as the long wars of religion slowly came to an end. At first, people tolerated each other because they could not do otherwise, for they had fought to a stalemate. Only slowly did they come to attach a positive value to tolerance itself.

However, with the subgroups who maintain what I call *reasonable outlooks:* outlooks which accept the well-established, widely and readily available scientific beliefs in our culture and time, where people having these outlooks have a respect for evidence, careful argument, and plausible presentation, care about and utilize in their reasoning the social and historical facts readily available to them, are people who are tolerant of others, respect democratic procedures, and, in many circumstances (I don't rule out Lenin and Trotsky) respect constitutional arrangements, who take all human beings as having an equal status and moral standing, and who care about human well-being and the avoidance of suffering for humankind: each is to count for one and none to count for more than one. *People in our culture—I do not say only in our culture—who share these things are people with a reasonable outlook.* It is here where we have the conditions for, and in part the achievement of, an overlapping consensus. (Note that people could be perfectly rational and not have some of those commitments. Rational people need not, in my non-eccentric sense, be reasonable, though reasonable people will also be rational.)

People with such reasonable outlooks (the above specification gives something of what I mean by "reasonable") will, at a given time and place at least, have, as a matter of fact, an overlapping consensus about a lot of shared moral truisms. And their being truistic does not make them unimportant; it is just that, since they are part of their shared background beliefs, they can be safely assumed. (I do not mean safely assumed to be true, but to be commonly held and their being so held to be something that would not be extinguished on reflection and with information.) None of the principles expressed in these beliefs are principles that never can be overridden, but they can only rightly be overridden in very extreme situations: situations where the principle in question conflicts extensively with enough of our other principles and beliefs of a similar status. But they all *generally*, that is, pervasively usually, hold and cannot in any circumstance be lightly set aside. Indeed, if the circumstances were not very rare where one or another of these moral truisms could be rightly set aside on a given occasion, we would be living in a moral wilderness. Our overriding one or another of them, where that becomes at all frequent, is symptomatic of our being in a moral wilderness. (For some of us, for some periods of time, this is our moral lot. As I write this [1993], Bosnia is a moral wilderness.)

In speaking of these moral truisms, I refer to such things as pain and suffering being bad things and pleasure and happiness being good things, of freedom, autonomy, and self-direction being good things and oppression, subordination, and dictatorship being bad things. In this cluster of truisms, self-respect, the value of having a sense of who we are, and the value of recognition are similarly good things and alienation, isolation, and a lack of any sense of human bonding, love, and reciprocity are similarly bad things. Likewise, that promises are generally to be kept, that truth be told, that people live up to their commitments and are not indifferent to the well-being and interests of others are similar moral truisms.

We start with such things; they are part of our overlapping consensus and they serve as background assumptions and beliefs in live moral and social deliberation when we wrestle with the problems of life. Only rarely do any of them come up for live challenge and then never *holus bolus*. If we tried to reject them all at once we would have no place to stand in reasoning morally: we would be utterly at sea. But particular circumstances can and do arise—though it is important to see that they are both rare and exceptional circumstances—when *one or another* of them can and sometimes do come into question. But it is crucial to see that when they do, the others (or at least the very great majority of them) hold fast. It is only by their holding fast that in certain circumstances they could come to be problematic, and then only problematic in those specific circumstances. (They do not thereby become generally problematic.) There are, to illustrate, rather plainly circumstances when we might think lying or deception is justified or (to go to something more extreme) where we might even think torture is justified or a reliance on constitutional procedures should be temporarily overridden.[24]

That we might so reason in extreme situations does not show that such clusters of moral truisms, along with certain beliefs about how constitutions work, or at least should work, along with plainly available scientific beliefs and some firm common sense factual beliefs, are not all part of our overlapping consensus in modern societies (and most particularly in liberal democracies). What it shows is that extreme situations can arise where a moral truism—in this case, that we must not torture—is overridden in a particular context. But, where this happens, other beliefs in the overlapping consensus hold fast in that circumstance and all of them, the overridden belief included, *generally* hold fast. This rather messy cluster serves as background beliefs in our reasoning about the problems of life. We will, just routinely assuming them, argue in ordinary life circumstances to distinct moral or political positions, articulating as conclusions, or as close to conclusions, normative beliefs that are often tendentious or at least would be tendentious without a carefully constructed argument-cum-narrative being clearly in the public space. We argue to these perhaps tendentious conclusions or near conclusions from the beliefs of the overlapping consensus, trying to show that these tendentious beliefs are all the same justified in the light of other untendentious things we believe. The truisms, or at least most of them, in these circumstances stand fast for us.

In so arguing, we seek to fit these conclusions in with these background beliefs, moral and factual. We seek to show how they square better than opposed beliefs with whatever relevant factual evidence we have about the situation and, as well, resolve more adequately, given our common background beliefs and convictions, the problem or problems that generated the articulating of the new moral or political claims in the first place. Sometimes, indeed most of the time, these new moral claims are just the conclusions that we came to in resolving the problem at hand by getting our beliefs—factual, moral, and political—into the most coherent pattern presently attainable. They are what we must, or at least should, believe, given the other things we believe or know, including, of course, that great mass of uncontested background beliefs, including among them our moral truisms.

X

It is sometimes thought that such a procedure leads to relativism or ethnocentrism, starting as it does with our considered convictions. But that is not so, for, using the full array of factual (scientific and commonsensical) beliefs and considered moral and other normative judgments we have available, we have plenty of material for the critique of our mores. Moreover, we have in our repertoire factual anthropological beliefs about the considered moral convictions of others in other societies together with, if our anthropology is at all sophisticated, the rationale they have for their beliefs and convictions.   Along with this, we have psychological and sociological theories about belief formation, the function of institutions, the role of ideology, and the like. We have this and more available to us in getting our beliefs into a coherent pattern.   This will yield a critical morality and not a conservative, conventional, *status quo* morality. We do indeed start with our considered moral judgments. Where else, after all, could we plausibly or perhaps even possibly start?[25] But any considered judgment, to say nothing of more contestable moral beliefs less firmly fixed, is subject to at least the possibility of critical overhaul and sometimes to outright rejection when we seek, as the Deweyian approach does, the most extensive, clearly articulated, coherent (consistent) conception of belief and conviction that we can attain. In doing this, we seek to have beliefs and convictions reflective of everything we know or can consistently believe, where no reasonably available fact, conception, or conviction can simply be ignored and no conviction or conception can be reasonably and justifiably held onto no matter how badly it fits with our other beliefs, conceptions, or convictions. This is not ethnocentrism or parochiality but reasonableness.

Notes

1. This conception was articulated by John Dewey. See his "The Need for a Recovery of Philosophy" in John Dewey et al., eds., *Creative Intelligence: Essays in the Pragmatic Attitude* (New York: Henry Holt, 1917), 3-69; John Dewey, *Reconstruction in Philosophy* (Boston: Beacon Press, 1957); John Dewey, *The Quest for Certainty* (New York: Capricorn Books, 1960); and John Dewey, *Intelligence in the Modern World* (New York: The Modern Library, 1939), 245-342.

2. In a masterful survey essay written jointly with John Darwall, Allan Gibbard, and Peter Railton, "Toward *Fin de siecle* Ethics: Some Trends," *Philosophical Review* 101, no. 1 (January 1992), 115-89, they survey and comment on the contemporary metaethical scene. W. K. Frankena, also masterfully, did it for the "classical" period of metaethics. See W. K. Frankena, "Ethical Theory" in Roderick M. Chisholm, et al., eds., *Philosophy* (Englewood Cliffs, New Jersey: Prentice-Hall, 1964). See, as well, my "Problems of Ethics" and my "Twentieth Century Ethics" both in Paul Edwards, ed., *The Encyclopedia of Philosophy* Vol. 3 (New York: Macmillan, 1967), 117-34 and 100-17.

3. Hilary Putnam, *Realism with a Human Face* (Cambridge, Massachusetts: Harvard University Press, 1990); Hilary Putnam, *Renewing Philosophy* (Cambridge, Massachusetts: Harvard University Press, 1992); Richard Rorty, *Consequences of*

Pragmatism (Minneapolis, Minnesota: University of Minnesota Press, 1982); Richard Rorty, *Contingency, Irony and Solidarity* (Cambridge: Cambridge University Press, 1989).

4. John Dewey, *Problems of Men* (New York: Philosophical Library), 3-20, Part I, 211-49.

5. Michael Williams, *Unnatural Doubts* (Oxford: Basil Blackwell, 1991) and Kai Nielsen, *After the Demise of the Tradition* (Boulder, Colorado: Westview Press, 1991).

6. Ernst Tugendhat, "Reflections on Philosophical Method from an Analytic Point of View" in Axel Hanneth, et al., eds., *Philosophical Interventions in the Unfinished Project of Enlightenment* (Cambridge, Massachusetts: MIT Press, 1992), 113-24.

7. Kai Nielsen, "Philosophy and the Search for Wisdom," *Teaching Philosophy* 16, no. 1 (March 1993), 5-20.

8. Kai Nielsen, "Philosophy and *Weltanschauung*," *The Journal of Value Inquiry* 27 (1993), 179-86.

9. Nielsen, *After the Demise of the Tradition.*

10. Ernest Gellmer, "What Do We Need Now?" *Times Literary Supplement* no. 4711 (July 16, 1993), 3-4.

11. Simone de Beauvoir, *Old Age*, trans. Patrick O'Brian (Harmondsworth, Middlesex, England: Penguin Books, 1972).

12. Linda J. Nicholson, ed., *Feminism/Postmodernism* (London: Routledge and Kegan Paul, 1990) and Sean Sayers and Peter Osborne, eds., *Socialism, Feminism and Philosophy* (London: Routledge and Kegan Paul, 1990).

13. Isaiah Berlin, *Against the Current* (New York: Viking Press, 1980), 333-55 and Isaiah Berlin, *The Crooked Timber of Humanity* (New York, Alfred A. Knopf, 1991), 238-61.

14. I try to do a bit of the actual arguing for such a position in my "Secession: The Case of Quebec," *Journal of Applied Philosophy* 10, no. 1 (1993), 29-43.

15. G. A. Cohen, *History, Labour and Freedom* (Oxford: Clarendon Press, 1988), 132-54.

16. Amartya Sen is very informative on India. See his discussion in the *New York Review of Books* (1993).

17. Isaiah Berlin, *Concept and Categories* (Oxford: Oxford University Press, 1980), 103-42.

18. Edward Westermarck, *Ethical Relativity* (Paterson, New Jersey: Littlefield Adams, 1967); J. L. Mackie, *Ethics: Inventing Right and Wrong* (Harmondsworth, Middlesex, England: Penguin Books, 1977); and Simon Blackburn, *Essays in Quasi-Realism* (New York: Oxford University Press, 1993), 52-74 and 111-212.

19. A. J. Ayer, *Philosophical Essays* (London: Macmillan, 1963), 250-70 and Kai Nielsen, "On Liberty and Equality: A Case for Radical Egalitarianism," *The Windsor Yearbook of Access to Justice* 4 (1984), 121-42.

20. The desirability of shifting from talk of preferences to talk of needs is made evident in David Braybrooke's *Meeting Needs* (Princeton, New Jersey: Princeton University Press, 1987). See also Kai Nielsen, "Justice, Equality and Needs," *Dalhousie Review* 69, no. 2 (Summer 1989).

21. Something of a start was made in facing these problems by David Braybrooke in *Meeting Needs.*

22. Martha Nussbaum, "Virtue Revived: Habit, Passion, Reflection in the Aristotelian Tradition," *Times Literary Supplement* (July 3,1992), 9-11; Martha Nussbaum, "Non-Relative Virtues: An Aristotelian Approach" in Martha Nussbaum and Amartya Sen, eds., *The Quality of Life* (Oxford: Clarendon Press, 1993), 242-69; and Amartya Sen, "Capability and Well-Being" in Nussbaum and Sen, eds., *The Quality of Life*, 30-53.

23. John Rawls, *Political Liberalism* (New York: Columbia University Press, 1993) and Kai Nielsen, "Philosophy within the Limits of Reflective Equilibrium Alone," *Iyyun* (January 1994).

24. Kai Nielsen, "Revolution" in Lawrence Becker, ed., *Encyclopedia of Ethics* II (New York: Garland, 1992), 1095-99 and Kai Nielsen, "On Justifying Violence," *Inquiry* 25 (1982), 16-35.

25. Suppose one says instead we should start with our preferences or at least our considered preferences instead. But to try to so circumvent considered judgments or convictions just causes needless complications. Suppose I try to ignore my considered convictions and only consider my wants and preferences. I may see a friend at a distance on the street and wish to avoid him so as to not have to pay him the twenty dollars I borrowed last week. I may prefer not to tell the person walking before me whose wallet has fallen out of his pocket that it has fallen out and pocket the wallet myself instead. I may prefer playing music very loudly late at night though it will keep my neighbor from sleeping. I may prefer to turn my eyes from extensive misery before me when I could, without extensive trouble to myself, do something about it. But all these preferences should be discounted as morally irrelevant in deciding what to do, even if they are considered preferences. If we try to bring them in we will just have the complication of explaining why my moral preferences (my considered convictions) should override, at least in normal circumstances, my other preferences.

6

Critique and Meta-Inquiries

I

In the previous chapter I argued that philosophy should centrally concern itself with the problems of life: the moral, political, social, and recurrent personal problems that we come up against in our actual lives. It should, I argued, set aside the perennial problems of philosophy, metaphysical, epistemological, normative ethical (as in foundational normative ethical theories) and set aside, as well, metaethical inquiries and inquiries into the philosophy of logic and concentrate on the problems of human beings. To this it is not unreasonable to respond that just as both traditional metaphysically oriented philosophy and systematic analytical philosophy, with its putting logic, the philosophy of logic, the philosophy of language, and the philosophy of science at the core of philosophical endeavours, was one sided, and in effect partisan, losing a lot with its partisanship of what in the past had made philosophy a vital human activity and what could make it vital now, so this pragmatist Deweyian turn of mine is equally one sided, taking a part of philosophy, admittedly a neglected part of philosophy, and unjustifiably taking it to be the whole of philosophy or the really important thing for philosophers to be doing. It is indeed important, but at least some of these other more traditional activities, or at least the standard analytical ones, have an importance of their own, though a quite different importance than the Deweyian one. I blinker myself and do our intellectual life a disservice if I do not acknowledge that and, mistakenly setting such traditional philosophical tasks aside, take this problems of life conception of philosophy as *the task* of philosophy.

In the first place, there is no such thing as *the* task of philosophy, any more than there is such a thing as *the* task of science, education or art. Philosophy, like these other activities, is many things. Philosophers do many different things and have many different tasks. Philosophy, not being a natural kind, has no essence. I have spotted one important, neglected and often scoffed at or patronized task, and I have explained it and defended it. Perhaps I have even succeeded in showing that when we think carefully about the problems of life that this does not require foundations in metaphysics, epistemology, normative ethical theory, or metaethics, or, alternatively, a perspicuous general representation of our reasoning and thinking: a saying of what practical reason is. The latter even Dewey tried, but we do not need an elucidation of what practical reason is, Deweyian or otherwise, to do the Deweyian thing I characterized in the previous chapter.[1] But such considerations, even if well taken, do not show that these other activities are not legitimate and do not have an importance in their own right: that is, that there are not distinctive tasks that are theirs that are important to our intellectual and cultural life. To deny that is as narrow minded and intellectually blocked as is the philosopher who thinks that logic and philosophy of science is philosophy enough or the traditionalist who thinks that the heart of philosophy is metaphysics. The reasonable thing is to let many flowers bloom, to encourage many different philosophical tasks and not to engage in any attempted imperialistic cornering of the market and, by a *persuasive* definition of "philosophy," to attempt to make a part of philosophy the sole legitimate philosophical activity. That certain systematic analytical philosophers, full of scientistic ideology, did that does not justify reverse discrimination.

I am sure this traditionalist response in a very plain sense is right. Certainly, at least as a practical matter, we should let many flowers bloom. If we do, we can perhaps expect that a rather Darwinian survival of the fittest will result. Let them all compete in the open intellectual marketplace and let the fittest survive. But against the traditionalist, given the spectacular lack of progress in gaining anything more than a local and temporary consensus concerning theories developed in the traditional domains of philosophy, it is perhaps not out of line to be deeply skeptical about the legitimacy and point of these activities, particularly when they are no longer seen as foundational to the problems of human beings or the moral life and concerns of *Weltanschauung* more generally.[2] If they lack such relevance, then it is not unreasonable to ask "Why do them?". Is it just that some people get a kick out of doing them and that that is reason enough to go on with such activities in a tolerably wealthy society? Perhaps? But then again perhaps not, and do not the people—or at least most of them—who do them themselves expect something more of them? We have here a series of legitimate questions, or at least apparently legitimate questions, and they fuel metaphilosophical inquisitiveness and perplexity. So let us see what more, if anything, philosophy can legitimately be.

II

One thing more—and quite distant from a Deweyian problems-of-life conception of philosophy—is the task given to philosophy by linguistic philosophers. It is that philosophy is to be a distinctive type of conceptual investigation. It, taking a linguistic turn, and engaging in semantic ascent, does not directly talk about the world but talks about the talk about the world, or, more accurately, about the *uses* (meanings, sense) of our talk about the world.[3] Where we are speaking English, we, in practising philosophy, talk about the uses of "knowledge," "thought," "truth," "belief," "cause," "good," and the like.[4] We try to ascertain what sense or senses these terms have.   And, if we are using another language, we would similarly talk about the uses of the equivalent expressions in those languages. This conceptual investigation, which some linguistic philosophers see as constituting philosophy, is a *second-order* activity (talking about the talk about the world) as distinct from a *first-order* activity which talks about the world (including the moral and political world). Physicists, for example, talk about neutrinos or use the term "neutrino" to make claims about the world. Philosophers, and sometimes physicists themselves, when they are doing philosophy as distinct from physics, talk about whether or not "neutrino" is a theoretical term with a purely instrumental use.

Philosophers need not be as partisan as purist linguistic philosophers. They can acknowledge that philosophy does other things as well, and legitimately so, so that we cannot rightly say that these conceptual investigations *constitute* philosophy.[5]   Other things, as well, count as philosophical.   But it is nonetheless a very characteristic philosophical activity. Moreover, it is a legitimate one and, the claim goes, a useful and enlightening one as well. This *second-order* work gives, or tries to give, us criteria for such concepts as knowledge, belief, identity, good, truth, and the like.[6] To speak of concepts is to speak of the use of our terms.   Our access to concepts is through the use of the terms that express them.[7] Thus to elucidate the concept of knowledge is to elucidate the use of "knowledge" and its equivalents in other languages. We, as native speakers, standardly correctly operate *with* these terms, e.g., "knowledge," "belief," "good," but to philosophize we must cultivate the ability to do something we do not often do, namely, to operate *upon* these terms: to come to learn how to specify and articulate the conditions of their use rather than just to use the terms with the easy assurance and authority gained by speakers who have thoroughly learned the language in question.

Native speakers and like practiced persons in a given language standardly correctly use the terms of their language. The philosopher with such a practiced ability, namely, someone with the linguistic competence of a native speaker, provides (if only in his own thoughts) sample utterances, in doing these conceptual investigations, investigations that are at least partly definitive of what it is to do philosophy, and attends to them, carefully reflecting on his linguistic intuitions concerning them.[8] We take note of what we would say when and of what we mean when we say these things. And this comes to gaining a sense of the use of the term or terms in question. The philosopher, practising this method, looks at the way the terms are used in their characteristic contexts and in unusual contexts as well and carefully reflects on their use in these varied situations. Repeatedly noting what we would say in such and such situations and in relying on our linguistic intuitions in that noting, we, if we are such philosophers, proceed by contrasting and comparing and reflecting carefully on the workings on the site and in action of the language we use.

Philosophy—at least on this conception—is in this way a reflective armchair activity. Thought experiments aside, it does not make experiments or carry out or engage in observations of what the facts of the matter are. And it certainly is not in the fact-collecting business. Instead, it reflects on and elucidates our language—the employments of our language—as a way of reflecting on and elucidating our thought. This is the kind of reflective activity that philosophical research comes to. (It makes it, for people standing outside it, seem like no research at all.)

We, standardly and typically, use language competently but we often do not command a clear view of that use. The philosophical task, on such a linguistic conception of philosophy, is to enable us, at least for certain purposes, to come to command a clear view of the uses of our words when they are philosophically troubling, i. e., when we get into conceptual perplexities over them.[9] We speak of concepts here and of conceptual clarification through the elucidation of our uses of words, for with concepts, hopefully, we will get something which is not specific language-parochial, but something which captures linguistic universals: something, that is, which gets expressed, though often in different ways, in all languages. Indeed it is something which not only in fact gets expressed, but would have to be expressed in one way or another in anything that could count as a language. We also speak of concepts to get away from just speaking of words and to focus instead on the various *uses* of words and the causal factors behind these uses. To speak of the concept of knowledge is to speak of the use (meaning, sense) of "knowledge." The use presumptively, and expectedly, would be the same for equivalent words in different languages. (That there are such equivalent words or roughly equivalent words is again an empirical issue.)

To be a master of the uses of our terms need not at all to be someone who knows the reasons for, or the rationale of, these uses. We may have no theoretical understanding of them at all even though we know how to use them, to operate with them, perfectly. But it is this theoretical understanding that a philosopher seeks to discover by reflecting on that use: reflecting on a use that she, like other practiced speakers, knows by *wont*. What native speakers say when they are actually employing their language, operating with their language, in live contexts, determines what is the correct use. The philosopher, the linguist, the grammarian, must just bow their heads to an acknowledgement of the correctness of the native speaker's employment of the language, though not at all to his account of that employment.[10] It is in the giving of an account of *why* this use is correct—the *second-order* job—that philosophy and linguistic theory come into play. The native speaker in such a *second-order* context is no longer the authority as he is in the *first-order* contexts in which he is using language or saying (reporting on) what that use is, saying, that is, that that is the use, e.g., we can say "talks faster" but not "sleeps faster." (More accurately, it is the collective "we" of a linguistic community which is such an authority. But normally the individual speaker can rely on his sense of language here: on his actual use, though not on his talk about that use.) Philosophy, on such a construal, is *conceptual investigation: a reflective examination of the uses of our language.*

On some such accounts, accounts of a Wittgensteinian sort, there is no attempt to systematically chart the uses of language and construct a *theory* of language to perspicuously represent our thought and language. Rather, the elucidations are, by contrast, on the spot clarifications where some particular concept, say, what it is to have a sudden thought and whether it is intrinsically private, is perplexing us, leading us, perhaps even obsessively leading us, to wonder whether we can ever really know the thoughts and feelings of another. The conceptual elucidation makes clear to us what a thought, including a sudden thought, is by making it clear to us how we use "thought," "to have a sudden thought" and related terms in the live contexts of our living of our lives: contexts where the engine isn't idling.

Such conceptual elucidation is therapeutic.[11] By this I mean it is used to relieve perplexity and to overcome confusion engendered by having a mistaken picture of how our language works. In this instance it might be a picture which represents a sudden thought as a "private entity" that one is just directly aware of and that is distinct from anything that is going on in the body, as a part of the workings of the body, or from any of the ways the person having the thought might act. A sudden thought, it is sometimes believed, is not just contingently private, but essentially and necessarily private, being a mental event which is quite distinct from any physical event that others might observe or in any way take note of. Such a picture of thought—a very pervasive picture of thought in the history of Western philosophy—leads to strange views about there being two radically different realities: physical realities, which are public and intersubjectively examinable, and mental realities which are private and are not inter-subjectively examinable. And with the latter—of which a sudden thought is an exemplification—goes the wild philosophical thought that we can never know—or never *really* know—the thoughts and feelings—the mind—of another.

Conceptual elucidation as theraphy seeks to show the mistakenness of such thinking by showing how we actually use "thought" and the like and for what purposes. (Recall something closely related to this was going on when we discussed "private language" arguments.) In the careful doing of this, it shows that such a philosophical picture does not square with our actual uses of "thought," is not a correct conceptualization of our common concept of thinking. The philosophical task is to so assemble reminders of what we say and think when we are actually operating with our language and by perspicuously displaying them (making us see how they actually work) to dispel confused and false images (pictures) of our language when we try to say what we mean by "thought," "truth," "justice," "good," "knowledge," "belief," and the like.

This Wittgensteinian therapeutic approach is not the only form that philosophy as *second-order* conceptual elucidation takes. Philosophers such as Peter Strawson, Stuart Hampshire, and Zeno Vendler, who, like Wittgensteinians, have a deep respect for ordinary language and do not believe with W. O. Quine and Donald Davidson that formal logic affords the or even a canonical notation which reveals the deep logical structure of our thought and language, still think, as Wittgenstein and Wittgenstein-ians do not, that we can, and usefully so, systematically chart the uses of our language—order our fundamental concepts—by showing which concepts are absolutely indispensable to any coherent conception of experience.[12]

For anything of any complexity at all, language serves for the expression of thought—what we can't say, we can't think. A person who has gained linguistic competency in a language can generate and understand a seemingly limitless repertoire of sentences in that language. Consider, Strawson remarks,

> the idea of the thoughts lying there, in potentiality, in the language—in its vocabulary and syntax. Our language seems like a highly structured, autonomous realm of significance—yet still a realm of which we are in a sense masters. It is *our* language. There are limitless sentences and combinations of sentences of which we know, in advance, the sense, the significance, though we shall only ever use, or hear, or read, a compara-tively insignificant portion of them.[13]

We clearly, through stimulus response, do not learn every new sentence independently.   We   can—independently   of   such   stimulus   and response—generate new sentences at will: sentences we have never heard before, such as, to take a random example, my writing "Purple porcupines are rare." Perhaps this absurdly false but still perfectly intelligible sentence has never been written before and may never be written or uttered again. Yet I readily generated it and you readily understood it.

How is it that we have this vast and potentially limitless understanding and mastery? To account for this we seem, at least, to have to postulate that we have an implicit mastery of *underlying structural principles of our language*. Because we have such a mastery we have the ability to so spontaneously generate and understand sentences in that language. Given that this obtains for all people with a linguistic competence in a particular language, no matter what that language is, and, given that, in spite of their surface differences, all languages are inter-translatable, no matter what that language is, it is plausible to believe that these structural principles, of which we have a tacit mastery, are structural principles which underlie not only that language but any language. The variant grammars of particular languages are variant realizations of something more general. That something more general is an underlying linguistic structure expressing itself in different forms in particular languages. In this way we have linguistic universals.

However, typically, people with linguistic competence, even full linguistic competence, cannot state even the grammatical rules of their particular language let alone these underlying structural principles; still, they have, again typically, a perfectly sound implicit or tacit knowledge of them: they can, as we have put it, operate with them but not upon them, not even to the extent of saying what these principles are. Still, since they have this linguistic competence, they must have an implicit or tacit knowledge of these underlying structural principles.

There must—or so the argument goes—be such general structural principles, since people with linguistic competence can so spontaneously and effortlessly generate new sentences. The job of the philosopher, on such a conception of linguistic philosophy, is to state and clearly display such underlying structural principles of language and therefore of thought. Strawson's suggestion is that we start by "concerning ourselves with the basic type of *matter* of our discourse and with the types of situation which we articulate in speech."[14] We need carefully to reflect on our situation in the world which is also to reflect on the basic features of our conceptual scheme. In evaluating them, through locating the basic features of our language, such as predication, identity, and quantification, we identify the central governing categories of our language, categories which are ahistorical: that is to say, they do not change significantly over time and are categories of all other languages as well. They are—and that is why we call them governing categories—categories without which people could have

no understanding of themselves, of others or of the world, and could not
act in the world. I have in mind, in addition to predication, attribution,
and identity, notions such as existence, knowledge, truth, and value. These
categories and concepts are the central governing concepts or organizing
notions of any system of thought and action.[15] The central philosophical
task, on such a Strawsonian and Hampshirean conception, is to elucidate
such governing concepts—say clearly what we mean by "existence,""identity,"
"attribute" (as in predication), "knowledge," "truth," and "value" and show
how they *connect* and the roles they play in our lives—in our systems of
thought and action. We, in doing philosophy, should also reflect on, and
come clearly to articulate, how we are acting, perceiving, corporeal beings
in a spatio-temporal world that we ineluctably experience as spacial and
temporal. It is a world with other human beings where all these human
beings, including, of course, ourselves, not only mutually interact but are
liable to change. Such a situation—such a condition in the world, a
condition which is inescapable—will give our governing concepts a certain
character and "this will be reflected in the basic semantic types of element
which will figure in...[our] discourse and in the basic types of semantically
significant combinations of which they will there be susceptible."[16] To
clearly articulate these things in their interconnections will be to articulate
what those deep structural features of our language and of our system of
ideas are. But these structural features will not only be of *our* system of
ideas and of *our* language but of any actual or even possible system of
ideas in any possible language. This is so since these features are
"absolutely indispensable to any coherent conception of experience."[17]

This is a way of doing a more systematic *second-order* job of describing
and displaying our uses of language than the Wittgensteinian one, but it
still has the same *second-order* logical status. It is still talk about our talk
about the world. It is possible—and indeed some Wittgensteinians will
think that—that the belief in such deep structures is mythical.[18] We have
no good reason to believe, they think, that there are such structures
underlying all languages or indeed any language and explaining linguistic
competence, to say nothing of anything that intelligibly could count as "a
language." Moreover, Wittgensteinians will add, we do not need them
(even if we could have them or do in fact have them) to carry out
conceptual theraphy. We do not use such conceptions in clearing up
misconceptions about what it is to think, to believe or to act morally. It is
also not implausible to think, as Richard Rorty does, that even if we could
carry out something like Strawson's Kantian charting of our language and
thought that this would yield little more than platitudes concerning our
system of thought and action.[19]

I shall not enter into these controversies here, but shall simply note
that both of these *second-order* philosophical activities—more obviously the

first one than the second—are at least apparently legitimate enough activities and activities that can be seen readily enough as philosophical while still being distinct from, and indeed distant from, both the Deweyian one I characterized and defended in the previous chapter and from the metaphysical or epistemological pursuits such as I described in Part One. If the Strawsonian one is called "descriptive metaphysics," then it should be said, as I remarked in Chapter 2, to be more *descriptive* than metaphysical, for it makes no transcendental moves, provides no strictly transcendental arguments or transcendental hypotheses, and claims no synthetic *a priori* truths. It is through and through empirical.[20]

However, what I particularly want to draw attention to now is how, in a way that is often not noticed by their adherents, both of these *second-order* activities are thoroughly empirical. They are empirical in this way: the statements made by these philosophers are empirical statements about our uses of words, the function of sentences, and the structure of language. They very frequently are generalizations about linguistic regularities and could be absorbed into the science of linguistics.[21] There is no *a priori* way or transcendental way here and philosophy on such an approach, the self-images of these philosophers to the contrary notwithstanding, loses its autonomy. It becomes an empirical enterprise not in principle distinct from linguistics. With such a conceptual investigation of the uses of words, there is nothing metaphysical or even epistemological, where epistemology is conceived as setting out the *a priori* (allegedly *a priori*) conditions for our knowing. That all language is claimed to have a certain feature, that even anything that could count as a language is said to have such and such a feature, is still a claim about how we speak and about what we find conceivable and inconceivable. And these are empirical claims. Philosophy so practiced gains its clear legitimacy by dropping its transcendental and allegedly super-scientific appeals and by becoming through and through empirical and with that the dropping of any claims that the structures it discloses have any *a priori* necessity.[22]. It is indeed a reflective armchair activity, but the *test* for the truth of its claims about the uses of words is empirical. We can typically rely on our nose for language concerning what can and cannot be said, but where there is doubt we can put the matter to test by surveying what native speakers say and in that way put the matter to empirical test.[23] That we usually do not have to do it, and that doing that would normally be a waste of intellectual effort, does not mean that where doubts actually arise we cannot and should not do it.

III

Metaethics is plainly such a *second-order* conceptual and philosophical investigation and it can and has taken both the forms characterized in the previous section.[24] Moreover, its claims about the uses of moral and other normative terms and sentences is itself, like the other bits of *second-order* philosophizing, not normative but, in the way I have just explained, empirical. I want here, after characterizing metaethics and stating some of the problems of metaethics, to inquire into whether there is much point in it, even when well done, and, in the light of that, and as part of that inquiring, to reconsider the point discussed in the previous chapter: to wit, whether metaethics supplies the rational underpinning for either our ordinary moral thought or for more systematic normative ethical theories or other substantive ethical theorizing.

Philosophy on such a view is thought to be a detached *second-order* commentary upon *first-order* judgments and activity. Indeed this view was the prevalent view in the Anglo-American and Scandinavian philosophical ambience during the high period of the linguistic turn, when first logical empiricism and then linguistic philosophy was at the cutting edge in philosophy. I refer to the period roughly from 1930-1970. Concerning this period, W. K. Frankena puts it well when he says, "the main concern of ethical theory or moral philosophy in our period [1930-1970] has been with so-called metaethical questions rather than with normative or practical ones. That is, the primary concern has been, not with propounding judgments about what is right or good, but with analyzing the meaning or nature of such judgments and of the logic of their justification."[25] This, of course, fits perfectly the conception of philosophy as *second-order* discourse that we have been discussing. Indeed some linguistic philosophers (A. J. Ayer, Charles Stevenson, Rudolf Carnap, Hans Reichenbach) boldly asserted that such metaethics was the only thing a moral philosopher could legitimately do *qua* moral philosopher, though *qua* interested citizen or moral agent she was, of course, quite free to engage in moral argumentation designed to establish or defend certain moral positions or beliefs and that there need be nothing unreasonable about this at all. Only she should be quite clear that this is not a philosophical activity.[26]

Philosophy, even moral philosophy, on such a conception, is exclusively a *second-order* activity: talk about the talk about the world—in this case *first-order* moral talk—rather than itself being talk of the world, including moral talk. Their task is to talk about moral discourse, not to engage, while doing philosophy, in moral discourse itself. Not all analytical philosophers who did moral philosophy were so restrictive. Not, for example, W. K. Frankena, whom I have just quoted. But whether or not metaethics was regarded as the only legitimate philosophical investigation where ethics was concerned, it was widely regarded during that period as the central concern of moral philosophy and, rather typically, as its only legitimate concern.

The publication of John Rawls's *A Theory of Justice* in 1971 was widely thought to have brought an end to the hegemony of metaethics (and the metapolitical in a parallel fashion, as well) among philosophers. Until the late 1960s, philosophers in Britain, America and Scandinavia were working mainly on analytical issues. They were cautiously unpacking the meanings or uses of "good," "right," "ought," "obligation," "freedom," and authority" and examining how these terms, and the concepts they express, connect and the logical status of sentences employing these moral terms. They did this metaethical and metapolitical work while studiously, as Jeremy Waldron puts it, "avoiding the temptations of grand normative theory in the tradition of Hobbes, Locke and T. H. Green."[27] But, Waldron continues, "*A Theory of Justice* changed all that for it was not an analysis of the word 'justice', but a presentation of broad egalitarian principles for the whole institutional structure of modern society, together with a complex methodology for their elaboration and defense."[28] It was this, and activities like it, that became the central task of moral and political philosophy. This was, to put it mildly, a great sea-change from a tradition of short duration—some 40 or 50 years—back to the historically dominate tradition of moral and political philosophizing and theorizing. Philosophers had found their normative voice once more, but, as in the past, it was an argument-based, narrative-based, elucidation-rooted normative voice.

However, there are those who think that even after the great expansion (as the Rawlsian counter-revolution has been called) there is still room for metaethics and indeed some even think that "to get to the bottom of things" we must carefully engage in such metaethical and metapolitical issues.[29] So, on their conception, philosophy as a *second-order* activity retains its pride of place even in the domains of moral and political philosophy. This plainly cuts against my Deweyian conception of philosophy. So it is necessary for me to examine this issue to see both what legitimacy and point metaethics has in its own right and to see if we really need it to find a rational underpinning for Rawlsian or any other substantive moral and political theory or for a Deweyian problems-of-life-conception of philosophy, another conception which is plainly substantive.

IV

Where philosophy is construed in the *second-order* way we have been discussing, it is neither metaphysical nor empirical science nor moral or otherwise normative guidance or theory construction. It is, rather, the attempt to achieve conceptual and methodological clarity in the various domains of discourse and, given the way words are related to the world, in the various domains of life, including, of course, morality and politics. We do this by becoming clear about how moral and political discourse functions. Here questions of meaning—questions of use or sense—have center stage. (That the test for what the use is is empirical does not gainsay that.)

I will speak of the new metaethics and the old metaethics. The old metaethics is what many philosophers, perhaps most philosophers, think of as metaethics *period*. It, as a distinct subject, was created during the rise of logical positivism and linguistic philosophy. The new metaethics—a rather expanded conception of metaethics—is the subject as it was articulated after the great expansion and after Quine's rejection of any significant analytic/synthetic distinction.[30]

The old metaethics is clearly a *second-order* activity, and standardly, in intent at least, normatively neutral. It is the analysis or elucidation of the uses or meanings of moral terms, utterances, or, put differently, an examination of the nature of moral concepts and discourse. The meta-ethicist does not set out a moral system and try to show how such a system is justified; she does not articulate moral principles and show how they are justified. She does not try to tell us what the good life for human beings is or what are just institutions or just and decent relations between human beings. That normative ethical or moral task is not that of the metaethicist, who sometimes will even think that normative ethics, as we have noted, is not a proper *philosophical* subject at all.[31] Rather, the metaethicist will analyze (elucidate) moral concepts, including the key notions of various normative ethical systems. Such philosophers will not in their philosophical work (except incidentally and in ways which could readily be excised) make moral judgments themselves.[32] They will, instead, discuss the meaning and function of moral statements. In metaethical works moral terms and sentences occur in *mention* and not in *use*. Put more fully, the old metaethics takes its activity to be a form of reflective *second-order* discourse in which statements are made about the uses or meanings of moral utterances, principles or terms, about the logical status of moral sentences, about the nature of moral argument and practical reasoning more generally and about what constitutes a morality. In short, the metaethicist tries to elucidate (analyze) and perspicuously display moral discourse or portions of moral discourse. His intent is not to engage in moral argument, reasoning or normative ethical discourse at all, but, as a kind of conceptual cartographer, or, to switch the metaphor, as a "mental geographer," to give a clear description and/or elucidation of that discourse. His aim is not, even in the most general terms, to tell us how to live or what the good life for human beings is, but to make clear what morality is all about, to show how moral discourse works and what is the "logic" of moral reasoning.

Just as philosophy conceived of as conceptual elucidation is a considerable change from traditional philosophy, so metaethics (as a part of that) is a considerable shift from traditional moral philosophy. The traditional task of moral philosophy was not to content itself simply with clarifying the uses of moral discourse, but, moral skeptics and subjectivists aside, it sought to give us objective, rationally justified, knowledge of how we should live and of what the good life for human beings is. Even the skeptics and subjectivists lived in the shadow of this goal, for their primary purpose was to show that the moral philosophers defending an objective normative ethics could not achieve their goal. (Here Edward Westermarck is an exemplary example of such a moral skeptic.)[33] What we, of course, would want, such moral skeptics believe, is to have such objective moral knowledge, but such knowledge is not to be had. So the only thing left to do for the moral philosopher, who sees this, is, honoring truth, to make it clear that this is our situation.

However, throughout most of our history the skeptic has remained very much in the minority and the traditional task of moral philosophy remained in place and that was to set forth systematically the first principles of morality and in doing that to show that and how these principles are justified and to show how there is a system of moral thought which hangs together and is a justified system of thought. Indeed in some instances they claimed to have established that the system of ideas they articulated was "the one true moral system."

Such a conception of the task of a moral philosopher would not only be to give a theoretical articulation and an account of the limits of moral justification, but, as well, to give an articulation and defense of what a, or perhaps even *the*, good life for human beings is and of how it is that we ought to live our lives. Traditionally, moral philosophy, so construed, had a *practical aim;* moral knowledge was not conceived as a purely theoretical knowledge of moral phenomena or moral data, but, as well, and most essentially, as a practical knowledge of how to live. The goal was not that we should simply know what goodness and rightness is but that we should become good persons of moral principle who can be relied on to act rightly. *Practice* not theory was the aim of traditional moral philosophy, though practice informed by theory. Their theoretical interests, which were considerable, were instrumental to that aim.[34]

This traditional conception of moral philosophy is very distant from metaethics, which, as a *second-order* elucidatory activity, contents itself with being clarificatory. It does not tell us what it is to live a good life, let alone advocate our living of that life, but analyzes or elucidates what it means, among other things, to speak of "a good life." It can and has been asked if there is much point to that metaethical activity. Well, there is, I believe, a Wittgensteinian theraphy point, or what I think comes to much the same thing, a Lockean underlaborer point, on the not unreasonable assumption that we human beings would like to free ourselves, to the extent we can, of confusions, even if the confusions in question are caused by our entanglement with our own language resulting from a mistaken picture of how it works. The point, of course, is the achievement of clarity.[35] (Clarity may not be enough, but it is clearly something.)

Consider three oversimplified examples deployed simply to illustrate how such an elucidation works. To believe that something is the right thing to do is just, some have said, to have a pro-attitude toward doing it. That just is what it *means* to say something is the right thing to do. "Right thing to do" has no other intelligible meaning. But to say this is a mistake and attention to how language works can show that this is so. Someone, without the slightest linguistic or conceptual deviance or incongruity, can say "I want to do it, I have a very strong pro-attitude toward doing it indeed, but I know that it would be wrong to do it." If being the right thing to do just meant having a pro-attitude toward doing it, then the above mentioned sentence would be self-contradictory, but it plainly is not, so "being the right thing to do" cannot mean "I (or we) have a pro-attitude toward doing it" or anything like that, such as having a disposition to do it. So it cannot be correct to simply assert that norms are pro-attitudes or dispositions to act in a certain way or anything like that.

Similarly, to take my second example, suppose someone says that to fail to see or recognize the truth of "Inflicting pain without point is evil," "Pleasure is good," "Failing to keep faith with friends is a very grave wrong," or "Self respect is good" is a definite cognitive fault: it is to be *morally blind*. It is just as much an objective error, the claim goes, as are errors in color discrimination due to color-blindness. But this, the metaethicist should respond, is a mistaken analogy for we have objective tests such that even the color-blind person can come to recognize that he is color-blind and does not, in certain areas, make the correct color discriminations. The color-blind person himself can know this. But the person who is said to be morally blind, because he does not accept the truth of the above mentioned moral sentences either cannot be brought to acknowledge that he is morally blind or, if he does acknowledge it, then he is then no longer morally blind, for he no longer fails to assent to the truth or at least correctness of those moral sentences and so no longer, at least on these grounds, can rightly be said to be morally blind. Color-blind people can come, on quite objective grounds, to acknowledge that they are color blind; so-called morally blind people cannot on either objective or subjective grounds. If someone says "Formerly I was morally blind" he is just giving to understand that he has changed his moral views. Talk of "moral blindness" is just a useless and obscuring metaphor. It makes it sound like we have, in having moral sensibilities, a kind of cognitive factuality when there is no good reason to think that we have such a faculty. It is quite unlike color blindness or tone deafness. Again, attention to how our language works can show us such things.[36]

Take, as a third and final example, a somewhat more complicated and more interesting case. Suppose that it is claimed that belief in morals rests on a mistake. Moral claims make claims to objectivity, but that belief is mistaken, for all moral beliefs are false. They are just the objectivizing of moral emotions, the assigning of objectivity to subjective experience. If we examine carefully the use of moral judgments and are not misled by their surface grammar, we will come to see that they are actually used to make claims of objectivity, where this is essentially a claim of objective prescriptivity in the world, but the very use of our language here is in error for morality is in reality based on emotions and not intellect and the very idea of such a "objectivity prescriptivity" is an incoherency. There is and can be no such "moral entity" in the world or, for that matter, "beyond the world." Belief in morals, therefore, rests on massive error. All our moral judgments are false. We objectivize our emotions: we, that is, project our emotions onto the world and mistakenly think there is some mysterious, non-natural, normative quality or characteristic there that makes our moral judgments true. But there is no such quality; there is just our projected or objectivized emotions.[37]

Again, staying on a *second-order* metaethical level, this account, it could be agreed, cannot be correct for objective truth is a redundancy and only if we understand what it would be like for some moral utterances to be true could we intelligibly say that they are all false. However, since on the above account they are just objectivized (projected) emotions and can be nothing else, we have no understanding of what it could be for them to be true. But, if there is no idea of what it could be for them to be true, then we do not understand what it means for them to be false either. So we have lost our grounds for saying that belief in morality is an error because all moral beliefs are false. On such an account we have no idea of what it would be like for them to be either true or false. Yet we are asserting (trying to assert) incoherently on our very own account that they all are false.[38]

These three examples of the therapeutic use of metaethics are deliberately oversimplified and in particular the last claim to be so therapized—the claim of what has been called the error theory—cannot be so easily disposed of. (We shall see something of this later.) But, from our three illustrative examples, we can see how by attention to the way that our language works we can sometimes undermine the grip that mistaken philosophical pictures of morality have on our consciousness. So it seems to be fairly evident that this Wittgensteinian deployment of metaethical remarks—this debunkingly, clarificatory underlaborer work—can at times be good conceptual theraphy. We can clear away some of the underbrush and, in the extreme cases, the rubbage that gets in the way of thinking and sometimes, perhaps, even of acting in a reasonable way. We can, that is, set aside some of the things that impede our making sense of our moral lives and perhaps even stand in the way of our acting and responding as reasonable moral persons. But even these therapeutic claims may be exaggerated. On the spot conceptual elucidation may not have such desirable therapeutic results.

However, metaethicists, both the old breed and the new, have generally wanted to do more than that. They have wanted to construct and justify systematic metaethical theories. This is just what the Wittgensteinian, but not the Strawsonian, approach regards as unnecessary and, more than that, impossible. With this systematic aim, a wide variety of metaethical theories have been propounded: intuitionism and varieties of ethical naturalism, among the cognitive theories, that is, theories that claim moral utterances are genuine propositions true or false in some substantial way. Among the non-cognitive theories, there have been emotive theories, prescriptive theories, and error-theories. All these non-cognitive theories are theories which deny that moral utterances and sentences can be usefully thought to be substantially either true or false and as making claims to a distinct kind of moral or normative knowledge or belief.[39] Then, in addition to these more traditional metaethical theories, there are a number of theories, all thought, on a generous construal of "metaethics," to be metaethical theories, namely, practical reasoning theories, constructivist theories, and sensibility theories.[40] For all these theories there have been varieties, some of the newer varieties meeting objections that were directed against the earlier versions. But one thing is plain: there is no substantial consensus about which of these theories is the more adequate and even little consensus concerning how we might best proceed to determine this or over whether there is much point in so constructing them. Intuitionism has few takers today. Ethical naturalism, in its new non-reductive forms, has somewhat more attraction now than it had at mid-century. Still it remains very controversial, with many philosophers thinking it through and through mistaken. Non-cognitivist accounts, with the work of J. L. Mackie, Simon Blackburn, and Alan Gibbard, have been given new and subtle formulations, but again there is little consensus concerning them.[41] Similar things should be said for sensibility theories and practical reasoning theories and constructivist theories. With David Wiggens, David Gauthier, Thomas Nagel, T. M. Scanlon, and John Rawls, all of these accounts have received impressive formulations.[42] Yet, as much as the other theories, they remain controversial and with the added difficulty that it is anything but clear whether at least some of them should even be regarded as metaethical theories. Rawls, for example, makes it clear that his account is not a metaethical account and, while Gauthier, Nagel, Scanlon, and even Rawls sometimes make, in the course of articulating their theories, remarks that reasonably could be classified as metaethical, that is not the thrust, the main import and point, of their theories. To call these theories metaethical is very tendentious indeed. But, metaethical or not, there is no more consensus over them than there is over the explicitly and uncontroversially metaethical theories.

With such a lack of consensus, it certainly does not, to understate it, seem very reasonable to claim truth or warrantedness for any of these theories. Being, where they are clearly metaethical, empirical claims about our moral discourse, there is, unlike with metaphysics or perhaps even foundationalist epistemology, no in principle reason why one of them could not, along the usual fallibilistic lines of our empirically oriented thinking, be judged to be true or found to be better warranted than the others. But, in fact, none have. There have been some temporary and rather local victories, but that is all. And there seems at least to be no reason to believe that anything like a convergence to consensus, or even anything approximating consensus, will come onto the scene. We will continue to have disputing, and sometimes warring, schools of metaethics as we do of metaphysics, epistemology and normative ethics (perhaps better labelled so-called normative ethics).

V

Edward Westermarck powerfully argued that the traditional moral theories (normative ethical theories, if you will) "including hedonism, utilitarianism, evolutionary ethics, rationalism and various accounts of a special 'moral faculty', are quite unable to defend their basic principles."[43] There is even less consensus concerning which, if any, of these traditional theories is the more adequate than there is concerning metaethics. Moreover, unless some form of ethical naturalism is true, these substantial moral theories, like metaphysical theories, are not, even in principle, the sorts of activities concerning which we even could reach a consensus *by way of empirical theory construction and testing.*[44] This being so, Westermarck argued, we do not have good grounds for believing moral judgments state objective truths. (We would do better to just say truths because "subjective *truth*" is an incoherent notion.)

However, returning to metaethics, this much similarity with traditional moral theories should be claimed concerning metaethical theories. We have no good reasons at all for believing any of them to be true or warranted. Still, it is important to keep in mind here that that does not entail or establish that some particular metaethical statements, e.g., "Moral utterances are universalizable," "'Good' is a general term of commendation," or "'Good' signifies a supervenient property," are not true and sometimes could be used therapeutically to cure certain philosophical perplexities. But it is a long way from such truths to establishing the truth of metaethical theories.

We are very likely to go around with something like the following picture of moral philosophy in our heads. Philosophers should engage in substantive moral philosophizing. We should not only try to characterize moral reasoning, we should also use it to criticize irrational and otherwise mistaken or problematic moral beliefs and practices and to search for general, rationally justifiable moral principles. The aim of moral philosophy, linguistic philosophy to the contrary notwithstanding, should be to either discover or construct, and, with that discovering or construction, clearly to articulate, a sound system of morality, with clearly stated justified moral principles, practices and particular moral claims and judgments. However, it is also not unnatural (going along with some linguistic philosophy) to believe that when questions arise about justifying such a moral system, or even just about justifying certain moral principles, particular moral practices or even particular moral judgments, that we, if we push our moral or normative inquiries far enough and hard enough, will see that what we can rationally conclude will turn on certain metaethical presuppositions or considerations. It is also not unnatural to think that if these metaethical issues cannot be rationally resolved, then these moral issues cannot be rationally resolved either. The whole thing, it is sometimes thought, depends on metaethics. We must go in a linear pattern of justification (as in a deductive system) from metaethical propositions to propositions of substantive normative ethics to the particular Deweyian type moral issues (problems-of-life issues). Which of these problems-of-life resolutions are justified or are the more reasonable to accept depends on what is established up the line with these prior metaethical and normative ethical issues. If we get truth or warrantability there, then we can go deductively down the line to the justification of the particular problems-of-life claims; if not, not.

I think this picture of philosophical moral reasoning and justification—a picture of how things should go in thinking about morality and in moral thinking as well—is fundamentally wrong. It is unrealistic and keeps us from seeing what really goes on when we engage in moral and practical reasoning, when we deliberate and try to think out and resolve moral problems. It is surely utterly at odds with the coherentist model of wide reflective equilibrium that I utilized in the previous chapter and elsewhere, as has John Rawls and Norman Daniels.[45] But this traditional way of looking at things with its linear model of justification is certainly a natural way to look at things or, at least, a natural model, to give us a picture of how we reason philosophically. And it is well entrenched in our philosophical culture. I shall argue that, as intuitively plausible as it at first sight may seem, it is thoroughly mistaken and that, if we try to appeal to it, we will unrealistically, and unnecessarily, end up in moral skepticism.

Starting with metaethics in such a service, this much can and should be said on the justificatory role of metaethics: it appears at least to be the case that we can justifiably make certain normative ethical claims only if certain metaethical claims are justified (justifiably believed to be true). The truth of these metaethical claims does not ensure the truth of these normative ethical or substantively moral claims, but the normative ethical claims cannot be true unless the metaethical claims are. In this respect metaethics does not *seem* to be normatively neutral. It plays, or seems to play, a weak justificatory role. Still it is not enough for it to be in a linear chain of justification. *Suppose*, to illustrate, a very strong form of non-cognitivism is justified and that it makes no sense to say that a moral utterance or sentence is true or false any more than it makes sense to say that an imperative or an optative is true or false. This being so, the moral (normative ethical) sentence "It is true that abortion is murder" could not intelligibly be asserted. It could not even falsely be asserted. On such an account, it would not be false but senseless, just as "It is false that abortion is murder" would not be true but also senseless. The metaethical claim rules out as senseless both putative truth-claims, rather than siding with one or the other, claiming one is true and the other false.

However, this consequence is more trivial than it at first might appear. The metaethical claim does not rule on the sense—the intelligibility—of either "Abortion is murder" or "Abortion is not murder." It does not at all give to understand that there is something illegitimate about either of them. More than that, as is clear in the metaethical accounts of such prominent non-cognitivists as A. J. Ayer and C. L. Stevenson, they do not even deny the *linguistic* propriety of applying "true" or "false" to declarative sentences such as "Abortion is murder."[46] They are only concerned to deny that such utterances can be *substantially* true in the sense that there is a fact or a state of affairs, either normative or non-normative, that statements made by the use of the sentence "Abortion is murder" correspond to such that such a fact or state of affairs makes that sentence true. They are only concerned to deny that there is some reality or fact—fact of any sort—that makes such sentences true. If we want to say that it is true that abortion is murder, we do not fall into any linguistic or conceptual deviancy and we, as well, will fall into no confusion as long as we are quite clear that we are not trying to assert the existence of some realm of fact that our sentence, when seriously used, is supposed to correspond to. (But perhaps à la Davidson and Rorty we have no truth makers anywhere along the way?)[47]

So what the metaethical statement rules out is pretty minimal. Perhaps it only rules out another metaethical statement of a different type belonging to a different metaethical or perhaps even normative ethical *theory*. At least when we reflect on the above complications, that seems to be the case. The claim that moral utterances can be neither true nor false, suitably interpreted, seems not even to rule out, when properly understood, "It is false that abortion is murder." It only rules out as unintelligible "It is false that abortion is murder" when "false" is construed in a substantive sense as standing for some natural property or some strange property and the sentence, in being held to be true, is thought to correspond to some "normative fact"−some "true maker"− somehow mysteriously just there in the world or "beyond the world." But it need not be so interpreted and there is nothing in the linguistic facts, as both Ayer and Stevenson well realized, that requires that interpretation. Moreover, that complication about truth aside, the metaethical statement does not enable us to decide that any normative ethical or substantially moral statement is warranted. It, at best, rules certain types of allegedly normative ethical sentences out as senseless and then only rather theoretically encrusted ones at that, e.g., "It is true that abortion is murder" but not "Abortion is murder."

Some, while remaining utterly skeptical about metaethical *theory*, could still argue, as a Wittgensteinian would, that sometimes metaethical elucidations, when we are confused about a moral belief, embedded as they always are in a stretch of moral language, can break or at least relieve that perplexity. We need not try to do what appears, at least, to be the impossible, namely, to create a metaethical *theory* to do that. But *second-order* elucidation of bits of our moral-talk, when sensitively and carefully done, can still be valuable in helping us to achieve a greater clarity in what we are doing when we think and act morally. In that way it can perhaps (if it can really do these things) still serve as an instrument for greater rationality and adequacy in our actual moral lives. Given the fact that we want to be more rational and more reasonable in our moral thinking and acting, in our sense of ourselves as moral persons, and, given the fact that we can, at least to some degree, do these things, metaethical elucidation sometimes can be moderately useful. This is most obvious in its capacity to undermine obscure beliefs about morality and perhaps certain moral beliefs themselves, in a way that can further our moral lives. Consider the following illustrative examples. Suppose someone thinks that "x is right" has the same meaning as "God commands x". But then a little reflection on our use of moral language, a use shared by believers and non-believers alike, will show us that that cannot be right, for the believer, as readily as the non-believer, recognizes that the following sentences make sense and, on a little reflection, they both can be brought to recognize that they would not make sense if the equivalents postulated by such a believer actually held. It makes sense to say "God has not commanded me to refuse conscription, but still that is the only right course of action for me." It is, that is, no deviation from the linguistic regularities of English to say this. That moral claim may be mistaken, but it is perfectly intelligible as a moral claim (assuming "God" and "God commands" are intelligible). But it could not be if "x is right" means "God commands x." But its intelligibility shows that such an equivalence does not hold. Similarly, someone, including a believer, could believe that God had commanded him to kill his son and still believe that it is the wrong thing to do. Again that belief may be mistaken, but it is intelligible and so the equivalents in meaning that such a believer asserts—a believer in a divine command theory metaethics—could not hold.

Still, I think this clarification counts for less than philosophers are generally wont to believe. Someone who believes that he ought to do whatever God commands may very well not hold such an absurd meta-ethical view as described above. He may have no metaethical views at all. He may believe that God, in His wisdom, may often deliberately be silent concerning what people should do because God wants human beings to have a certain autonomy. Where He is silent He wants us to make up our own minds concerning what to do and how to respond to others. He wants us there, in line with our understanding of our own religion and in accordance with a network of our own moral beliefs, to make up our own minds about what to do and how to try to live certain portions of our lives. Similarly, God, being God—the God of love and goodness—would not command certain things. He certainly, since He is perfectly good, would not command things, like killing one's son, which go so firmly against our very moral sense—a sense that comes, he believes, from God. There are these and a lot of similar moral resources available to the believer, and indeed to the unbeliever (though rather less directly) as well. A person who believers that he should do what God commands need not have the absurd metaethical view that "x is right" means "God commands x" or, even if he does, he can give it a reading, in accordance with his other views, including his reflective moral conscience that would deny that it was *God* who was commanding it if it went against his firm moral sense. God, being *God*, would not command him to do anything horrendous.

My second example intends to establish much the same point, though in a way that makes it quite clear that such argumentation need not use religious examples: examples which might be thought to be in some other way fishy, mixed up, as religion seems at least to be, with metaphysics. Suppose someone says that "x is good" means "I (the utterer of the utterance) prefer x." But again that seems—to go way back to G. E. Moore—plainly mistaken and simple metaethical considerations, similar to those used by Moore in *Principia Ethica* (1903) will show that is so. I can perfectly intelligibly say or think "I know that I prefer x but I still wonder whether I should." I can wonder whether it is really a good thing to prefer.

I can quite firmly know that a certain person, or even people more generally, prefer something and still think such preferences are bad, but in thinking they are bad I am not thinking that they are not preferences or, necessarily, that I do not have these preferences myself. Going to the first person case changes nothing, for, if I can think others' preferences are bad, or that their having a preference does not establish its goodness, I can think this about myself as well. I can very well know what my preferences are, even what my considered preferences are, and still intelligibly ask if they are good, if having them is a good thing. And asking those things I am not at all asking if they are my preferences or are really my preferences. Knowing that I prefer something is one thing; knowing that it is good to have that preference is another.

Again these metaethical considerations, while to the point, and I believe well taken, do not establish as much as they might appear at first glance to establish. The person talking so incautiously about preference and good might readily retract her explicit semantical claims—that was not what she was really interested in in the first place—and say something non-semantical instead that is substantially very similar, though without the same *semantical* import. She could say that she should not have said that "X is good" has the same meaning as, or is logically equivalent to "I prefer x," but what she should have said is that when she believes something to be intrinsically good (worth having or experiencing for its own sake) she can, on honest reflection, find no better reason for believing that then recognizing it is a considered preference of hers, something she wants or prefers when she is aware of the causes of her preferring it and the consequences of her having her preferences satisfied and when she also recognizes that she continues to have that preference when she in a cool hour is being reflective and is well informed about her preferences: when she knows, for example, what alternatives she might have preferred instead and why and has taken the whole matter to heart.

What better reasons could anyone have for saying that something is *intrinsically* good then that it is such a considered preference of theirs.[48] This claim may still be mistaken, or at least not sufficiently nuanced, but it is not a claim about the meaning or the use of terms or the logical status of sentences. It is making no claims about equivalents of meaning or, more generally, concerning or in the semantics of moral or practical discourse. And it may be something that not a few people, when they are thinking about what is intrinsically good, would reflectively assent to. Moreover, when the person makes that claim about preferences and intrinsic goodness, it is not evident that any metaethical considerations have been appealed to or show, or even go any distance toward showing, such a claim to be either true or false.

These are simple cases, but they serve to cast doubt on whether metaethical reasonings or elucidations will, in any very important sense, yield greater clarity about our moral lives or what a good life or an acceptable set of practices or principles would be. Metaethical elucidation can help us dispose of simple theses that probably few believe anyway and, even when they do (if they do), where they can, easily setting them aside, readily fall back on a similar substantive position that does not have these difficulties. My two examples illustrated this. Where metaethical analysis settles something, some conceptual theraphy aside, it is not needed. Where the case is sufficiently difficult to be of moral interest or significance or of theoretical interest, the metaethical judgment is either irrelevant—or at least apparently irrelevant—or what should be said metaethically speaking is something concerning which there is little consensus and little prospect of consensus. Indeed here—over such metaethical issues—there is no more consensus, and perhaps even less, than there is over plainly substantive moral issues. So it is not obvious, or perhaps even true, that metaethics can serve as an instrument for greater rationality or adequacy in our moral lives. It is not clear what we need these clarifications for or how much they actually clarify. Do they do much more than give us a new jargon for talking about morality? Alternatively if we try to say we need metaethics as a new foundational account for ethics—there being, without it, no prospect for consensus on foundational normative ethical theories or even for plausibly claiming any of them are true—we seem to say something that does not track truth and is not even clearly intelligible.

VI

Before I further query the philosophical import of metaethics, I need to contrast the new metaethics that has emerged in the 1970s and 80s with the old metaethics—the, if you will, standard metaethics that I have just described and raised questions about its import. In their masterful review article of the state of the art in current ethical theory, "Toward *Fin Siècle* Ethics," Stephen Darwall, Alan Gibbard and Peter Railton write,

> Slowly, the landscape of moral philosophy, which had become stark, even desiccated, during the final years of the reign of analytic metaethics, was being populated by a richer variety of views, many of which placed substantive and normative questions at the fore.[49]

They go on to add:

...one such view became the reference point for all others, thanks in part
to its systematic character and normative attractiveness: John Rawls's
Theory of Justice, with its method of "reflective equilibrium." The narrowly
language-oriented agenda of analytic metaethics was fully displaced, not
so much because of a refutation of, say, noncognitivism, but because of an
uneasiness about the notions of "meaning" or "analytic truth," and because
reflective equilibrium arguments, which tended to set aside metaethical
questions, promised to shed much greater light on substantive—and in
many cases socially pressing—moral questions.[50]

This is what they call the period of the Great Expansion. But they also
claim that, paradoxically, "the Great Expansion partly contributed to the
contemporary revival of metaethics."[51] But this, as they are well aware, is
an expanded conception of metaethics. It is what I have called the new
metaethics.

Let us see how, as they have it, metaethics returned to the scene.
Reflective equilibrium, as we saw in the previous chapter, appealed to
considered judgments, what some critics misleadingly called intuitions,
though, as Darwall *et al.* point out, these considered judgments, these (if
you will) intuitions, were "not Moorean insights into the forms but
substantive moral responses that strike us as compelling."[52] But, be that
as it may, there was this central appeal to considered judgments or
considered convictions.   And they were quickly, though I believe
misleadingly, labelled by not a few philosophers as "intuitions."

Reflective equilibrium, Darwall *et al.* continue, was not just a coherence
model, with all its familiar objections, because of the role played in it by
considered judgments. But these considered judgments, as Darwall *et al.*
note, did flow abundantly. Over time, as they also point out, reflective
equilibrium became clearly wide reflective equilibrium, where it appealed
to various empirical matters and empirical theories. Still, integral to the
method, the conception was, that competing normative theories were to be
tested dialectically against these considered judgments or considered
convictions. This seemed to many philosophers problematic, reviving old
questions about the status of intuitions. How is it, it was asked, that these
considered judgments themselves have any initial credibility or warrant?
Why should we—or should we—accept them or appeal to them, and so use
them in justificatory and explanatory argumentation? And what are they
anyway? What are we talking about here? Would it not be better to
develop a moral methodology that made no such appeal? But, in turn it
was asked, is that really possible, if one's moral theory is to make any
genuine contact with morality?

Here we have a cluster of metaethical questions that in turn generated
still others. The questions they generated included questions about the

meaning of "rationality" and "reasonableness" and the rethinking of questions about practical reasoning and practical justification. It, as Darwall *et al.* aver, is difficult to speak unblushingly of metaethical issues now, yet blushing or not, they return to them now under a wider dispensation, a dispensation setting aside what they regard as the obsession with "analytic metaethics" which they take to be of pre-Quinean inspiration.

How, then, do they continue "metaethics"? They remark

> We use this term broadly, not assuming that one can avoid normative commitments in doing metaethics and not restricting metaethics to the analysis of moral language; we include under "metaethics" studies of the justification and justifiability of ethical claims as well as their meaning, and also the metaphysics and epistemology of morals and like matters.[53]

In a footnote, they add, however, and I think revealingly and significantly, perhaps taking away with the left hand what they gave with the right, that it

> remains true—and one might well ask how it could be otherwise—that an approach to the semantics of moral language typically plays a central role in current discussions of metaphysics and justification.[54]

David Copp proceeds along a similar path in his encyclopedia article "Metaethics."[55] After remarking that the distinction and the alleged mutual exclusivity and independence of each other of normative ethics and metaethics has become controversial, he still goes on to describe metaethics as "the philosophical study of the nature, justification, rationality, truth-conditions, and status of moral codes, standards, judgments, and principles, abstracting from their specific content."[56] He then adds that, because metaethics "takes morality and moral principles as its subject matter in this way, it is sometimes called 'second order' ethics."[57] He, in a way that is useful, contrasts normative ethics, which he calls *first-order* ethics, because it actually yields conclusions and theories which are themselves substantive ethical statements and theories, with *second-order* ethics which is metaethics. So, new metaethics or not, the contrast between metaethics and normative ethics, for Copp at least, crucially involves a contrast between *second-order* and *first-order* activities, though it is also stressed that the former (the *second-order* activity) abstracts from the particular content of any actual morality or moral claim. "Normative ethics," he adds, "includes the philosophical defense of positions and principles concerning specific moral issues such as capital punishment, as well as the formulation and defense of general moral principles and normative moral theories such as forms of utilitarian theory, virtue theory and rights based theory."[58] But again, like

Darwall *et al.*, Copp remarks that even with its more holistic approach, "issues about meaning can still be regarded as pivotal."[59] Any adequate metaethical theory, Copp believes, "must *include* an account of the semantics of moral discourse."[60]

So we see here how, as in the old metaethics, questions concerning meaning (use, sense) remain center stage. However, it is also true that discussions of meaning are placed in a wider framework. The import of this comes out clearly and helpfully when Darwall *et al.* applaudingly remark that W. O. Quine and Nelson Goodman have "urged a conception of the task of philosophy in which theory, metatheory, evidence, and inferential norm or, alternatively, content and framework, were not sharply distinguished."[61] This, they think, relieves metaethics of the pressure of fixating its efforts on attaining "conceptual truth" and removes discussions of meaning from being discussed in a vacuum. It keeps metaethics from being desiccated.

As with the method of wide reflective equilibrium, the new metaethics, abandoning what they regard as the old metaethics analytical obsessions, includes in its scope "a broad range of empirical and philosophical questions."[62] Indeed Darwall *et al.* go on to remark that "it would be misleading to attempt to draw a clear distinction between the revival of metaethics in recent years and what broad reflective equilibrium was becoming during the Great Expansion. For what does broad [wide] reflective equilibrium demand if not that we bring morality into some congruence with whatever else we hold in our going view of the world."[63]

First we are told that reflective equilibrium (including wide reflective equilibrium) tends to set aside metaethical questions and then we are told, properly pursued, wide reflective equilibrium and the new metaethics come to much the same thing. I think that this shows that "metaethics," on the new dispensation, is slowly becoming deprived of any significant contrast with an ethics that is not meta and that we had better just junk the old contrast "metaethics"/"normative ethics" and, if we need moral theory at all, to construe it rather differently than the proponents of either metaethics or normative ethics do. This, I think, is being done rather quietly by many philosophers now–Annette Baier, Jean Hampton, Martha Nussbaum, and Cora Diamond among them.[64]

VII

However, I want here to return to the issue I am centrally concerned with in this chapter. Does someone who takes a Deweyian problems-of-life conception of philosophy really need to ground, or at least link, his account to a metaethics (old or new), if he is not to stop short and be intellectually evasive? If he wants to really get to the bottom of things, must he do that?

Will the adoption or rejection of any of these metaethical theories—new or old—or any of their conceptions make any important difference to how we are to live or to how we are to resolve the problems of life? Will such an adoption or rejection of any of these metaethical positions lead to our begging any controversial questions about how to live? My hypothesis—or at least hunch—is that it will not. Metaethical theory will not help in the resolution of questions about the problems of life. However, as is always the case with any philosophical perplexity, what exactly is at issue and what would resolve our perplexities is anything but evident. Some, Copp and Darwall *et al.*, think that metaethics makes a difference normatively speaking. Indeed it even looks like, for them, an occupational presupposition, and, they think, rightly so, of a well-equipped modern moral philosopher. But that that is so is very problematic. Perhaps the heavens will not fall if we do not work out the right metaethics.

Copp writes, "...metaethical theories about the justification of moral standards, together with relevant empirical information, substantiate or undermine moral standards we otherwise might have been inclined to accept."[65] Suppose I believe, as not unsurprisingly I in fact do, that the life of everyone matters and matters equally and that human life has intrinsic value and should be respected. These are key moral notions for me and they are for me moral standards that govern my behavior. Suppose, while keeping these moral beliefs, this bit of *first-order* ethics, I come to accept, as a metaethical theory, a rather simplified version of emotivism. I think moral utterances express the feelings of the utterer and tend to evoke like feelings in hearers. I think they, no more than imperatives, can be properly said to be true or false and that what finally resolves moral disagreement is the achievement of agreement *in* attitude. What, that is, makes a disagreement a moral disagreement is that it is a disagreement *in* attitude. What makes something a normative matter is that it is attitude expressing and evoking.

Will that metaethical theory—that simple emotivism—undermine the moral belief and moral standard I just expressed about the intrinsic value of life? Believing that it, like any other moral utterance, is just expressive and evocative of feelings, I will not expect that it, or any other moral belief, can be seen to be true, to empirically, or in any other way, be established to be true or, for that matter, false. I am not, note, saying all moral beliefs are in error. That, as we have seen, is, if taken straightforwardly, no metaethical remark at all. If I have these emotions, have a pro-attitude towards so regarding and treating people, then these are my moral beliefs and convictions. Recognizing that they have this non-cognitive status gives me no reason for abandoning them, being skeptical about them or adopting other standards or rejecting the idea that there are standards or to regard them all as optional. To the response: "But they are not objective, they finally rest on what pro-attitudes you just happen to have." The proper response to this comes easily, "So then they are not objective. Indeed, with objectivity *so conceived*, no moral standard is or can be objective. So, this being so, they are not worse off than any other moral standard; still they are my standards and I cherish them and will stick with them." To the charge that I am being irrational, I can readily reply: "Not at all. Such standards, if my metaethical account is correct, do indeed depend, if they are to be acceptable to me, on my having certain pro-attitudes and, if you are going to share them, you will have to have these pro-attitudes too." The same thing obtains, and must obtain, if emotivism is justified, for all moral standards for all people. But such semantical considerations do not, in themselves, make my choice or anyone's choice irrational, though it does make them, or at least the fundamental ones, non-rational. But non-rational choices do not have to be, and very often are not, irrational. My choice here is non-rational, not irrational. I need make no mistake in so reasoning nor need I make any factual mistake or be blind to any information in so adopting them, sticking with them and cherishing them, in not taking them to be at all optional.

Or suppose, while keeping the same moral standards, I change, not my morality, but my metaethics and become instead an ethical naturalist who believes that all moral utterances are a subspecies of empirical factual utterance whose truth or falsity is empirically testable. Standards are, I now believe, properly regarded as empirical hypotheses capable of being confirmed or infirmed. So I now take "The life of everyone matters and matters equally" and "Life has intrinsic value" to be such empirical hypotheses. I might think I know how to confirm them and, if I believe that, my standards will not be undermined by my becoming an ethical naturalist. And there is nothing in the *metaethical theory itself* which requires me, if I do not think they have been confirmed, to think they have been *disconfirmed* as distinct from thinking they are *disconfirmable* just as they are *confirmable*. So, in becoming an ethical naturalist, I am not by that very fact rationally required to abandon my standards. I might very well think that while they are confirmable and infirmable they have not yet been confirmed and that I do not myself know how to confirm them. But this again does not rationally require, or in any other way require, me to abandon them any more than a scientist need abandon a pet hypothesis of his because he has not yet confirmed it and does not yet know how to confirm it.

Suppose I do another metaethical flip-flop and I become a Moorean intuitionist. I think I am just directly and non-empirically intuitively aware of the truth of "Life has intrinsic value" and of "The life of everyone matters and matters equally." They, I believe, are synthetic *a priori* propositions, clear to the light of reason, and that what makes them true are some Platonic forms of which I am just directly aware. Coming to doubt such an intuitionism and switching, again, as Bertrand Russell did after a brief alliance with Moore, to a form of emotivism, will not, or at least need not, produce a switch in my actual moral standards, though it does, of course, produce a switch in my metaethical standards.[66] With such an intuitionism, I can, of course, readily claim that I am just directly aware of the truth of "The life of everyone matters and matters equally" and "Life has intrinsic value." But, with the shifting of my metaethical views, they can, without any illogicality of my part, remain fundamental convictions of mine, firmly embedded in my moral being, even after I become persuaded of emotivism. I just do not think any more that they are *synthetic a priori truths* clear to the light of reason. I can go back and forth between different metaethical theories without any shift of or undermining of my actual moral views.

The sample metaethical theories trotted out are absurdly simple ones and any metaethical theory which is even a plausible candidate for acceptance must be much more sophisticated and nuanced than that. But it is also true that it would be something like the first two simple meta-ethical theories that would be the most plausible candidates for metaethical theories which, if accepted, would do that undermining. But they do not, as I have been at pains to show.

It might in turn be responded that I can only come to this comfortable conclusion by ignoring a form of moral skepticism that John Mackie called error-theory.[67] (In my illustrative use of Wittgensteinian therapeutic analysis an oversimplified version of it was stated and criticized. I now turn to a more robust version.) Mackie, like Westermarck before him, who also articulated and defended an error-theory (though Westermarck did not so label it), denies that moral judgments are or could be objective.[68] Given the very nature of what these so-called objective values are supposed to be, there cannot, error-theorists argue, be any such values. People who believe in morals believe that certain actions are just wrong in themselves quite independently of how we happen to feel or of what we approve of or disapprove of. Certain things—the common belief goes—just must be done full stop. But *all* such views, Mackie believes, as did Westermarck as well, are in error. That error consists in—and the claim is that it is perva-sive—believing that certain things are just right or wrong quite independent-ly of the dispositions of human beings. There just is, it is widely believed, and it is what it is "to believe in morals," some "moral entity," some moral reality—some moral truth-maker—in the universe which constitutes the rightness of things. A moral proposition is true when it corresponds to such a moral state of affairs or entity. When it does not, it is false. Moral truth is determined by that "moral stuff." They are the truth-makers for morals. But such views are a bit of incoherent metaphysics and thus are mistaken. There neither is nor can there be such a moral entity, such an objective prescriptivity.

That claim has a paradoxical side, for moral beliefs are said to be mistaken, not because moral beliefs are not the sort of thing that could be either true or false, but because *all moral beliefs are false*. This is said to be so because to believe that just in the very fabric of the universe things are right or wrong is what Mackie takes to be believing in morals and such believing in morals rests on a mistake. To so believe in morals, Mackie thinks, is a presupposition that is built into our very *first-order* moral language—the language we use when the engine is not idling. But this built in presupposition, he also argues, is false thus rendering all our actual, and indeed all our possible, moral beliefs false.

If this argument goes through, and it really is the case that all moral beliefs are false, then my belief that the life of everyone matters and matters equally and that life has intrinsic value would, of course, be false, along with all the rest of our moral beliefs. But this means, paradoxically, that their denials would be false as well, e.g., that life has no intrinsic value or that the lives of all people do not matter equally. These denials of these central moral beliefs of mine are themselves also moral beliefs and again, along with all other moral beliefs, would, on such an account, be false. Aside from my previously argued point about what it could mean to speak of falsity here, where we have no non-vacuous contrast, there is another consideration, turning on the paradoxicality of the claim, that also puts the error-theory in question. When error-theorists are not doing metaethics (*second-order* ethics) or the "ontology of morals," they, in engaging, as they do, in moral deliberations, are doing *first-order* ethics. They are propounding and carefully arguing for certain moral views as Mackie does in Part Two of his *Ethics: Inventing Right and Wrong.*[69] But here they are arguing morally, trying carefully to establish the correctness of certain moral beliefs. They plainly take their *first-order* moral beliefs very seriously indeed and they certainly do not regard their own moral beliefs as errors or all the moral theories (*first-order* ethics) they critically examine (as, say, when Mackie examines Sidgwick) as only making false claims.[70] Rather, they treat some moral views has having beliefs which they think are true or at least as rationally warranted or at the very least as rationally warrantable. They seek, in their actual moral argumentation, to show that some moral beliefs are rationally warranted. But this makes perplexing and problematical their claim that *all* moral beliefs are false. It looks like, appearances to the contrary notwithstanding, that they actually expect the error-theory to be only a *second-order* theory and not a claim of, or in, *first-order* ethics. (Talk of the ontology [metaphysics] of morals muddies things, for it is not clear, *if* ontological claims are intelligible at all, what kind of status such claims have.)

What they are actually saying, I believe, in so speaking, though they put the matter in a misleading way, is (1) that there is no objective prescriptivity (no normative entity, no moral truth-makers) in the world or, for that matter, "out of the world" and (2) that, all the same, people rather massively and tenaciously, for psychologically understandable reasons, believe that there are and that that last belief is in error. That is the great and pervasive error of people (great masses of people) who believe in morals. What, by contrast, for great masses of people (including objectivist philosophers) need not be false, or at least not invariably false, are their actual moral beliefs; some may be true, some false, or maybe they are the sort of thing that, like imperatives, are neither true nor false; but they need not invariably or necessarily be false. What is invariably false, is their *objectivist metaethical belief or metaphysical belief that there is such normative objectivity (objective prescriptivity in, or "out of", the world.* There is, and can be, no such objective prescriptivity. Such a conception is incoherent, or at least a conception for which we have no evidence or even have a good understanding. Massively, error-theorists claim, people have a meta-belief or an ontological belief in a very queer something, they know not what. The error—the false view—is having this mixed up philosophical view, a view which, in one form or another, Mackie believes, is pervasive. If we want to call that "believing in morals" and say that such a metaethical or metaphysical belief is in error, we can do so and perhaps that view is correct. Indeed, it seems to me very plausible. But that is a view in metaethics or in the ontology (metaphysics) of morals. (On the new metaethics it is both.) But it—and this is crucial—is not itself a moral belief, a part of *first-order* morality. Moreover, it does not follow because in that sense there are no objective values—no objective prescriptivity out there in the world—that nothing is valuable, nothing is worth doing or having or worth struggling for. Taken straightforwardly—but in a way error-theorists do *not* intend—the claim that all moral beliefs are false does indeed conflict with my belief that life has intrinsic value. But so taken it is not itself a metaethical belief (a *second-order* belief) but is itself a moral belief (a claim in *first-order* ethics) which, if true is false, sharing the logical features of the liar paradox. So understood it undermines itself and thus does nothing to show that it is a mistake to think life has intrinsic value. More to the present point, if the claim that all believing in morality is in error is taken, as error-theorists seem to intend it, as a metaethical or ontological thesis, it also does nothing to undermine the belief that the life of everyone matters and matters equally and the belief that life has intrinsic value. Taken, as it was actually taken by error-theorists, as the metaethical or ontological belief (assuming for the moment the latter notion is intelligible), that there is in the world no objective prescriptivity, it does not undermine the *first-order* view that life has intrinsic value, that we should respect life, that the life of everyone matters and matters equally, or indeed any *first-order* moral belief at all. Many philosophers, including Westermarck and Mackie, do not believe in objective prescriptivity or even find the notion coherent, yet they have moral beliefs: they believe one should keep one's promises, keep faith with one's friends, that having certain of one's needs met is a good thing and that torturing people for the fun of it is vile. They just reject, and perhaps correctly, certain meta-theories or ontological theories and certain pictures of what rightness and wrongness or goodness and badness consist in. But they do not reject the moral beliefs themselves; they are as much their convictions as they are of the plainest of plain women and men.

We still have no reason to believe that any metaethical view could legitimately undermine our moral standards or our *first-order* moral commitments. What could be undermined is some metaethical dangler fortuitously attached to a *first-order* moral view. Suppose, for example, in thinking that life has intrinsic value I also believe, or even *think* that in believing that I *must* also believe, that, in some Platonist or moral realist way, there must be intrinsic value in the universe. I must believe, that is, that there is in the universe some strange kind of ultimate moral reality. This Platonism is the metaphysical and metaethical dangler attached to my *first-order* moral view that life has intrinsic value. But I could, as Russell came to, moving away from his earlier intuitionism, see that such Platonism is moonshine, or at least come to believe, however mistakenly, that it is, without abandoning my *first-order* moral belief. I just excise the dangler. There is no reason, if we are tolerably clear-headed, to abandon any moral belief that is straightforwardly *first-order* because of some metaethical view, some *second-order* conception concerning morals.

VIII

Assuming (what is to assume a lot) that we could achieve agreement about it, would the best philosophical clarification of the nature of morality lead us to accept or reject morality? I cannot see that it would. The previous arguments were intended to push in the direction of showing that only by a confusion could it have such an effect. But let us try to push a little further. Only metaethical theories at the subjectivist end of the metaethical spectrum would be even plausible candidates for such upsetting theories. Supposing (for the sake of the present discussion) they yield the best clarification of the nature of morality, that might, some might argue, lead us to *reject* morality when we finally come to see what its real nature is. We have seen, *au contraire*, how neither an emotive theory nor an error-theory (paradigms of upsetting theories) afford any sound ground for rejecting morality. Perhaps a Hobbesian reductive ethical naturalism would? "Good" and "bad" states of affairs or objects are defined, on such an account, by a person's desires and aversions. What we have an aversion for is bad; what we seek out, desire or want is good. Desire, in short, determines both good and bad. We, as well, understand both right and rational actions purely instrumentally as those actions which are the most effective of the alternatives available in attaining the objects or states of affairs that we regard as good, namely, those that we desire. This is a thorough naturalism with no reference being made to strange powers of human reason (some substantial rationality) or to non-material objects, properties or relations.

This Hobbesian naturalism is, as well, entirely congruent with an utterly physicalist or materialist view of the world and rejects, just as firmly as an error-theory, any conception of an objective prescriptivity or a "moral entity" just built into the fabric of the universe or any conception of a *summum bonum* (highest good) requiring any such metaphysical conception. There are just the goods which are the objects of our desires, some of the desires being basic desires (where the object of the basic desire is desired for its own sake) the other desires being non-basic desires where we desire something as a means to something else which we desire for its own sake. These basic desires are, as well, very persistent and pervasive desires. The objects of these basic desires are said to be intrinsically good, for they are desired for their own sake, but they do not, singly or together, constitute an Aristotelian *summum bonum*, an objective value, that ought to be desired for its own sake. Moreover, these things wanted in themselves are not something some mysterious reason or rational faculty just tells us that we ought to desire, whether we in fact desire them or not. No such imputation of such a mysterious faculty is required or even needed. Reason, on such an Aristotelian conception, but not on a Hobbesian conception, has, somehow, an end of its own which can conflict with ends resulting from our desires and rightly, according to the rationalist Aristotelian view, when this happens, override our desires. A Hobbesian naturalism cannot consistently accept such an Aristotelian doctrine, though it does believe that there are intrinsic goods in the perfectly ordinary sense that some things are desired for their own sakes or wanted in themselves. No end—not even self-preservation and life—if it is not actually desired, on a Hobbesian account, can be rational to pursue. And when two ends rooted in two conflicting desires conflict, the strongest desire—the strongest desire that we have at the time—determines at that time what is good and what is to be done. Contrary to Aristotle, and many non-naturalists and rationalists, a Hobbesian naturalism cannot attribute to reason a goal or end of its own which is taken to be objectively valuable and which can be opposed to the goals or ends of desire. There is no such rationality any more than there is an objective prescriptivity. Hobbes does indeed say that those glory prone people who do not pursue their self-preservation are irrational. This sounds Aristotelian, but it is not, for self-preservation is an instrumental good, on his account, necessary for getting the things we want, for satisfying our basic desires, i.e., things wanted in themselves of which one very insistent one is life. But self-preservation, like security, is instrumentally valuable only. It is not a basic desire, but life is. Where something is desired as a means to something else we desire, and that something else is intensely desired, then it is irrational to not also desire the necessary means to what we so strongly desire.

Presumably there are many things we intensely desire, some of them for their own sakes. Being alive is a necessary condition for having them, so it would be irrational not to desire our self-preservation for without it we could not have the things we so intensely want. Hobbes's core naturalistic metaethical account is summed up in a famous passage from his *Leviathan*:

> ...whatsoever is the object of any mans Appetite or Desire; that is it, which he for his part calleth *Good:* And the object of his *Hate*, and Aversion, Evill; And of his Contempt, *Vile* and *Inconsiderable*. For these words, Good, Evil, and Contemptable, are ever used with relation to the person that useth them: there being nothing simply and absolutely so; nor any common rule of Good and Evill, to be taken from the objects them-selves...[71]

Here we have an austere metaethic: a naturalism that might be labelled, where it is sympathized with, a moral science, and, where not an object of sympathy, a scientistic conception of morality, foreign to our reflective moral sensibilities. Unlike an Aristotelianism, a Kantian conception of morality or a Moorean or Sidgwickean non-naturalism, there is nothing on Hobbes's account that reason itself determines, or just discerns, to be good.

If this Hobbesian naturalism is clearheadedly accepted will it not lead us to reject morality or at least the morality that is embedded in our civilization? Well, it did not as a matter of fact lead Hobbes to make such a rejection or contemporary Hobbesians either (though they usually soften, in one way or another, Hobbes's austere metaethics); and it did not lead Adam Smith, David Hume or Edward Westermarck to such a rejection, who in similar but not identical ways were subjectivist about values and skeptical of the whole tradition of moral rationalism. Though all these philosophers were ethical skeptics or moral skeptics in the metaethical or the ontological sense just specified, they nonetheless accepted most of the tablets of conventional morality (Hume less so than Hobbes). They just put them on a different metaethical foundation. As Westermarck put it, in a very un-Platonistic and un-Aristotelian way, morality rests on *feeling* rather than on *reason*. But our feelings in fact turn out to be such that we get the good old morality back, but on a different philosophical foundation. There is no Stirnerian, Nietzschean, or Foucaultian transvaluation of our actual values. Indeed Hobbes was not content until he got back into his system the natural moral laws of the Medieval tradition, but now as axioms of prudence. There is no Aristotelian *summum bonum* but there is what he called a common good.[72] Though human beings differ rather extensively in what they desire, they all agree that "Peace is good."[73] There are, that is, some things that all human beings in fact want. Here we have common goods, though no common measure to be taken from the objects themselves. Moreover, to the extent that we are rational—instrumentally rational—(for Hobbes there is no other rationality) we, desiring peace, and therefore finding it good, will also desire the "means of Peace, which...are Justice, Gratitude, Modesty, Equity, Mercy and the rest of Laws of Nature," i.e., the natural moral laws of the Medieval tradition. We will recognize in this way that these natural laws are good. The natural laws of the Medieval tradition are not self-evident truths clear to the light of reason, but are prudential imperatives, and, as such, with their hypothetical status, they are empirical truths or falsehoods. They assert a causal connection between cooperative forms of behavior and self-preservation because these forms of behavior effect peace and thereby help us to achieve what we all want, namely, a longer, more secure life and a more commodious life. If these causal connections actually obtain, the natural moral laws are true; otherwise, they are false. They are not, to repeat, truths of reason. There are no such truths. To believe in such truths is to be caught up in myth.

However, we will act in accordance with these laws only if generally others are willing to do so. Thus, as Jean Hampton puts it, the natural moral laws have the following logical structure: "If you seek peace (which is a means to your preservation), provided that others are willing to do x, then do action x."[74] So understood, as she continues, "the laws [the natural moral laws] can be taken to be accurate axioms of prudence, and not directives that generate obligations that are opposed to self-interest."[75] So, as Schopenhauer and Nietzsche could have scoffed, as they actually did at Kant, we have with Hobbes, in spite of his seeming tough mindedness, a full acceptance of traditional morality. We get a rejection of alternative rationalistic metaethics, and some normative ethical *theories* (certain pictures of morality), but no rejection of, or even modification of, morality. And contemporary Hobbesians have been no more rejectful or iconoclastic.[76] So, if our object is to gain a critical morality that might reject all or (more plausibly) part of traditional morality, we have no basis for it here. Someone, wrestling with the problems of life, might learn to talk Hobbesian, if she likes, but it would have no effect on her actual arguments about what is to be done or about what concretely and contextually it is a good thing to do or have or what kind of person it would be good to be.

If it is implausible to believe that metaethical theories could give us sound reasons for rejecting morality, it is also implausible to think that metaethical theories, even those giving us the best clarification of the nature of morality, could give us grounds for accepting morality. Unless some theory might plausibly threaten to upset morality, there is nothing that we need a theory for to show us that after all it is alright to accept morality. Morality has not been shaking, at least not for these philosophical reasons, such that we need philosophy to show us that, after all, it rests on a secure foundation. Perhaps even a shiny new foundation. This should be a subject of Kierkegaardian irony. Still many metaethicists, probably not great fans of Kierkegaard, have thought they would, and should, provide us with the underlying rationale for such an acceptance, showing us that an acceptance of morality can be demonstrated by "philosophical reason." But it looks like nothing like this is in the offing or needed.

IX

Certain rather rationalistic metaethicists at the other end of the metaethical spectrum from Hobbes or the emotivists believe that there are sound transcendental arguments that can, and should, be deployed which will show that rationality requires the acceptance of morality, or at least the crucial structure of morality that these philosophers describe. So we are back to the kinds of arguments we found reasons for rejecting in discussing metaphysics. Let us see if in this ethical context they will work any better. In speaking of transcendental arguments, I am speaking of arguments, as I discussed in Chapter 2, which seek to show that for a given domain of discourse there are certain features which are necessary, logically necessary, for that form of discourse to be possible. Thus, if there is to be sensible experience at all, it is sometimes claimed, there must be embodied beings having the experience and for them to have any experience at all, that experience must be in spatial and temporal terms. Similarly some have said that for there to be something recognizable as a morality it must—logically "must"—have certain features or characteristics. These features set *a priori* constraints on what moral principles are justified, or indeed can be justified, and what considerations can legitimately be appealed to in morality. Such a metaethic is a form of objectivism, but it is not like Sidgwickean, Moorean or Rossian intuitionism. We do not just intuit—non-sensorily become directly aware of—the truth, indeed the necessary truth, of moral propositions which themselves are synthetic *a priori* principles. We do not have any such non-sensory perception at all. We do indeed, such philosophers argue, justify certain ultimate moral principles and in doing so show that they are necessary truths, while also being synthetic, but they are established to be necessary truths not by intuitive insight, but by a transcendental argument that show they are necessary to the very possibility of morality and that morality is inescapable for rational agents. Careful reasoning, the claim goes, leads us to the acknowledgement of such principles. The idea is not that we find moral principles which are objective because they afford an accurate representation of an independent metaphysical or moral order—as with intuitionism or natural moral law theories—but moral principles are instead universal *rational* demands yielding moral principles that are imposed by our very practical reasoning, i.e., reasoning about what to do and what to be. If we think carefully and reason consistently, we will come to acknowledge that there are sound reasons which specify that we must act in certain ways and must try to become or remain a certain sort of person.

Such conceptions are on the objectivist end of what Darwall *et al.* call Practical Reasoning Theories.[77] Kant's account is such a metaethic, as is Stephen Darwall's, Alan Gewirth's, Marcus Singer's, and A. Phillips Griffiths's.[78] As the polar opposite of a Hobbesian, Humean, error-theory (Westermarck, Mackie) or an emotivist metaethic, such rationalist Practical Reasoning Theories argue that certain reasons are good reasons—in some instances morally and rationally compelling reasons—for an agent to act in a certain way quite independently of what desires or feelings she may have or not have. Even though she may have no desire to do x it may be the case that it would be both immoral and irrational of her not to do x or not, at least, to try to do x. There is the vaulting ambition here to show that *morality can be grounded in practical reason: in reason as it is employed in agency.* The thing that such moral philosophers sought to establish is that morality confronts us with categorical demands—demands that are in this way objective—which nonetheless "ultimately issue from deep within the moral agent" but not from his sentiments, or not necessarily from his sentiments or ever *just* from his sentiments, but, and necessarily, from his very rationality.

Griffiths's, to consider a brief but reasonably clear articulation of such an account, tries to show that certain substantive moral principles are so transcendentally required by our very practical reason.[79] Unlike Sidgwick, Moore, and Ross, Griffiths is a rationalist who eschews appeals to intuition and seeks to articulate, as we have remarked, transcendental arguments designed to show that certain substantive moral principles are required by the very formal character of morality itself. Put differently, he seeks to show that certain moral principles must be taken to be correct, if moral discourse is to be possible. And since moral discourse is actual, it must be possible, and so such moral principles must be justified, must be correct. Careful reasoning, staying within the circle of moral principles, judgments and considerations, will show that certain moral principles or standards or judgments are true or are warranted in such a way that there is no rational or even coherent alternative to accepting and seeking to act in accordance with them. There is nothing rationally *optional* about them. It is not just that morality is in *accordance* with reason; it is *required* by reason.

Griffiths believes he can establish three fundamental substantive moral principles in this way: (1) a principle of impartiality, (2) a principle of rational benevolence, and (3) a principle of liberty. These, he argues, are *ultimate principles that are necessarily presupposed in all moral reasoning.* Their assumption is necessary, though not sufficient, for the justification of all particular, contextually determinate, moral judgments.

Put most simply, to consider it first, *the principle of impartiality* requires that similar cases must be treated similarly. Any form of treatment that is taken to be right for one person must be right for all others unless the others are significantly different. Why is this so and why is it a presupposition of the very possibility of moral discourse? It is so and is such a presupposition because morality is a form of discourse that requires a form of objectivity, where in judging actions to be right or wrong, we so reason that a correct practical principle is one that could in principle be reached by anybody. But for this in turn to be so, such judgments must be made in terms of features that the actions or the situations in which they are done actually possess and not on any other factors arbitrarily introduced by the person making the judgment.[80] Any feature that we pick out in justifying a moral judgment must always be relevant to moral judgments of that type unless something has changed about the situation or the persons involved (but not just a change in their pro-or-con attitudes but something like their becoming ill, impoverished, or the like). "It follows that any action which is right or wrong for one person to do is right or wrong for every person to do unless there are some special factors present in the other cases."[81] So what "anyone ought to do in any given set of circumstances is what anyone else ought to do, as long as his case is not relevantly different," and anything one ought to do on "any given occasion is what one ought to do in every occasion unless there are factors present which are relevantly different."[82] Put simply: the principle of impartiality is that similar cases are to be treated similarly. I will state his argument for his other two principles before I turn to critical assessment.

The principle of rational benevolence, stated crudely, as Griffiths initially states it himself, is the principle that "one ought in action to consider the interests of all beings in the universe."[83] Stated just like that, the principle is absurd, but Griffiths gives a rational reconstruction of it in such a way that it becomes a more plausible candidate for a principle that might be a necessary feature of all moral discourse. His argument here is rather indirect. He starts by reminding us that moral discourse is public objective discourse. I cannot, conceptually cannot, in setting out moral principles, set secret principles which are not available to everyone. Such principles could not count as moral principles; they could not be part of my, or any other person's, *moral* code. This is so because every rational being will wish to see his interests protected and satisfied. It would be irrational for him to "participate in a form of discourse the practical effect of which would be to deny his interests..."[84] But a secret code could very well do this. There would be no way with such a code of assuring that it answers to the interests of everyone involved. But then a rational moral agent would not, and indeed could not, accept it.

For a moral agent, assuming she acts rationally, to engage in moral discourse, it must not be the case that a consideration of her interests is being ruled out. Moreover, any rational being is in principle a possible interlocutor in a moral discussion, given that morality is an objective public discourse. So what is determined by such means cannot, Griffiths tells us, neglect the interests of any rational being. *In deciding what is to be done the interests of every rational agent involved in the situation must be taken into account.* That, rationally reconstructed, is the *principle of rational benevolence* and, his claim is that it just follows from what moral discourse, and hence morality, is. It is a necessary presupposition of morality.

The *principle of liberty*, to move on to his last transcendental principle, says "that one ought not to interfere, without special justification, in the chosen course of any rational being or impose on any rational being conditions which will prevent him from pursuing his chosen courses of action."[85] Moral discourse is a form of discourse in which we try to guide action *rationally*, but to do so "we try to determine action on the basis of a rational consideration of the nature of the action and its context."[86] But, in determination of the course of action of an agent, to interfere with his choice imposes something by force rather than to allow it to be up for rational determination. For rational determination to obtain the moral agent must be free to choose his course of action. He may, of course, choose irrationally; still, as a necessary condition for the action to be rationally determined, it must, all the same, be an action where he is free to choose what course of action to take. "Such interference must then be presupposed as absent in public objective practical discourse in which action is determined by reason, and hence in using such discourse, in participating in it as an institution, one is presupposing that one ought not interfere by force, but only by rational persuasion, in the chosen course of any rational being."[87]

Suppose these three principles are, as Griffiths believes, transcendentally secured. No rational agent, let us now assume, could deny or reject them. And there is no engaging in moral discourse without presupposing them. Indeed let us assume that we would not even understand how a discourse could be a moral discourse without these principles being in place in it. Does this mean any rational agent will accept morality? Of course, any rational *moral* agent must accept morality, for trivially, if he did not, he would then not be a *moral* agent. But we cannot get from what a rational *moral* agent must accept to what any rational agent must accept, for it remains possible that some amoralists or nihilists might be rational. At the very least, Griffiths has given us no reason for ruling that out. It is quite possible that a clever free-rider might not be a fool. *Perhaps* arguments like those of Hobbes or, building on him, those of Kurt Baier or David Gauthier, will establish that the rational agent will abandon or, from the very beginning, will not engage in free-riding or egoism, but then again perhaps not.[88] But there is nothing in the above three principles or in Griffiths's arguments to show that reason requires the abandoning of free riding and the accepting of morality. He doesn't show why, in certain favored circumstances, a purely self-interested person should abandon the perspective of rational self-interest and accept – and not just for what he can milk out of it – morality. Perhaps he should accept only the *rhetoric* of morality and falsely swear to those principles while continuing judiciously to free-ride? Hobbes's *foole* may not be a fool after all. He may be a tough-minded, very clear-sighted individual. Griffiths has at best only shown that *if* we are to be persons of moral principle, then we must accept these three principles. He has not shown why a rational person, no matter how she is situated, must comply with the dictates of morality. Morality might be in *accordance* with reason without being *required* by reason. So in the most fundamental sense Griffiths has not shown why rational agents must accept rational morality.[89]

However, even if such amoralist, why-be-moral? considerations can be legitimately set aside, Griffiths's transcendental argumentation still has its inadequacies. It suffers from another quite different difficulty: a difficulty which, I believe, afflicts all such accounts. It is that such accounts, to preserve their *necessity*, have to be so vague and indeterminate that they yield nothing with any genuine substance. In articulating the principle of impartiality, for example, we have no non-contextual account of what features make for relevant or non-arbitrary differences and what do not.[90] Or what is to count as a "special explanation" which will change our assessment of what is relevant and what is not? Or when are "special features" sufficiently special such that we should now say that we have relevantly different cases so that we should now realize that we do not really have similar cases which we must treat similarly? Treat similar cases similarly is practically devoid of content. It is not sufficiently determinate to guide conduct. What is right for John must be right for Joan, unless John and Joan are significantly different or significantly differently situated, but whether they are or are not cannot be determined by transcendental argument or from inspecting the principle of impartiality itself. To get something that is a necessary presupposition of moral discourse, we get something so thin in content that it cannot do what moral principles are supposed to do, namely, guide conduct.

If to try to rectify this, we fill in the content by specifying "significantly different," "relevantly different," or "special factors" and the like. But then we will get something that cannot be specified non-contextually and cannot be determined by transcendental argument. The transcendental arguments, even if sound, give us, as might be expected, not morality, not even a minimal morality, or moral discourse, but some skeletal, more or less, formal features of morality or moral discourse. Accepting them will not be accepting (or for that matter rejecting) morality, for moralities are full-bodied things, and not infrequently conflicting things. Even if these transcendental arguments are sound, all the at least apparently conflicting moralities remain in place. If Griffiths's transcendental arguments are sound, all these moralities will have some identical somewhat formal features. But such transcendental argumentation will yield no principle or basis for choosing between these conflicting moralities, so that we can determine what "true morality" is. Formal structures do not determine content; and surely accepting morality is not just accepting the formal structure, even the more or less formal structure, of all moralities, including the at least apparently conflicting moralities.

Generally, such a rationalistic metaethics, with its transcendental argumentation, suffers from the difficulties common to all such rationalism, ethical and non-ethical: whatever principles, if any, which are transcendentally secured are so thin as to be devoid of substance. In the "Practical Reasoning Theories" cases, for example, we get principles so devoid of content as to be worthless in the establishment or defense of any substantive ethics.[91] A Deweyian problems-of-life philosophy can, and should, ignore such accounts and it should itself eschew all utilization of transcendental argument. Perhaps, just perhaps, some such accounts do validly articulate some necessary presuppositions of moral discourse. Still they are utterly useless in reasoning in trying to decide what to do or in reflecting on what kind of person to try to become or on what kind of conception of the moral life we should have. They are free spinning wheels that turn no machinery.

X

I have neither suggested nor is it my belief that metaethical theories are without intrinsic interest. On the contrary, the best work going on here seems to me subtle, complex and, with writers such as Allan Gibbard and David Wiggens, deeply reflective.[92] What I have argued is that it has minimal relevance in thinking about the problems of life, such as facing the issues discussed in the previous chapter, or even in thinking about what principles of social justice to adhere to or what a good life for human beings would be.   Where done in an astute Wittgensteinian manner, metaethical elucidation (I did not say metaethical *theory*) can break obsessive confusions about what our moral discourse must be like. Confusions that can become, when people are in the grip of philosophy, obsessions standing in the way of serious moral thinking.   Doing that elucidatory work is, of course, not nothing.   But it is, all the same, a therapeutic underlaborer job.   It does not reveal "the foundations of the moral life," but, among other things, points to the senselessness or at least non-necessity of looking for such foundations.   I have not even argued, or claimed without argument, that now, as metaethics, a Strawsonian conception of philosophy, as a form of *second-order* discourse, charting systematically the structure of moral discourse, is impossible.   It has not been systematically done and perhaps cannot be.   But I was not concerned to argue that.   But what I did say at the end of the previous section about Practical Reason Theories does suggest that such an account, if true, would provide us only with platitudes.   But I have, in discussing these theories and others as well – emotivism, Hobbesian naturalism, the error-theory – argued for their *normative impotence.*   It is this claim that is essential for me. Someone doing moral and social philosophy after the fashion of Rawls or Dewey and the conception I have defended, can and should ignore such theorizing.   Again it stands in the way of serious moral and political thinking.

However, the metaethicist, or his metaphilosophical defender, might respond: you ignore the question of *moral skepticism*.   Given the pervasive, persistent and at least apparently fundamental differences in moral belief in the world, moral skepticism is a real problem.   Perhaps, such a critic could continue, you are right in thinking that *epistemological* skepticism is a pseudo-problem subject to Moorean dissolution, but *moral* skepticism is not analogous.   It is more like religious skepticism.   There is no real problem about whether we can know that the external world exists or whether there are other minds, but there is a real problem about whether God exists.   Indeed skepticism here is surely not unreasonable and it is very likely thoroughly justified.   Moral skepticism, such a philosopher is claiming, is in the same boat as religious skepticism.   It needs to be taken seriously and, if it is to be defeated, we must succeed in articulating a sound normative ethical or moral theory backed up by a sound metaethics. Moral skepticism is corrosive of the Deweyian enterprise I articulated in the last chapter.   So metaethics, after all, cannot be benignly neglected.[93]

I shall now argue that this claim is false.   Where we are talking about a global moral skepticism, where the claim is that we can never know or warrantedly believe that *any* moral standard or *any* belief is justified, this skepticism can be defeated by arguments similar to the reconstructed Moorean arguments I deployed in the third chapter. Moreover, metaethical argumentation is, I believe, more likely, along with misconceptions about its relevance, to fuel moral skepticism than to dissolve it or refute it. We do not need, I shall argue, a sound normative ethical theory backed up by a sound metaethic to refute moral skepticism. Moreover—or so I shall argue—my Moorean arguments are more plausible—more likely to be right—than any metaethical defense of or refutation of moral skepticism.

However, unlike intuitions about epistemological skepticism, intuitions about moral skepticism, I believe, run against me. My impression is that most intellectuals think moral skepticism is very real. It, like religious skepticism, needs, they believe, to be nonevasively faced in our cultural life. I shall argue that the reason why this seems plausible, and indeed is plausible, rests on a confusion about *scope* in considering moral skepticism. There is a problem—a real problem, with real doubts, not merely Cartesian doubts—about morality. And it generates, and rightly so, I shall argue, a form of moral skepticism—a less than global moral skepticism—that I shall discuss later in this chapter. But that moral skepticism, it is vital to realize, is not the global moral skepticism that is the object of concern of some metaethicists or normative ethical theoreticians. That problem (that global moral skepticism), I shall argue, should go the way of epistemological skepticism or global skepticism more generally. It should be up for Wittgensteinian dissolution and Kierkegaardian irony and perhaps even positivist scorn.

However, this should be argued, not just declaimed. I shall do this, before taking my Moorean turn, by examining the most intelligent and reflective recent argument with which I am acquainted for taking moral skepticism (global moral skepticism) seriously, namely, the argument in David Copp's "Moral Skepticism."[94] Copp argues, rightly it seems to me, that, unlike epistemological skepticism, moral skepticism has no standard and accepted form. There are, as he remarks, various challenges to morality that have engaged different philosophers and other intellectuals throughout history. No one of them has been generally taken to be "the problem of moral skepticism."[95] He sees, among moral philosophers, the more typical view as being the belief that "moral skepticism can be responsibly ignored..."[96] Still, moral skepticism "expresses widespread intuitive doubts about morality. It has moral significance because it can lead a person to view moral commitment as optional, in the way that we think daily exercise is optional."[97]

My disagreement with Copp could be put, following that remark, in a nutshell. Nothing of the sort has been shown. Moral skepticism, of the type he will articulate, casts doubts on ethical *theories* (metaethical and substantive). And indeed we may have good reasons to be skeptical about ethical *theories:* about whether any of them are true or warranted or even have much of a point. We may not even have a clear idea about how to go about establishing that some have greater plausibility than others.[98] We might be quite at a loss here. But these things would not entail skepticism about the firmest of our actual moral beliefs or necessarily, or even plausibly, lead to the belief that these moral beliefs may be just arbitrary constructions and that we can never know or reasonably believe that anything at all is right or wrong, good or bad, desirable or undesirable. A skeptic about *theory* might very well think *such* moral skepticism absurd. The parallel *here* with epistemology is, as far as I can see, exact. We could be – and I believe we should be – through and through skeptical about the soundness of any of the proposed epistemological *theories* without being at all skeptical that we sometimes know that the water is running, the light has been left on, that it is snowing, that there are many rocks in Iceland, that it is usually hotter in South Carolina in summer than it is in the Northwest Territories and the like. Skepticism about epistemological theories is completely compatible with utter non-skepticism about our commonsense beliefs about matters of fact and utter non-skepticism about our knowledge of the external world and of other minds. Similarly utter skepticism about the soundness of moral theories, even skepticism concerning the coherence of some, is completely compatible with complete non-skepticism about many of our actual moral beliefs, e.g., that we should keep faith with our friends, that we should try to avoid inflicting unnecessary suffering, that we should try to protect the bases for self-respect, and the like. Only if it could be shown that skepticism about moral theories should, or even will, where rationally and correctly dwelt on, generate moral skepticism of the sort I have just described should we think that moral skepticism is a serious problem that needs our urgent attention rather than our benign neglect or something, if we like unravelling these puzzles, we might, just for the fun of it, turn our attention to. So I am at a loss to see why moral skepticism and its refutation has philosophical or any other kind of significance.

Yet Copp, like Barry Stroud among epistemologists and for epistemological skepticism, thinks that moral skepticism needs a strong response. Moral theories (metaethical and normative ethical or some amalgam) "aim to explain the nature and justification of morality [and they] must be evaluated as responses to it."[99] "Anti-skeptical philosophers," of which he is one, "need to investigate skepticism, and provide it with a formulation, in order to be able to argue that it is untenable."[100] Moreover, we cannot know that we already have a theory which defeats moral skepticism until we have stated moral skepticism in its strongest and most plausible form; "we cannot evaluate a theory as a reply to skepticism until we know how best to express the skeptic's position."[101]   And that is what he sets out to do.

He thinks that people like myself have been as complacent about the problem as we have because we think moral skepticism is either skepticism about reasons for being moral—the "why be moral?" problem—or epistemological skepticism as applied to morals and that both of these forms of skepticism can be rather easily disposed of. Copp will define a form of moral skepticism—the form he thinks we should take really seriously—that "is not a skepticism about reasons to be moral, nor is it simply a form of epistemological skepticism."[102]

He first sets out what he takes to be a set of plausible intuitions that the skeptic has about morality and then he gives a formulation—an abstract formulation—of moral skepticism that "expresses these intuitions."[103] First Copp points out that

> the skeptic recognizes that a moral code is part of the culture of most if not every society, and she recognizes that most people subscribe to certain moral standards and strive to conform to them. She acknowledges as well that people typically believe that the standards they subscribe to are justified, credible or warranted. There are perhaps uncountably many imaginable moral standards, most of which no one is likely ever to subscribe to. But the skeptic denies that any moral standard has any genuine credibility, and she is not swayed from her position by the fact that many people regard some of them as credible. She thinks that no moral standard has any adequate and appropriate warrant, grounding, certification, or justification....[104]

Given that moral codes are often deeply entrenched and that the outsider or the rebel who does not conform will pay dearly for non-conformity, the moral skeptic will conform, as a matter of prudence, to the moral code and its standards while still denying, at least to herself, that these standards are morally justified. She may not be at all like the free-rider who asks why should he be moral and concerning whom there will be a problem of compliance. The moral skeptic may perfectly comply and think it stupid not to. She need not, and typically will not, deny that morality and being a person of good morals is instrumentally rational. In addition, the moral skeptic need not deny, Copp argues, that "people in her society may be able to bring their moral views into a structured and reflective state of coherence, in which their moral views are internally coherent, and coherent with their other beliefs."[105] Moreover, Copp's ideal moral skeptic will, like most of us, have certain moral standards that will likely continue to figure in her life and she "will continue to have values and standards that [she will] subscribe to, without thereby exhibiting any kind of irrationality."[106] People, who like that sort of thing, or want a moral order to prevail, including a moral order in their lives, can reasonably continue to subscribe to moral standards, but, the moral skeptic, unlike the non-skeptic, will hold "that no moral standard as such has an adequate and appropriate justification, yet she holds that subscription to a moral standard is an option even for a skeptic."[107] Whether, on the skeptic's view of things, we are rational to subscribe to it—to commit ourselves to that, or any, moral standard, not just instrumentally but for its own sake as well—will depend on what our desires happen to be. For some, moral subscription will be rational; for others, it will not. Moral subscription, she holds, is *rationally optional* but not irrational. Whether or not one subscribes to a moral standard, the moral skeptic believes, "one cannot be convicted on that basis alone of any epistemic or cognitive failure...."[108] A moral skeptic, on Copp's conception, could be morally exemplary. She could be committed to all the things non-skeptics are committed to. She could live, without the slightest wavering, a thoroughly virtuous, principled and caring life, committed to the very *first-order* specifically moral things that Kantians, Rawlsians and Aristotelians, among others, are committed to. She may take the same things as required and forbidden, as we staunch moralists do, but, Copp has it, she will not "share our moral *beliefs* as to what is required and what is forbidden...for to say that she believes some way of acting is morally required would suggest...that she believes some moral standard is justified which calls on people to act in that way."[109] She will differ from the non-skeptic in the important way that she will believe that there are no standards that are justified which just call on people to act in a certain way. To be a moral skeptic is to believe "that no moral code or moral standard is or could be objectively justified."[110]

Here the really telling question becomes: What would it be for a moral code, standard, or belief to be *objectively justified*? The skeptic denies—or at least questions—that any of them are, or even could be, so justified, but in denying, or questioning, that they are or even could be so justified, the skeptic must have some idea, for her denial or questioning to be intelligible, what it would be like for a moral code, standard or belief to be objectively justified—a desideratum none of them, if the moral skeptic is right, actually achieve or at least are not known or justifiability believed to have achieved. (Presumably, it should not be *logically* impossible for them to achieve it. For then "moral skepticism" would lack a non-vacuous contrast and thus would be unintelligible.) So what is objective justification in morals?

For there to be objective justification, in the sense Copp conceives of it, we must be able to specify the circumstances under which the code or the standards themselves would be so justified and not just the circumstances in which certain people would be justified in complying with or accepting the moral code or standards. What the non-skeptical moral philosopher should be doing is to appraise or evaluate the various moral standards that are believed in in order to see whether these standards *are themselves* justified. "A moral code or standard," on Copp's account, is "objectively justified just in case it is itself adequately justified, certified or supported on the basis of relevant evidence, arguments, considerations, or reasons."[111] Copp, in trying to show what this comes to, stresses the parallel, as we have already noted but not detailed, between moral skepticism and religious skepticism. "A skeptic," he remarks, "about the existence of God...is concerned to deny that there is any argument or evidence which, all things considered, establishes or has any significant tendency to show, the existence of God."[112] But the religious skeptic is not thereby claiming that people who believe in God are failing in their epistemic responsibilities. These are different issues. There was no more evidence, and the arguments for the existence of God were no better than they are now, in the Middle Ages, but most people living then, including most particularly medieval intellectuals, would have been justified in believing in God. But His existence was no better or worse established then than it is now, when it is anything but obvious that we, particularly we intellectuals, are justified in believing in God. In a parallel way, the moral skeptic "denies that any moral code is established as true, or significantly supported, taking into account all the available evidence and arguments...."[113] But in so reasoning she, Copp tells us, "need not be concerned about the possibility that someone has moral views that are coherent with his other beliefs in a wide reflective equilibrium."[114] Gaining such reflective equilibrium, he has it, does nothing to justify *the codes or standards themselves.* Moreover, she need not think that it is unreasonable for someone to be morally committed. In looking for objective justification of moral codes and moral standards, we are not concerned with ascertaining whether it is reasonable for us to believe that torture is wrong or whether we are justified in believing it to be wrong. In being concerned with objective justification we want to know whether for a given theory or proposition—in this case, the proposition that torture is wrong—there is either evidence or an argument that that would support its truth.[115] What Copp wants to get at is the distinction between, and a setting out of clear cases of, "where a person is (really) justified in believing something" and where he is not, where the former is where the person has "grounds for his belief which succeed in showing or significant supporting the truth of his belief...."[116] He wants to distinguish that situation from "cases where the person has met all the requirements of responsible belief, but does not have such grounds."[117] The moral skeptic, on his reading, is only interested in denying that anyone is ever justified in having moral beliefs in the sense that he has good grounds for believing they are true. The moral skeptic, as Copp defines her, is concerned to deny that moral agents ever have grounds that justify or support the truth of any moral belief, including the belief that torture is wrong.

We must, in seeing clearly what is involved here, keep firmly in mind the distinction between a *person being justified in believing a proposition and justifying the proposition itself*. The moral skeptic is only concerned with the latter. She denies that any moral *proposition* or *belief* is itself ever justified. "We are often interested," Copp remarks, " in the credentials of theories and propositions as potential objects of belief, rather than in the cognitive or epistemic credentials of those who believe them. If we look for or offer a justification of a proposition or theory, then, in my terminology, we are looking for or purporting to offer an objective justification, a justification of the potential object of belief."[118] The moral skeptic is denying that in morals we ever get such objective justification. Sometimes scientists and detectives, for example, have evidence sufficient to justify their beliefs in just this sense of objective justification. They do not, of course, get certainty, but that is another matter. The moral skeptic denies, or at least doubts, that we have or ever could have anything analogous in the moral case. The remarks about the scientist and detective show that we understand well enough what it is to have objective justification, but that we see, the skeptic has it, that we do not get such justification in morals or at least do not have adequate reasons for thinking we have it.

What we need to meet the moral skeptic, Copp claims, is a moral theory (metaethical or otherwise) which would tell us under what "circum-stances...a moral code or standard would be justified."[119] To be "an account of objective moral justification...[it] must specify justifying data, arguments, circumstances, or conditions of rational choice, in order that they can serve to justify it..."[120] This is what we need to confirm or disconfirm (infirm) a moral standard and without that confirmation for some moral standards, moral skepticism will remain live and well. Moreover, the moral skeptic's case, as Copp avers, is very strong for "it is not obvious what a justification of a moral code would consist in."[121] We do not have much in the way of consensus here. We have, as we have seen, many competing theories giving very different accounts of what a justification of a moral code or a moral standard would consist in. We should look at each theory of moral justification as "an attempt to explain what would count as the justification of a moral code."[122] We should look at the rationale and structure of each theory and then evaluate them individually. Only after we have rather carefully done that can we be confident that any of these theories have refuted moral skepticism.[123] The nagging question comes immediately to the fore: with what criteria do we do this evaluation? Is there a non-question begging place to stand here? Be that as it may, Copp's general moral is that "moral skepticism can only be defeated by *a theory of moral justification*."[124] We need—and this, he has it, is the central task of ethical theory—to develop a moral theory which can do that. Without it, all moral codes, moral standards, moral beliefs, moral commitments are at risk for they all lack objective justification. A philosophy as a problems-of-life approach could not yield moral or normatively political claims that are rationally justified unless it is under the umbrella of, that is, it is backed up by, a moral theory which has legitimately set aside moral skepticism. So my benign neglect of metaethical theory and systematic normative ethics, after all, rests on a mistake.

XI

Copp's argument here is powerful, more intricate than I have been able to convey, and he locates well, *in the traditional pattern of moral theory*, how moral skepticism should be placed and articulated. That notwithstanding, it seems to me, as I remarked initially, that his account is mistaken and importantly so; mistaken not just in detail but, as well, in its very conception. First, accepting more of his account for starters than I would in fact be prepared to accept, it seems he goes invalidly from a claim that we need a moral *theory* to refute the claim that no moral *theories* have been, or even could be, objectively justified, to the claim that we need a moral theory to show that it is a mistake to believe that no moral codes, standards or beliefs are justified. (For the rest of this discussion I will just use "justified" to mean "objectively justified" *in Copp's sense*.) I do not think that Copp has shown that it is true that moral skepticism can only be defeated by a *theory* of moral justification. We can, I shall argue, have no *theory* of moral justification at all—no moral theory at all—and indeed be deeply skeptical that we can even have a sound theory and still reasonably reject moral skepticism. Skepticism about *theories* of moral justification does not imply moral skepticism, i.e., a belief that no moral code, standard or belief (all of themselves importantly different things) is justified (plausibly believed to be true or warranted). It is just a skepticism about *theory*. Someone, say, someone skeptical about the power of traditional philosophical argumentation and theory construction (say, a Wittgenstein, a Rorty, a Dewey, or a Hume), might be completely (and consistently so) unskeptical about the justifiability of some moral codes, standards and beliefs. Indeed, he might think—though this is not necessary here—that any theory of justification that did not take as given certain moral beliefs could not possibly be a justified moral theory. But again he might not claim that. He might simply be very skeptical about moral theories, while not being skeptical at all about some moral beliefs or standards. He might rightly partition his skepticism here.

His skepticism—including his moral skepticism—might not be at all global.

Can we show that that is so, as distinct from just showing, as we have, it to be a logical and conceptual possibility, i.e., it does not follow because we have no sound theory of moral justification that no moral beliefs are justified or reasonably believed to be justifiable? The Moorean argument I alluded to, parallel to the Moorean argument I used in arguing against epistemological skepticism in Chapter 4, will, I believe, do the trick. Copp acknowledges that someone completely skeptical about the validity and viability of moral theories can consistently believe that torture is wrong and indeed, through and through, commit herself to act on that belief. It is so deeply embedded as an element in her structure of moral belief, so central to her moral sensibilities, to her sense of being a decent person, that she will not abandon it come what may. There her spade is turned. Her moral belief is not at all optional. She may indeed come to think that in some horrible circumstances of war, revolution or counter-revolution torture *in certain very special circumstances* may be justified, but always as the lesser of two very great evils, and, as such, it is always wrong only sometimes, to feel the wrenchingness of this, even greater wrongs will obtain if the torturing does not occur. Her sense that torture is evil and wrong is not something that will be undermined for her by any ethical *theory*. Just the reverse. An ethical theory (substantive, *first-order* ethical theory) which had as one of its beliefs that torture was not wrong would thereby discredit itself in her eyes as a viable ethical theory. It would not, even if it is acceptable to her on other grounds, be acceptable to her until it was so modified so as not to contain such a belief as a moral element or as a morally acceptable possibility.

In such a situation my Moorean will reason in the following manner. The belief that torture is wrong is more plausibly held than any moral theory, skeptical or otherwise, which would deny it. Faced with the choice between accepting and believing in the correctness of such a moral theory and believing that, after all, torture is not wrong, or may not be wrong, it is always more reasonable to reject the theory, no matter how tightly woven and logically cogent the theory seems, then to reject the belief that torture is wrong. It is more reasonable to believe that a mistake in reasoning has been made somewhere or a questionable premise has been unwittingly assumed in the theory in question than to believe that it is not true or firmly warranted that torture is wrong. Rather than accept the repugnant conclusion—that torture is not wrong or that it is not true or warranted that torture is wrong—it is better, more reasonable, to send the ethical theory, with such a repugnant conclusion, back to the drawing board for reworking until it no longer has that repugnant conclusion.

This is not *just* an argument about what it is more reasonable for a moral agent to believe, though it is that too, but, meeting Copp's conception of objective justification head on, it is an argument that the proposition that torture is wrong is more plausibly believed to be true or otherwise justified than the propositions given by an ethical theory for denying that or saying we cannot be justified in believing that or even that we should doubt whether it is so.   The argument here is strictly parallel to my Moorean argument against the epistemological skeptic who believes that we cannot know or be justified in believing that there is an external world, but must take it, if we take it at all, as a matter of animal faith.   Copp is right in thinking that in certain ways epistemological skepticism and moral skepticism are distinct, but the differences are not such as to effect the soundness and relevance of both of these parallel arguments.

There is another way of thinking about morality that fits badly with what Copp says about moral skepticism. A person, he rightly tells us, "can value something without believing that some corresponding standard is justified."[125]   But in valuing something, he might very well think that either there was no clearly identifiable corresponding standard justifying it or that, though he did not think the corresponding standard was justified, he did not think that it was unjustified either. He thought, rather, that the standard in question was so deeply embedded that no question coherently, or even intelligibly, arises about it either being justified or unjustified. Such conceptions he thinks have no grip here. Suppose, to translate into the concrete, he values being a certain kind of person, namely, a person who keeps trust with those with whom he interacts. If he tells a neighbor he will mail a letter for her, he will, though not though the heavens fall; there can, of course, be overriding circumstances. But normally, even at some inconvenience to himself, he will mail it. Indeed he can be relied on to mail it barring unforeseen extraordinary circumstances. That is a part of what integrity comes to and he values integrity and being the kind of person who has integrity and acts consistently with integrity. He might, of course, discover or construct a rationale for his convictions here, say, a utilitarian one or a Kantian one: a standard or cluster of standards which he thinks are justified and which justifies his valuing as he does integrity. But again he might not. He might think any such claimed justification would be less reliable than his own conviction that this is the way he and others should act. He might be mistaken; he might be too skeptical about theory and too trusting of his convictions. But mistaken or not, still he plainly is not a moral skeptic, though in Copp's sense he must be, but this shows that there is something problematic in Copp's conceptualization and way of reasoning here. The person might, skeptical as he is about theory, still quite *categorically* value integrity, be *categorically* committed to trying to be a person of integrity. For this person, his moral beliefs are anything but *optional*. (To say "Well, not *morally* optional, but *intellectually* optional" is at best hollow, more likely question begging, and at worse incoherent.)

Certainly it is very strange indeed to regard this as moral skepticism. He doesn't think his so valuing integrity has been justified, but from that he does not conclude it is unjustified either, but that no such questions arise for him here and he is very skeptical that they can intelligibly arise. How would we show, after all, that we are really not justified in keeping faith with people we know are our friends?

Though he says, and believes, as we non-skeptics Copp style do, that it is always wrong to break trust with our friends, the moral skeptic, Copp tells us, does not share our moral *beliefs* as to what is required and what is forbidden for he does not believe that "some moral standard is justified which calls on people to act in that way."[126] Since that is so, Copp thinks, he cannot, as we do, think that some way of acting is morally required. But, of course, the above reasoner about integrity (a skeptic Copp-style) believes that, for he thinks it is required of him and of all of us to keep faith with our friends. Integrity, he believes, is not optional for a moral being. But he has no *theory* to back this conviction up or any opinion that there is a justified standard which could be unearthed or constructed which would justify his belief in integrity. He remains skeptical about *that*. But whether (*contra* Copp) he shares our moral beliefs—in this case our belief in keeping faith with our friends—is shown by how he acts and reacts and what he commits himself to and not in his beliefs *about* justified or justifying standards or even that a certain standard is justified.

Copp would probably respond that this *only* shows that we have a person here with moral beliefs, indeed with moral beliefs that are deep convictions. Many people, he might add, have moral beliefs, some even have coherent moral beliefs, neatly synchronized with their other beliefs, moral and otherwise, which, some few may get into wide reflective equilibrium, but this does not show that any of these beliefs, including, of course, the moral ones, are justified. Even if we can show he is being reasonable in so valuing integrity, it does nothing to show his beliefs are themselves justified. That he does not think that there is a standard he can appeal to here which is either justified or unjustified, shows, with respect to this belief at least, that at heart he is really a moral skeptic and, if he so regards all his moral beliefs, he is, Copp would have it, a veritable paradigm of someone who is, through and through, a moral skeptic.

I think, on the contrary, that this only shows the arbitrariness of Copp's conception of moral skepticism. But even sticking with it for the purpose of this argument, Copp's belief is still not justified that a moral belief held in the way I described it above is not justified. Copp grants that such an agent could be reasonable in having such commitments if that agent maintains them in a certain way, namely, that they are reflectively held when he is aware of the causes of his commitments, something of the consequences of acting on them and how they fit with other things he believes and, as well, with the reflective and informed beliefs of others in his society and in similar societies and the like. But reasonably so committing himself, or being reasonable in doing so, is not the same as being justified in doing so, Copp has it, because he can do that without knowing that, or being justified in believing that, his moral beliefs are true or are backed up by standards he knows are true or justified. Because he does not know that this is so, reasonable though he may be, he still, on Copp's account, remains a moral skeptic or at least he has not deflected moral skepticism.

However, he may well, in being reasonable in this manner, as Copp agrees he can, have gotten his beliefs—including crucially here his beliefs expressing or signalling his moral commitments—into wide reflectively equilibrium. That can be so, for to get them into wide reflective equilib-rium is to get them into a consistent and coherent pattern with all his other beliefs, and all the relevant beliefs reasonably available in the world (the cluster of societies) in which he lives or stands in contact with, including, in this wide reflective equilibrium, the commonsensical and scientific (including social scientific) beliefs readily available in his society. To get his moral convictions in such a pattern of coherence is to square them with (render them logically consistent with) everything that is reasonably known in such societies at such a moment in time. *But this just is to justify his beliefs,* including crucially here his moral beliefs, for we justify our beliefs by so consistently meshing them in our web of beliefs, never breaking out of the web of our beliefs (a very wide circle of beliefs indeed). This will justify his beliefs, including his moral beliefs, if anything will, for it appeals to everything that could be reasonably known at a given time. Indeed this is the only thing that a full justification could come to. But in so justifying his moral beliefs, he need have no conception that there is a corresponding standard justified because known to be true. There may be such a corresponding standard or there may not, indeed what we are even talking about here may be bafflingly obscure, but to the extent that sense can be made of it and to the extent that it actually plays a justificatory role at all, it is in virtue of going with the rest of his—that is, our—beliefs into the hopper of wide reflective equilibrium. Wide reflective equilibrium requires that we bring morality, and with that, of course, our moral beliefs and convictions, into congruence with whatever else we hold in our ongoing view of the world. When we have done that in the best way—the fullest, most complete, consistent and perspicuous way that can be done at a given point in time—what more could be done by way of justifying our beliefs? As far as I can see, nothing.[127]

Someone with the kind of moral commitments I have spoken of a few paragraphs back, but with no corresponding conception about true moral norms, could no more leave subscription to a moral code optional than

Copp's non-skeptic. (Her imperative "Turn off the gas" is neither true nor false, but it can be through and through justified in the same manner as moral standards.) So skepticism, even in his sense, need not leave subscription to a moral code optional. People, again *contra* Copp, can be consistently opposed to capital punishment and still be moral skeptics *in Copp's special sense.*[128] They probably would not take it as a fundamental moral belief of theirs, but as a moral belief that is dependent both on certain factual beliefs (e.g., capital punishment is not an effective deterrent) and what they take to be more fundamental moral beliefs, perhaps something vague, but all the same important, such as the sanctity of life. But they could, and some do, quite consistently hold capital punishment to be wrong as a dependant belief based on a more fundamental moral belief which is for them up for subscription though a firm, indeed even categorical, commitment. There is nothing inconsistent in that or even necessarily irrational. (Non-rational commitments are not thereby irrational.) But it is, on Copp's conception, but not on mine, an expression of moral skepticism. But the above considerations show it, I believe, to be an arbitrary conception of moral skepticism.

Even more deeply, a Kierkegaardian, Sartrean, or Camusian will have very passionate and firm moral convictions, but they also think that intellectually speaking, from the perspective of a neutral spectator or observer of the world, that they are arbitrary.[129] There is, they believe, not knowing of wide reflective equilibrium or anything like it, no way of justifying their moral convictions or any other convictions. Yet they have, all the same, very intense and firmly held moral convictions that guide, indeed engulf, their lives and which they are not about to abandon. They, on Copp's counting, are moral skeptics for they do not see how any moral standard—any moral standard at all—could have an objective justification. (And recall that "objective justification" is pleonastic.) Indeed they think that it is foolish to look for one or to try to construct one. Only someone, they believe, who was deeply self-deceived could think such a rationalistic project plausible. But they do not thereby, or in fact, take morality as optional and say one can just as well be an amoralist, moral cynic, a nihilist or simply remain indifferent to morality. They remain deeply, very deeply, committed moral persons. What they take to be the rational arbitrariness of that commitment does not leave room for the "the *abandonment* of subscription to any moral standard as an option for a rational and informed person..."[130] Not everything we do, we do for a reason; not everything we reasonably commit ourselves to we commit ourselves to because we can see that it is *rationally* mandatory or even believe that if only we knew enough we would come to see that it is rationally mandatory. Reason is an important factor in life, but it is surely not everything. The lives of people such as de Beauvoir and Sartre were tied up with their distinctive moral and political commitments, as was Bertrand Russell's, whose live moral and political commitments, though surely not his philosophical views, were very similar to theirs. Moreover, de Beauvoir, Sartre and Russell wished to see such commitments obtain generally in society and they struggled for their attainment. They were, that is, politically and morally engaged intellectuals. Were the exemplification of their views in social life to come into existence and then be threatened, they would have resisted with all their might their undermining. Like Hume, Westermarck, Santayana, and Mackie, they think that morality is rooted fundamentally in feelings and not in reason and that people who do not have their convictions (moral convictions, not meta-moral convictions), or indeed any moral convictions, need not have made any *intellectual* mistake, i.e., incorrect deductive or inductive inferences, or have made any mistaken observations or neglected to observe empirical data which are readily at hand. Such intellectual clarity, they are sadly aware, is at least logically compatible with a complete lack of moral sensibility or even with indifference to morality. Moreover, they believe, one can be intellectually skeptical through and through about how to justify moral beliefs, or about their even being justifiable, and still not be a moral skeptic, i.e., someone who has no firm moral commitments and who thinks rather that morality is optional for clear-headed human beings or indeed perhaps for any human being. Such an existentialist, and Russell as well, would, I think, should they become aware of them, be skeptical about principally coherentist projects of justification in ethics, such as wide reflective equilibrium, believing that they are just the old rationalistic illusions all over again. But they can—rightly or wrongly—think that without at all being moral skeptics. Acting in accordance with moral standards is not at all *optional* for them. Intellectual skepticism about various philosophical, theological or scientific projects to justify moral standards and moral beliefs need not at all add up to moral skepticism, i.e., to the belief that nothing is morally required of us. Such skepticism about moral theory and moral philosophy often goes with intense, reflective, emotionally stable and indeed categorical moral commitment. This is something that Wittgenstein and many Wittgensteinians have both seen and exemplified very clearly.

However, I am not defending such a non-rationalist existentialist conception of ethics. I was concerned only to show that, even if we come to subscribe, and even rightly so, to such a non-cognitivist commitment oriented conception of morality, it does not at all add up to moral skepticism or even indirectly support it or condone it.[131] But my contextualist broadly Deweyian problems-of-life oriented way of doing moral and political philosophy, with its use of wide reflective equilibrium, gives far more scope for deliberation and reasoning in ethics than does existentialism. Indeed it seems to me a mistake to say, as Copp does, that "we have few intellectual resources to rely on, when we find the justification of our moral convictions challenged by someone who disagrees with us at a fundamental level."[132] I think that on the contrary we have too many resources so that a central problem becomes to order them, sort them out and clearly relate them to each other. In disputes like those over nationalism, discussed in the previous chapter, or over abortion and euthanasia, we are, if anything, overwhelmed by the number of at least putatively relevant considerations and intellectual resources at our disposal, even though, over these issues, there is in our society at this time fundamental disagreement. How much can be done in discussing abortion, even when there is such disagreement, is impressively shown by both Ronald Dworkin and T. M. Scanlon.[133] In discussing nationalism, euthanasia and abortion, as well as many issues like this, there is plenty of scope to use our brains and our moral reflectiveness, even without—and perhaps better without—a grand philosophical moral theory, either skeptical or non-skeptical. It is not at all evident that "to defeat moral skepticism, it must be attacked at its roots, and for this, an adequate non-skeptical conception of morality must be established."[134] Morality and politics do not totter while they await the construction of a non-skeptical ethical theory that will defeat moral skepticism. Morality and politics requires, for their legitimacy, no such grounding. They no more totter in the absence of such a theory than mathematics totters while awaiting a refutation of Gödel.

Faithful to the underlying metaphilosophical thrust of this volume, I have been concerned to argue against Copp's rationalistic defense of ethical theory and its role in our social life. In accordance with that metaphilosophical conception, though I hope not dictated by it, I have argued that we do not need a moral *theory* (metaethical, normative ethical or some amalgam) to make sense of our moral lives or to pursue philosophy as a context dependent, historically and culturally situated normative treatment of the problems of life, where philosophy, so transformed, engages in actual social and moral critique. It tries to say, though surely not to declaim, what can and should be done about pressing human problems. It makes arguments, formulates hypotheses, and makes suggestions here. It certainly does not try to lay down the law. This would be both foolish and arrogant and not within the vocation of a philosopher or any other kind of intellectual.

Metaethical theory, normative ethical theory and the grand moral theories of traditional philosophy can and should be put on the sidelines when we engage in such philosophizing. Therapeutic conceptual analysis apart, such activities block inquiry, stand in the way of resolving, or at best are just irrelevant to the examination of, these problems of human beings and to the development of sound and effective social critique.

XII

Copp, and many other more tradition oriented moral philosophers, might still persist in saying that traditional moral philosophy cannot rightly be set aside. For all I have said above, I still have not treated moral skepticism seriously enough. I have treated it too much like epistemological skepticism. But when we see clearly how disanalogous it is, they will claim, we will see how my various arguments fail and, most crucially, how my Moorean argument, on which a lot of my argumentation hinges, fails. I think this counter-claim is mistaken. Copp indeed rightly points to differences between moral skepticism and epistemological skepticism (Cartesian skepticism, if you will). Moral skepticism, as we have seen, is more like skepticism about the existence of God. But the acknowledgement of these things does not affect the soundness of the arguments I have articulated above against taking moral skepticism seriously when "moral skepticism" is construed as Copp construes it.

Epistemological skepticism is indeed argument driven, while moral skepticism, like religious skepticism, is not. Rather it wells up out of modern cultural life. People have to be vigorously talked into epistemological skepticism (skepticism about the external world or about other minds) and even then, as we have seen, even for those who have been taken by it—Locke and Hume, to take the classical examples—it has a kind of unreal quality. It gives rise to what Charles Peirce called "paper doubts," not real doubts. But moral skepticism, though often in an inchoate form, is common among many thoughtful people. Indeed it may even be pervasively common. They do not need philosophy to talk them into it, though sometimes philosophy will help them more clearly articulate their skepticism or even deepen it. Here it seems exactly like religious skepticism. Indeed for many people moral skepticism just seems obvious. They see a lot of emotion driven, ideology driven, religion or anti-religion driven, moralizing around them with wide, and seemingly intractable disagreements abounding and with very little idea of how these disagreements could be reasonably resolved. How, in such a circumstance, they ask, could any moral standard have an objective justification, how could moral skepticism *fail* to be true? Moreover, since moral skepticism is culture driven, the defeat of a philosophical argument for it, on the one hand, or an appeal to common sense, on the other, will not settle things. The cultural source remains after the philosophical argument is defeated. (Here moral skepticism is very different than epistemological skepticism.) And since common sense—the culture—is complicit in moral skepticism, it cannot be appealed to in rejecting it as it can against epistemological skepticism. Common sense, as Copp puts it, is not unequivocally against moral skepticism and, he concludes, it cannot be appealed to in an attempt legitimately to set moral skepticism aside.[135]

A qualification on the last part aside, I substantially agree with most of this, though I think some points are overstated. And I also agree that it is important to say and see that there are differences between epistemological skepticism and moral skepticism. But why does it not—or so I believe—touch my Moorean argument, an argument which, after all, is modelled after Moore's use of it in epistemological and metaphysical contexts? (Moore did not apply it himself in moral contexts.) To see that it does not, recall first the argument. I argued that it was more reasonable to believe that certain moral truisms are true or otherwise warranted than to accept as true or otherwise justified any moral theory, no matter how carefully argued, which rejected these truisms as being untrue, otherwise unwarranted. The moral truisms I had in mind were things like torture is wrong, truth is to be told, promises are to be kept, integrity is humanly important, unnecessary suffering is bad, pain is bad, pleasure is good, friendships are to be prized, security is good, and the like. My Moorean point was that it is more reasonable to accept them than any theory which rejects them or says that they are optional for a moral agent. My claim, to repeat and to simplify, was that it is more reasonable to accept these truisms than any theory that would reject them or say that they are not essential to morality. But this does not require treating moral skepticism as an epistemological or metaphysical skepticism, though it is compatible with such skepticism. This Moorean argument does not require that moral skepticism be a creature of a philosophical theory or be in any way theory driven; it could instead very well up out of our common life. It only says that a moral skepticism which rejects these moral propositions (these moral truisms) as false, otherwise unwarranted, unjustified or as something not to be taken as morally required is mistaken. However moral skeptics come by their skeptical beliefs, the Moorean argument is that it is more reasonable to reject moral skepticism than to reject these moral truisms. None of the disanalogies that Copp locates between moral skepticism and epistemological skepticism effect that point, except perhaps the point about common sense.

I shall now argue that even that isn't effected. Common sense, he says, and rightly, is not unequivocally against moral skepticism. There is, I agree, a sense in which common sense—including reflective common sense—is not against moral skepticism, a sense that I will specify in a moment, but common sense is against a moral skepticism of Copp's sort (moral skepticism as he defines it), when common sense recognizes that that skepticism requires the rejection of these moral truisms. Common sense accepts these moral truisms or will after some elementary philosophy 101 *second-order* clarification, e.g., distinguishing for "Pleasure is good" between intrinsic goods and instrumental goods and by making it quite clear that in accepting "Pleasure is good" one is not committed to accepting that pleasure is the *sole* intrinsic good or the most important intrinsic good or anything of the kind, or, for "Promises are to be kept" and "Truth is to be told," to distinguish between conditional oughts and unconditional ones. But subject to some minimal elementary and uncontroversial metaethical clarification (Wittgensteinian *second-order* conceptual theraphy), common sense accepts, without any ambivalence at all, these moral truisms and so rejects moral skepticism Copp-style. Moreover, it accepts them in such a way that it does not take them to be *optional* beliefs or commitments.

Suppose someone says: But why go with common sense here? Why accept these truisms? I think honest reflection and psychological realism would lead us to accept them.[136] We do as a matter of fact accept them and, after reflection, our beliefs here are not weakened. They are not, for most of us, subject to psychological extinction. Moreover, we can think of no actual reason for rejecting them or even really doubting them. What could make you really believe that pleasure is not good and pain is not bad? What evidence could you have which would make it the slightest bit problematical or what argument would show you that after all you only thought that pain was bad but now you see that you had made a mistake in believing that pain is bad. If we are honest with ourselves we will have to admit that there are none. To echo Henry Sidgwick, you just find pleasure good and pain bad and on reflection you continue to do so and can honestly conceive of no reason for not continuing to find them so. Similar things could, and should, be said for torturing is wrong and the other moral truisms. We accept them—indeed as moral agents they leave us with no options—and we, on reflection, continue to accept them even when we come to see the world clearly. We are, of course, seeing things by our own lights, but what other lights could we see things by? And there is no reason to think that anthropology or history or anything else shows that these beliefs—these general truisms, vague as they are—are at all ethnocentric or culturally particular.

However, Copp points to the sociological fact that in our modern or modernizing societies or (if you will) postmodernist societies moral skepticism is very pervasive. But the moral skepticism which is culturally pervasive is not the skepticism of which Copp speaks. It is not the moral skepticism which he sees as a menace and thinks we must refute, if we can, and which I have just argued is no such threat. The moral skepticism I have in mind is something else again. It is, I think, very pervasive culturally and is, I also believe, a very reasonable skepticism. Indeed it is, I am inclined to think, a justified skepticism. In that sense, in what I shall describe as its weak form, I am a moral skeptic and, I suspect, or at least hope, that Copp is too. The moral skepticism I have in mind has no doubts at all about the moral truisms being true or otherwise warranted, but it thinks, except in their deployment in defeating paradoxical philosophical theses and theories, such as moral skepticism Copp-style, these truisms are pretty useless morally speaking. If someone says something absurd like we never know whether anything is good or bad or right or wrong these truisms can be trotted out Moore-like to refute such a claim. But otherwise they are just rather useless but still unproblematical background beliefs in our moral lives. The genuine moral skepticism of which I speak comes out about the resolution of live complex moral problems, such as those I described in the previous chapter. We have seen, again and again, throughout history and in our actual lives, that complex moral problems are very difficult to resolve. (Indeed, we would probably not even call them complex unless they had that feature.) Deep entrenched moral differences between people often remain even after their extensive airing. People still, even after extensive critical examination and controversy, see the contested issue or issues very differently. Though they agree about a lot (there is a mass of shared background beliefs moral and otherwise), they still disagree about these taxing moral problems. These differences often remain even after continued thoughtful and honest discussion. The disputants agree about the moral truisms. They are just sitting there as unquestioned background assumptions accepted by all parties to the dispute. Moreover, *sometimes* the disputants are not hung up on grand philosophical or theological theories or theses, are not suffering in any serious way from conceptual confusion, have a rather clear picture of the relevant facts and, even to some considerable extent, agree on the relevant facts, and yet they continue, to a significant extent, to disagree morally over such taxing moral problems. Their moral sensibilities differ, sometimes even deeply differ, here; they "see" the situation significantly differently and they do not agree about what to do or about what would be the good or desirable reaction and response here. Even after careful and honest deliberation, their differences, though perhaps narrowed to a certain extent, remain and they cannot see, and others—third parties—cannot see either, how their moral differences can be reasonably resolved. They agree about a lot of things, including about the moral truisms, but they give things a different weighting, interpretation and package things differently. Perhaps, though we should beware of exaggeration here, they even have, as Iris Murdoch would put it, different moral visions.[137]

Both sides are trying to be reasonable and to some extent they are succeeding. Still they do not agree—they do not see eye to eye—and see no way of their coming to agree. The moral skepticism of which I speak is the feeling, perhaps even the conviction, that this is just the way the moral life is—the serious real moral life, not textbook horsing around. We cannot expect rational resolution, the attaining of the same or meshing moral sensibilities, over many serious moral issues, and, without this meshing of sensibilities, we cannot expect agreement on what is to be done in these concrete complex situations. Sometimes the force of circumstances bring compromises, but compromises that satisfy no one and leave the moral differences just standing there unresolved. People, even when they honestly seek moral agreement, find that in many circumstances they cannot get it and cannot see how to proceed to gain it another day. It is this kind of moral skepticism which is pervasive in at least modern societies. And it is difficult for me to understand how any thoughtful person would not feel its force. And it is not unreasonable that many will come to regard it as the sad truth about morals. But this should not be confused with the moral skepticism of the philosophers, the skepticism of which Copp speaks.

There is a stronger way and a weaker way in which the moral skepticism described above may be held. The *stronger* way takes it as a settled conviction that such moral differences are inescapable and not rationally resolvable. No matter how informed or how reasonable and thoughtful people will come to be, these differences will remain. There just is, the stronger reading has it, no rational basis for the resolution of such complex moral differences. Moral skepticism's *weaker* form, which is skeptical of its very skepticism, is the belief—the, if you like, factual belief—that such differences persist and are very intractable and, along with this factual belief, goes as well, the suspicion or hunch that, even after thoughtful, honest, fairminded, reasonable and informed deliberation, these differences in moral sensibility and resolution are very likely to persist. The weaker form of moral skepticism does not have the firm conviction (metaethical conviction or sociological conviction) that such differences will persist, let alone that they must persist. It rather suspects, its hopes to the contrary notwithstanding, that such moral disagreement will remain: that serious moral disputes will often, perhaps always, remain intractable. But it remains, as I remarked initially, skeptical of its own skepticism.

The Deweyian pragmatist will tend to be more optimistic. She will think that by the resolute use of our intelligence—by the application of scientific method (broadly conceived) in moral and social domains, by the careful use of wide reflective equilibrium—the problems of human living can be addressed and reasonably resolved. She need not think they all will be resolved, but she will believe that none of them are in principle irresolvable and, she will further believe, that we will not know whether they can be resolved until we resolutely apply the pragmatic method (the systematic application of our intelligence to the problems of life). John Dewey himself, his followers, including his contemporary followers (Sidney Hook, Ernest Nagel, Isaac Levi), were all perhaps too optimistic about our problem solving capacities in such domains. (Reinholdt Niebuhr overstated his case against Dewey's optimism, but he had a point.) But it is true, on Dewey's side, that we have not systematically employed such methods or procedures and thus we are hardly in a good position to make claims about the expectable outcomes of such procedures. Yet it is certainly possible to feel, or at least suspect, that this Deweyian thing is too rationalistic, has too much of a cheerful faith in the Enlightenment in the face of the horrors of our time and against the power of human irrationality. A somewhat more pessimistic Deweyian, of which I am one, will agree, of course, that these at least seemingly intractable moral disagreements are not *in principle* rationally irresolvable. There is no principle of sufficient reason in morality, but, we should also remember that there is no principle that reason must always be insufficient either. The pessimistic Deweyian will just remain skeptical that many of them will in fact be reasonably resolved or sometimes even resolved at all. If he had to bet, he would bet that, again and again, they will not be: that things will go on pretty much as they are now. The heavenly city of the Enlightenment will not be ours. Pessimistic Deweyianism and weak skepticism go in tandem. But we are also actors, agents in the world, with hopes and fears as well as detached observers of the actual and speculators about the possible. As observers and speculators, we should be weak moral skeptics; as actors, agents in our world, we should be broadly Deweyian problems-of-life philosophers using and refining the pragmatic method (the method of intelligence) to try reasonably to resolve our problems and in so proceeding to try to refine this method as we go along. Again, Otto Neurath's metaphor of rebuilding the ship at sea is a very insightful one. The core of the pragmatic method (where it is also what Peirce called a critical commonsensism) is to start with our own considered convictions and, while appealing to them, to use them really intelligently in applying the method of wide reflective equilibrium.

XIII

I should guard against ways in which I may be misunderstood. I am not suggesting that most moral disputes are as reasonable and as fairminded as I have portrayed moral disputes as being capable of being. Much, perhaps most, actual moral dispute, both public and private, is passion driven, ideologically beclouded, religiously and metaphysically entangled, partisan, sometimes even fanatical, twisted by irrational fears and wildly unrealistic hopes and the like. It is very distant from undistorted discourse. But noting how pervasive this is should not lead us to exaggerate. Sometimes, both in private and in public arenas, people thoughtfully, dispassionately, and reasonably dispute with each other, inform themselves and seek fairmindedly to resolve their disputes. Sometimes they even succeed. But even when they do not, or do so only faintly, they can, and sometimes do, continue to disagree in a reasonable and human way and do not foreclose the possibility of future agreements.   Sometimes such discussion, so reasonably conducted, goes on in the pages of some of our cultural journals, e.g., frequently in *The New York Review of Books* or *Le Monde diplomatique*.   It is not always, or even usually, ideological point counterpoint.   Moreover, to make a Marxian observation, where social life becomes more secure with a considerable increase and more equal distribution of social wealth, and with increasing levels of education as well, it is not unreasonable to expect that the percentage of reasonable disputes will increase and the number of irrational disputes will decrease.   Admittedly, things are not going very well now, but we are going through, on a world scale, a very rapid, unexpected, and gigantic social change with all the wrenchings and dislocations that we can expect from this.   We should not take this time as the norm.   Moreover, let me stress again that we are actors in the world and not just spectators and observers.   What reasonable alternatives are there to this broadly Deweyian-Rawlsian thing?

So I think we should be weak skeptics resolutely tackling the problems of life with as much intelligence and thoughtfulness as we can muster. Given how bankrupt metaphysics (including the ontology of ethics) and foundationalist epistemology (including foundationalist epistemology of morals) is, we should be skeptics about grand ethical theory (utilitarianism, perfectionism, Kantianism, Platonism, or Aristotelianism).   Skepticism here should be both about the results and about whether there is much point in *such* theory construction.

Even if my arguments directed against metaphysics and epistemology do not seem persuasive and are not, in fact, sound, we still have to contend with the often noted fact that in such domains—the domain of grand ethical theory, metaphysics and epistemology—we have nothing even approaching a consensus, no agreed on conception for what it would be like to get a rational consensus and little prospect of attaining consensus, rational or otherwise, in the foreseeable future.[138]   Just this, by itself, should make a fairminded person, not trapped by a surplus of self-confidence, skeptical of any metaphysical or epistemological plunking or grand theory construction in ethics, or, for that matter, elsewhere.   Why should any of us think that we have got it right when there is such a lack of consensus?   To think we have smacks of *hubris* and some considerable distance from reflective common sense.

Exactly the same thing, as we have said about metaphysics and epistemology, should be said for metaethical theory, normative ethical theory or ethical theory—grand ethical theory—more generally.   Darwall *et al.* point to a lot of impressive work in metaethics, but the upshot has not been toward a convergence of views but to a proliferation of theories with, if anything, an even more impressive lack of consensus.[139]   Some things get resolved—perhaps only for a time and only rather locally—only for still more disagreements to pop up in the wake of these agreements. The same thing is true for normative ethics and moral philosophy more generally. We repeatedly, though not all at once, have calls for "Back to Kant," then after a time a call for "Back to Hobbes," followed by a "Back to Aristotle" in turned followed by a "Back to Hegel" or a "Back to Hume" or a "Back to the pragmatists." We have, or seem at least to have, a merry-go-round, or, perhaps better, a whirligig, of fashion. Philosophy professors stick with something for a while until they get bored—more hopefully, get stuck—and then the fashion swings again. Philosophy, as Peirce observed, in this crucial respect is very different from science. There is disagreement and sometimes even partisanship there too, but it is not so extensive. There is no such whirligig of fashions, no disagreement all over the place going on all at once, and theories tend to succeed one another rather than prolifer- ate or chase their tails. One does not have to be scientistic to be very skeptical about the Philosophical Tradition.

In the face of this, I made, in the previous chapter, a proposal. Philosophy, I proposed, should reconstruct or reconstitute itself in a broadly Deweyian-Rawlsian direction to become an engagement with the problems of life in the way I have described. In doing so it should benignly neglect the perennial problems of philosophy (the problems of metaphysics, epistemology and grand moral theory, theory after the fashion of Kant, Sidgwick and W. D. Ross), as well as metaethical theory (old and new). I have *perhaps* treated metaphysical and epistemological problems—the hang up (as I see it) of The Tradition—too cavalierly with too much of something like a logical positivist scorn or a too easy Rorty-like dis- missal.[140]   If so—and if my claims have actually been unwittingly too partisan here—the proposal could still stand. We do not need, and indeed should not, in doing this Deweyian- Rawlsian thing, take stands concerning controversial metaphysical, epistemological, metaethical or normative ethical issues or theories. Whatever the merits, or lack thereof, of these theories or putative theories, we can ignore them, and, in this way, travelling philosophically light, turn our critical and reflective scrutiny to the problems of life.[141]   To engage in careful, reflective inquiry here, we do not need resolutions of the perennial problems of philosophy (if such there can be) or in metaethical theory.   We can, and should, tackle, and possibly reasonably resolve, these problems without the aid of such theories. Attending to these problems of the tradition actually blocks inquiry here rather than furthers it. The central thrust of this chapter was to show that this obtained for metaethical theory. Reflective contextual moral inquiry and moral and social critique can and should neglect metaethical theory, though, as a rather ancillary activity, *second-order* conceptual clarifica- tion—Wittgensteinian theraphy—may be occasionally useful to break conceptual confusions which stand in the way of pursuing such moral and social inquiry and critique.

Notes

1. John Dewey, *Essays in Experimental Logic* (New York: Dover, 1953), 335-442.

2. Kai Nielsen, "Philosophy within the Limits of Wide Reflective Equilibrium Alone," *Iyyun* (January 1994).

3. Gilbert Ryle, *Collected Essays* Vol II (London: Hutchinson, 1971), 194-211, 319-25, 250-72.

4. Kai Nielsen, "On there being Philosophical Knowledge," *Philosophical Investigations* 15 (April 1992), 147-77.

5. John Passmore, *Philosophical Reasoning* (London: Duckworth, 1961) and Stuart Hampshire, "The Interpretation of Language: Words and Concepts" in C. A. Mace, ed., *British Philosophical in the Mid-Century* (London: Allen and Unwin, 1957), 267-79.

6. Stuart Hampshire, "Identification and Existence" in H. D. Lewis, ed., *Contemporary British Philosophy* (London: Allen and Unwin, 1956), 191-208; Stuart Hampshire, "A Statement about Philosophy" in Charles Bontempo and S. Jack Odell, eds., *The Owl of Minerva* (New York: McGraw-Hill, 1985), 89; Isaiah Berlin, *Concepts and Categories* (Oxford: Oxford University Press, 1980), 143-72.

7. Ryle, *Collected Papers* Vol II, 350-72, 446-50.

8. Stanley Cavell, *Must We Mean What We Say?* (New York: Scribner's, 1969), 1-43; Nielsen, "On there being Philosophical Knowledge," 147-77.

9. Ludwig Wittgenstein, *Philosophical Investigations* (Oxford: Basil Blackwell, 1953) and John Wisdom, *Philosophy and Psycho-Analysis* (Oxford: Basil Blackwell, 1953), 36-148.

10. Cavell, *Must We Mean What We Say?*, 1-43 and Kai Nielsen, "Formalists and Informalists: Some Methodological Turnings," *Critica* XXV, no. 73 (April 1993), 71-82.

11. See references in note 9.

12. Peter Strawson, *Individuals: An Essay in Descriptive Metaphysics* (London: Methuen, 1959); Peter Strawson, *Logico-Linguistic Papers* (London: Methuen, 1971); Peter Strawson, *Analyses and Metaphysics: An Introduction to Philosophy* (Oxford: Oxford University Press, 1992); and Stuart Hampshire, *Thought and Action* (London: Chatto and Windus, 1960).

13. Strawson, *Analysis and Metaphysics*, 98.

14. Ibid., 106.

15. Hampshire, "Identification and Existence," 191-92.

16. Strawson, *Analyses and Metaphysics*, 107.

17. Ibid., 97. You can call this descriptive metaphysics, if you like, but note that it is more descriptive than metaphysical.

18. Cora Diamond, *The Realistic Spirit: Wittgenstein, Philosophy, and the Mind* (Cambridge, Massachusetts: MIT Press, 1991), 13-72.

19. Richard Rorty, *Consequences of Pragmatism* (Minneapolis, Minnesota: University of Minnesota Press, 1982).

20. But see Peter Strawson, *Skepticism and Naturalism* (London: Methuen, 1985), 21-23.

21. Nielsen, "On there being Philosophical Knowledge," 147-77 and "Formalists and Informalists: Some Methodological Turnings," 71-82.

22. Rorty, *Consequences of Pragmatism*, 19-36.

23. See references in note 21.

24. David Copp, "Metaethics" in Lawrence C. Becker, ed., *Encyclopedia of Ethics* Vol II (New York: Garland, 1992), 790-98 and Kai Nielsen, "Problems of Ethics" in Paul Edwards, ed., *Encyclopedia of Philosophy* Vol III (New York: Macmillan, 1967), 117-34.

25. W. K. Frankena, "Ethical Theory" in Chisholm *et al.*, eds., *Philosophy* (Englewood Cliffs, New Jersey: Prentice-Hall, 1964), 347.

26. Charles Stevenson, *Ethics and Language* (New Haven, Connecticut: Yale University Press, 1944), 1; A. J. Ayer, *Philosophical Essays* (London: Macmillan, 1963), 231-49.

27. Jeremy Waldron, "Justice Revisited," *Times Literary Supplement* (June 16, 1993), 5.

28. Ibid.

29. Stephen Darwall, Alan Gibbard, and Peter Railton, "Toward *Fin de siècle* Ethics," *The Philosophical Review* 101, no. 1 (January 1992), 115-89; Copp, "Metaethics," 790-98.

30. Ibid.

31. Hans Reichenbach, *The Rise of Scientific Philosophy* (Berkeley, California: University of California Press, 1951), 276-302.

32. Charles Stevenson, *Facts and Values* (New Haven, Connecticut: Yale University Press, 1963), viii-ix.

33. Edward Westermarck, *The Origin and Development of the Moral Ideas* (London: Macmillan, 1932); J. L. Mackie, "Westermarck" in Paul Edwards, ed., *Encyclopedia of Philosophy* Vol. 8 (New York: Macmillan, 1967), 284-86; Kai Nielsen, "Problems for Westermarck's Subjectivism" in Timothy Stroup, ed., *Edward Westermarck: Essays on His Life and Works* (Helsinki, Finland: Acta Philophica Fennica, 1982), 122-43; Timothy Stroup, "In Defense of Westermarck," *Journal of the History of Philosophy* III, no. 2 (April 1981), 213-34; and Timothy Stroup, *Westermarck's Ethics* (Abo, Finland: Abo Akademi, 1982).

34. P. H. Nowell-Smith shows very clearly how this has been the central aim of traditional moral philosophy. Traditionally, as Nowell-Smith brings out, moral philosophers sought to give us objective knowledge about how we should live. But, as R. M. Hare points out in his discussion of Nowell-Smith's views, Nowell-Smith was a champion of traditional moral philosophy but not an imitator of it. Hare rightly describes Nowell-Smith's *Ethics* as "a study of the words and concepts we use for making decisions, advising, warning, and appraising conduct." In short, it is the standard *second-order* normatively neutral description and analysis of analytical metaethics. P. H. Nowell-Smith, *Ethics* (London: Penguin Books, 1954); Kai Nielsen, "Problems of Ethics," 117-18.

35. But skepticism about what moral philosophy should be runs much deeper. Diamond, *The Realistic Spirit*, 367-81 and Annette Baier, *Postures of the Mind: Essays on Mind and Morals* (Minneapolis, Minnesota: University of Minnesota Press, 1985), 135-38, 207-47.

36. This is well argued by P. H. Nowell-Smith, *Ethics*, 23-60.

37. John Mackie, "A Refutation of Morals," *Australasian Journal of Psychology and Philosophy* 29, nos. 1-2 (September 1946), 77-90; John Mackie, *Ethics: Inventing Right and Wrong* (Harmondsworth, Middlesex, England: Penguin Books, 1985). Mackie not only reads, correctly I believe, Westermarck as an error-theorist, but he so reads Hume as well. John Mackie, *Hume's Moral Theory* (London: Routledge and Kegan Paul, 1980).

38. Paul Edwards, *The Logic of Moral Discourse* (Glencoe, Illinois: Free Press, 1955), 67-82.

39. The error-theory is in a bit of a confusion here, for it actually claims that all moral beliefs are false and yet, like those moral philosophers who are explicitly non-cognitivists, error theorists claim that moral statements cannot possibly be true. They have a *metabelief*, as those of who reject belief in morals actually do, that no moral belief could possibly be true. But for that to be coherent, it needs a non-cognitivist metaethic denying that it makes sense to say that moral beliefs could be either true or false. But the error-theorist is also saying they are all false.

40. For comparative accounts of them see Darwall *et al.*, "Toward *Fin de siècle* Ethics," 131-44, 152-65.

41. For an extensive discussion of Mackie's views, including a defence of the error-theory by Simon Blackburn, see Ted Honderich, ed., *Morality and Objectivity: A Tribute to J. L. Mackie* (London: Routledge and Kegan Paul, 1985). See as well Simon Blackburn, *Essays in Quasi-Realism* (New York: Oxford University Press, 1993), Part Two. See also the essays in Part IV of John Haldane and Crispin Wright, eds., *Reality, Representation and Projection* (Oxford: Oxford University Press, 1993) and Alan Gibbard, *Wise Choices, Apt Feelings: A Theory of Normative Judgment* (Cambridge, Massachusetts: Harvard University Press, 1990).

42. David Wiggins, *Needs, Values and Truth: Essays in the Philosophy of Value* (Oxford: Basil Blackwell, 1986); Thomas Nagel, *The View From Nowhere* (New York: Oxford University Press, 1986); T. M. Scanlon, "Contractualism and Utilitarianism" in Amartya Sen and Bernard Williams, eds., *Utilitarianism and Beyond* (Cambridge: Cambridge University Press, 1982), 103-28; John Rawls, *A Theory of Justice* (Cambridge, Massachusetts: Harvard University Press, 1971); and John Rawls, *Political Liberalism* (New York: Columbia University Press, 1993).

43. Mackie, "Westermarck," 285.

44. But this just assumes, as is standardly done, that Dewey's analogies between ethics and science are mistaken. Dewey argued for the use of the scientific method in ethics, while repudiating reductionism or any derivation of the ought from the is. John Dewey, "Logical Conditions of the Scientific Treatment of Morality" in his *Problems of Men* (New York: Philosophical Library, 1948), 211-49. There is need for further argument here. But, for the sake of the discussion above, I make that traditional assumption.

45. On reflective equilibrium see Rawls, *A Theory of Justice*, 19-21, 48-51, 577-87; Rawls, "The Independence of Moral Theory," *Proceedings and Addresses of the American Philosophical Association* XLVII (1974/75), 7-10; Rawls, *Political Liberalism*, 8, 28, 43-45, 72, 92-96, 113-19, 124-28, 210; Norman Daniels, "Wide Reflective Equilibrium and Theory Acceptance in Ethics," *Journal of Philosophy* 76 (1979); Daniels, "Two Approaches to Theory Acceptance in Ethics" in David Copp and David Zimmerman, eds., *Morality, Reason, and Truth* (Totowa, New Jersey: Rowman and Allanheld, 1985); Kai Nielsen, *After the Demise of the Tradition* (Boulder, Colorado: Westview Press, 1991), 195-248; and Kai Nielsen, "Philosophy Within the Limits of Wide Reflective Equilibrium Alone," *Iyyun* (January 1994).

46. See references in note 26.

47. Rorty, "Putnam on Truth," *Philosophy and Phenomenological Research* LII, no. 2 (June 1992), 415-18.

48. Georg Henrik von Wright, *The Varieties of Goodness* (London: Routledge and Kegan Paul, 1963), 118.

49. Darwall *et al.*, "Toward *Fin de siècle* Ethics," 122.

50. Ibid., 128.

51. Ibid., 123.

52. Ibid.

53. Ibid., 125.

54. Ibid., 125-26.

55. David Copp, "Metaethics," 790-98.

56. Ibid., 790.

57. Ibid.

58. Ibid., 790.

59. Ibid., 795.

60. Ibid.

61. Darwall *et al.*, "Toward *Fin de siècle* Ethics," 121-22.

62. Ibid., 123.

63. Ibid., 125-26.

64. Annette Baier, *Postures of the Mind*; Jean Hampton, *Hobbes and the Social Contract Tradition* (Cambridge: Cambridge University Press, 1986); Martha Nussbaum, *Love's Knowledge* (Oxford: Oxford University Press, 1990); Martha Nussbaum, "Non-Relative Virtues: An Aristotelian Approach" in Martha Nussbaum and Amartya Sen, eds., *The Quality of Life* (Oxford: Oxford University Press, 1993), 242-69. Cora Diamond, *The Realistic Spirit*, chapters 13, 14, 15; Cora Diamond, "Ethics, Imagination and the Method of Wittgenstein's *Tractatus*" in R. Heinrich and H. Vetter, eds., *Bilder der Philosophie* (Vienna, 1991).

65. Copp, "Metaethics," 791.

66. For Russell's Moorean account see Bertrand Russell, "The Elements of Ethics" in Wilfrid Sellars and John Hospers, *Readings in Ethical Theory* (New York: Appleton Century Crofts, 1952), 1-32. This essay was written in 1910. On the reprinting of this paper, Russell points out that he no longer thinks that "good" is indefinable and that he thinks "whatever objectively the concept [concept of good] may possess is political rather than logical." Russell's mature views in ethical theory

occur in his *Human Society in Ethics and Politics* (New York: Simon and Schuster, 1955). The account is rather similar to an emotive theory.

67. See reference to Mackie in note 37.

68. See references to Westermarck in note 33.

69. J. L. Mackie, *Ethics: Inventing Right and Wrong*, 105-235. See also his *Persons and Values*.

70. See Mackie, *Persons and Values*, 77-90.

71. Thomas Hobbes, *Leviathan*, chapter 6.

72. Thomas Hobbes, *De Homine*, chapter 11.

73. Hobbes, *Leviathan*, chapter 15.

74. Jean Hampton, "Hobbes" in Lawrence C. Becker, ed., *Encyclopedia of Ethics* Vol I (New York: Garland, 1992), 547.

75. Ibid.

76. In speaking of contemporary Hobbesians, I have in mind Jean Hampton, Gregory Kavka, and David Gauthier. See Hampton, *Hobbes and the Social Contract Tradition*; Kavka, *Hobbesian Moral and Political Theory* (Princeton, New Jersey: Princeton University Press, 1986); Gauthier, *Morals By Agreement* (Oxford: Clarendon Press, 1986); and Gauthier, *Moral Dealing* (Ithaca, New York: Cornell University Press, 1990). 11-44.

77. Darwall *et al.*, "Toward *Fin de siècle* Ethics," 131.

78. Stephen L. Darwall, *Impartial Reason* (Ithaca, New York: Cornell University Press, 1983); Alan Gewirth, *Reason and Morality* (Chicago, Illinois: University of Chicago Press, 1978); Marcus Singer, *Generalization in Ethics* (New York: Alfred A. Knopf, 1961); and A. Phillips Griffiths, "Ultimate Moral Principles: Their Justification" in Paul Edwards ed., *Encyclopedia of Philosophy* Vol 8 (New York: Macmillan, 1967), 177-82.

79. Griffiths, "Ultimate Moral Principles: Their Justification," 177-82.

80. Ibid., 180.

81. Ibid.

82. Ibid.

83. Ibid.

84. Ibid., 181.

85. Ibid.

86. Ibid.

87. Ibid.

88. Kurt Baier, "Egoism" in Peter Singer, ed., *A Companion to Ethics* (Oxford: Basil Blackwell, 1991), 197-204; David Gauthier, *Moral Dealing*, 234-73; David Copp and David Zimmerman, eds., *Morality, Reason, and Truth* (Totowa, New Jersey: Rowman and Allanheld, 1984) Part Two and particularly the essays by Baier, Nielsen, and Kavka; Kai Nielsen, *Why Be Moral?* (Buffalo, New York: Prometheus Books, 1989), 143-227, 269-302.

89. Nielsen, *Why Be Moral?*, 207-27 and Nielsen, "Reason and Sentiment" in Theodore F. Geraets, ed., *Rationality Today* (Ottawa, Ontario: University of Ottawa Press, 1979), 249-79.

90. Kai Nielsen, "Universalizability and the Commitment to Impartiality" in Nelson T. Potter and Mark Timmons, eds., *Morality and Universality* (Dordrecht, Holland: D. Reidel, 1985), 91-102.

91. In this context note my critique of Alan Gewirth in *Why Be Moral?*, 245-68.

92. Alan Gibbard, *Wise Choices, Apt Feelings* and David Wiggins, *Needs, Value and Truth.*

93. Such a view is powerfully argued by David Copp, "Moral Skepticism," *Philosophical Studies* 62 (1991), 203-33. See also his "Skepticism in Ethics," *Encyclopedia of Ethics* Vol II, 1156-58.

94. Copp, "Moral Skepticism," 203-233.

95. Ibid., 203.

96. Ibid.

97. Ibid.

98. Diamond, *The Realistic Spirit*, 367-81.

99. Copp, "Moral Skepticism," 204.

100. Ibid.

101. Ibid.

102. Ibid.

103. Ibid., 205.

104. Ibid., 206-207.

105. Ibid., 207.

106. Ibid.

107. Ibid.

108. Ibid.

109. Ibid., 208.

110. Ibid.

111. Ibid., 221.

112. Ibid., 222.

113. Ibid.

114. Ibid.

115. Ibid., 223.

116. Ibid., 225.

117. Ibid.

118. Ibid., 226.

119. Ibid., 227.

120. Ibid., 221.

121. Ibid., 227.

122. Ibid.

123. Ibid.

124. Ibid., 208. Italics mine.

125. Ibid.

126. Ibid.

127. *Pace* Copp, a reflective equilibrium could not be a wide reflective equilibrium if it was backed by a threat. So Copp's counter-example fails.

128. Ibid., 210.

129. For just one of many examples where Sartre expresses firm and passionate moral convictions see his discussion with Simone de Beauvoir recorded in her *Adieux Sartre* (London: Penguin Books, 1985), 367.

130. Copp, "Moral Skepticism," 211.

131. A. J. Ayer, "Novelist-philosophers: Jean-Paul Sartre," *Horizon* (1946); Ayer, "Albert Camus, Novelist philosopher," *Horizon* (1946); and Ayer, "Philosophy at Absolute Zero," *Encounter* (1955), 24-33.

132. Copp, "Moral Skepticism," 211-12.

133. Ronald Dworkin, *Life's Domain* (New York: Alfred A. Knopf, 1993) and T. M. Scanlon, "Ronald Dworkin and the 'Sanctity of Life'," *New York Review of Books* XL, no. 13 (July 15, 1993), 45-51.

134. Copp, "Moral Skepticism," 212.

135. Ibid.

136. E. W. Hall, *Categorial Analysis* (Chapel Hill, North Carolina: University of North Carolina Press, 1964), 93-131.

137. Iris Murdoch, "Metaphysics and Ethics" in D. F. Pears, ed., *The Nature of Metaphysics* (London: Macmillan, 1957), 99-123; Murdoch, "Vision and Choice in Morality," *Proceedings of the Aristotelian Society* Supplementary Vol. 30 (1956), 32-58; and Murdoch, *The Sovereignty of Good* (London: Routledge and Kegan Paul, 1970), 1-45.

138. Kai Nielsen, "Can there be Justified Philosophical Beliefs?" *Iyyun* 40 (July 1991), 235-70. On the lack of consensus in philosophy see also Henry Sidgwick, *Philosophy: Its Scope and Relations* (London: Macmillan, 1902) and C. D. Broad, "Two Lectures on the Nature of Philosophy" in H. D. Lewis, eds., *Clarity is Not Enough* (New York: Humanities Press, 1963), 42-75. Kai Nielsen, "What is Philosophy?" *History of Philosophy Quarterly* 10, no. 4 (October 1993), 389-404.

139. Rorty, *Consequences of Pragmatism*, 211-30.

140. Hampshire, "Liberalism: The New Twist," *The New York Review of Books* XI, no. 14 (August 12, 1993), 43-47.

141. Rawls, *Political Liberalism*.

CONCLUDING REMARKS

An Anticipatory Postscript

I

This book, while remaining a text, is intended to be a challenge to doing business as usual in philosophy. It is meant to be a provocation to the profession.[1] I think it will touch philosophy students and their teachers where they are ambivalent and unsettled concerning philosophy, caught up by it, but still perplexed by it and rather distrustful of it, wondering if it makes much sense or has much point. But there are a number of philosophers, perhaps by far the majority of them, who will neither be provoked nor be the least bit unsettled by what I say.

I shall very briefly say why they will not be unsettled and then, going against the grain, argue that, their complacency about the state of philosophy to the contrary notwithstanding, they should be. Many philosophers, and some of their students already aiming to be part of the profession and thinking of themselves as future professionals, are generally quite content with the state of their subject. They recognize, correctly, that the clarity, rigor, argumentative agility and systematic articulation of arguments and the clear statement of philosophical theses has very considerably, and rather steadily, increased in the last fifty years. Many articles and books are being written in Europe, North America, Australia, New Zealand, and South Africa which display these virtues (virtues I neither deny nor belittle), so that philosophy, more and more, is just becoming systematic analytic philosophy. This is by now not only true in English speaking and Scandinavian societies, but more broadly in other places in Europe as well. We have, it is widely believed among philosophers, good grounds, if not for celebration, at least for a quiet confidence in and an optimism about the state and prospects for our profession. It is, they believe, no time, and besides there is no point, in going around knocking and debunking philosophy and calling either for its demise or for its transformation. It is a quite healthy and eminently worthwhile discipline just as it is.

Moreover, it will be added, the tradition bashing I engage in and transformation I propose–the theses I push–are old hat. The nay-saying thesis is just more stale, old Wittgensteinian therapy and my yeah-saying is essentially an updated version, sensitive to the linguistic turn, of what Dewey argued in his *Reconstruction in Philosophy*.[2] The Deweyian thesis that philosophers should set aside the traditional problems of philosophy and concern themselves with the problems of life is certainly not new. And the critique of metaphysics and epistemology that I engage in, while generally sound (or so these critics are inclined to believe), is hardly news. It is mainly a flogging of dead horses. That, of course, does not make it mistaken, but it does make it, it is at least natural to believe, rather pointless.

So rather than be provoked by it, to say nothing of being unsettled, my argumentatively rooted narrative will actually produce yawns rather than provocations. "So what else is new?" the thought will be.

II

The dismissal of what I have argued in this book will not stop there. On the yea-saying side, where I argue for a transformed philosophy centred in normative critique and concerning itself with the problems of life, I utilize, as an underlying method, an appeal to considered judgments in wide reflective equilibrium. Here some will say, though not nearly as many as those who will respond in the ways I described in the previous section, that this method, at least as I deploy it, is little more than pontificating. It is no more than what has been called "The New Casuistry": the assembling and orchestrating of currently fashionable moral opinions to yield answers to our current concerns. If this is all that philosophy as dealing with the problems of life can come to, then we might just as well say goodbye to philosophy and stick with newspaper pundits.

III

These are some of the ways that some philosophers will respond to my argument for transforming philosophy. We have, they will think, small potatoes here and cooked over ones at that. Why do I think that such a response is so fundamentally mistaken? Perhaps I protest too much? I will start with the last mentioned issue about pontifications, "The New Casuistry" and wide reflective equilibrium. The coherentist model of wide reflective equilibrium and the New Casuistry do not come even nearly to the same thing, or even to similar things, either in my deployment of the former or more generally. It is indeed the case that central to the method of wide reflective equilibrium is an appeal to considered convictions or judgments. Moreover, I make that appeal with a new twist that involves a transposition of a Moorean argument, usually used in epistemological contexts, to the context of moral philosophy. One of our firmest considered judgments, to return to an example I used in articulating my account of wide reflective equilibrium, is that torture is wrong. This is one of the judgments that we seek to collect together into a reflective equilibrium.[3] To the moral skeptic who would challenge us by asking "Why accept that belief?" I respond by showing how firmly it fits with the other things we believe: how it fits very well in a very wide reflective equilibrium. But, I respond, as well, by arguing that it is also the case that it is more reasonable to believe that torture is wrong than to accept any skeptical philosophy theory which tells us that we just arbitrarily, without any good reason, accept that belief about the wrongness of torture. Why so? We certainly should not rely on pontifical declarations.

Such thinking, not a few will argue, is ethnocentric, overly complacent and rationally unmotivated. Moreover, such complacency is not adequate to cases of serious moral disagreement. When we take proper note of such disagreements, we will come to see that such a Moorean defence of common sense in morals, whatever its force in epistemology, will not work. The Pope, for example, may very well be more confident that abortion is wrong than he is of any philosophical theory which would deny it or cast doubt on it. Some Moslem Fundamentalists may be more confident of the moral obligation to kill Salmon Rushdie than of any philosophical theory which would deny that there is such an obligation or even put it in question. But, if the Pope's or a Fundamentalist's certainties do not prove anything here, as surely they do not, why should my confidence about the wrongness of torture prove anything either? Isn't it just foot stamping and pontificating on my part?

I think not. There is a world of difference between believing that torture is wrong and believing that abortion is wrong or believing that we must kill Salmon Rushdie. The latter two views could not be part of a wide reflective equilibrium for (1) they are the *parti-pris* beliefs of a certain subsection of modern Western societies and there would certainly be no overlapping consensus about them in such societies, as there is about the wrongness of torturing and (2) the Catholic and the Moslem Fundamentalist beliefs rest on contestable metaphysical and theological doctrines in a way that the belief that torture is wrong does not.[4] Wide reflective equilibrium requires that our beliefs, including our moral beliefs, cohere with all the other things that we know or reasonably believe, where the "we" is ubiquitous in such societies. This, among other things, requires our getting the empirical facts of the matter right (or as to close to being right as we can, given what is known, or reasonably believed, in our society at our time). It also requires us to only rely on general theories that are (a) well warranted and, as well, (b) in a situation where there is an inter-subjective test for, and an agreement about, that warrant within our society and other societies similarly situated: literate societies with long scientific and philosophical traditions and with reasonably well functioning demo-cratic institutions where conflicting views can be, and are, thoroughly aired. The Pope's views about abortion and a Moslem Fundamentalist's belief about the duty to kill Rushdie fail those tests; the belief about the wrongness of torture does not.

Even *if* it is the case that there are some societies, say Iroquois or Medieval Icelandic societies, where people do not believe that it is wrong to torture, this would only show that, stretched back through historical time and cultural space, we do not have an overlapping consensus on the wrongness of torture in contrast with the consensus that exists about its wrongness in modern constitutional democracies. (Sometimes it is done in those societies–during the Algerian war, for example, by the French–for "reasons of state", but it is still widely thought to be wrong even when certain members of the state apparatus carry it out for such purposes.) Still a defender of wide reflective equilibrium could, and should, argue that beliefs about the acceptability of torture could not be set in wide reflective equilibrium even when–indeed most particularly when–we so widen the scope of the "we". They would not even cohere with many other moral beliefs central to these societies (Iroquois or Medieval Icelandic societies). And a denial that torture is wrong certainly does not square with the deepest considered convictions of people in most of the other societies coming within the scope of our extended "we". So there is no possibility of having here the overlapping consensus necessary, but, of course, not sufficient, for a wide reflective equilibrium. Moreover, even if on the moral convictions side it did (surely speaking now counterfactually), the accepta-bility of torture requires, for it to be rationalized, the acceptance of factual or metaphysical beliefs that are either false or incoherent. People in such societies, for example, might believe that torture is justified for it is necessary to endure in order to steel one's soul or to achieve human perfection or to purge one's soul of the influence of the Devil or of other evil spirits. It has even been thought, now reasoning on a rather different track, that some people are necessarily so morally and cognitively enfeebled that they do not count: they have no moral standing, and thus we do no wrong in torturing them or doing with them what we will. But morality, differing under the sweep of culture and history, aside, these beliefs could not be part of a wide reflective equilibrium for us, that is, for people living in present day Western societies, for (among other things) they run against firmly established factual considerations or involve the acceptance of incoherent, or at the very least of thoroughly contestable, theological considerations. So our belief that torture is vile is not *just* a matter of our strong moral disapproval. That such beliefs are historically conditioned does not distinguish them from any other beliefs, factual or moral, that we have, or might come to have, for this is true, and unavoidably so, of all beliefs.

Considerations of this sort reveal the great difference between wide reflective equilibrium and the New Casuistry. In seeking to gain a wide reflective equilibrium, we, in a Quinean holist and coherentist manner, weave and unweave the web of our beliefs, excising here and amending there, in an endless never finally completable manner, as we seek to maximize coherence.[5] Wide reflective equilibrium in that way yields a critical morality. The New Casuistry, by contrast, is simply an assembling and orchestrating of currently fashionable opinion to yield answers to questions of current concern. That one should stay loose is for us now one such currently fashionable view and that one should play it cool politically and not get involved is another. Going back a bit in time, that socialism is evil is one such view and that children should be seen and not heard is another. There are, indeed, such things as fashionable moral opinions, though the fashions tend to be rather local and, historically speaking, rather transient. Even the social world that Katherine Mansfield (1888-1923) so sensitively and perceptively displays differs in important respects from ours; some of the standard (for a time currently fashionable) moral opinions have shifted. Though it should also be remarked that when those having them come actually to view them as "currently fashionable opinions," they then cease to be moral convictions for them and become simply some of their transient and localized mores and they are recognized as such by them. But to believe that torture is wrong is a currently fashionable "moral opinion" is both silly and, if taken at all seriously, morally offensive. (If to say this is to pontificate, then make the most of it.)

IV

I turn now to the first cluster of reasons that will be given for not being unsettled or even provoked by my challenge to the Tradition. Contrary to the way the critique of my account ran, what is new, in my setting forth and arguing for a cluster of theses, is principally in the way in which they are put together such that with the resulting narrative we get a fresh perspective on how things stand in philosophy. It is a perspective which, if persuasive, justifies saying goodbye and good riddance to the Tradition (including its latest phase: systematic analytic philosophy), while still preserving, for both my nay-saying and yeah-saying, certain ways of proceeding that have been characteristic of analytic philosophers and for utilizing them in transforming philosophy in a broadly Deweyian direction and, as well, in that transformed philosophy itself.[6] What is new here is principally in narrative and arrangement and, in a way Dewey does not do, in *arguing* in a straightforwardly philosophical way for the setting aside of metaphysics, epistemology and foundationalist normative ethical theory.[7] It is also the case that substantively in arguing for the normative impotence and irrelevance of metaethics and systematic normative ethical theory, I cover new ground, again going against against the grain.

In my nay-saying, I stick principally, though not entirely (recall the critique of Quine and Smart), with a critique of traditional metaphysics (metaphysics relying on transcendental arguments and claiming to establish *synthetic a priori* truths) and foundationalist epistemology. I do this because it is only these accounts which even try to be either more than simply descriptive or handmaidens to science. Instead they try to find a foundation for knowledge (knowledge in general) or give an account of "ultimate reality" or of "The Truth" such that with these we could have a ground for assessing culture, showing "the real ground" of science, religion, morality, politics and the like, so that the philosopher could justifiably claim to know something substantial that no one else could know so well and that, with this distinctively philosophical knowledge, they could establish the rational foundation for all our forms of life. Philosophers, on such a traditionalist conception, would not be super-scientists, but, instead, super-assessors or judges of what is to be believed and done. Philosophy, on such an account, would be foundational for culture. If metaphysics and/or epistemology could achieve that, or even hold out a reasonable hope that it could be achieved or even approximated, it would be worth devoting a life to. But nothing like this is involved or claimed in the metaphysics or epistemology of present day systematic analytic philosophy. Indeed such an enterprise appears to them, as it does to me as well, at best hopeless and at worst incoherent. But they seem, at least, to have no sense of how much has been lost of the aspirations of philosophy–the things that drive so many people to passionately study philosophy–with such a demise of the Tradition.

However, traditional metaphysicians (including some who argued very carefully indeed) and some of the first wave of analytic philosophers–the non-positivist contingent of the first wave (Bertrand Russell, C. D. Broad, C. I. Lewis, H. H. Price, Curt Ducasse, Roderick Chisholm)–thought that something like that could be achieved and sought to achieve it or at least something of it[8]. I fasten on that kind of metaphysics and epistemology for that kind, and only that kind, holds out something of such a hope: a hope that in the past has fuelled philosophy. With physicalist metaphysics (what Hilary Putnam ironically calls metaphysics within the limits of science alone) and naturalized epistemology such a project is abandoned. I try to show how much is lost in abandoning those projects and how what remains, where sound, is platitudinous.[9]   Reductionist views, for example, are invariably mistaken; non-reductionist views, though sometimes sound, are platitudinous giving us additional reasons for believing what we believe with good reason anyway and could hardly coherently not believe. And, if the idea is to get the certainty of self-evidence, that isn't to be had anyway with any matter of substance.

If such foundationalist metaphysics and epistemology are dead horses, as many, though not all, present day systematic analytical philosophers believe (sometimes just assume), then my thesis is strengthened, for I too think such metaphysics and epistemology is impossible and that it is long since time that they be set aside or viewed as historical curiosities. But I also stress, as I remarked above, that then we have lost with that some of our most compelling reasons to philosophize. I tried to make clear how much we have lost and, as well, because of that, wishing to make as certain as I could that we really had lost it, I tried not just to assume the deadness of these views, but, given what is at stake, to argue the case still again, giving such metaphysicians and epistemologists a run for their money, trying to make sure that such rejections are not just something that is now currently fashionable among analytic philosophers and some post-modernist French intellectuals.

It is also important to recognize that such a regarding of traditional metaphysics and epistemology as dead horses that can just be forgotten about or treated as having historical interest only, is not *the view* of systematic analytic philosophy, but the currently dominant and currently fashionable view among *most* systematic analytic philosophers.[10] But the consensus is anything but complete. Fashions may change (they repeatedly have in the past in philosophy) and such a fashionable view is not itself a view that at present at least is in a wide reflective equilibrium. It does not have the necessary overlapping consensus among systematic analytic philosophers. It does not have the necessary ubiquity, let alone the intersubjective testing, to make it a *considered* conviction of systematic analytic philosophy. Moreover, and distinctly, where we allow ourselves to go back a few decades, and include those analytic philosophers of that time in the scope of systematic analytical philosophy, it will be evident that we do not have an overlapping consensus. We are blinkered to the present if we think otherwise.[11]

V

Where there is something which I think may be more worrisome concerning what I have argued in this book, it is in what *may* be a conflict between the Wittgensteinian therapeutic side and the Deweyian side of my conception of the proper office of philosophy; a possible conflict, that is, between the nay-saying and the yeah-saying side of my account. A Wittgensteinian will, and not without reason, be skeptical about whether philosophers can do anything very worthwhile towards getting a grip on the problems of life. Some Wittgensteinians will be inclined to think that a philosopher hard at work on the problems of life (something that itself, he will feel, sounds a little fishy) will create more fog, beclouding the issues even more than they already are.   Nobody, of course, who has much sense, thinks that the philosopher can go it alone over such matters. But the reasonable worry is whether they can, beyond a little elementary and often not really needed clarification, do, *qua* philosophers, something that has much value here. Some Wittgensteinians will think that they are very likely, if they manage to do anything at all, to do more harm than good, but that is probably too extreme a view.

I tried in Chapter 5 to make my own ambivalence clear. It is not obvious that philosophers, including we Deweyian or Marxian philosophers, have much to offer here. It is not clear to me, for example, that the philosophers and social scientists who discuss the question of nationalism in Québec and the possible secession of Québec have, in many important respects, done a better job, or even as good a job, in giving insightful and in depth analyses, and in arguing what they think should be done, than have some of the journalists in *Le Devoir* and *The Globe and Mail*.[12] Moreover, I do not think that there is some difference in *kind between* the philosopher's and social scientist's analyses and critiques, on the one hand, and those of the journalists, on the other.[13]   The former tend, hardly unsurprisingly, to be more theoretical, more caught up with what is taken to be (mistakenly, I believe) a disciplinary expertise and some philosophical problematic, than the latter, but the difference in theoreticity between their writings is one of degree and not of kind.   Perhaps what needs to be dropped, in addition to the assumption of some disciplinary expertise, is talk of what philosophers, *qua* philosophers, can do, along with the essentialist assumptions behind it. "Philosophy" is not a label for a natural kind.

I think there is room for Wittgensteinian skepticism here about such a Deweyian approach. I remain, speaking for myself, ambivalent. What I did try to do, using the problem of nationalism as an illustrative case to facilitate the making of the underlying method of my transformed philosophy clearer, was to show how to use the coherentist model of wide reflective equilibrium to gain something of a reasonable purchase on that problem. Staying on the surface in the attempt to make the underlying method clear, I tried to show how we would put together considered convictions (principally moral ones), theories about morality (including its functions), theories about political structure, social science, legal and social psychological thinking, plus (always and essentially) giving careful attention to the empirical facts, including historical ones, to give a coherent, interconnected account of what is at issue concerning such a political problem.   In showing how the method of wide reflective equilibrium operates, in such a specific context, we show, among other things, how in a putative reflective equilibrium some rather general moral beliefs (say, something like Rawls's two principles of justice) function in a way broadly similar to hypotheses, but "hypotheses" concerning what is to be done or what attitude to take toward what is to be done, by showing how they, better than the extant alternative hypotheses (say, the principle of utility), help in maximizing the coherence of our beliefs by getting them into wide reflective equilibrium.[14]   (They also give us an explanation of how it is that these various moral beliefs hang together.)

I am at least moderately optimistic that philosophers, historians, social scientists, and journalists working together can achieve something here. Philosophers, as Jürgen Habermas believes they are, might be particularly good at suggesting "hypotheses."[15]   If that is so, we have good place in the broader context of our intellectual life for philosophy transformed and reconstructed in the way I advocate.   But we surely do not need, and should not have, the philosopher as a lone ranger here or, for that matter, any place else.

VI

Many of those more content with the Tradition than I am, or at least about its last systematic analytic phase, will agree that systematic analytical philosophy will not solve the problems that traditional metaphysics and foundationalist epistemology tried and failed to solve.   Indeed they think that it should not even try to.   Many of them will even agree that systematic normative ethics or metaethics, or the two together, will not shed much light on the problems of life. (Some would add that they should not be seen as even trying to.)   But, they will claim, systematic analytical philosophy is worthwhile, important and even useful in other ways. But–once the foundationalist quest is abandoned–I ask in what other ways? Analytic philosophy can, upon occasion, as I have remarked and illustrated, usefully clear up, doing a little under laborer work, some on-the-spot conceptual confusions and it can, also along the same line, sometimes, by deploying Wittgensteinian therapy, dispel some philosophical obsessions. But this does not leave us with a positive view.   It does not leave us with a *philosophical* theory.

Systematic analytical philosophy, in search of a *positive* philosophical theory, has had, as perhaps its most fundamental component, what has been called descriptive metaphysics (what Simon Blackburn has ironically labelled

"Oxford Science") and revisionist metaphysics as a handmaiden to science à la Quine or Smart. But neither descriptive metaphysics nor revisionist metaphysics have given us anything but platitudes. If there are any great insights here, just what are they? Similar things can be said about systematic ethical theory. The various forms of utilitarianism, perfectionism, contractarianism, and communitarianism have given us different and often conflicting accounts of what the good life would be or what a just society would be. But there is no consensus, let alone a rational consensus, on which, if any, of these grand accounts, are sound or come closer to being sound among these views. Moreover, as I argued in Chapters 5 and 6, none of them aid us in getting a better grip on the problems of life. For the most part, they just get in the way of reflective moral thinking. Accounts more limited in scope, such as those of John Rawls, Norman Daniels and Ronald Dworkin, do sometimes help us in the gaining of some reasonable purchase on such human problems, but only by, in effect, transforming philosophy in the direction I advocate.

VII

It in turn could be responded that I suffer from a one-sided diet. If I would turn my metaphilosophical gaze on different kinds of work in the tradition of systematic analytical philosophy, work I have shown in my own work that I admire and try to build on, I could, removing the mote from my eye, see how systematic analytical philosophy does things that are worthwhile and insightful.[16] I refer to works such as G. A. Cohen's *Karl Marx's Theory of History: A Defence* and his *History, Labour and Freedom*, Andrew Levine's *Arguing for Socialism: Theoretical Considerations*, and Alan Garfinkel's *Forms of Explanation: Rethinking the Questions in Social Theory*.[17] These works are systematic, carefully argued and generally display the virtues of analytic philosophy, while avoiding its vices, *and*, as well, have something to say that is humanly important. They do not serve us up a nicely arranged plate of platitudes.

In transforming philosophy in a pragmatic direction, I have also argued that this transformation is into a critical social theory with an emancipatory interest and intent, where philosophers in conjunction with social scientists develop a thoroughly empirically based critical social theory.[18] That is, they develop something that is firmly a part of social science, though at its theoretical end. Conceptual clarification, I further argued, is an essential part of this. The three philosophers mentioned above are all rather adept at, without deploying a lot of unnecessary philosophical machinery, providing insightful conceptual clarifications and elucidations that have in turn been utilized by critical social theory–again, I stress an empirical social theory.

Cohen and Levine, for example, have clarified historical materialism showing how it is a falsifiable theory of epochal social change and showing how Marxianism, free of claims of historical inevitability and dialectical materialism, as well as Althusserian scientistic obfuscation, is an empirical social theory with an emancipatory intent, free of metaphysical encumbrances and of distinctive philosophical epistemological claims. Levine and Garfinkel do similar things in discussing methodological individualism, though they seek to set it aside, not to rationally reconstruct it, as Cohen and Levine seek to rationally reconstruct historical materialism. Levine and Garfinkel show the conceptual confusions, including the pointless and groundless metaphysical confusion, in much, if not all, methodological individualist theorizing and assumption and, as well, how sometimes methodological holism is just the confused mirror image of that. They, that is, not infrequently, take in each other's dirty linen. Levine and Garfinkel also show that there are coherent forms of social explanation and talk about society that are not reducible to individualist explanations or individualist ways of talking about institutions and practices. Moreover, all this can be, and should be, done, without any ontological commitment to "social entities." (Neither "ontological commitment" nor "social entities" are labels for anything that has much, if anything, in the way of a clear articulation.) Garfinkel also does other clarificatory things for the concept of explanation. He elucidates the concept with a full sense of its contextuality and its actual roles in the various sciences and, more generally, in our lives. In doing so, he makes evident the rigidity, inapplicability and unrealistic quality of the standard positivist conception of explanation that we have inherited from Carl Hempel.

All of the above mentioned accounts, like that of Rawls, travel philosophically light. They neither invoke nor presuppose any controversial philosophical theses, though they do make some logical conceptual claims. But none of them involve controversial philosophical theses. Either all talk about what institutions do (say, banks) can be paraphrased without remainder into talk about what individuals do or it cannot. Whichever, if either, claim is made, it is a logical or conceptual claim and requires no appeal to philosophical claims such as realism or anti-realism or Hegelian claims about social entities or the contention that all relations are internal relations or anything of the sort. They engage, and engagingly and perceptively, in conceptual elucidation and classification, distinction drawing (where useful) and mapping (for particular purposes) of contested terrain. But in doing so, they invoke no metaphysical or distinctively epistemological claims or philosophical theses or theories. In this respect, they stand in marked contrast to Quine, Davidson, Kripke, Fodor, Goldman, and Dummett and systematic analytical philosophy more generally.

They do, what in reality, though not in programmatic articulation, is Lockean under laborer work in the service of empirical social theory and good common sense, though common sense cleansed of ideology. They do not construct philosophical theories, not even normative ethical theories, but are content to make clarificatory contributions to the articulation and construction of social theory and to the understanding of our moral and political lives. In the case of Cohen and Levine, they develop, stressing the conceptual side, in what is plainly a division of labor, an analytical Marxian social theory jointly with economists, political scientists and sociologists.[19] But it is not a defence of some "philosophical Marxism" or "philosophical socialism," as if we even understood what we are talking about here. They are not giving us a philosophical social theory.

We have with Cohen, Levine and Garfinkel clear illustrations of the very transformed philosophy whose conception I have articulated and which I have defended. But the under laborer clarification pursued here also fits well with Wittgensteinian conceptual therapy (my nay-saying) and with my Deweyian pragmatism (my yeah-saying). There is some difference concerning the scope of critical social theory between such a pragmatism and such a Marxianism.[20] But this does not come to a difference in principle; between them, the question of scope is something that can be worked out in the practice of social theorizing and social action. We, in doing that, try to see to what extent a rather generalized social theory such as a Marxian theory can still yield testable predictions and retrodictions, be otherwise informative and can articulate things perspicuously, while remaining an emancipatory account that would guide social practice. But, vis-à-vis the question of scope, there is no room for *a priori* restrictions, one way or the other, though a good dose of Wittgensteinian skepticism about theories of grand scale, and, more generally, about the scientific substantiation of social theory, is not unreasonable. Still, no matter what we think about the scope of critical theory, we have philosophers, along with other intellectuals, directing their attention to trying to intelligently come to grips with the problems of life, including, of course, with getting a grip on what a just, efficient and flourishing social order would be and on how it could be achieved and sustained. In so directing their endeavors, they set aside the grand old philosophical issues as well as newer issues in the philosophy of logic and the philosophy of language. This includes not only the traditional "questions" about other minds, the external world and the issues (cloudy as they are) between realism and anti-realism, but, as well, the turning away from questions about whether rational persons must also be persons of moral principle (whether, that is, indifference to moral commitment *must* be some kind of cognitive mistake, some failure to be as intelligent as one might be), questions about the nature of moral obligation and the "foundations of ethics." Philosophy in so transforming itself frees itself both from general skepticism and from the construction of arcane *a priori* philosophical theories, theories that can come to obsess philosophers, and, with these obsessions, block the road to inquiry.[21]   But these traditional philosophical theories are conceptions and speculations–houses of cards, as Wittgenstein put it–that turn no machinery either in theory or in the living of our lives. We should take to heart Fredrick Waismann's dictum that the heart of rationalism is irrational.

Notes

1. Even so speaking of "the profession"–and it is a standard way of talking among present day philosophers–suggests a scientization or, at least, a bureaucratization of philosophy. When the self-image of philosophers is that of "being a professional" rather than "being a critical intellectual," we have already gone down the scientistic, or at least the bureaucratic, garden path. Of course they could be both, but then the important thing is which is the dominant or more compelling part of their self-image. This is not a trivial matter of labels, but is deeply a matter of how they see their role, or try to forge their role, in society.

2. Actually with Dewey it is even somewhat older. See his path breaking 1917 essay "The Need for a Recovery of Philosophy" in John Dewey et al., *Creative Intelligence: Essays in the Pragmatic Attitude* (New York: Henry Holt, 1917), 3-69.

3. It is necessary to be cautious how one puts matters here, for, though torture is always wrong, still in some terrible situations, where we are forced to choose between two or more very great evils, it may be, in certain circumstances, the lesser evil. See and note carefully Walzer's detailed example in Michael Walzer, "Political Action: The Problem of Dirty Hands," *Philosophy and Public Affairs* Vol 2 (1973).

4. There are certain people who place their belief in the wrongness of torture in the frame of an account which appeals to such contestable doctrines. But many others do not. Such a belief is compatible with such doctrines, but, mercifully, does require them. For a generalization of that, see John Rawls, *Political Liberalism* (New York: Columbia University Press, 1993).

5. John Rawls remarks: "...as to how we find the correct procedure [in moral and political deliberation], the constructivist says: by reflection, using our powers of reason. But since we are using our reason to describe itself, we can misdescribe our reason as we can anything else. The struggle for reflective equilibrium continues indefinitely, in this case as in others." *Ibid.*, 96-7. As always, fallibilism is the name of the game.

6. It is only broadly Deweyian and differs from Dewey in many important details. It is, that is, "Deweyian" in a way analogous to the way Rawls's account is "Kantian."

7. It is not that Dewey does not argue at all and contents himself, seer-like, with dishing out the insight with a take it or leave it attitude. That "seer-ism" is very distant from Dewey's approach to things as it is from philosophy generally. Still it has been frustrating to many of his critics how little he argues and the manner in which he argues when he does. Given the kind of arguments that philosophers have come to expect, there is little argument in Dewey and often, when he does argue, it is not in a typical philosophical manner. He refuses to play the philosopher's game. Rather, he characteristically sets out a narrative and a framework in which the problems, the ways

philosophers have done and are doing things, and the social situations in the background of their doings, are reconceptualized so that we come to see things in a fresh light and, if the new picture is to us compelling, or even strikingly suggestive, our intellectual energies and often even our political/moral energies are redirected. There remains, of course, the question of which pictures are the more plausible and how we could find out. But Dewey, in his characteristic way, addresses himself to these things too. Holistic considerations of reflective equilibrium are not irrelevant here.

8. I critically consider the metaphilosophical views of one such first generation non-positivist analytic philosopher (C. D. Broad) in my "What is Philosophy?" *History of Philosophy Quarterly* 10, no. 4 (October 1993), 389-404.

9. It might be asked, if these grand traditional claims are at best false and at worst incoherent (the latter being probably the most likely scenario), how then can anything really be lost? All we ever really had anyway was "a house of cards." The only difference is that now we know that. But what is lost is a very deep aspiration of philosophy, namely, to be able to see the world rightly–to see how it is and indeed must be–and to see, as well, how, in accordance with this view of the world, our lives should be lived and how, if we so live our lives, this will yield something that is deeply and finally fulfilling, answering to what is deepest in us. The loss of such a hope, the showing it to be an illusion, the recognizing and taking to heart, that such a state of things is not, and cannot be, on the agenda, is, to understate it, to lose a lot. It is analogous to recognizing that God is dead or that real communism is impossible.

10. There could, of course, be such a thing, over such matters, as *the view* of systematic analytic philosophy, but, as a matter of fact, there is not.

11. This blinkering is graphically exemplified in the remark of a tolerably well known systematic analytic philosopher that he never reads any philosophy that is more than a decade old.

12. *Le Devoir* and *The Globe and Mail* are Canada's national newspapers of record, roughly comparable in their role in Québec and in English Canada respectively to the role of *The New York Times* in the United States and *Le Monde* in France.

13. Not infrequently, particularly in *Le Devoir*, articles appearing on political and social issues are written by social scientists, historians, and sometimes even by philosophers. So there is an overlap here between the professor and the journalist. This is even more strikingly, and more frequently, true of *Le Monde Diplomatique*. The moral here is that we should see all these writers as critical intellectuals (not the newspaper pundit we typically get in the vulgar press) and not worry about the cubbyholes "philosopher *qua* philosopher" or "sociologist *qua* sociologist" or journalist *qua* journalist."

14. I try to put this method to work in discussing the national issue and the secession of Québec in my "Secession: The Case of Québec," *Journal of Applied Philosophy* 10, no. 1 (1993), 29-43.

15. See here Jürgen Habermas, "Philosophy as Stand-in and Interpreter" in Kenneth Baynes, et al., eds., *After Philosophy* (Cambridge, MA: MIT Press, 1987), 296-315. But see, as well, my "Sceptical Remarks on the Scope of Philosophy: Rorty v. Habermas," *Social Theory and Practice* 19, no. 2 (Summer 1993), 117-60.

16. Kai Nielsen: "Analytical Marxism: A Form of Critical Theory,"*Erkenntnis* 39 (1993), 1-21; "Analytical Marxism as Critical Theory: A Theory in Crisis,"*Annals of Scholarship* 9, no. 4 (1992), 375-402; "Afterword: Remarks on the Roots of Progress" in Robert Ware and Kai Nielsen, eds.,*Analyzing Marxism: New Essays on Analytical Marxism* (Calgary, Alberta: University of Calgary Press, 1989), 497-539; and *After the Demise of The Tradition* (Boulder, CO: Westview Press, 1991), Part Two.

17. G. A. Cohen, *Karl Marx's Theory of History: A Defence* (Oxford, England: Clarendon Press, 1978); G. A. Cohen, *History, Labour and Freedom* (Oxford, England: Clarendon Press, 1988); Andrew Levine, *Arguing for Socialism* (London, England: Routledge & Kegan Paul, 1984); and Alan Garfinkel,*Forms of Explanation: Rethinking the Questions in Social Theory* (New Haven, CT: Yale University Press, 1981). See also Andrew Levine, "Althusser's Marxism," *Economy and Society* 10, no. 1 (1981), 243-83. For a splendid example of such work, which only came to my attention after I had drafted this, see Rajeev Bhargava,*Individualism in Social Science: Forms and Limits of a Methodology* (Oxford, England: Clarendon Press, 1992).

18. See references in note 16 and my "Philosophy as Critical Theory,"*Proceedings of the American Philosophical Association* (1987), 89-108.

19. For striking examples of this cooperative work see John Roemer, eds., *Analytical Marxism* (Cambridge, England: Cambridge University Press, 1986); Erik Olin Wright, Andrew Levine and Elliot Sober,*Reconstructing Marxism* (London: Verso, 1992); Robert Ware and Kai Nielsen, eds.,*Analyzing Marxism: New Essays on Analytical Marxism* (Calgary, Alberta: University of Calgary Press, 1989); Jon Elster and Karl Ove Moene, eds. *Alternatives to Capitalism* (Cambridge, England: Cambridge University Press, 1989); and David Copp, Jean Hampton and John Roemer, eds., *The Idea of Democracy* (Cambridge, England: Cambridge University Press, 1993).

20. See particularly the last section of my "Philosophy as Critical Theory." See also my "Sceptical Remarks on the Scope of Philosophy: Rorty v. Habermas."

21. For a non-transformed philosophy, "*a priori* philosophical" may well be pleonastic. Wittingly or at least unwittingly, that was what traditionalists were about. However, if the *a priori/non-a priori* distinction does not make much sense or is, as Putnam believes that Quine in effect shows, a distinction that is without theoretical and critical import, then traditionalist philosophy is even more deeply mired in the mud.

Bibliography

Achinstein, Peter and Barker, Stephen F., eds. 1969. *The Legacy of Logical Positivism*. Baltimore: John Hopkins Press.

Aiken, Henry. 1962. "The Fate of Philosophy in the Twentieth Century." *The Kenyon Review* XXIV:233-52.

Ajdukiewicz, Kasimir. 1949. "The Scientific World-Perspective," in Herbert Feigl and Wilfrid Sellars, eds., *Readings in Philosophical Analysis*. Pp. 182-88. New York: Appleton-Century-Crofts.

Albert, Hans. 1985. *Treatise on Critical Reason*. Translated by Mary Varney Rorty. Princeton, NJ: Princeton University Press.

Allen, Barry. 1994. "Difference Unlimited," in G. B. Madison, ed., *Working Through Derrida*. Evanston, IL: Northwestern University Press.

_____. 1994. *Truth in Philosophy*. Cambridge, MA: Harvard University Press.

Ambrose, Alice. 1960. "Philosophical Doubts." *The Massachusetts Review* 111 (1):270-80.

Anderson, John. 1962. *Studies in Empirical Philosophy*. Sydney, Australia: Angus & Robertson.

Armstrong, D. M. 1973. "Continuity and Change in Philosophy." *Quadrant* XVII (56):19-23.

_____. 1978. "Naturalism, Materialism and First Philosophy." *Philosophia* 8.

Austin, John. 1961. *Philosophical Papers*. Oxford: Clarendon Press.

Ayer, A. J., ed. 1959. *Logical Positivism*. Glencoe, IL: Free Press.

_____. 1990. *The Meaning of Life*. New York: Charles Scribner's Sons.

_____. 1991. "A Defense of Empiricism," in A. Phillips Griffiths, ed., *A. J. Ayer Memorial Essays*. Pp. 1-16. Cambridge, England: Cambridge University Press.

Ayers, Michael. 1978. "Analytical Philosophy and the History of Philosophy," in *Philosophy and Its Past*. Pp. 41-66. Atlantic Highlands, NJ: Humanities Press.

Barber, Benjamin. 1988. *The Conquest of Politics*. Princeton, NJ: Princeton University Press.

Beehler, Rodger, et al., eds. 1992. *On the Track of Reason*. Boulder, CO: Westview Press.

Berlin, Isaiah. 1973. "Austin and the Early Beginnings of Oxford Philosophy," in G. J. Warnock, ed., *Essays on J. L. Austin*. Pp. 1-16. Oxford: Clarendon Press.

_____. 1980. *Concepts and Categories: Philosophical Essays*. Oxford: Oxford University Press.

_____. 1991. *The Crooked Timber of Humanity*. New York: Alfred A. Knopf.

_____. 1992. "Reply to Ronald H. McKinney, 'Towards a Postmodern Ethics'." *Journal of Value Inquiry* 26:557-60.

Bernstein, Richard J. 1992. *The New Constellation*. Cambridge, MA: MIT Press.

_____. 1992. "The Resurgence of Pragmatism." *Social Research* 59(4).

Blackburn, Simon. 1993. *Essays in Quasi-Realism*. Oxford: Oxford University Press.

Blanshard, Brand. 1949. "The New Subjectivism in Ethics." *Philosophy and Phenomenological Research*.

_____. 1985. "The Philosophical Enterprise," in Charles Bontempo and S. Jack Odell, eds., *The Owl of Minerva*. Pp. 174-77. New York: McGraw-Hill.

Blake, Ralph. 1943. "Can Speculative Philosophy be Defended?" *The Philosophical Review* LII:127-34.

Bobik, Joseph, ed. 1970. *The Nature of Philosophic Inquiry*. Notre Dame, IN: University of Notre Dame Press.

Bolzano, Bernard. 1848. *Was ist Philosophie?* Vienna: Wilhelm Brausmüller.

Bouveresse, Jacques. 1976. *Le Mythe de l'intériorité*. Paris: Editions de Minuit.

Bouwsma, O. K. 1965. *Philosophical Essays*. Lincoln, NE: University of Nebraska Press.

_____. 1974. *Without Proof or Evidence*. Lincoln, NE: University of Nebraska Press.

Broad, C. D. 1923. *Scientific Thought*. London: Routledge & Kegan Paul.

_____. 1924. "Critical and Speculative Philosophy," in J. H. Muirhead, ed., *Contemporary Philosophy*. London: Allen & Unwin.

_____. 1958. "Philosophy." *Inquiry* I(2):99-129.

Burge, Tyler. 1992. "Philosophy of Language and Mind: 1950-1990." *The Philosophical Review* 101:3-51.

Burtt, E. A. 1946. "The Problem of Philosophic Method." *The Philosophical Review* LV:505-33.

Callinicos, Alex. 1983. *Marxism and Philosophy*. Oxford: Clarendon Press.

Carnap, Rudolf. 1950. "Empiricism, Semantics and Ontology." *Revue Internationale de Philosphie* 4.

_____. 1956. *Meaning and Necessary*. Chicago, IL: University of Chicago Press.

Cavell, Stanley. 1969. *Must We Mean What We Say?* New York: Charles Scribner's Sons.

_____. 1979. *The Claim of Reason*. New York: Oxford University Press.

_____. 1988. "The Uncanniness of the Ordinary," in Sterling M. McMurrin, ed., *The Tanner Lectures on Human Values, VII*. Pp. 83-112. Salt Lake City, UT: University of Utah Press.

_____. 1988. *In Quest of the Ordinary: Lines in Skepticism and Romaniticism*. Chicago, IL: University of Chicago Press.

_____. 1990. *Conditions Handsome and Unhandsome*. Chicago, IL: University of Chicago Press.

Cohen, T., P. Guyer, and H. Putnam, eds. 1993. *Pursuits of Reason: Essays in Honor of Stanley Cavell*. Lubbock, TX: Texas Tech University Press.

Cohen, Ted. 1993. "Some Philosophy, in Two Parts," in Ted Cohen, Paul Guyer, and Hilary Putnam, eds., *Pursuits of Reason: Essays in Honor of Stanley Cavell*. Pp. 185-401. Lubbock, TX: Texas Tech University Press.

Collingwood, R. G. 1924. *Speculum Mentis*. Oxford: Oxford University Press.

Conant, James. 1989. "An Interview With Stanley Cavell," in Richard Flemming and Michael Payne, eds., *The Senses of Stanley Cavell*. Pp. 21-72. Lewisburg, PA: Bucknell University Press.

_____. 1989. "Must We Show What We Cannot Say?" in Richard Flemming and Michael Payne, eds., *The Senses of Stanley Cavell*. Pp. 242-83. Lewisburg, PA: Bucknell University Press.

_____. 1991. "The Search for Logically Alien Thought: Descartes, Kant, Frege and the *Tractatus*." *Philosophical Topics* 20(1):100-66.

_____. 1993. "Kierkegaard, Wittgenstein, and Nonsense," in Ted Cohen, Paul Guyer, and Hilary Putnam, eds., *Pursuits of Reason: Essays in Honor of Stanley Cavell*. Pp. 195-224. Lubbock, TX: Texas Tech University Press.

Copleston, Frederick. 1956. *Contemporary Philosophy*. London: Burns & Oates.

_____. 1991. "Ayer and World Views," in A. Phillips Griffiths, ed., *A. J. Ayer Memorial Essays*. Pp. 63-75. Cambridge, England: Cambridge University Press.

Couture, Jocelyne. 1989. "Méta-éthique," in *l'Encyclopédie Philosophique Universelle, Tome I: L'univers philosophique*. Paris: Presses Universitaires de France.

_____, ed., 1992. *Ethique et rationalité*. Liège: Mardaga.

Davidson, Arnold. 1989. "Beginning Cavell," in Richard Flemming and Michael Payne, eds., *The Senses of Stanley Cavell*. Lewisburg, PA: Bucknell University Press.

Davidson, Donald. 1982. "The Myth of the Subjective," in Michael Krausz, ed., *Relativism*. Pp. 159-81. Notre Dame, IN: University of Notre Dame Press.

_____. 1984. *Inquiries into Truth and Meaning*. Oxford: Clarendon Press.

_____. 1990. "The Structure and Content of Truth." *Journal of Philosophy* LXXXVII(6):297-326.

_____. 1990. "Afterthoughts, 1987," in Alan Malachowski, ed., *Reading Rorty*. Pp. 134-37. Oxford: Basil Blackwell.

_____. 1991. "Three Varieties of Knowledge," in A. Phillips Griffiths, ed., *A. J. Ayer Memorial Essays*. Pp. 153-66. Cambridge: Cambridge University Press.

Dennes, William Ray. 1960. *Some Dilemmas of Naturalism*. New York: Columbia University Press.

Dewey, John. 1939. *Intelligence in the Modern World*. New York: Random House.

_____. 1957. *Reconstruction in Philosophy*. Boston, MA: Beacon Press.

Diamond, Cora. 1991. *The Realistic Spirit*. Cambridge, MA: MIT Press.

Ducasse, C. J. 1941. *Philosophy as a Science*. New York: Oskar Piest.

_____. 1946. "The Subject-Matter Distinctive of Philosophy." *Philosophy and Phenomenological Research* 6(3).

_____. 1950. "Qu'est-ce que la Philosophie." *Synthese* 8(6-7).

_____. 1956. "The Method of Knowledge in Philosophy," in Sidney Hook, ed., *American Philosophers at Work*. Pp. 207-24. New York: Criterion Books.

_____. 1959. "Philosophy can become a Science." *Revue Internationale de Philosophie* 1(47).

_____. 1961. "What Metaphysics is Good For," in Gerald E. Meyers, ed., *Self, Religion and Metaphysics*. Pp. 127-41. New York: Macmillan.

Dummett, Michael. 1988. "The Origins of Analytical Philosophy, Part I." *Lingua E Stile* 23:3-49.

———. 1988. "The Origins of Analytical Philosophy, Part II." *Lingua E Stile* 23: 171-210.

———. 1991. *The Logical Basis of Metaphysics*. Cambridge, MA: Harvard University Press.

Edwards, Paul. 1955. *The Logic of Moral Discourse*. Glencoe, IL: Free Press.

Farber, Marvin. 1940. "The Ideal of a Presuppositionless Philosophy," in M. Farber, ed., *Philosophical Essays in Memory of Edmund Husserl*. Pp. 49-64. Cambridge, MA: Harvard University Press.

———. 1951. "Reflections on the Nature and Method of Philosophy," in Paul Henle, ed., *Structure, Method and Meaning*. Pp. 183-206. New York: Liberal Arts Press.

Farrell, B. A. 1946. "An Appraisal of Therapeutic Positivism." *Mind* LV:25-48.

Feigl, Herbert. 1950. "*De Principiis Non Disputandum...?* On the Meaning and the Limits of Justification," in Max Black, ed., *Philosophical Analysis: A Collection of Essays*. Pp. 119-56. Ithaca, NY: Cornell University Press.

———. 1956. "Logical Empiricism," in Dagobert D. Runes, ed., *Living Schools of Philosophy*. Ames, IA: Littlefield Adams.

Fleming, Richard and Michael Payne, eds. 1989. *The Senses of Stanley Cavell*. Lewisburg, PA: Bucknell University Press.

Fraser, Nancy and Linda J. Nicholson. 1990. "Social Criticism Without Philosophy," in Linda J. Nicholson, ed., *Feminism/Postmodernism*. Pp. 19-38. New York: Routledge.

Gallie, W. B. 1949. "The Limitations of Analytical Philosophy." *Analysis* IX:35-44.

Gauthier, David. 1986. *Morals by Agreement*. Oxford: Clarendon Press.

Geach, Peter. 1964. "Assertion." *Philosophical Review* 74:449-65.

Geiger, Theodor. 1946. "Evaluative Nihilism." *Acta Sociologica* 1(1).

Gellner, Ernest. 1964. "The Crisis in the Humanities and the Mainstream of Philosophy," in J. H. Blumb, ed., *Crisis in the Humanities*. Pp. 45-81. Baltimore, MD: Penguin Books.

———. 1979. *Spectacles and Predicaments*. Cambridge: Cambridge University Press.

Gibbard, Allan. 1990. *Wise Choices, Apt Feelings*. Cambridge, MA: Harvard University Press.

Gitelman, Damon. 1991. *Conceptual Scheme Differentiation*. PhD Thesis, University of Calgary, Calgary, Alberta.

Goddard, L. 1962. *Philosophical Thinking*. Inaugural Public Lecture, October 17, Armidale, New South Wales.

Goodman, Nelson. 1956. "The Revision of Philosophy," in Sidney Hook, ed., *American Philosophers at Work*. Pp. 75-92. New York: Criterion Books.

Goodman, Nelson and Catherine Z. Elgin. 1988. *Reconceptions in Philosophy and Other Arts and Sciences*. Indianapolis, IN: Hackett Publishing.

Granger, Gilles-Gaston. 1959. "Sur la Connaissance Philosophique." *Revue Internationale de Philosophie* XIII:92-111.

———. 1967. *Pensée formelle et sciences de l'homme*. Paris: Aubier.

_____. 1982. "On the Notion of Formal Content." *Social Research* 49(2).

_____. 1988. *Pour la connaissance philosophique*. Paris: Odile Jacob.

_____. 1990. *Invitation à la lecture de Wittgenstein*. Aix-en-Provence: Alinéa.

Grice, G. R. 1972. *Philosophy as an Investigation of Meanings*. Inaugural Lecture, May 16, University of East Anglia.

Griffiths, A. Phillips, ed. 1991. *A. J. Ayer: Memorial Essays*. Cambridge: Cambridge University Press.

Grimshaw, Jean. 1986. *Philosophy and Feminist Thinking*. Minneapolis, MN: University of Minnesota Press.

Gunn, Giles. 1990. "Rorty's *Novum Organum*." *Raritan* X(1):80-103.

Habermas, Jürgen. 1970. *Toward a Rational Society*. Boston, MA: Beacon Press.

_____. 1983. "Does Philosophy Still have a Purpose?" *Philosophical-Political Profiles*. Pp. 1-20. Cambridge, MA: MIT Press.

_____. 1990. "Philosophy as Stand-In and Interpreter," in Jürgen Habermas, ed., *Moral Consciousness and Communicative Action*. Pp. 1-20. Cambridge, MA: MIT Press.

Hacking, Ian. 1985. "Styles of Scientific Reasoning," in John Rajchman and Cornel West, eds., *Post-Analytic Philosophy*. Pp. 145-65. New York: Columbia University Press.

Hägerstrom, Axel. 1953. *Inquiries into the Nature of Law and Morals*. Translated by C. D. Broad. Stockholm: Almqvist & Wiksell.

Hall, E. W. 19 "Is Philosophy a Science?" *Journal of Philosophy* XXXIX:113-18.

Hallden, Sören. 1954. *Emotive Propositions: A Study of Value*. Stockholm: Almqvist & Wiksell.

Hampshire, Stuart. 1946. "The Progress of Philosophy," *Polemic* 5:22-32.

_____. 1956. "Identification and Existence," in H. D. Lewis, ed., *Contemporary British Philosophy*. Pp. 191-208. London: Allen & Unwin.

_____. 1960. "Fredrich Waismann, 1896-1959." *Proceedings of the British Academy* XLVI:309-17.

_____. 1985. "A Statement About Philosophy," in Charles Bontempo and S. Jack Odell, eds., *The Owl of Minerva*. P. 89. New York: McGraw-Hill.

_____. 1989. *Innocence and Experience*. Cambridge, MA: Harvard University Press.

Harman, Gilbert. 1977. *The Nature of Morality*. New York: Oxford University Press.

Hartz, Carolyn G. 1991. "What Putnam Should Have Said: An Alternative Reply to Rorty." *Erkenntnis* 34:287-95.

Honderich, Ted. 19 . "An Interview with A. J. Ayer," in A. Phillips Griffiths, ed., *A. J. Ayer Memorial Essays*. Pp. 209-26. Cambridge: Cambridge University Press.

Hook, Sidney. 1956. "Naturalism and First Principles," in Sidney Hook, ed., *American Philosophers at Work*. Pp. 236-58. Criterion Books.

Horwich, Paul. 1993. "Gibbard's Theory of Norms." *Philosophy and Public Affairs* 22(1).

Jacob, Pierre. 1980. *L'empirisme logique, ses antécédents, ses critiques*. Paris: Editions de Minuit.

_____. 1989. "Qu'est-ce que l'autoritarisme épistémologique." *Epistémologie*, numéro thématique de *L'Age de la Science*. Paris: Editions Odile Jacob.

Jorgensen, Joergen. 1951. *The Development of Logical Empiricism*. Chicago, IL: University of Chicago Press.

Kitcher, Philip. 1992. "The Naturalists Return." *The Philosophical Review* 101(1):53-114.

_____. 1993. "Knowledge, Society, and History." *Canadian Journal of Philosophy* 23(2):155-76.

Kreisel, G. 1960. "Wittgenstein's Theory and Practice of Philosophy." *British Journal of the Philosophy of Science* XI:238-51.

Lange, John. 1970. *The Cognitivity Paradox: An Inquiry Concerning the Claims of Philosophy*. Princeton, NJ: Princeton University Press.

Lazerowitz, Morris. 1966. "Understanding Philosophy," in Frederick C. Dommeyer, ed., *Current Philosophical Issues*. Pp. 27-53. Springfield, IL: Charles C. Thomas.

Levi, Isaac. 1992. "Conflict and Inquiry." *Ethics* 102:814-34.

Lipkin, Robert Justin. 1990. "Beyond Skepticism, Foundationalism and the New Fuzziness." *Cornell Law Review* 75(4):811-77.

_____. 1991. "Kibitzers, Fuzzies and Apes Without Tails: Pragmatism and the Art of Conversation in Legal Theory." *Tulane Law Review* 66(1):69-139.

_____. 1993. "Pragmatism—The Unfinished Revolution: Doctrinaire and Reflective Pragmatism in Rorty's Thought." *Tulane Law Review* 67(5):1561-1630.

MacIntyre, Alasdair. 1987. "Relativism, Power and Philosophy," in Kenneth Baynes et al., eds., *After Philosophy: End or Transformation?* Pp. 385-421. Cambridge, MA: MIT Press.

Mackie, J. L. 1946. "A Refutation of Morals." *The Australasian Journal of Psychology and Philosophy* XXIV.

_____. 1956. *Contemporary Linguistic Philosophy—Its Strength and Its Weakness*. Australia: University of Otago Press.

_____. 1967. "Westermark," in Paul Edwards, ed., *The Encyclopedia of Philosophy* Vol 8. New York: Free Press.

_____. 1977. *Ethics: Inventing Right and Wrong*. Harmondsworth, England: Penguin Books.

_____. 1980. *Hume's Moral Theory*. London: Routledge & Kegan Paul.

_____. 1985. *Persons and Values*. Oxford: Clarendon Press.

Magee, Bryan. 1982. *Men of Ideas*. Oxford: Oxford University Press.

Marcuse, Herbert. 1964. *One-Demensional Man*. Boston: Beacon Press.

Mays, Wolfe and S. C. Brown, eds. 1972. *Linguistic Analysis and Phenomenology*. London: Macmillan.

McCarthy, Thomas. 1990. "Private Irony and Public Decency: Richard Rorty's New Pragmatism." *Critical Inquiry* 16:355-70.

_____. 1990. "Ironist Theory as a Vocation: A Response to Rorty's Reply." *Critical Inquiry* 16:644-55.

_____. 1991. *Ideals and Illusions: On Reconstruction and Deconstruction in Contemporary Critical Theory*. Cambridge, MA: MIT Press.

McDonald, Joseph F. 1993. *Wittgenstein's Therapeutic Conception of Philosophy*. PhD Thesis, University of Ottawa, Ottawa, Ontario.

Mehlberg, Henry. 1959. "Can Science Absorb Philosophy?" *Revue International de Philosophie* XIII:61-87.

Mézáros, István. 1966. "The Possibility of Dialogue," in Bernard Williams and Alan Montefiore, eds., *British Analytical Philosophy*. Pp. 311-34. London: Routledge & Kegan Paul.

Monro, D. H. 1967. *Empiricism and Ethics*. Cambridge: Cambridge University Press.

_____. 1973. "Relativism in Ethics," in P. P. Wiener, ed., *Dictionary of the History of Ideas* Vol IV. New York: Charles Scribner's Sons.

Moore, G. E. 1903. *Principia Ethica*. Cambridge: Cambridge University Press.

Murdoch, Iris. 1992. *Metaphysics as a Guide to Morals*. New York: Penguin Books.

Murphy, Arthur E. 1943. *The Uses of Reason*. New York: Macmillan.

_____. 1943. "Can Speculative Philosophy be Defended?" *The Philosophical Review* LII:135-43.

_____. 1965. *The Theory of Practical Reason*. La Salle, IL: Open Court.

Nagel, Ernest. 1956. *Logic Without Metaphysics*. Glencoe, IL: Free Press.

Nehamas, Alexander. 1990. "A Touch of the Poet." *Raritan* X(1):104-25.

Newell, R. W. 1967. *The Concept of Philosophy*. London: Methuen.

Nielsen, Kai. 1958. "Speaking of Morals." *The Centennial Review of Arts & Science* II:414-44.

_____. 1958. "Bertrand Russell's New Ethic." *Methodos* 10(37-38).

_____. 1960. "Dewey's Conception of Philosophy." *The Massachusetts Review* II (1):110-34.

_____. 1969. "Linguistic Philosophy and Beliefs," in Gerry H. Gill, ed., *Philosophy Today*. New York: Macmillan.

_____. 1980. "Linguistic Philosophy and 'The Meaning of Life'," in Steven Sanders and David Cheney, eds., *The Meaning of Life*. Pp. 129-54. Englewood Cliffs, NJ: Prentice-Hall.

_____. 1985. *Philosophy and Atheism*. Buffalo, NY: Prometheus Books.

_____. 1986. "On Finding One's Feet in Philosophy." *Metaphilosophy* 16(1).

_____. 1987. "Philosophy as Critical Theory." *Proceedings and Addresses of the American Philosophical Association* 61(1).

_____. 1989. "Transforming Philosophy." *Dalhousie Review*.

_____. 1990. "On There Being Philosophical Knowledge." *Theoria* LVI(4):193-225.

_____. 1990. *Ethics Without God*. Buffalo, NY: Prometheus Press.

_____. 1991. *After the Demise of the Tradition*. Boulder, CO: Westview Press.

_____. 1991. "Can There be Justified Philosophical Beliefs?" *Iyyun* 40:235-70.

_____. 1991. *God and the Grounding of Morality*. Ottawa, ON: University of Ottawa Press.

_____. 1993. "Philosophy and *Weltanschuung*." *The Journal of Value Inquiry* 27:179-86.

_____. 1993. "Analytical Marxism: A Form of Critical Theory." *Erkenntnis*.

_____. 1993. "Peirce, Pragmatism and the Challenge of Postmodernism." *Transactions of the Charles S. Peirce Society*. Pp. 513-60.

_____. 1993. "Formalists and Informalists: Some Methodological Turnings." *Critica* XX(73):71-82.

_____. 1993. "Is 'True Philosophy' Like 'True Art'?" *Philosophical Exchange.*

_____. 1994. "How to Proceed in Philosophy: Remarks After Habermas." *Theoria.*

_____. 1994. "Perspectivism and the Absolute Conception of the World." *Critica.*

_____. 1995. "Anti-Philosophy Philosophy: Some Programmatic Remarks." *Dialogos* 63.

_____. Forthcoming. "Jolting the Career of Reason: Absolute Idealism and Other Rationalisms Reconsidered." *The Journal of Speculative Philosophy.*

_____. Forthcoming. "Reconsidering the Platonic Conception of Philosophy." *International Studies in Philosophy.*

_____. Forthcoming. "What is Philosophy? The Reconsideration of Some Neglected Options." *History of Philosophy Quarterly.*

Passmore, John. 1943. "Logical Positivism I." *The Australasian Journal of Philosophy* XII.

_____. 1944. "Logical Positivism II." *The Australasian Journal of Philosophy* XXII.

_____. 1948. "Logical Positivism III." *The Australasian Journal of Philosophy* XXVI.

_____. 1961. *Philosophical Reasoning.* London: Duckworth.

_____. 1966. "The Place of Argument in Metaphysics," in W. E. Kennick and Morris Lazerowitz, eds., *Metaphysics.* Pp. 356-65. Englewood Cliffs, NJ: Prentice-Hall.

_____. 1967. "Philosophy," in Paul Edwards, ed., *The Encyclopedia of Philosophy.* Pp. 216-26. New York: Macmillan.

_____. 1969. *Philosophy in the Last Decade.* Occasional Paper 14. Sydney, Australia: Sydney University Press.

_____. 1985. *Recent Philosophers.* La Salle, Il: Open Court.

Paton, H. J. 1951. *In Defense of Reason.* London: Hutchinson's University Library.

Poirier, René. 1959. "La philosophie peut-Elle etre une science?" *Revue Internationale de Philosophie* XIII:33-60.

Price, H. H. 1963. "Clarity is Not Enough," in H. D. Lewis, ed., *Clarity is Not Enough.* Pp. 15-41. New York: Humanities Press.

Proust, Joëlle, ed. 1992. *La philosophie continent vue par la philosophie analytique.* Volume spécial de *Philosophie.* Paris: Les Editions de Minuit.

Putnam, Hilary. 1983. *Realism and Reason.* Cambridge: Cambridge University Press.

_____. 1987. *The Many Faces of Realism.* La Salle, IL: Open Court.

_____. 1989. *Representation and Reality.* Cambridge, MA: MIT Press.

_____. 1990. *Realism with a Human Face.* Cambridge, MA: Harvard University Press.

_____. 1991. "Replies and Comments." *Erkenntnis* 34:401-24.

_____. 1992. *Renewing Philosophy.* Cambridge, MA: Harvard University Press.

_____. 1993. "Introducing Cavell," in Ted Cohen, Paul Guyer, and Hilary Putnam, eds., *Pursuits of Reason: Essays in Honor of Stanley Cavell.* Pp. vii-xii. Lubbock, TX: Texas Tech University Press.

_____. 1993. "Pope's *Essay on Man* and Those 'Happy Pieties'," in Ted Cohen, Paul Guyer, and Hilary Putnam, eds., *Pursuits of Reason: Essays in Honor of Stanley Cavell.* Pp. 13-20. Lubbock, TX: Texas Tech University Press.

Putnam, Hilary and Anna Putnam. 1990. "Epistemology as Hypothesis." *Transactions of the Charles S. Peirce Society* 26:405-36.

Quine, W. V. 1978. "On the Nature of Moral Values," in Alvin Goldman and Jaegwon Kim, eds., *Values and Morals*. Pp. 37-45. Dordrect, Netherlands: D. Reidel.

_____. 1981. "The Pragmatist's Place in Empiricism," in Robert J. Mulvaney and Phillip M. Zeiltner, eds., *Pragmatism: Its Sources and Prospects*. Pp. 23-39. Springfield, SC: University of South Carolina Press.

_____. 1986. "Reply to Putnam," in L. E. Hahn and P. A. Schilpp, eds., *The Philosophy of W. V. Quine*. P 429. La Salle, IL: Open Court.

_____. 1992. "Words Are All We Have To Go On." *Times Literary Supplement* July 3, p. 8.

_____. 1993. "In Praise of Observation Sentences." *The Journal of Philosophy* XC(3):107-17.

Rawls, J. 1971. *A Theory of Justice*. Cambridge, MA: Harvard University Press.

_____. 1993. *Political Liberalism*. New York: Columbia University Press.

Recanati, François, ed. 1988. *Ethique et philosophie politique*, numéros thématique de *L'Age de la science*. Paris: Editions Odile Jacob.

Rée, Jonathan. 1978. "Philosophy and the History of Philosophy," in *Philosophy and Its Past*. Pp. 1-39. Atlantic Highlands, NJ: The Humanities Press.

_____. 1984. *Proletarian Philosophers*. Oxford: Clarendon Press.

Reichenbach, Hans. 1948. "Rationalism and Empiricism: An Inquiry into the Roots of Philosophical Error." *Philosophical Review* LVII:330-46.

_____. 1951. *The Rise of Scientific Philosophy*. Berkeley, CA: University of California Press.

Rescher, Nicholas. 1980. "Conceptual Schemes." *Midwest Studies in Philosophy*, Vol. 5. Pp. 323-45.

Robinson, Richard. 1948. "The Emotive Theory of Ethics." *Aristotelian Society Proceedings*, Supplementary Volume.

Romanos, George D. 1984. *Quine and Analytic Philosophy*. Cambridge, MA: MIT Press.

Rorty, Richard. 1979. "Transcendental Arguments, Self-Reference and Pragmatism," in Peter Bieri et al., eds., *Transcendental Arguments and Science: Essays in Epistemology*. Pp. 77-103. Dordrecht, Netherlands: D. Reidel.

_____. 1979. "The Unnaturaliness of Epistemology," in D. F. Gustafson and B. L. Tapscott, eds., *Body, Mind and Method*. Pp. 77-92. Dordrecht, Netherlands: D. Reidel.

_____. 1982. *Consequences of Pragmatism*. Minneapolis, MN: University of Minnesota Press.

_____. 1984. "Life at the End of Inquiry." *London Review of Books* 6(14-15):6-7.

_____. 1985. "Epistemological Behaviorism and the De-Transcendentalization of Analytic Philosophy," in Robert Hollinger, ed., *Hermeneutics and Praxis*. Pp. 89-121. Notre Dame, IN: University of Notre Dame Press.

_____. 1985. "Pragmatism Without Principles." *Critical Inquiry* 11(3):459-65.

_____. 1986. "Should Hume be Answered or Bypassed?" in A. Donagan et al., eds., *Human Nature and Natural Knowledge.* Pp. 341-52. Dordrecht, Netherlands: D. Reidel.

_____. 1990. "Truth and Freedom: A Reply to Thomas McCarthy." *Critical Inquiry* 16:633-43.

_____. 1990. "Pragmatism as Anti-Representationalism," in John P. Murphy, *Pragmatism from Peirce to Davidson.* Pp. 1-6. Boulder, CO: Westview Press.

_____. 1990. *Essays on Heidegger and Others.* Cambridge: Cambridge University Press.

_____. 1991. *Objectivity, Relativism and Truth.* Cambridge: Cambridge University Press.

_____. 1992. "Putnam on Truth." *Philosophy and Phenomenological Research* LII(2).

_____. 1992. "The Pragmatist's Progress," in Stefan Collins, ed., *Interpretation and Overinterpretation.* Pp. 89-108. Cambridge: Cambridge University Press.

_____. 1992. "Feminism and Pragmatism," in Gretke B. Petersen, ed., *The Tanner Lectures on Human Values.* Vol. 13. Pp. 3-35. Salt Lake City, UT: University of Utah Press.

_____. 1992. "The Professor and the Prophet." *Transition* 52.

_____. 1992. "What Can You Expect from Anti-Foundationalist Philosophers?" *Virginia Law Review* 78.

_____. Forthcoming. "Habermas, Derrida and the Function of Philosophy." *Revue Internationale de Philosophie.*

Ross, Alf. 1945. "On the Logical Nature of Propositions of Value." *Theoria* XI.

Russell, Bertrand. 1955. *Human Society in Ethics and Politics.* New York: Simon and Shuster.

Ryle, Gilbert et al., eds. 1963. *The Revolution in Philosophy.* London: Macmillan.

Ryle, Gilbert. 1971. *Collected Papers, Volume 2.* London: Hutchinson's.

Sayers, Sean and Peter Osborne, eds. 1990. *Socialism, Feminism and Philosophy.* New York: Routledge.

Schick, Frederic. 1992. "Liberty, Equality and Diversity: Some Reflections on Rorty." *Social Research* 59(2):297-314.

Schilpp, Paul Arthur. 1935. "Is Standpointless Philosophy Possible?" *The Philosophical Review* XLIV:227-53.

_____. 1959. "The Abdication of Philosophy." *Proceedings of the American Philosophical Association* XXXII:19-39.

Schlick, Moritz. 1932. "The Future of Philosophy." *College of the Pacific Publications in Philosophy* I:45-62.

Sellars, Wilfrid. 1963. "Philosophy and the Scientific Image of Man," in Wilfrid Sellars ed., *Science, Perception and Reality.* Pp. 1-40. London: Routledge & Kegan Paul.

Sidgwick, Henry. 1902. *Philosophy, Its Scope and Relations.* London: Macmillan.

Smart, J. J. C. 1957. "Plausible Reasoning in Philosophy." *Mind* 66:75-78.

_____. 1963. "The Province of Philosophy,"" in J. J. C. Smart, ed., *Philosophy and Scientific Realism.* Pp. 1-15. New York: Humanities Press.

_____. 1966. "Philosophy and Scientific Plausibility," in Paul K. Feyerabend and Grover Maxwell, eds., *Mind, Matter and Method*. Pp. 377-90. Minneapolis, MN: University of Minnesota Press.

Sparshott, F. E. 1972. *Looking for Philosophy*. Montréal: McGill-Queens University Press.

_____. 1975. "On Saying What Philosophy Is." *Philosophy in Context* 4:17-27.

Stace, W. T. 1943. "Can Speculative Philosophy be Defended?" *The Philosophical Review* LII:127-34.

Stebbing, L. Susan. 1933. "Logical Positivism and Analysis." *Annual Philosophical Lecture*. Herriette Hertz Trust, March 22.

Stevenson, Charles. 1944. *Ethics and Language*. New Haven, CT: Yale University Press.

_____. 1963. *Facts and Values*. New Haven, CT: Yale University Press.

Stroup, Timothy, ed. 1982. *Edward Westermark: Essays on His Life and Works*. Helsinki: Societas Philosophica Fennica.

Suchting, W. A. 1986. *Marx and Philosophy*. New York: New York University Press.

Taylor, Charles. 1985. *Human Agency and Language*. Cambridge: Cambridge University Press.

Toulmin, Stephen. 1958. *The Uses of Argument*. Cambridge: Cambridge University Press.

_____. 1990. *Cosmopolis*. Chicago, IL: Chicago University Press.

Tugendhat, Ernst. 1982. *Traditional and Analytical Philosophy*. Translated by P. A. Gorner. Cambridge: Cambridge University Press.

_____. 1986. *Self-Consciousness and Self-Determination*. Cambridge, MA: MIT Press.

_____. 1992. "Reflections on Philosophical Method from an Analytic Point of View," in Axel Honneth et al., eds., *Philosophical Interventions in the Unfinished Project of Enlightenment*. Pp. 113-24. Cambridge, MA: MIT Press.

Vuillemin, Jules. 1968. *Leçons sur la première philosophie de Russell*. Paris: A. Colin.

_____. 1976. "Le concept de significaton empirique chez Quine." *Revue Internationale de Philosophie*, 350-75.

_____. 1986. *What are Philosophical Systems?* Cambridge: Cambridge University Press.

Waismann, Frederich. 1965. *The Principles of Linguistic Philosophy*. New York: St. Martin's Press.

_____. 1968. *How I See Philosophy*. New York: St. Martin's Press.

Weil, Simone. 1959. *Leçon de Philosophie*. Paris: Librairie Plon.

Williams, Bernard. 1985. *Ethics and the Limits of Philosophy*. Cambridge, MA: Harvard University Press.

_____. 1993. *Shame and Necessity*. Berkeley, CA: University of California Press.

Williams, Michael. 1984. "The Elimination of Metaphysics," in Graham Macdonald and Crispin Wright, eds., *Fact, Science and Morality*. Pp. 20-24. Oxford: Basil Blackwell.

_____. 1991. *Unnatural Doubts*. Oxford: Blackwell.

Winch, Peter. 1955. "Contemporary British Philosophy and Its Critics." *Universities Quarterly* X:24-37.

Wittgenstein, Ludwig. 1953. *Philosphical Investigations*. Translated by G. E. M. Anscombe. Oxford: Basil Blackwell.

Wolfson, W. 1958. "What is Philosophy?" *Journal of Philosophy* LV:322-36.

Wollheim, Richard. 1955. "Modern Philosophy and Unreason." *Philosophical Quarterly* XXVI:246-57.

_____. 1984. *The Thread of Life*. Cambridge, MA: Harvard University Press.

_____. 1993. *The Mind and Its Depths*. Cambridge, MA: Harvard University Press.

Index

About the Book and Author

Since Rorty, the crisis of method and interests in philosophy has been at the forefront of metaphilosophy. In this book, Kai Nielsen, one of the most prominent critics of philosophy-as-usual, examines critically the most important claims made on behalf of philosophy. After rejecting as chimerical the ambitious claims of traditional, especially foundational, epistemology and metaphysics, he presents the case for a more modest view of what philosophy can accomplish.

Nielsen insists that philosophy must be devoted to actual problems of real people in everyday life. Influenced substantively by Dewey and more methodologically by Rawls, he carves out a defensible terrain for philosophy to inhabit–a terrain cleared of the more extravagant but implausible claims made by traditional philosophy.

Nielsen has been a major voice in debates about the scope of philosophy, and this latest work of his will be an important contribution to the "end of philosophy debate."

Kai Nielsen is emeritus professor of philosophy at the University of Calgary. He is the author of many books and articles on ethics, social and political philosophy, philosophy of religion, and metaphilosophy.